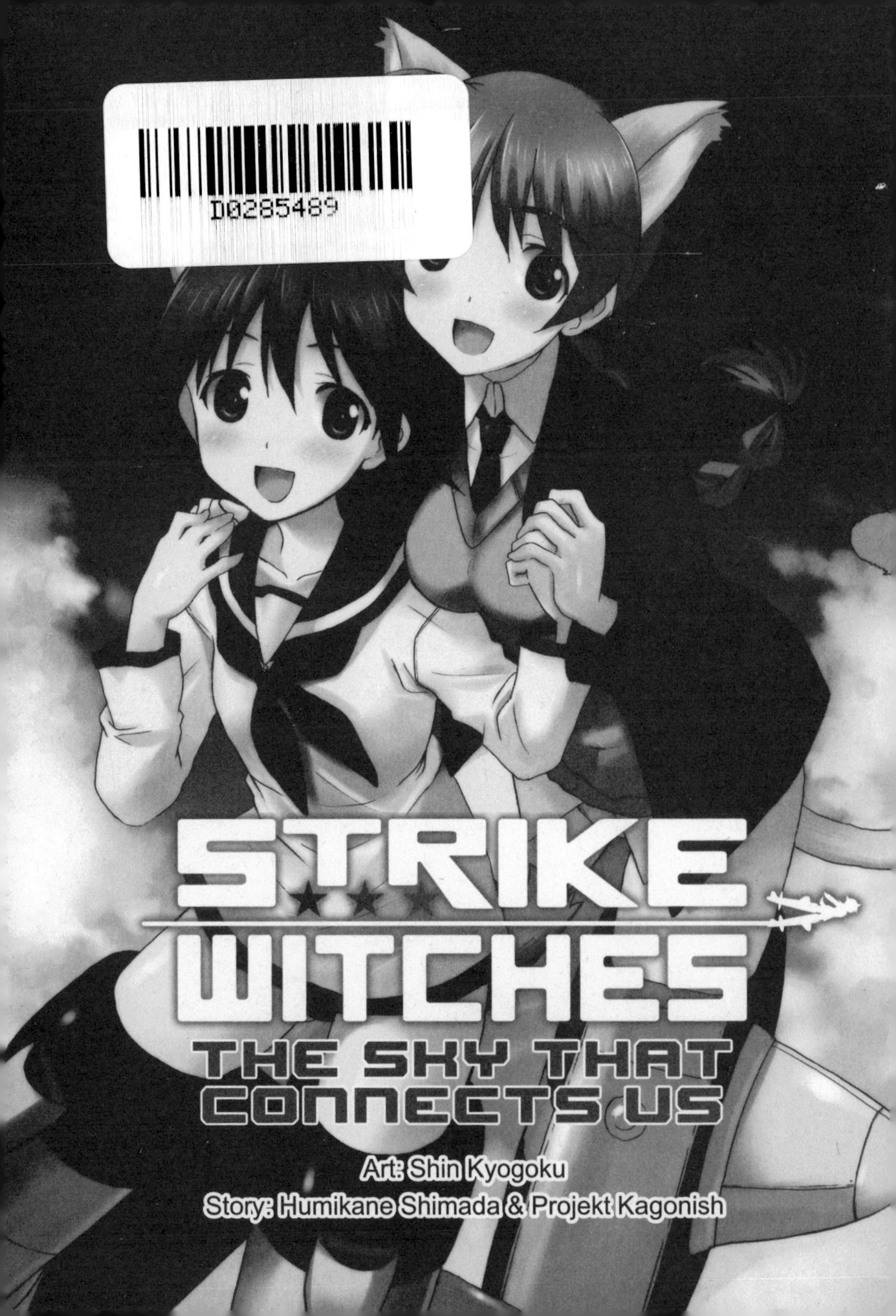
STRIKE WITCHES
THE SKY THAT CONNECTS US
Art: Shin Kyogoku
Story: Humikane Shimada & Projekt Kagonish

STRIKE WITCHES
OUTLINE

This is a world at war, and a world of magic. In 1939, the sudden invasion of the alien “Neuroi” nearly destroyed humanity. Thanks to the corrosive miasma they exude, Neuroi are nearly invulnerable to standard human weaponry. Their inexorable advance left nation after nation in ruins as people abandoned their homes, fleeing for their lives. The only force that can stand against the alien menace is a small group of young girls with unique magical abilities. Called “witches,” these girls have traded the traditional broomstick for mechanical “striker units,” which enable them to fly freely through the skies.

The girls of the 501st Joint Fighter Wing are an elite aerial unit known as the “Strike Witches.” Miyafuji Yoshika and her companions have destroyed countless Neuroi in the battle to protect the skies and people of Britannia, as well as battling the fearsome creatures in Gallia and elsewhere throughout the European continent.

But no battle lasts forever, and no band of sisters can fight together throughout an entire war. Missions end, assignments change, and even these brave comrades must eventually scatter to the four winds...

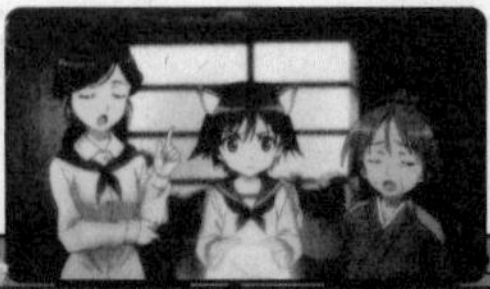

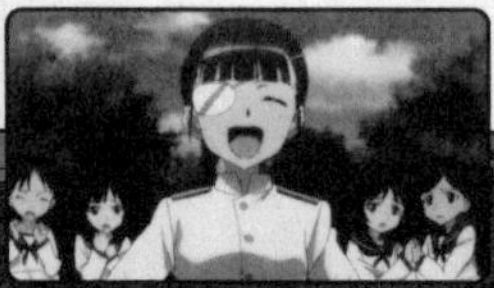

STRIKE WITCHES
WORLD MAP

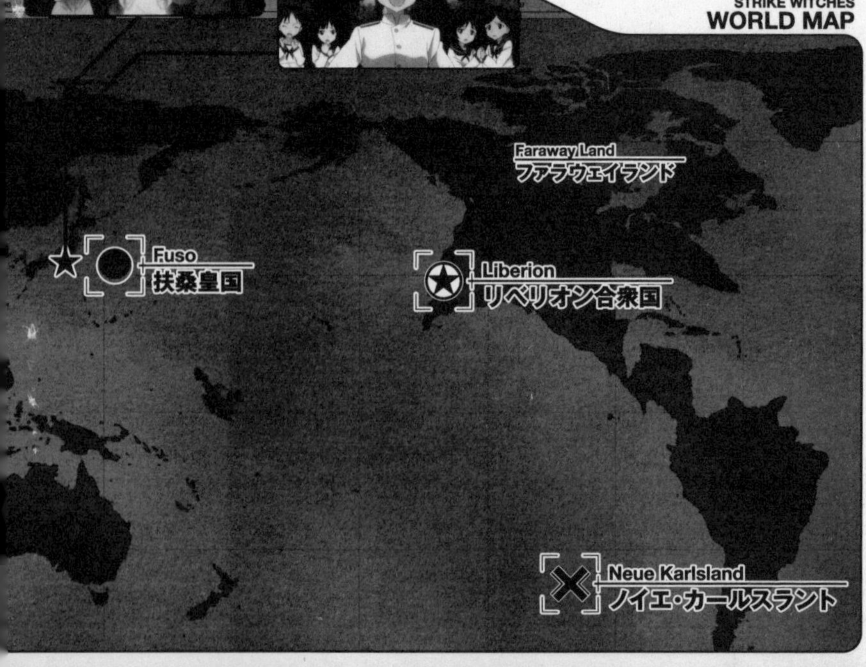
Faraway Land
ファラウェイランド
Fuso
扶桑皇国
Liberion
リベリオン合衆国
Neue Karlsland
ノイエ・カールスラント

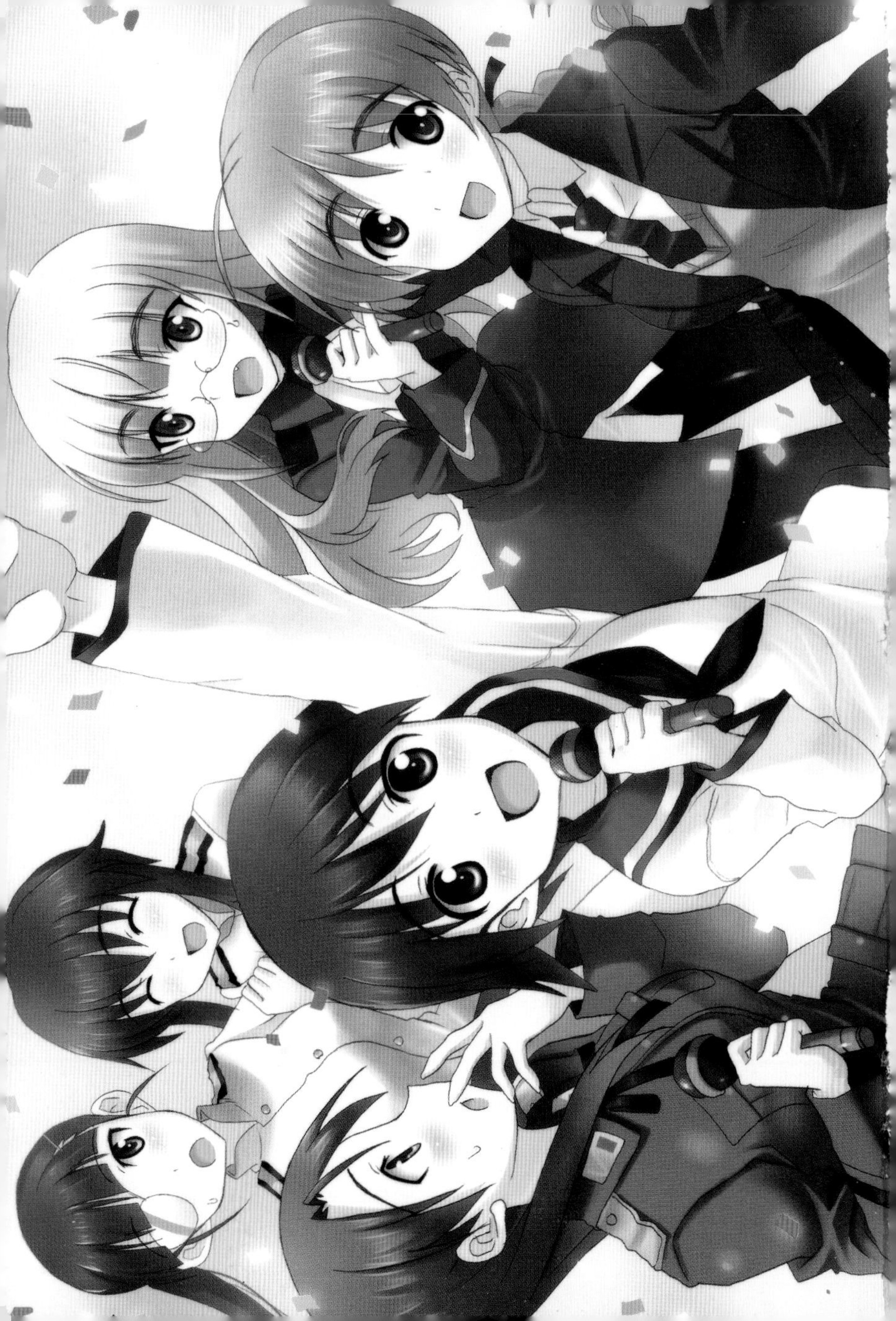

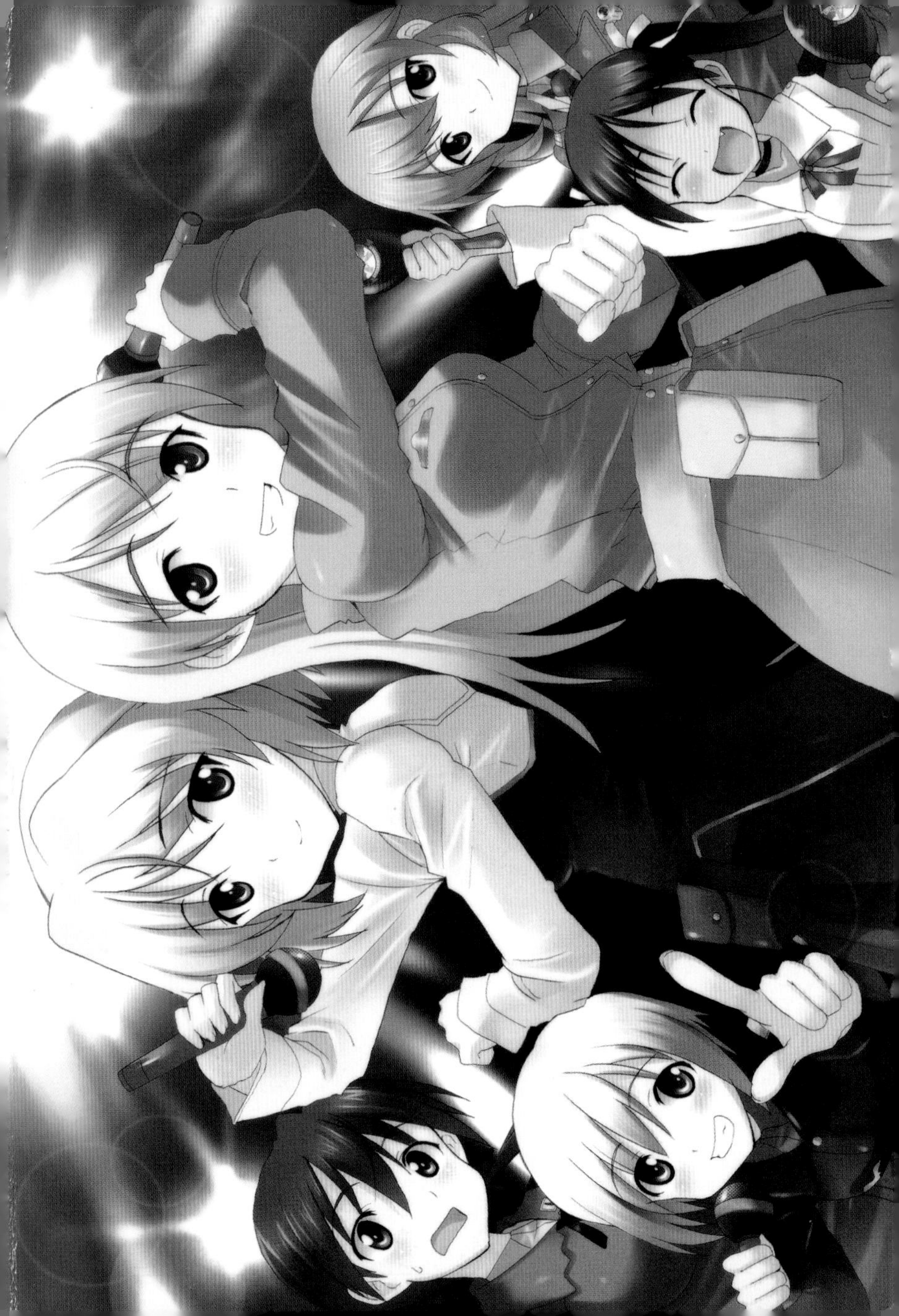

STRIKE WITCHES
THE SKY THAT CONNECTS US

SUMMARY & WORLD MAP

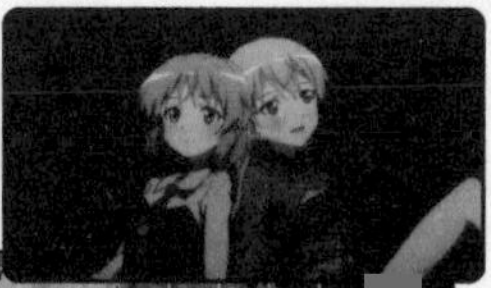

STRIKE WITCHES
EUROPE MAP

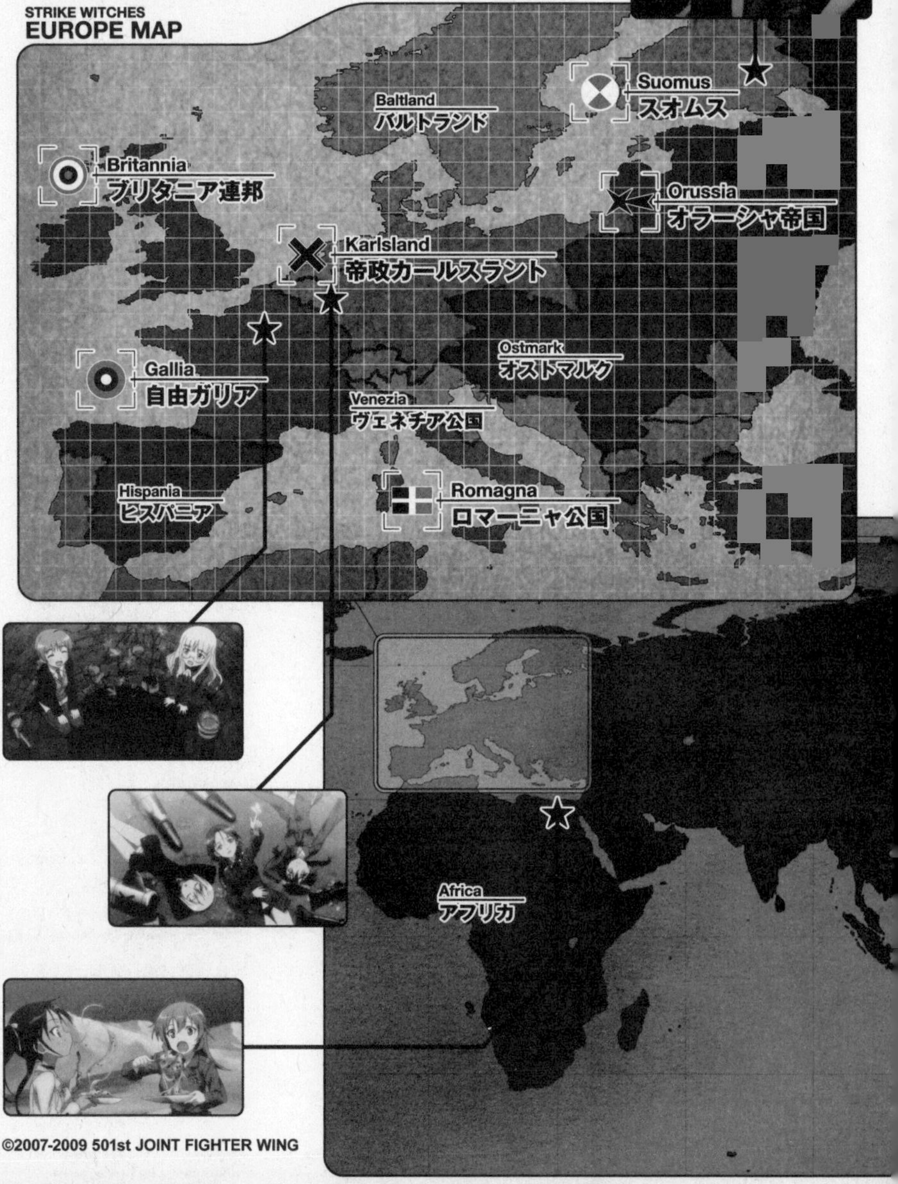
Baltland
バルトランド
Suomus
スオムス
Britannia
ブリタニア連邦
Orussia
オラーシャ帝国
Karlsland
帝政カールスラント
Ostmark
オストマルク
Gallia
自由ガリア
Venezia
ヴェネチア公国
Hispania
ヒスパニア
Romagna
ロマーニャ公国
Africa
アフリカ

CHAPTER 1:
THE GALLIA RECONSTRUCTION

Fg. Off. PERRINE H. CLOSTERMANN

Affiliation: Forces Aériennes Galliaises Libres 602nd Flying Corps
Rank: 1st Lieutenant **Age:** 15
Familiar: Chartreux
Unique Power: Tonnerre

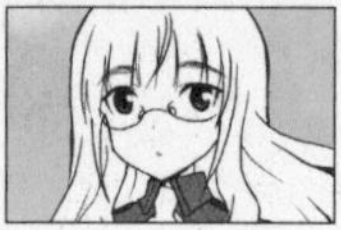

The proud and haughty daughter of a Gallian aristocrat. Very attached to Major Sakamoto.

Sgt. LYNETTE BISHOP

Affiliation: Britannia Air Force 610th Fighter Squadron
Rank: Sergeant **Age:** 15
Familiar: Scottish Fold
Unique Power: Stabilizing a bullet's trajectory and infusing objects with magic.

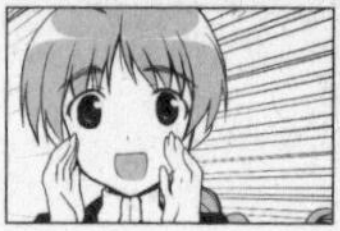

At first, Bishop was too shy to use her powers effectively, but becoming friends with Miyafuji helped her open up. She is an excellent sharpshooter.

Sgt. WILMA BISHOP

Affiliation: Royal Faraway Land Air Force (RFAF)
Rank: Sergeant **Age:** 21
Familiar: Scottish Fold
Unique Power: N/A

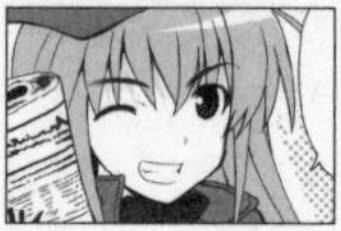

Lynette's older sister. Cheerful and mischievous, she is an energetic go-getter--quite the opposite of her little sister.

Sgt. AMELIE PLANCHARD

Affiliation: Forces Aériennes Galliaises Libres
Rank: Sergeant **Age:** 15
Familiar: European Rabbit
Unique Power: N/A

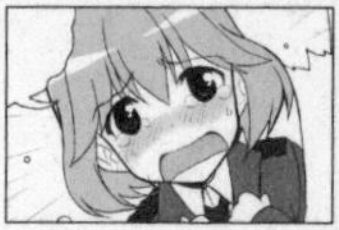

Perrine's friend from her days in the Gallian Alsace Flying Corps. A crybaby.

CHAPTER 2 & 3:
IN AFRICA

Flt. Lt. CHARLOTTE E. YEAGER (nickname: Shirley)

Affiliation: United States of Liberion Air Force 363rd Fighter Wing
Rank: Flight Lieutenant **Age:** 16
Familiar: Rabbit
Unique Power: Speed

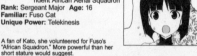

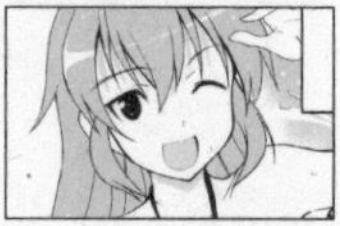

Glamorous and generous, she has a fascination with speed. She dreams of someday breaking the sound barrier.

Pit. Off. FRANCESCA LUCCHINI

Affiliation: Sovrana Aeronautica Romagniana 4th Air Unit, 10th Air Wing, 90th Squadron
Rank: Ensign **Age:** 12
Familiar: Black Leopard
Unique Power: White-hot burst attack and heavy shields.

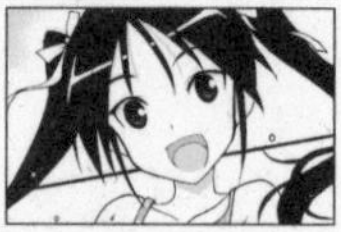

As innocent as a cat, and as intensely curious. She's also a big trouble-maker.

Sqn. Ldr. KEIKO KATO

Affiliation: Fuso Imperial Army Independent African Aerial Squadron
Rank: Major **Age:** 25
Familiar: Ezo Red Fox
Unique Power: Exceptionally sharp vision.

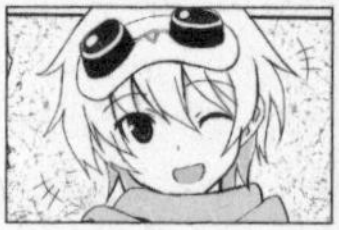

Though her Witch powers are fading, her leadership skills help unite her squadron.

Flt. Sgt. MAMI INAGAKI

Affiliation: Fuso Imperial Army Independent African Aerial Squadron
Rank: Sergeant Major **Age:** 16
Familiar: Fuso Cat
Unique Power: Telekinesis

A fan of Kato, she volunteered for Fuso's "African Squadron." More powerful than her short stature would suggest.

Flt. Lt. HANNA-JUSTINA MARSEILLE

Affiliation: Karlsland JG27 Luftwaffe, 3rd Squadron
Rank: Flight Lieutenant **Age:** 17
Familiar: Northern Goshawk
Unique Power: Ricochets

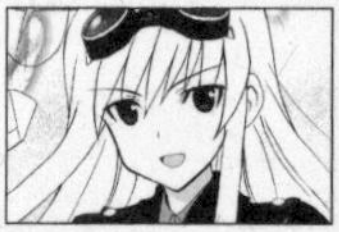

A natural dogfighter, she is an ultra-ace known as "The Star of Africa."

CHAPTER 4:
A SONG FROM SUOMUS

Fg. Off. EILA ILMATAR JUUTILAINEN

Affiliation: Suomus Air Force 24th Unit
Rank: Ensign **Age:** 15
Familiar: Black Fox
Unique Power: Prognostication

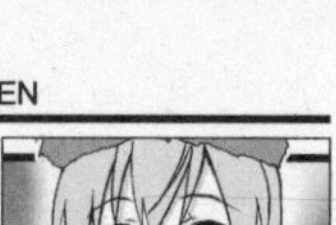

Exceptionally fond of Sanya, she is famous (in her own mind) for telling accurate (in her own mind) fortunes by reading Tarot cards.

Fg. Off. SANYA V. LITVYAK

Affiliation: Orussian Imperial Army 586th Fighter Regiment
Rank: 1st Lieutenant
Familiar: Black Cat
Unique Power: Omnidirectional wide-range search

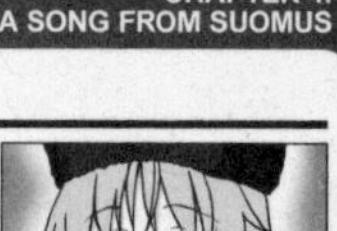

During the Neuroi's invasion of Orussia, she was separated from her father, a musician.

STRIKE WITCHES
THE SKY THAT CONNECTS US

CHARACTER INTRODUCTION

CHAPTER 4 & 5: THE KARLSLAND GHOST

Wg. Cdr. MINNA-DIETLINDE WILCKE

Affiliation: Karlsland JG3 Luftwaffe Command
Rank: Commander **Age:** 18
Familiar: Gray Wolf
Unique Power: Enhanced spatial awareness

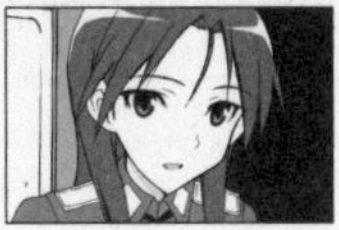

Commander of the Strike Witches, she has excellent judgment and very strong tactical and strategic abilities.

Fg. Off. ERICA HARTMANN

Affiliation: Karlsland JG52
Rank: 1st Lieutenant **Age:** 16
Familiar: Dachshund
Unique Power: Sturm

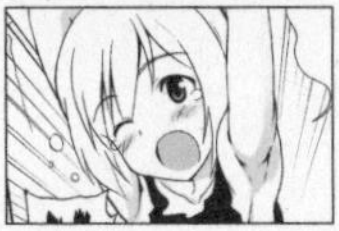

An ace on par with Gertrud, but her opposite personality-wise. Easy-going, messy, and loves her beauty sleep.

Flt. Lt. GERTRUD BARKHORN

Affiliation: Karlsland JG52 Luftwaffe, 2nd Squadron Command
Rank: Captain **Age:** 18
Familiar: German Pointer
Unique Power: Strength

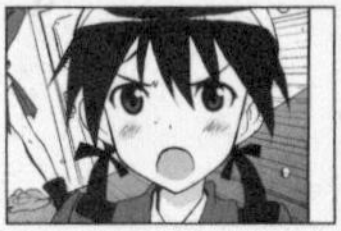

Serious, stubborn, and a perfectionist, she is a super-ace who has shot down over 250 enemies.

Flt. Lt. HEIDEMARIE W SCHNAUFER

Affiliation: Karlsland Luftwaffe
Rank: Flight Lieutenant **Age:** 16
Familiar: Gyrfalcon
Unique Power: Night vision

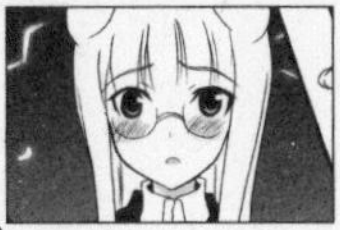

Her ability to see clearly even by starlight alone makes her Karlsland's greatest Night Witch.

Flt. Sgt. HELMA LENNARTZ

Affiliation: Karlsland Luftwaffe
Rank: Sergeant Major **Age:** 13
Familiar: Black Cat
Unique Power: N/A

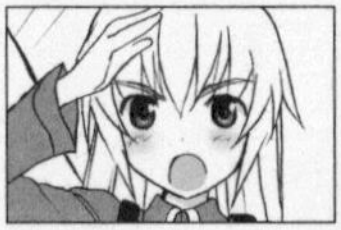

Serious, punctilious, and meddlesome, she idolizes Gertrud.

CHAPTER 7 A BATTLE IN FUSO

Sqn. Ldr. MIO SAKAMOTO

Affiliation: Fuso Imperial Navy, Europe Fleet 24th Fighter Unit 288th Squadron
Rank: Major **Age:** 19
Familiar: Doberman
Unique Power: Magic eye

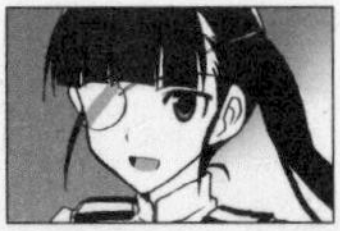

Her magical powers have faded, leaving her unable to use her shields.

Flt. Lt. AYAKA KUROE

Affiliation: Fuso Imperial Army Air Force Inspections Department, Prototypes
Rank: Flight Lieutenant **Age:** 23
Familiar: Satsuma Dog
Unique Power: Characteristic recognition

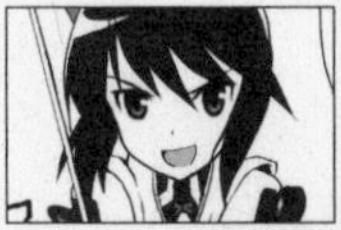

A specialist with the katana, she is one of Fuso's top Witches in close-quarters combat.

CHAPTER 8 UNDER THIS SKY

Sgt. YOSHIKA MIYAFUJI

Affiliation: Fuso Imperial Navy, Europe Fleet 24th Fighter Unit 288th Squadron
Rank: Sergeant **Age:** 15
Familiar: Miniature Shiba
Unique Power: Healing

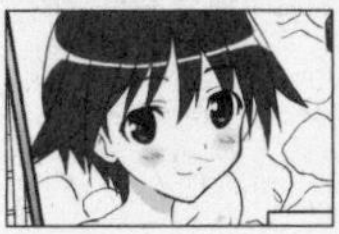

Originally wanted to become a doctor because of a message from Ichiro Miyafuji, her missing father.

Flt. Sgt. NIKKA EDVARDINE KATAJAINEN (nickname: Nipa

Affiliation: Suomus Air Force
Rank: Sergeant Major **Age:** 15
Familiar: White Mink
Unique Power: Regeneration

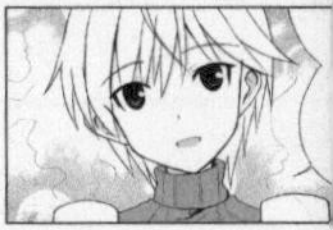

An old friend of Eila's. She is accident-prone, often destroying her Striker Unit.

STRIKE WITCHES

THE SKY THAT CONNECTS US

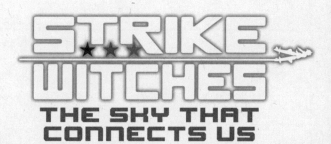

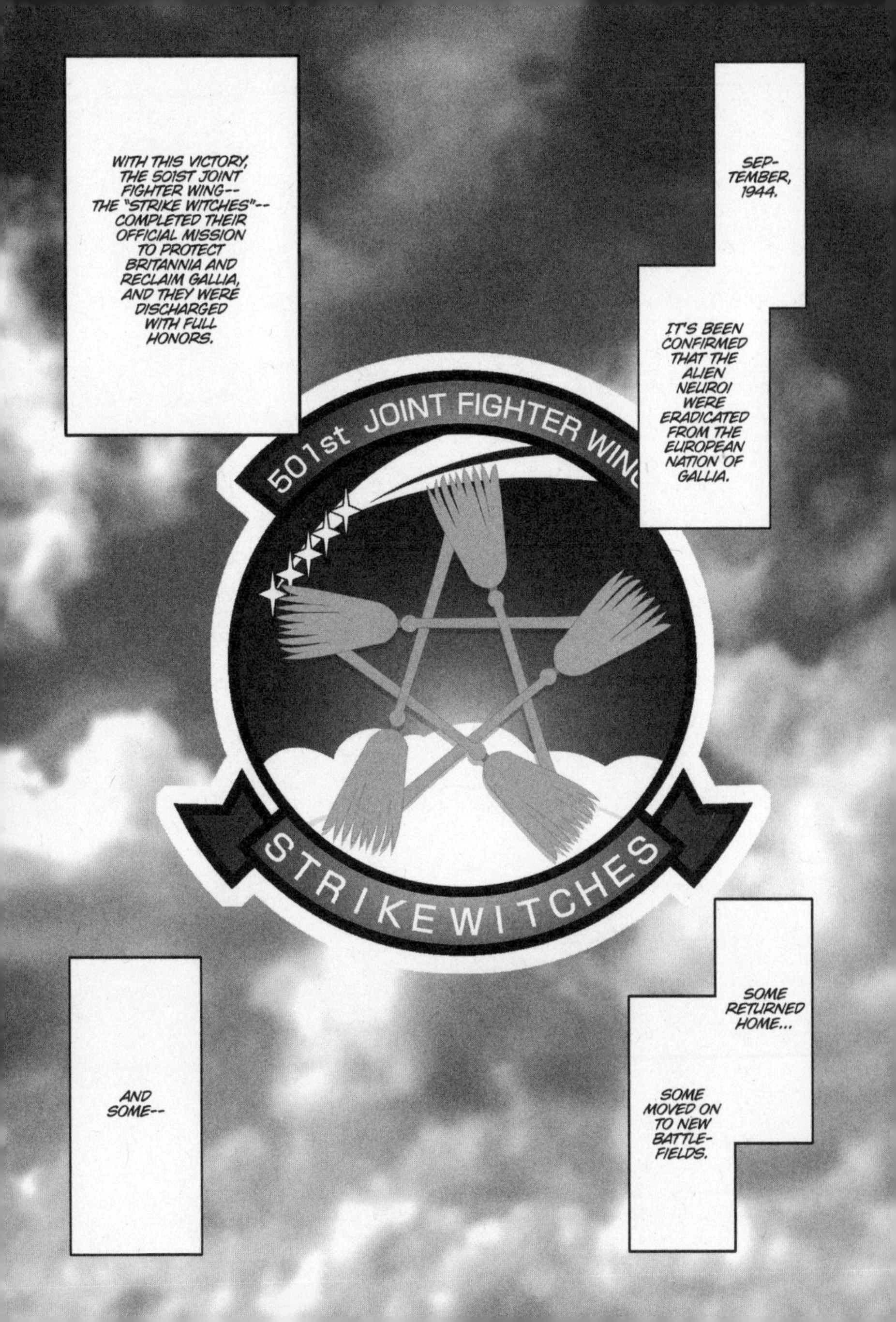
SEP-
TEMBER,
1944.
IT'S BEEN CONFIRMED THAT THE ALIEN NEUROI WERE ERADICATED FROM THE EUROPEAN NATION OF GALLIA.
WITH THIS VICTORY, THE 501ST JOINT FIGHTER WING-- THE "STRIKE WITCHES"-- COMPLETED THEIR OFFICIAL MISSION TO PROTECT BRITANNIA AND RECLAIM GALLIA, AND THEY WERE DISCHARGED WITH FULL HONORS.
501st JOINT FIGHTER WIN
STRIKEWITCHES
SOME RETURNED HOME...
SOME MOVED ON TO NEW BATTLE-FIELDS.
AND SOME--

CHAPTER 1

THE GALLIA RECONSTRUCTION

STRIKE WITCHES
THE SKY THAT CONNECTS US

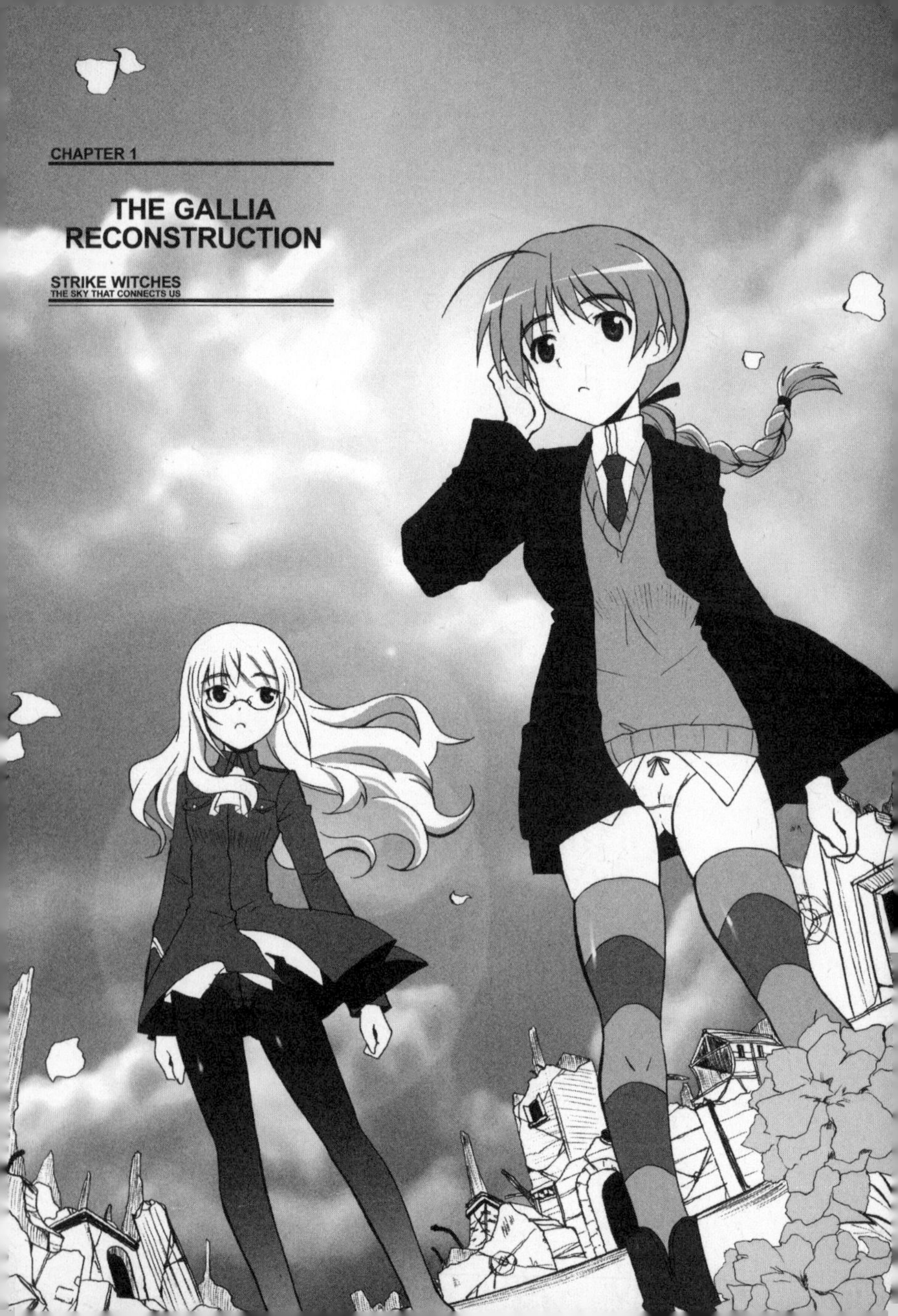

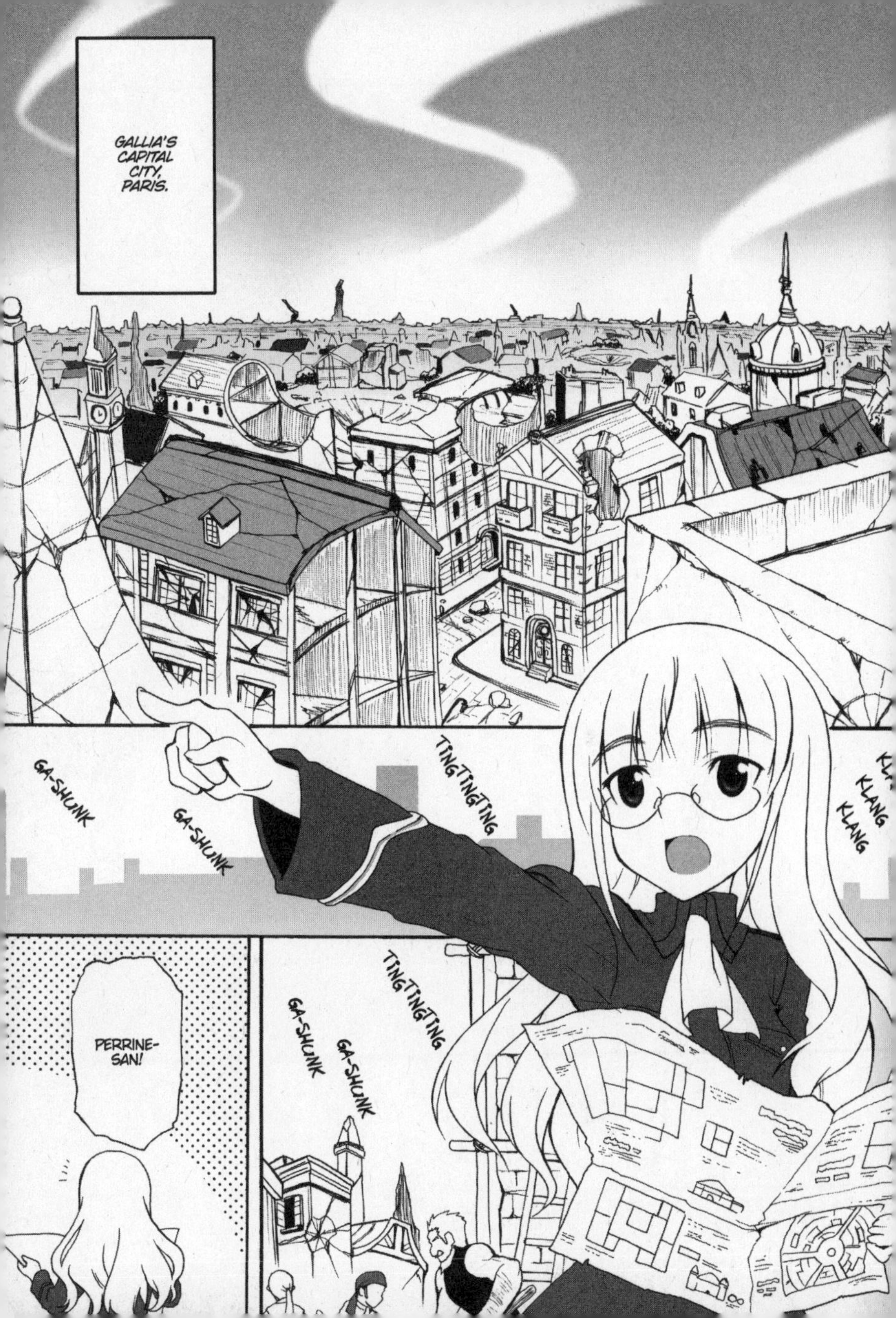
GALLIA'S CAPITAL CITY, PARIS.
KLANG
KLANG
TINGTINGTING
GA-SHUNK
GA-SHUNK
TINGTINGTING
GA-SHUNK
GA-SHUNK
PERRINE-SAN!

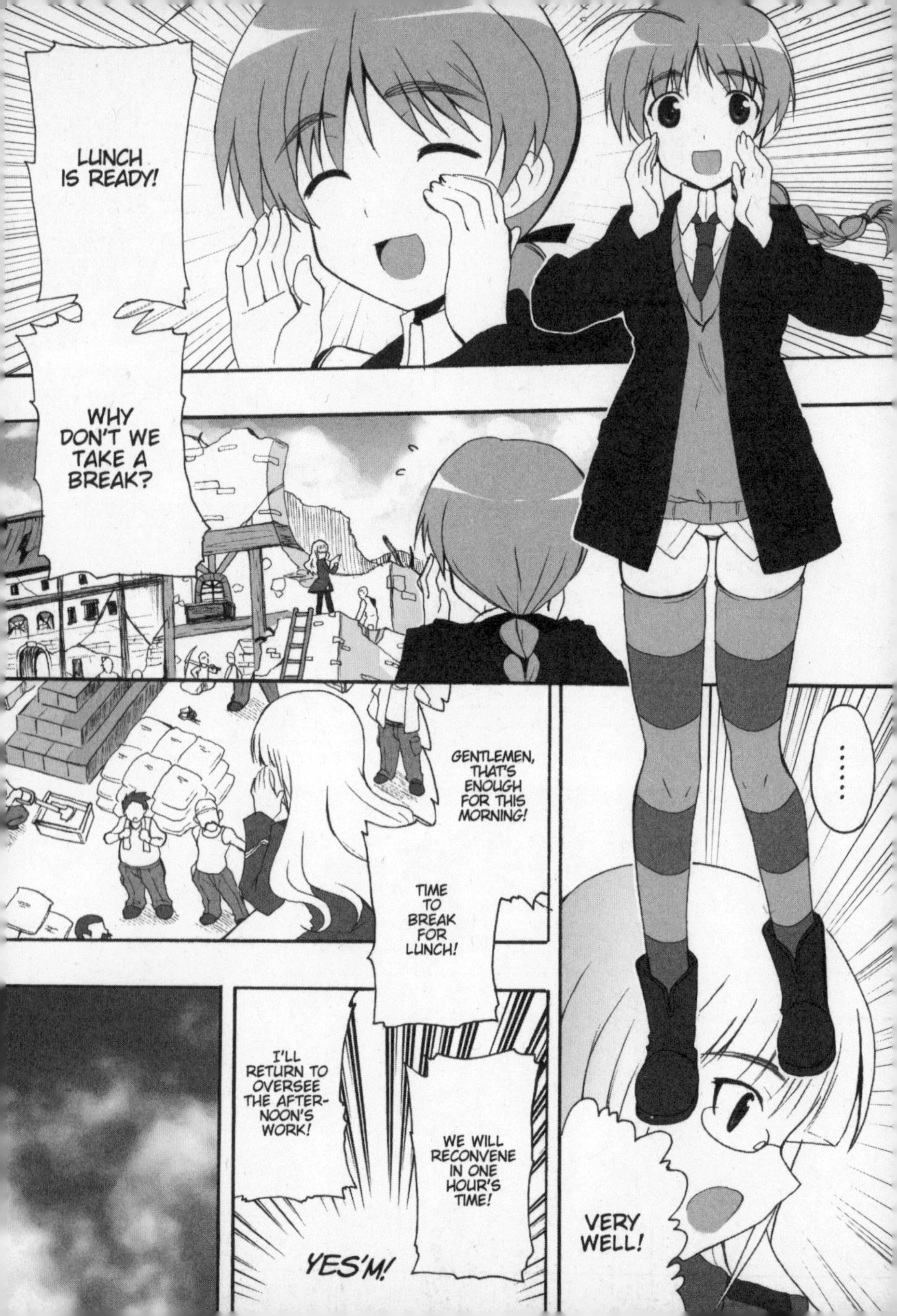
LUNCH IS READY!
WHY DON'T WE TAKE A BREAK?
......
GENTLEMEN, THAT'S ENOUGH FOR THIS MORNING!
TIME TO BREAK FOR LUNCH!
VERY WELL!
I'LL RETURN TO OVERSEE THE AFTER-NOON'S WORK!
WE WILL RECONVENE IN ONE HOUR'S TIME!
YES'M!

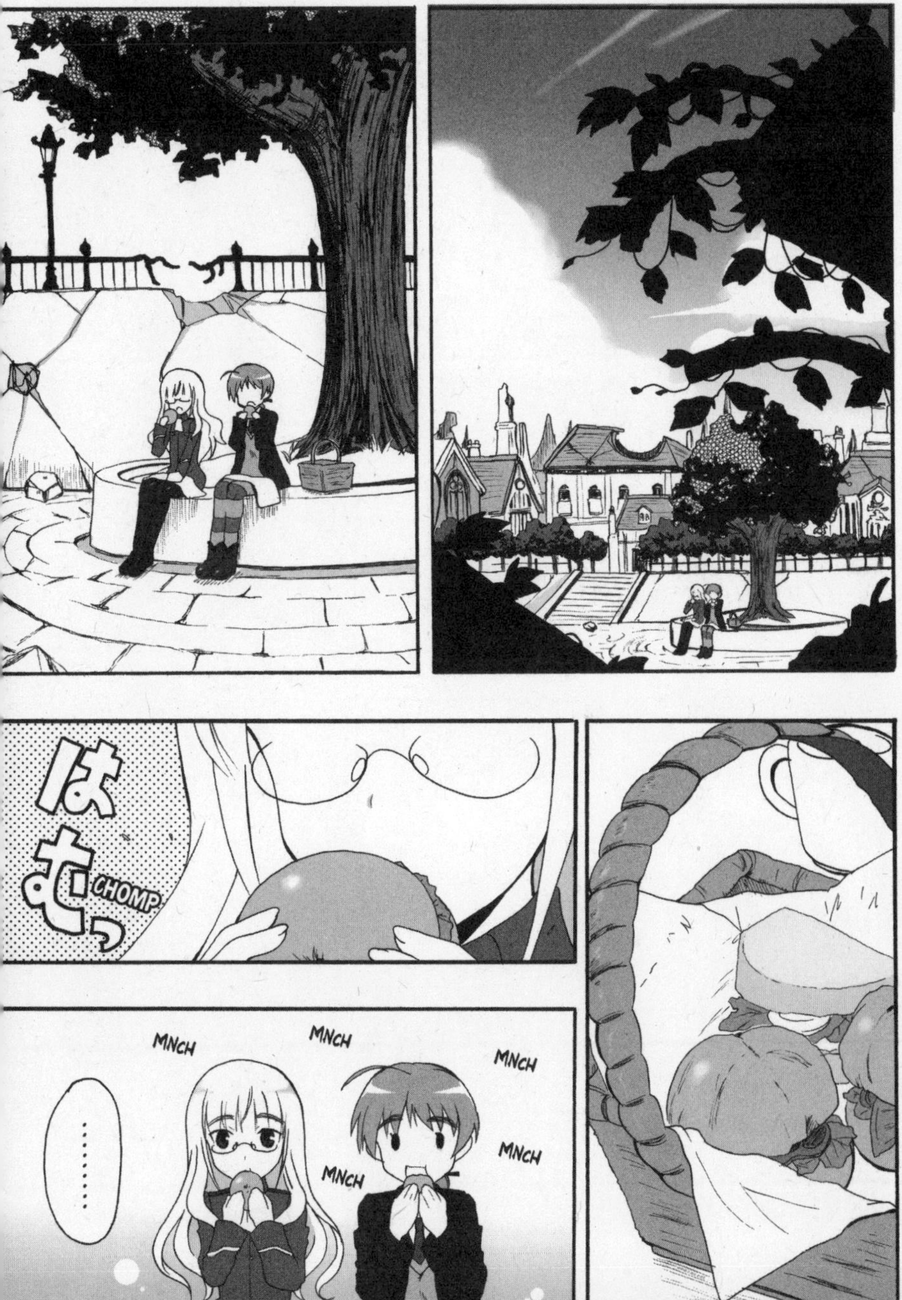
はむっ
CHOMP
MNCH
MNCH
MNCH
MNCH
MNCH
……

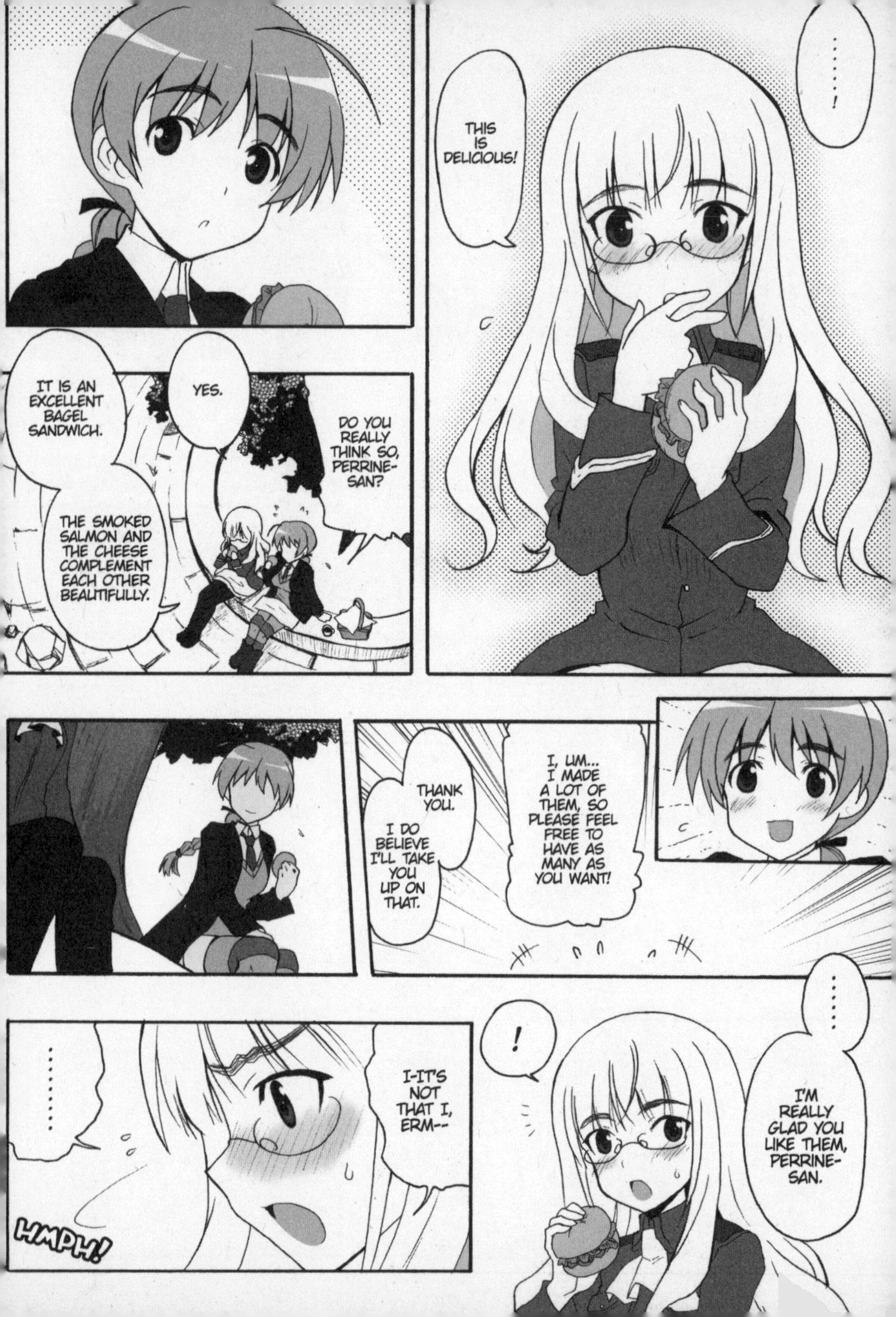
......!
THIS IS DELICIOUS!
DO YOU REALLY THINK SO, PERRINE-SAN?
YES.
IT IS AN EXCELLENT BAGEL SANDWICH.
THE SMOKED SALMON AND THE CHEESE COMPLEMENT EACH OTHER BEAUTIFULLY.
I, UM... I MADE A LOT OF THEM, SO PLEASE FEEL FREE TO HAVE AS MANY AS YOU WANT!
THANK YOU.
I DO BELIEVE I'LL TAKE YOU UP ON THAT.
......
I'M REALLY GLAD YOU LIKE THEM, PERRINE-SAN.
!
I-IT'S NOT THAT I, ERM--
......
HMPH!

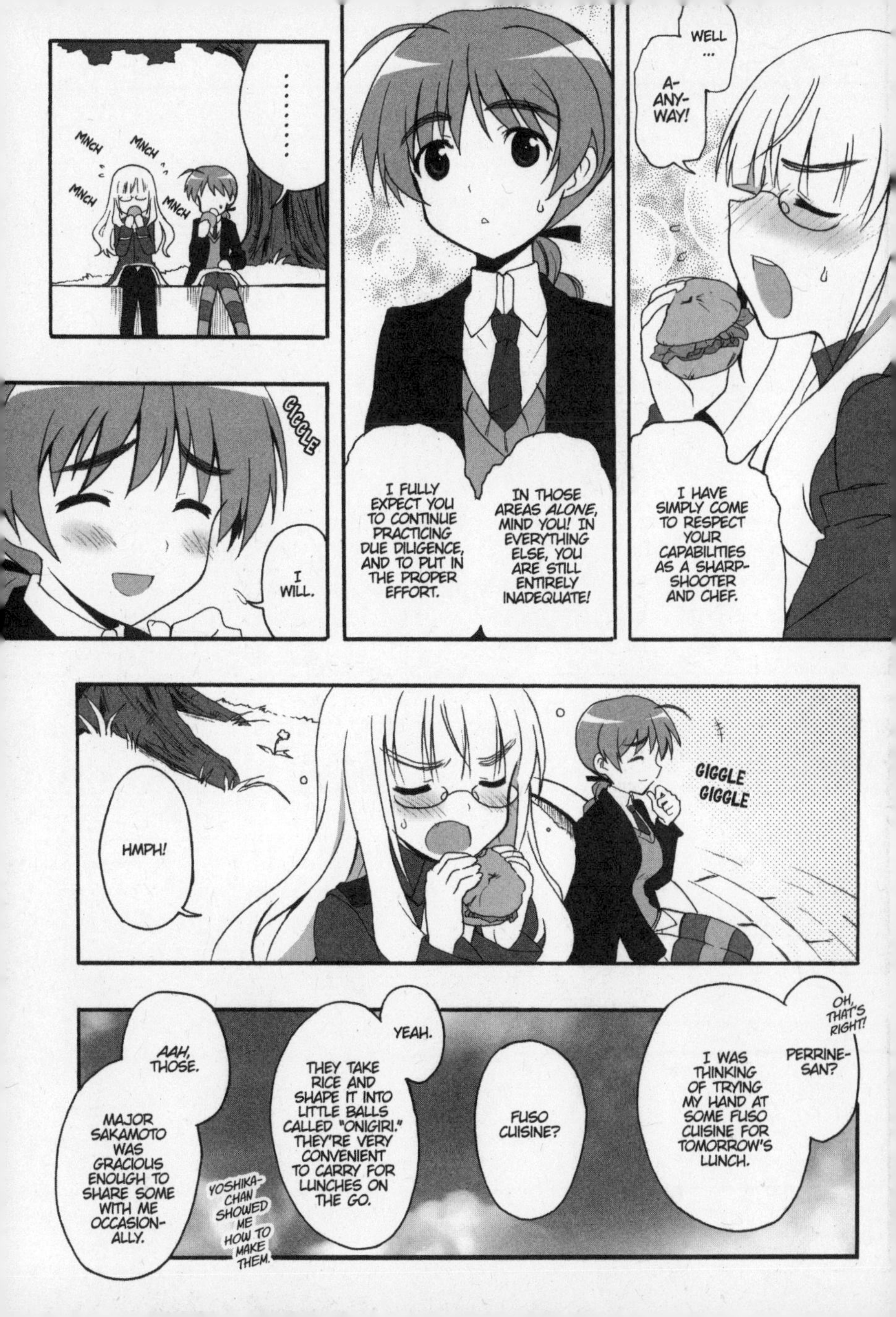
WELL ...
A- ANY- WAY!
I HAVE SIMPLY COME TO RESPECT YOUR CAPABILITIES AS A SHARP- SHOOTER AND CHEF.
IN THOSE AREAS *ALONE*, MIND YOU! IN EVERYTHING ELSE, YOU ARE STILL ENTIRELY INADEQUATE!
I FULLY EXPECT YOU TO CONTINUE PRACTICING DUE DILIGENCE, AND TO PUT IN THE PROPER EFFORT.
......
MNCH
MNCH
MNCH
MNCH
GIGGLE
I WILL.
GIGGLE GIGGLE
HMPH!
OH, THAT'S RIGHT!
PERRINE- SAN?
I WAS THINKING OF TRYING MY HAND AT SOME FUSO CUISINE FOR TOMORROW'S LUNCH.
FUSO CUISINE?
YEAH.
THEY TAKE RICE AND SHAPE IT INTO LITTLE BALLS CALLED "ONIGIRI." THEY'RE VERY CONVENIENT TO CARRY FOR LUNCHES ON THE GO.
YOSHIKA- CHAN SHOWED ME HOW TO MAKE THEM.
AAH, THOSE.
MAJOR SAKAMOTO WAS GRACIOUS ENOUGH TO SHARE SOME WITH ME OCCASION- ALLY.

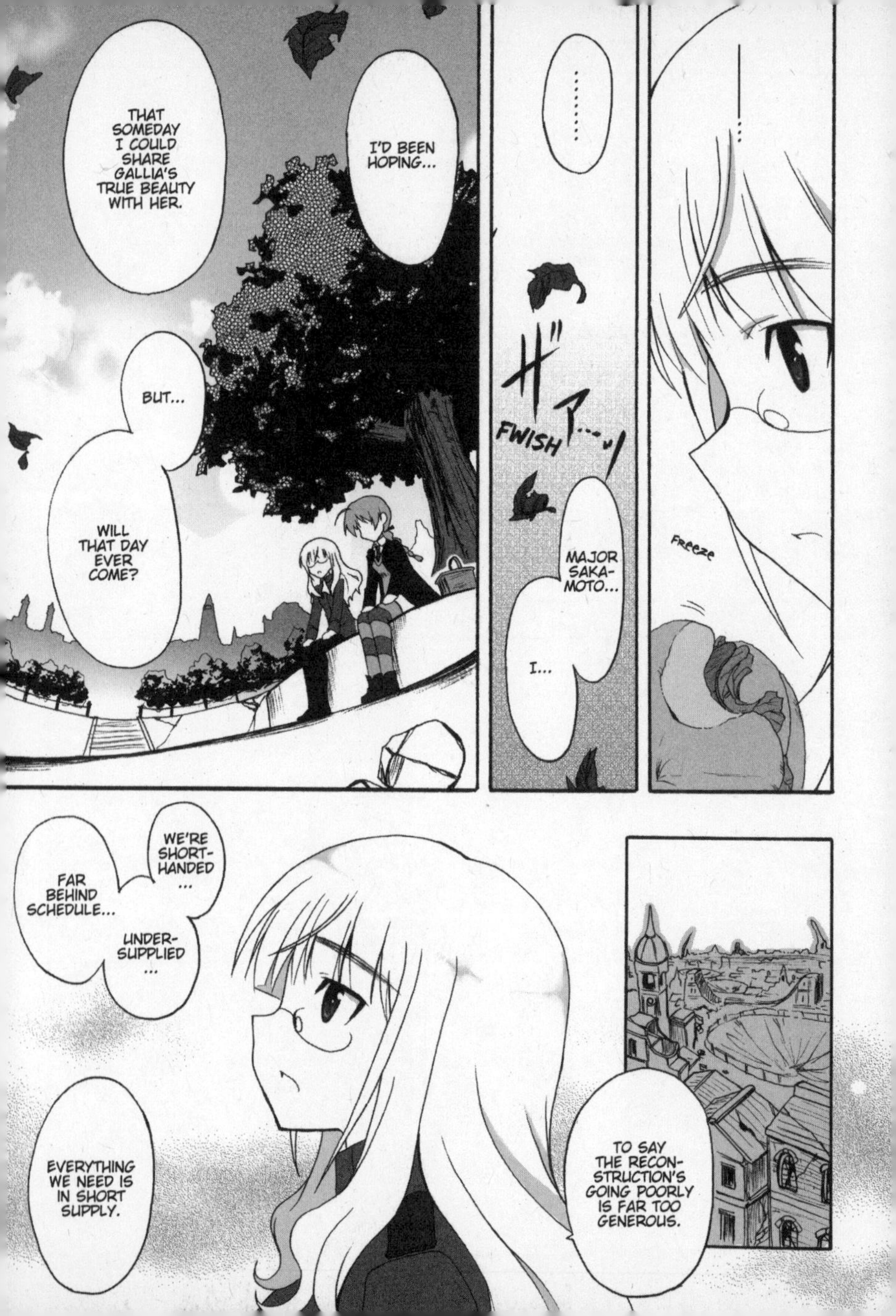

Freeze
......
ザァ…ッ
FWISH
MAJOR SAKAMOTO...
I...
I'D BEEN HOPING...
THAT SOMEDAY I COULD SHARE GALLIA'S TRUE BEAUTY WITH HER.
BUT...
WILL THAT DAY EVER COME?
TO SAY THE RECONSTRUCTION'S GOING POORLY IS FAR TOO GENEROUS.
WE'RE SHORT-HANDED ...
FAR BEHIND SCHEDULE...
UNDER-SUPPLIED ...
EVERYTHING WE NEED IS IN SHORT SUPPLY.

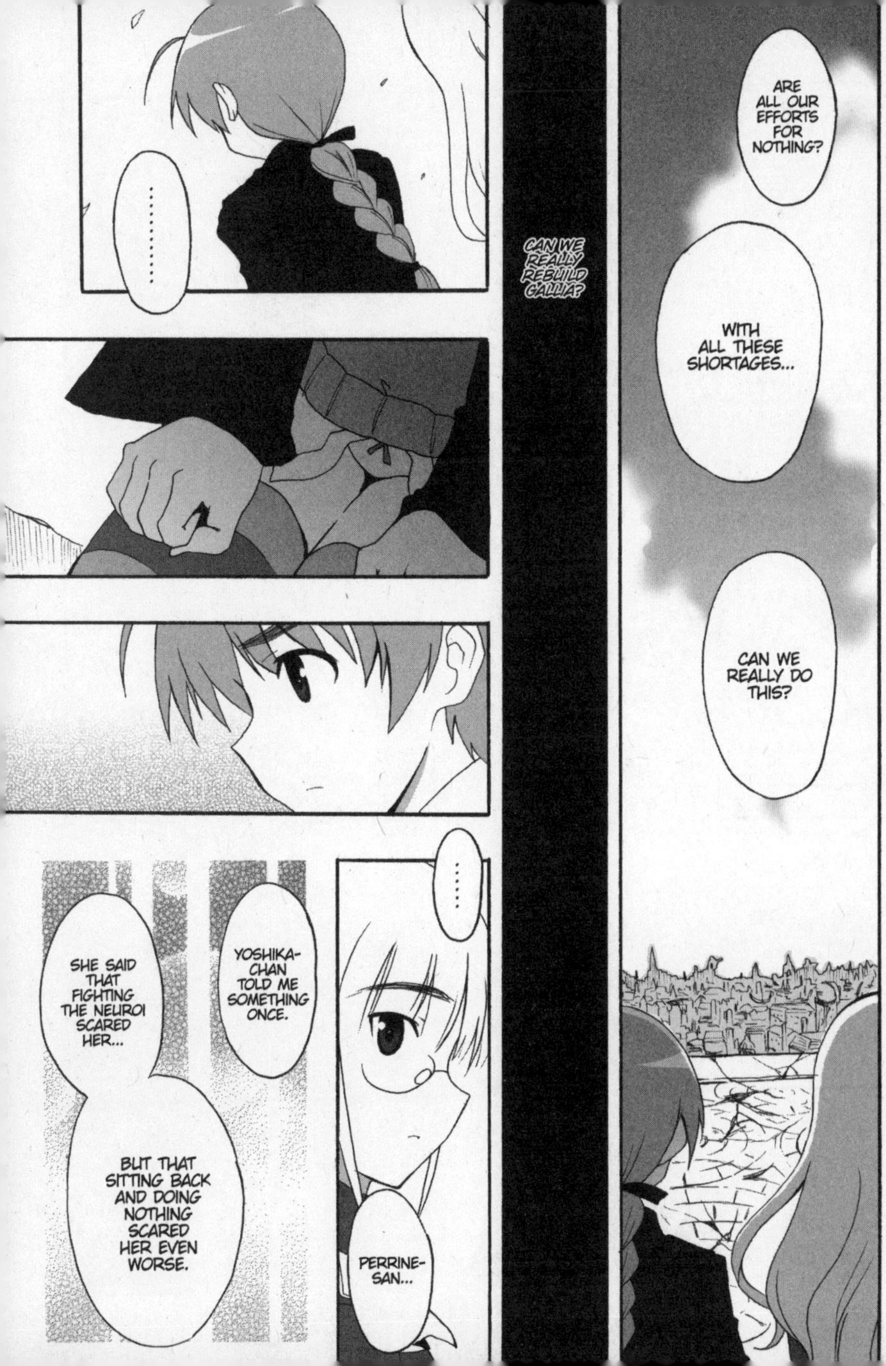
ARE ALL OUR EFFORTS FOR NOTHING?
WITH ALL THESE SHORTAGES...
CAN WE REALLY DO THIS?
CAN WE REALLY REBUILD GALLIA?
......
......
PERRINE-SAN...
YOSHIKA-CHAN TOLD ME SOMETHING ONCE.
SHE SAID THAT FIGHTING THE NEUROI SCARED HER...
BUT THAT SITTING BACK AND DOING NOTHING SCARED HER EVEN WORSE.

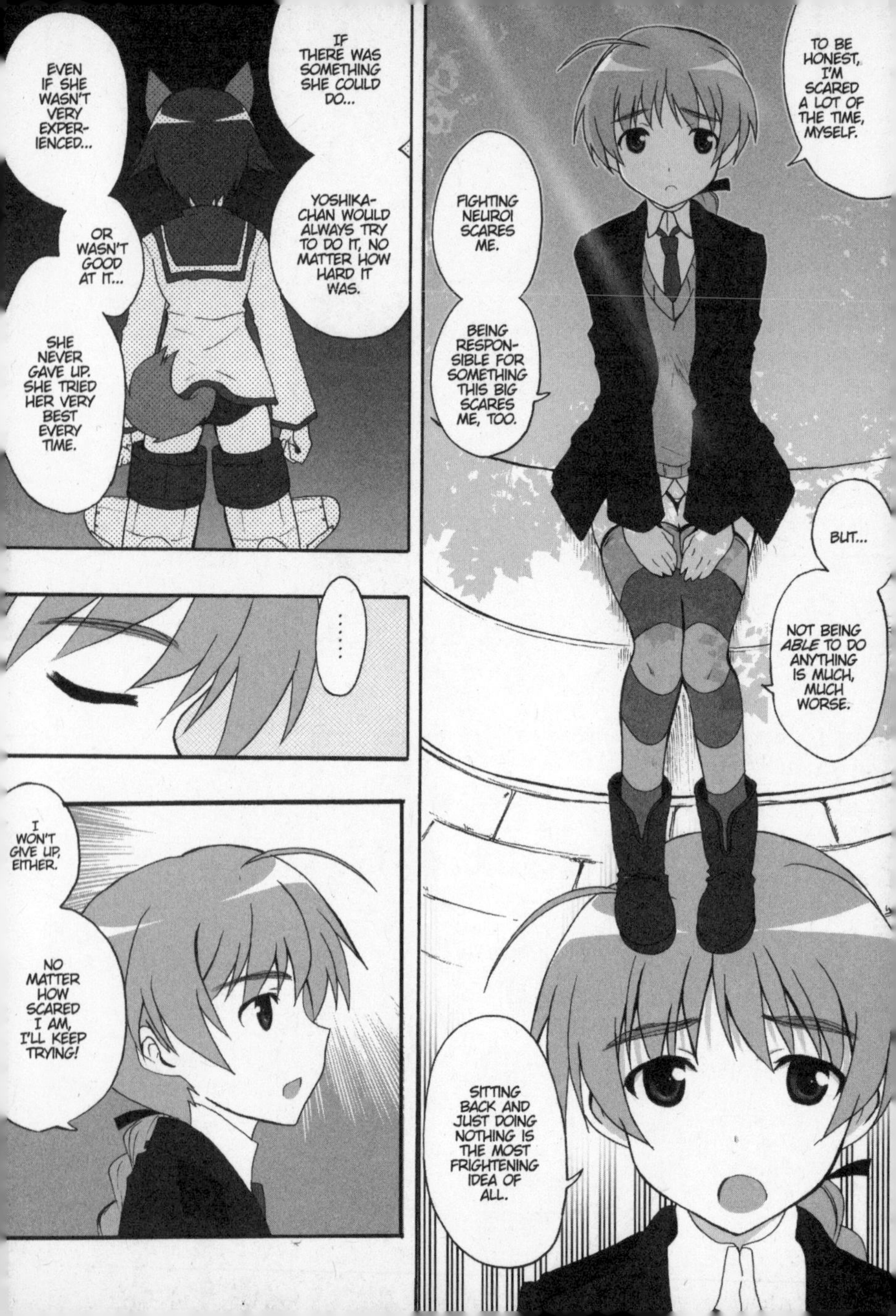
TO BE HONEST, I'M SCARED A LOT OF THE TIME, MYSELF.
FIGHTING NEUROI SCARES ME.
BEING RESPONSIBLE FOR SOMETHING THIS BIG SCARES ME, TOO.
BUT...
NOT BEING *ABLE* TO DO ANYTHING IS MUCH, MUCH WORSE.
SITTING BACK AND JUST DOING NOTHING IS THE MOST FRIGHTENING IDEA OF ALL.
IF THERE WAS SOMETHING SHE COULD DO...
YOSHIKA-CHAN WOULD ALWAYS TRY TO DO IT, NO MATTER HOW HARD IT WAS.
EVEN IF SHE WASN'T VERY EXPERIENCED...
OR WASN'T GOOD AT IT...
SHE NEVER GAVE UP. SHE TRIED HER VERY BEST EVERY TIME.
......
I WON'T GIVE UP, EITHER.
NO MATTER HOW SCARED I AM, I'LL KEEP TRYING!

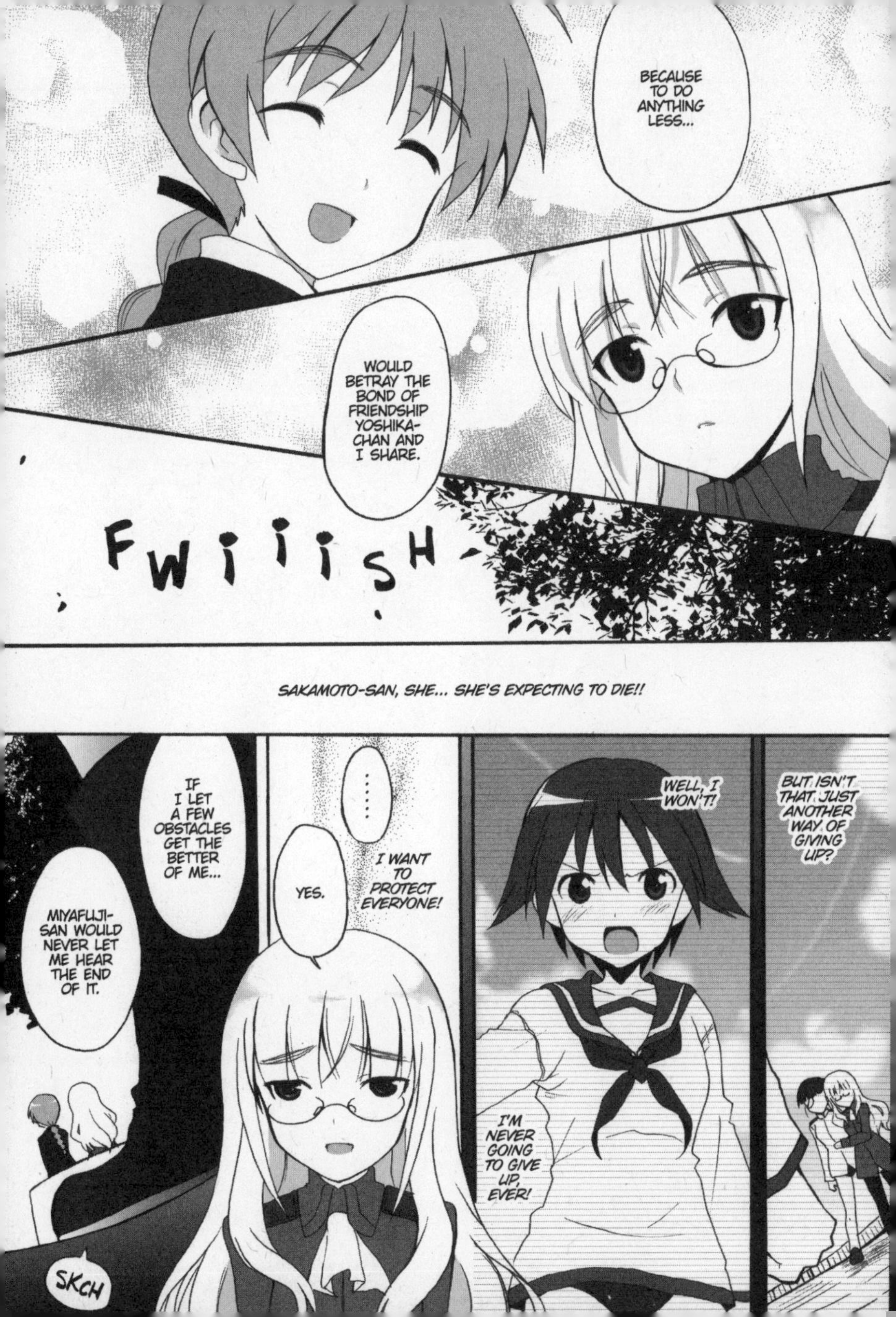
BECAUSE TO DO ANYTHING LESS...
WOULD BETRAY THE BOND OF FRIENDSHIP YOSHIKA-CHAN AND I SHARE.
FWIIISH
SAKAMOTO-SAN, SHE... SHE'S EXPECTING TO DIE!!
BUT ISN'T THAT JUST ANOTHER WAY OF GIVING UP?
WELL, I WON'T!
I'M NEVER GOING TO GIVE UP, EVER!
......
I WANT TO PROTECT EVERYONE!
YES.
IF I LET A FEW OBSTACLES GET THE BETTER OF ME...
MIYAFUJI-SAN WOULD NEVER LET ME HEAR THE END OF IT.
SKCH

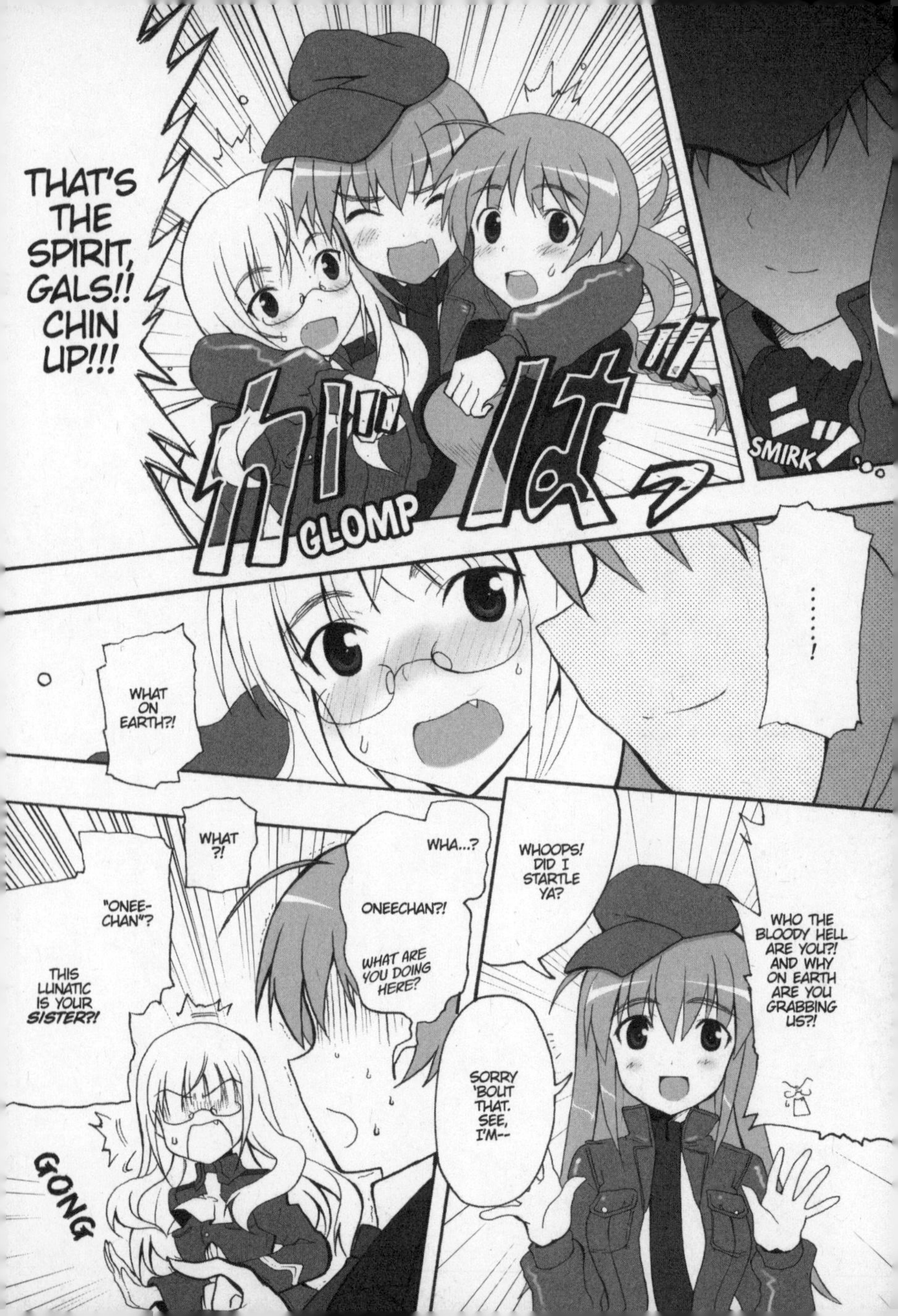
ニッ
SMIRK
THAT'S THE SPIRIT, GALS!! CHIN UP!!!
がばっ
GLOMP
......!
WHAT ON EARTH?!
WHOOPS! DID I STARTLE YA?
WHO THE BLOODY HELL ARE YOU?! AND WHY ON EARTH ARE YOU GRABBING US?!
SORRY 'BOUT THAT. SEE, I'M--
WHA...?
ONEECHAN?!
WHAT ARE YOU DOING HERE?
WHAT ?!
"ONEE-CHAN"?
THIS LUNATIC IS YOUR SISTER?!
GONG

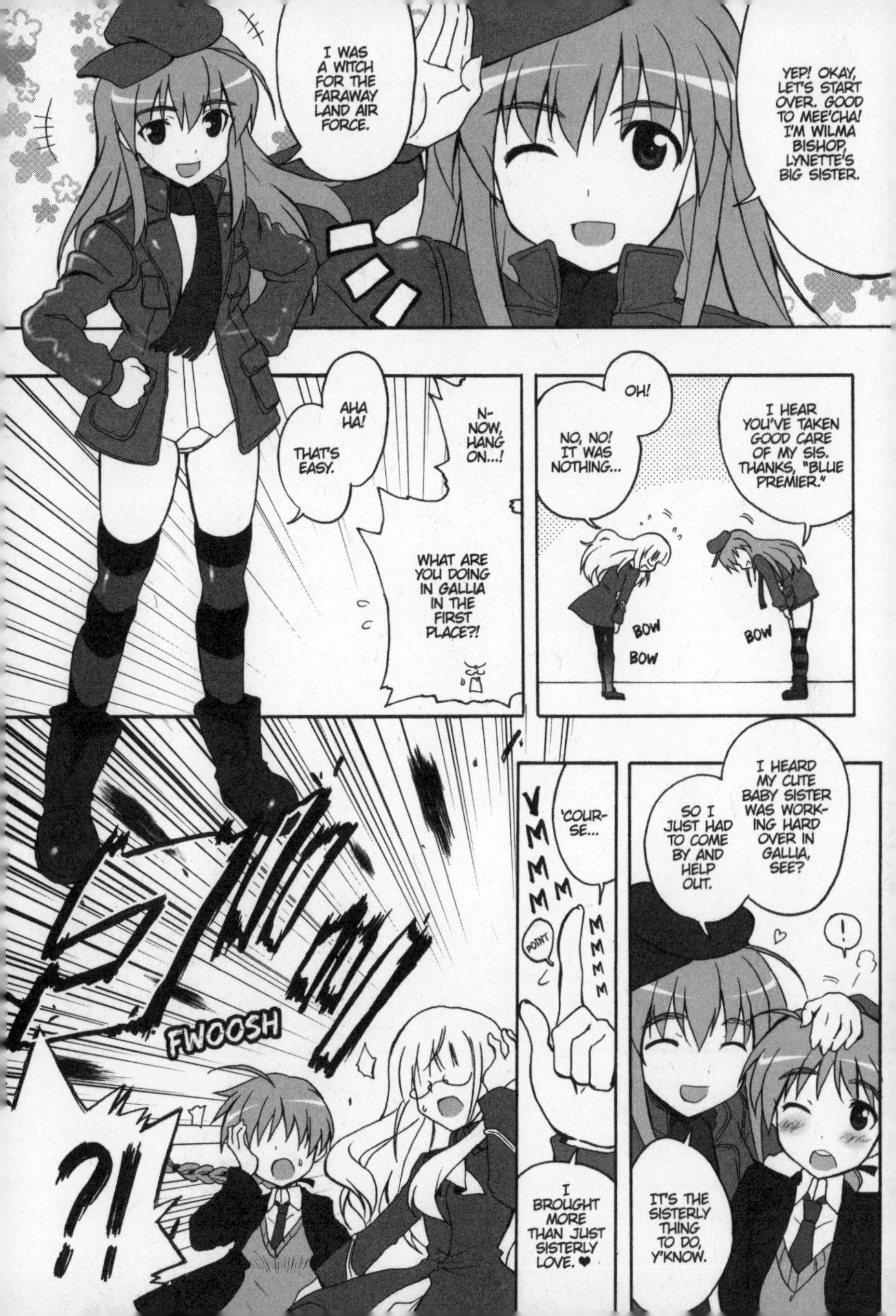
YEP! OKAY, LET'S START OVER. GOOD TO MEE'CHA! I'M WILMA BISHOP, LYNETTE'S BIG SISTER.
I WAS A WITCH FOR THE FARAWAY LAND AIR FORCE.
I HEAR YOU'VE TAKEN GOOD CARE OF MY SIS. THANKS, "BLUE PREMIER."
OH!
NO, NO! IT WAS NOTHING...
BOW
BOW
BOW
N-NOW, HANG ON...!
WHAT ARE YOU DOING IN GALLIA IN THE FIRST PLACE?!
AHA HA!
THAT'S EASY.
I HEARD MY CUTE BABY SISTER WAS WORKING HARD OVER IN GALLIA, SEE?
SO I JUST HAD TO COME BY AND HELP OUT.
!
IT'S THE SISTERLY THING TO DO, Y'KNOW.
'COURSE...
VMMMMM
MMMM
POINT
I BROUGHT MORE THAN JUST SISTERLY LOVE. ❤
FWOOSH
?!

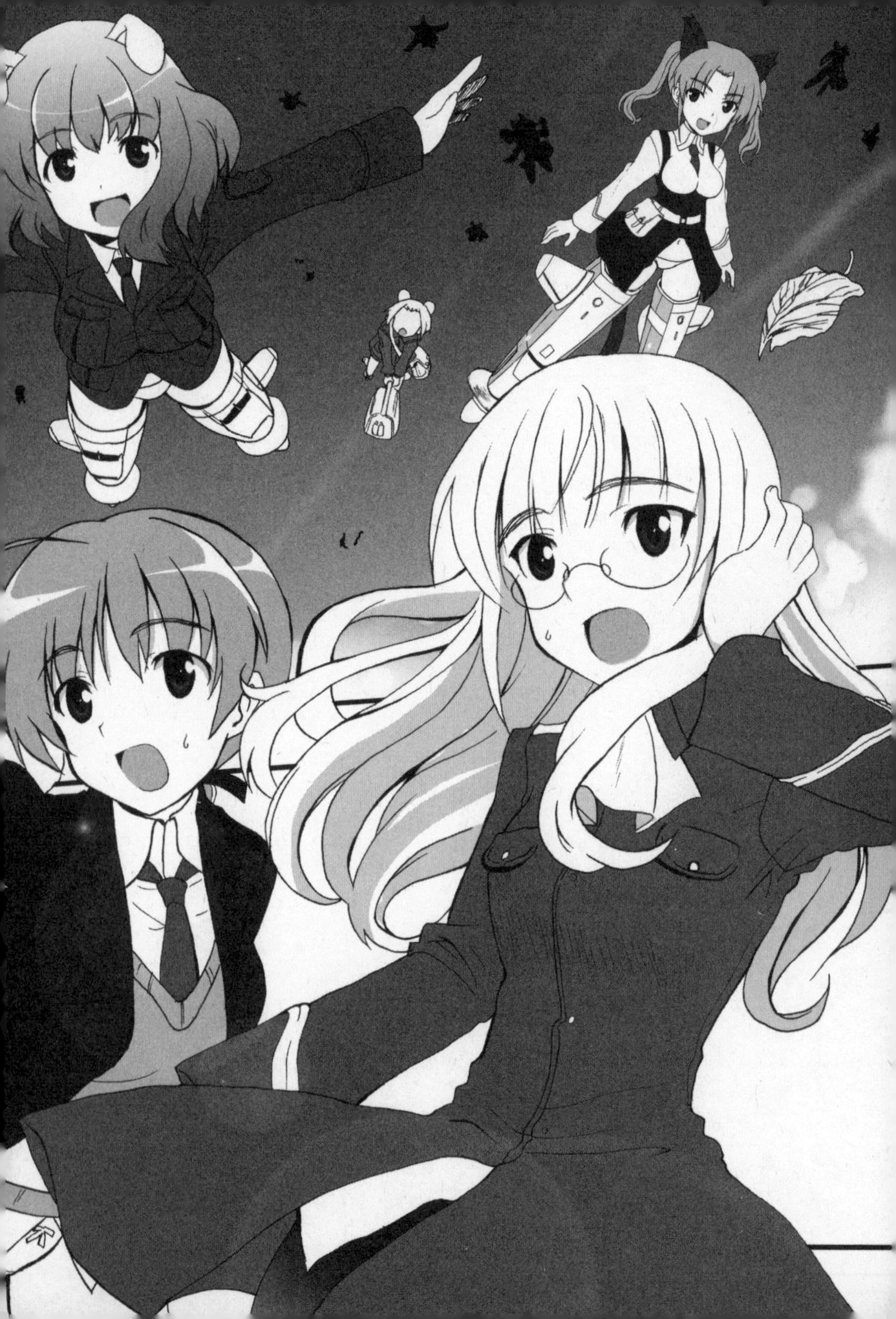

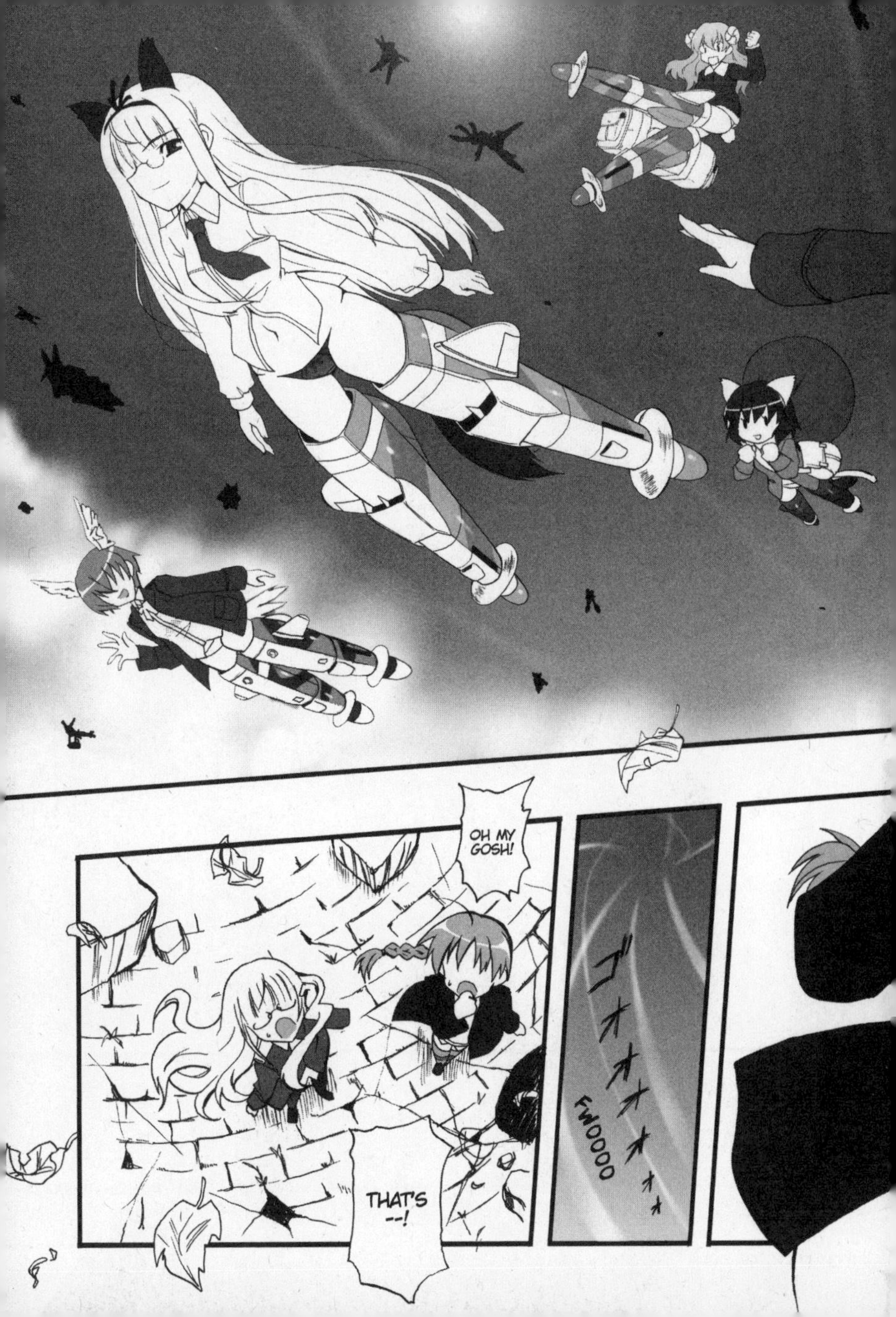
FWOOOO
OH MY GOSH!
THAT'S --!

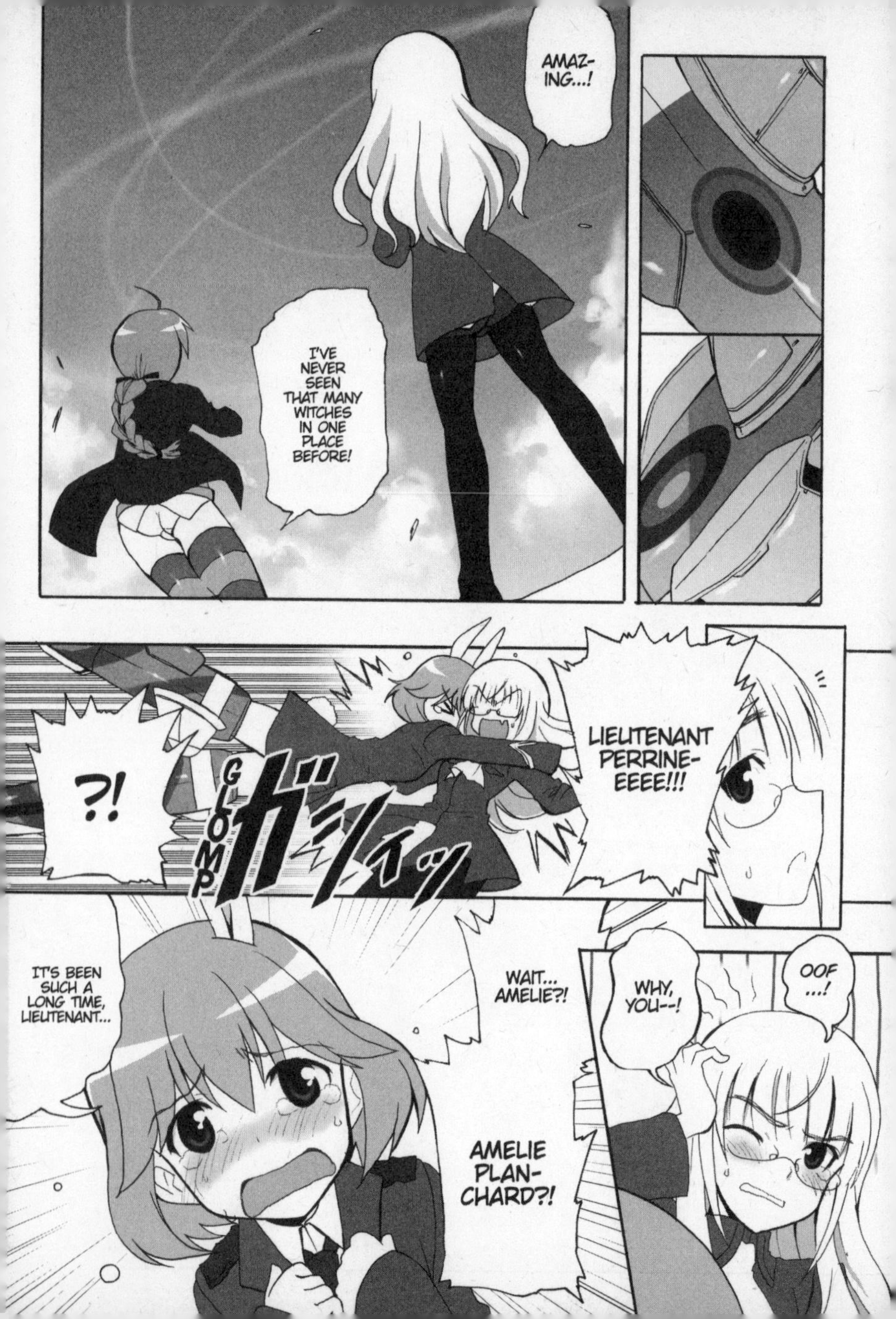
AMAZ-ING...!
I'VE NEVER SEEN THAT MANY WITCHES IN ONE PLACE BEFORE!
LIEUTENANT PERRINE-EEEE!!!
GLOMP
ガシィッ
?!
OOF ...!
WHY, YOU--!
WAIT... AMELIE?!
IT'S BEEN SUCH A LONG TIME, LIEUTENANT...
AMELIE PLAN-CHARD?!

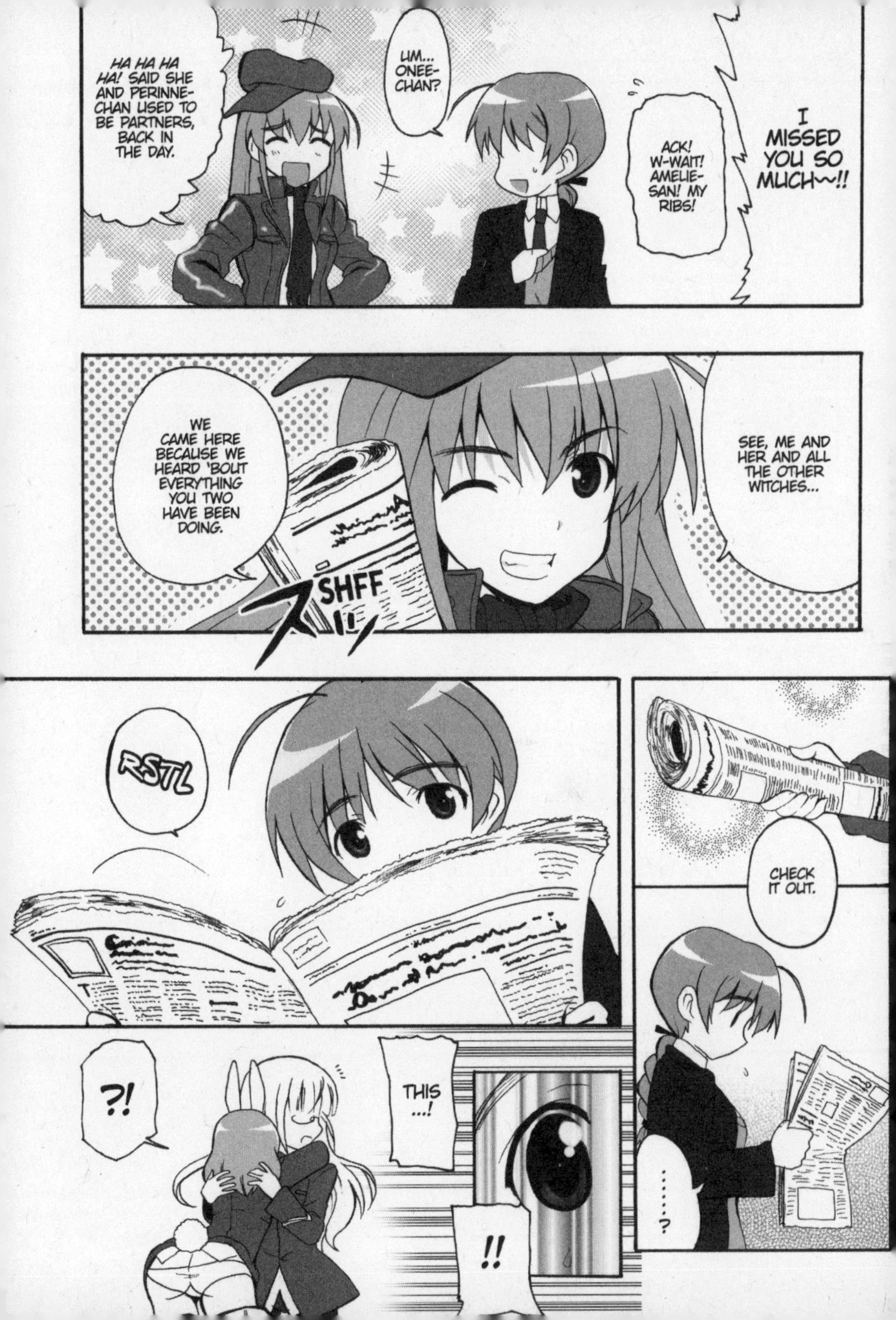
I MISSED YOU SO MUCH~!!
ACK! W-WAIT! AMELIE-SAN! MY RIBS!
UM... ONEE-CHAN?
HA HA HA HA! SAID SHE AND PERINNE-CHAN USED TO BE PARTNERS, BACK IN THE DAY.
SEE, ME AND HER AND ALL THE OTHER WITCHES...
WE CAME HERE BECAUSE WE HEARD 'BOUT EVERYTHING YOU TWO HAVE BEEN DOING.
SHFF
CHECK IT OUT.
......?
RSTL
THIS ...!
!!
?!

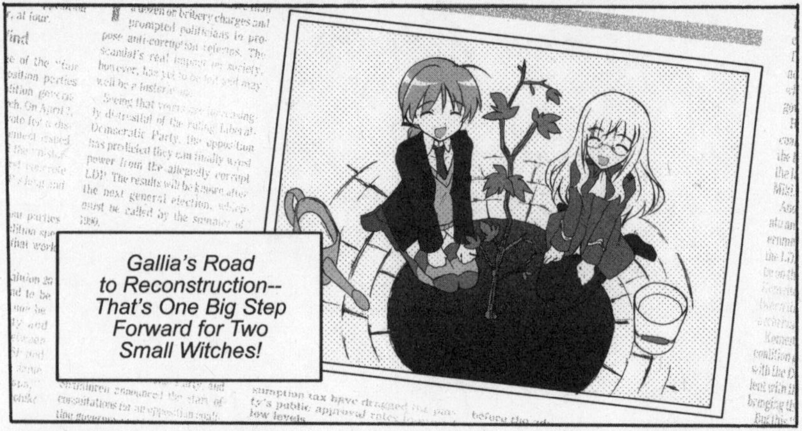
Gallia's Road to Reconstruction-- That's One Big Step Forward for Two Small Witches!

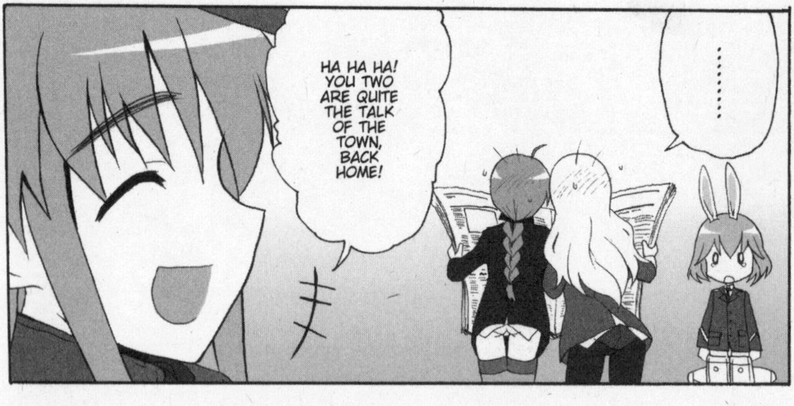
......
HA HA HA! YOU TWO ARE QUITE THE TALK OF THE TOWN, BACK HOME!

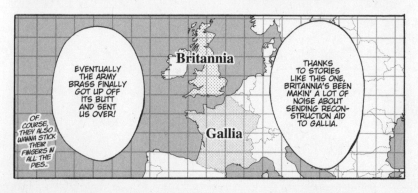

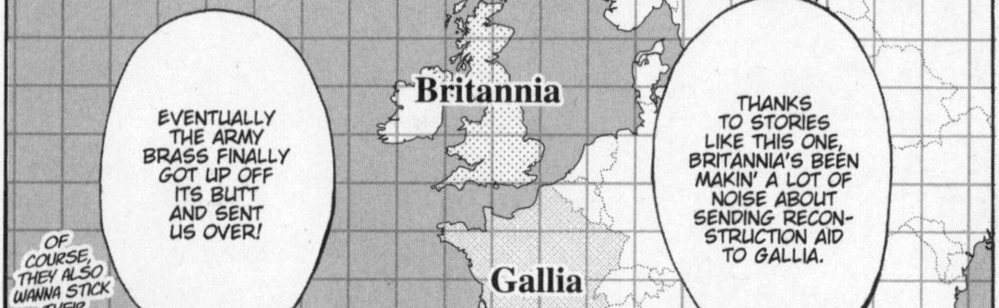
Britannia
Gallia
THANKS TO STORIES LIKE THIS ONE, BRITANNIA'S BEEN MAKIN' A LOT OF NOISE ABOUT SENDING RECON-STRUCTION AID TO GALLIA.
EVENTUALLY THE ARMY BRASS FINALLY GOT UP OFF ITS BUTT AND SENT US OVER!
OF COURSE, THEY ALSO WANNA STICK THEIR FINGERS IN ALL THE PIES...

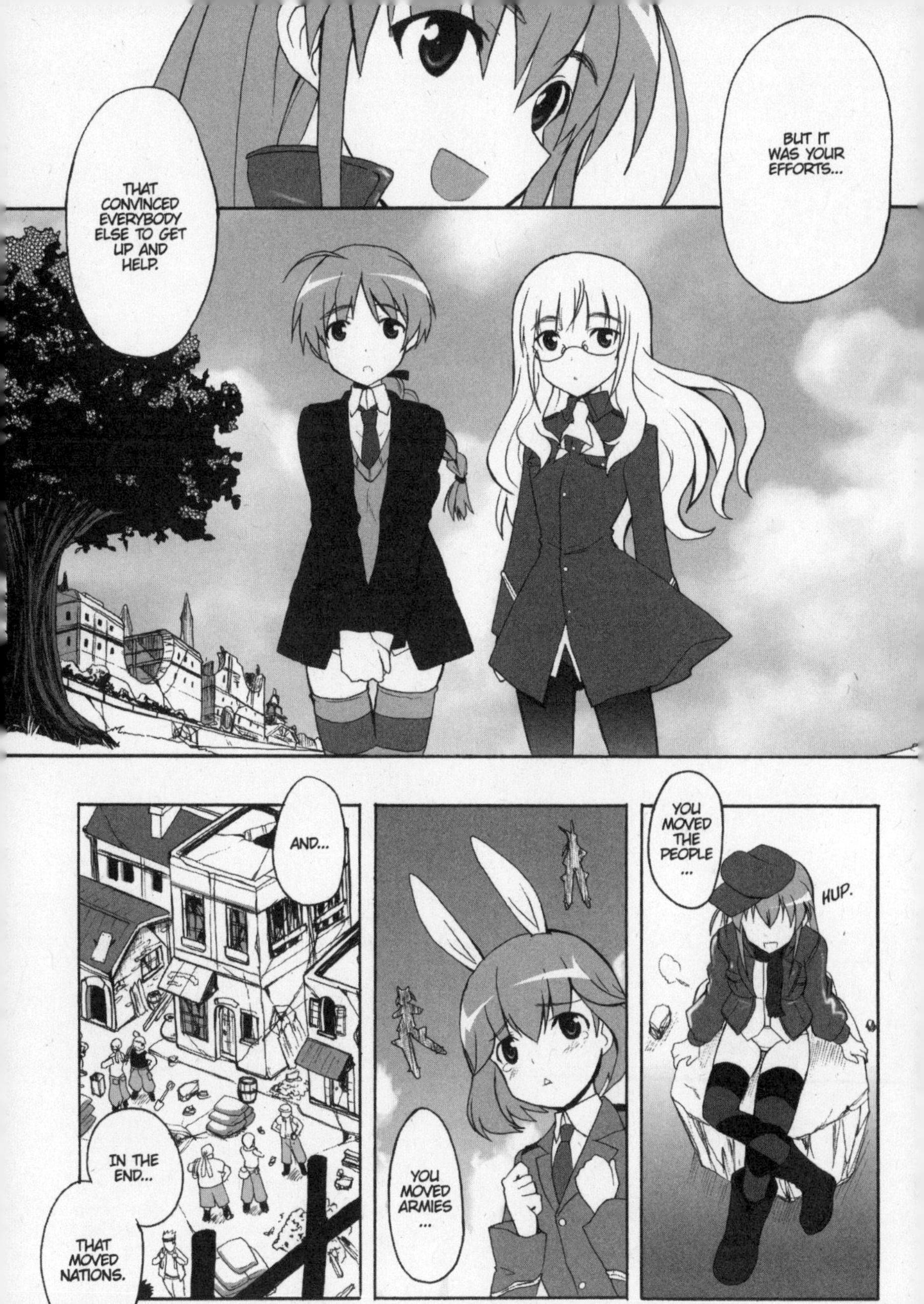
BUT IT WAS YOUR EFFORTS...
THAT CONVINCED EVERYBODY ELSE TO GET UP AND HELP.
YOU MOVED THE PEOPLE ...
HUP.
YOU MOVED ARMIES ...
AND...
IN THE END...
THAT MOVED NATIONS.

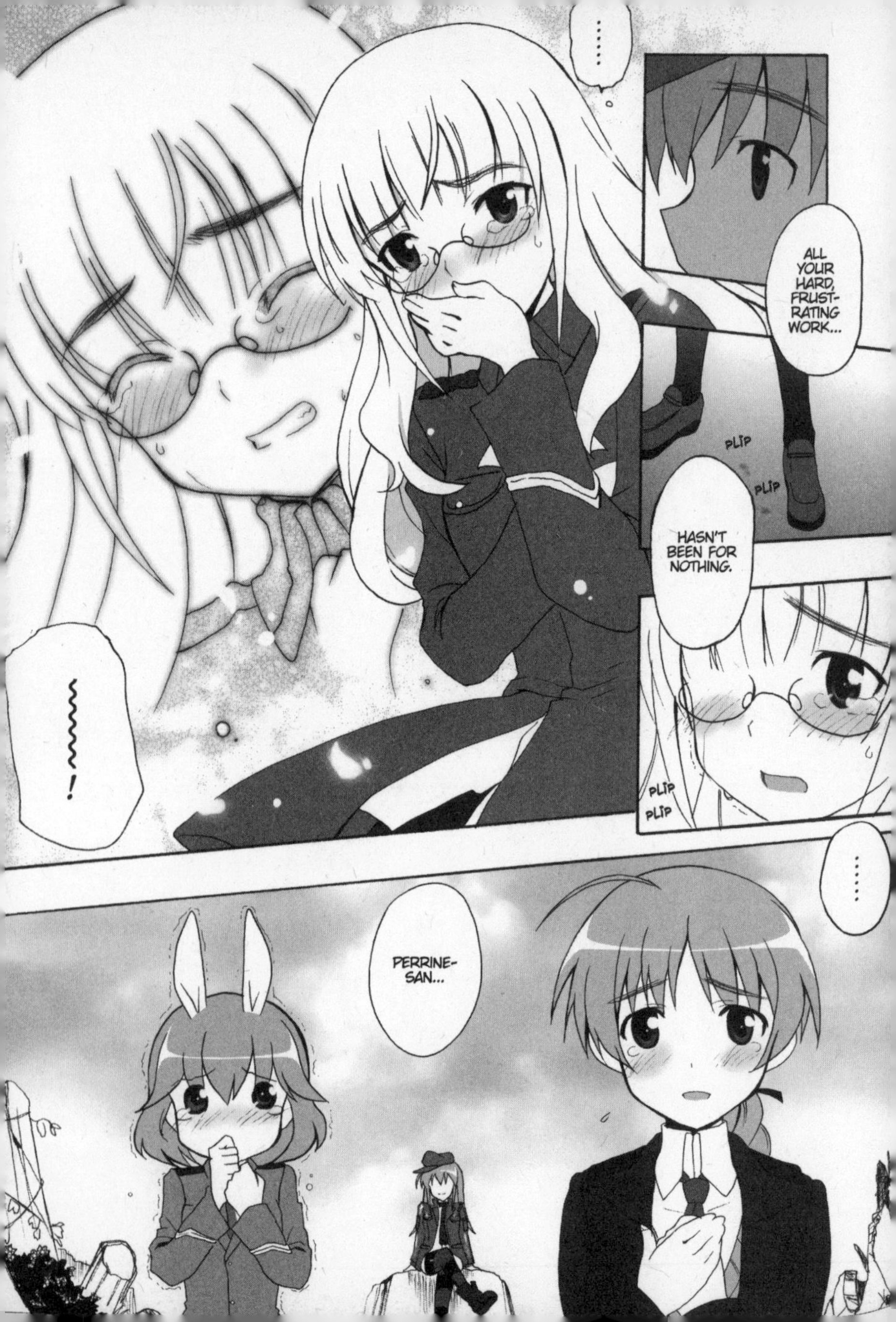
ALL YOUR HARD, FRUST-RATING WORK...
PLIP
PLIP
HASN'T BEEN FOR NOTHING.
PLIP
PLIP
......
~~~~~!
......
PERRINE-SAN...
~~~~~

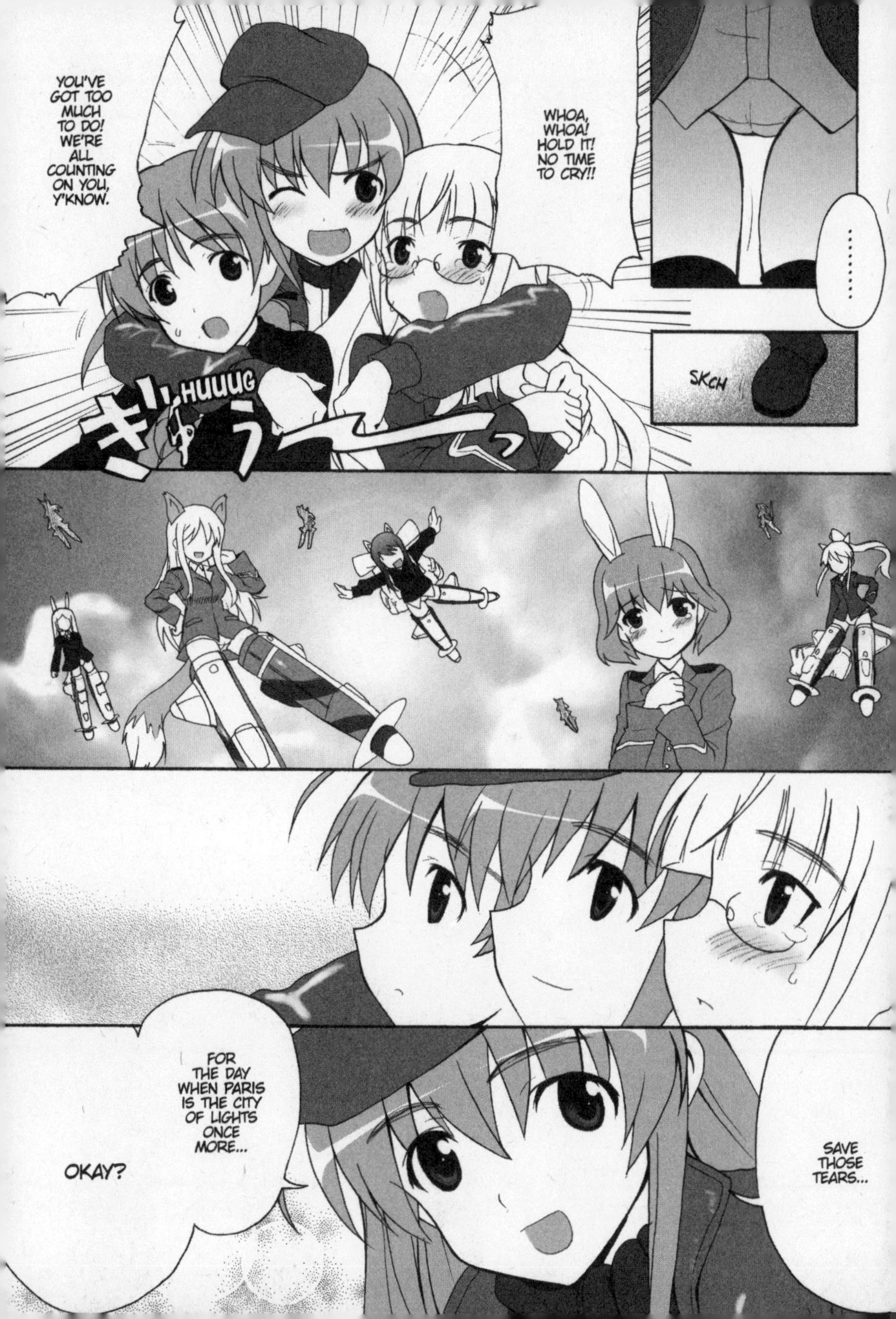
......
SKCH
WHOA, WHOA! HOLD IT! NO TIME TO CRY!!
YOU'VE GOT TOO MUCH TO DO! WE'RE ALL COUNTING ON YOU, Y'KNOW.
HUUUG
SAVE THOSE TEARS...
FOR THE DAY WHEN PARIS IS THE CITY OF LIGHTS ONCE MORE...
OKAY?

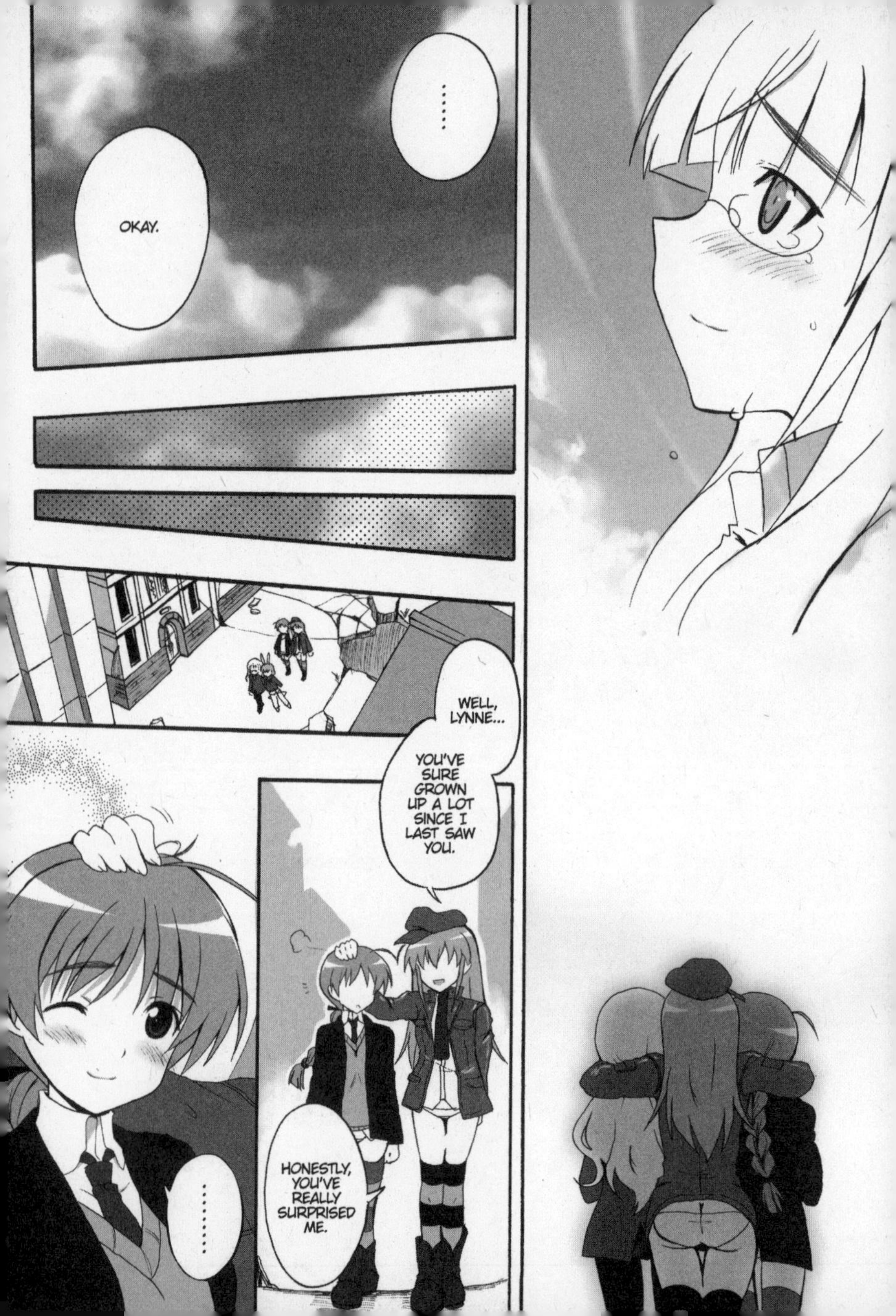
......
OKAY.
WELL, LYNNE...
YOU'VE SURE GROWN UP A LOT SINCE I LAST SAW YOU.
HONESTLY, YOU'VE REALLY SURPRISED ME.
......

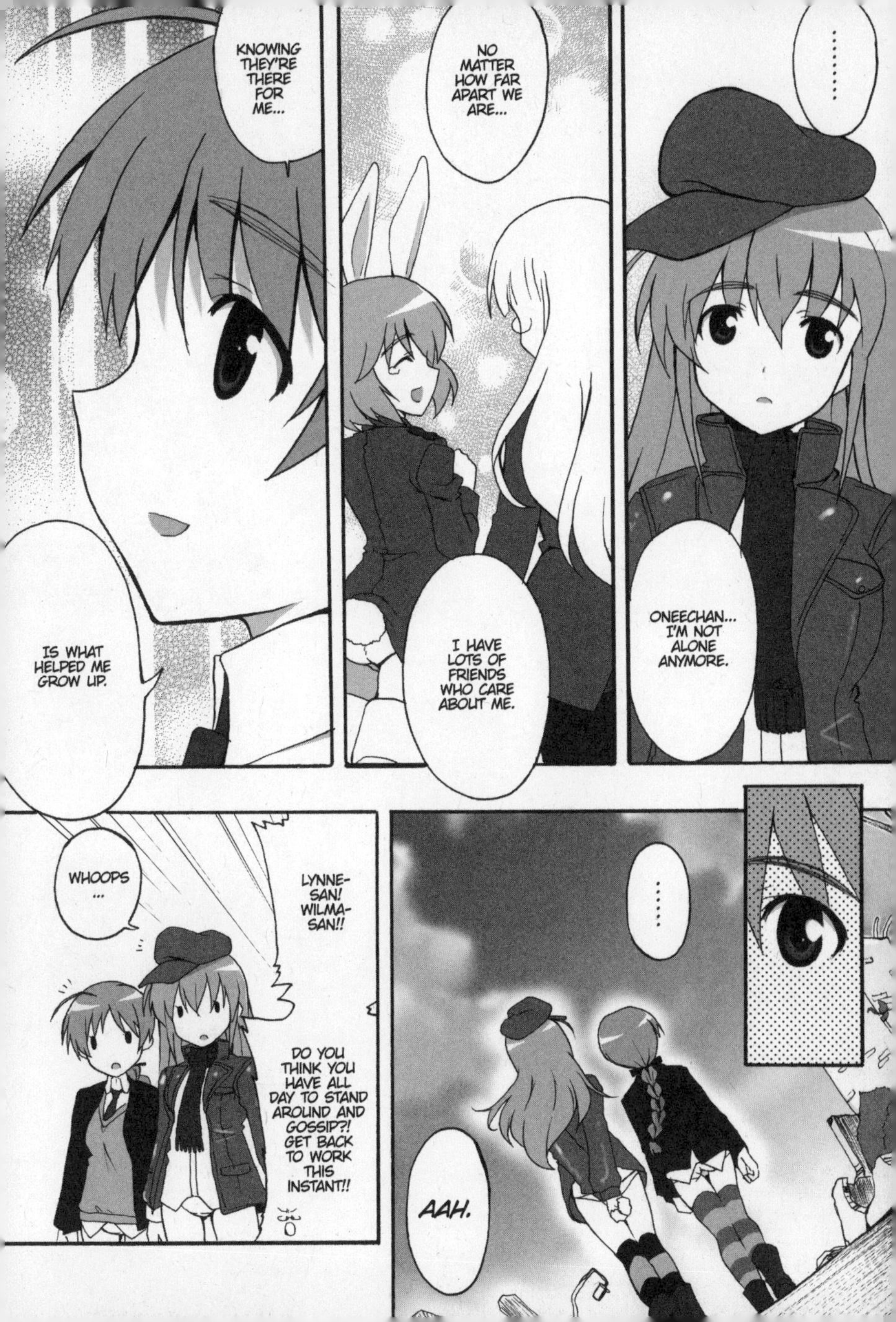
……
ONEECHAN... I'M NOT ALONE ANYMORE.
NO MATTER HOW FAR APART WE ARE...
I HAVE LOTS OF FRIENDS WHO CARE ABOUT ME.
KNOWING THEY'RE THERE FOR ME...
IS WHAT HELPED ME GROW UP.
……
AAH.
LYNNE-SAN! WILMA-SAN!!
DO YOU THINK YOU HAVE ALL DAY TO STAND AROUND AND GOSSIP?! GET BACK TO WORK THIS INSTANT!!
WHOOPS ...

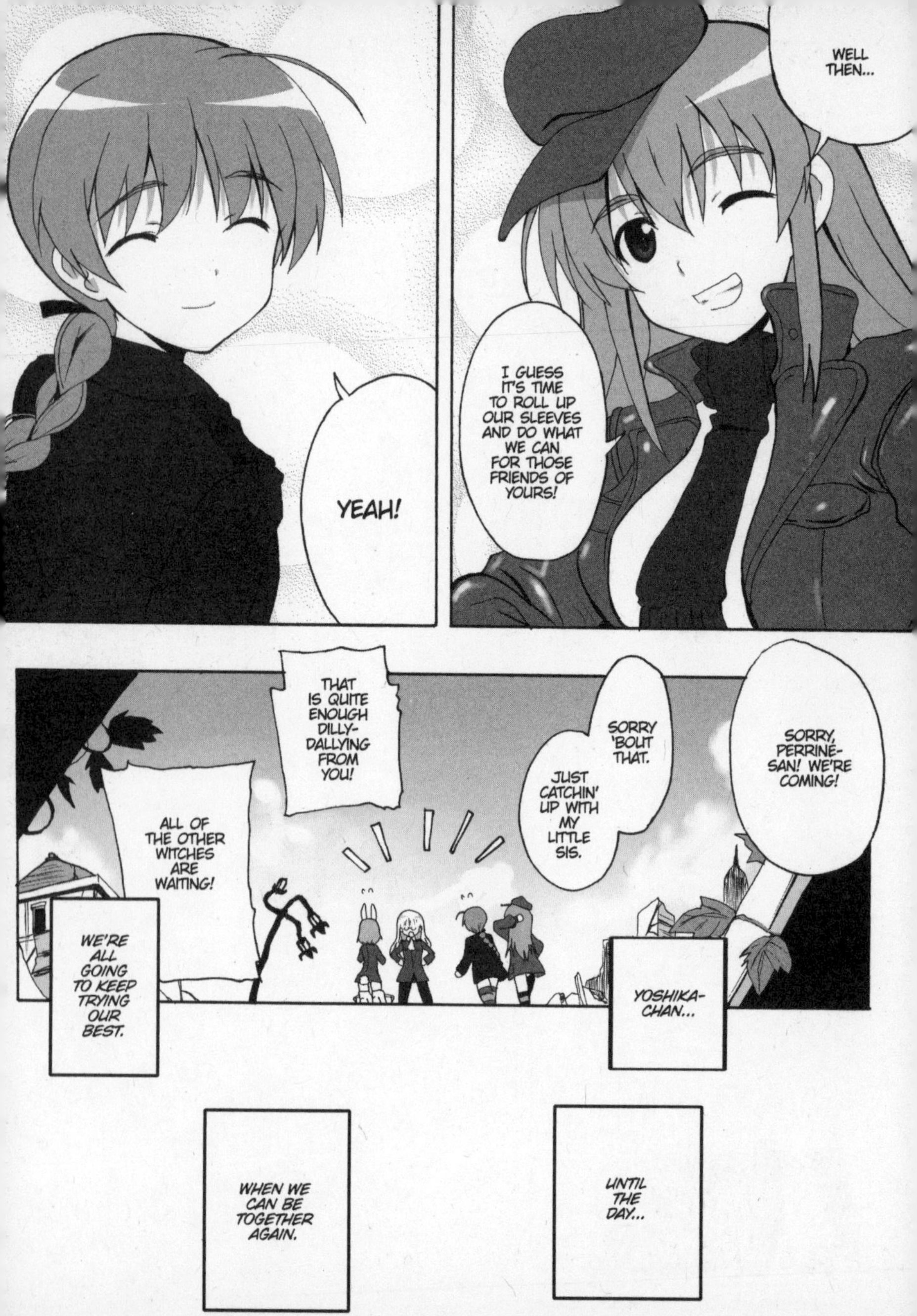
WELL THEN...
I GUESS IT'S TIME TO ROLL UP OUR SLEEVES AND DO WHAT WE CAN FOR THOSE FRIENDS OF YOURS!
YEAH!
SORRY, PERRINÉ-SAN! WE'RE COMING!
SORRY 'BOUT THAT.
JUST CATCHIN' UP WITH MY LITTLE SIS.
THAT IS QUITE ENOUGH DILLY-DALLYING FROM YOU!
ALL OF THE OTHER WITCHES ARE WAITING!
YOSHIKA-CHAN...
WE'RE ALL GOING TO KEEP TRYING OUR BEST.
UNTIL THE DAY...
WHEN WE CAN BE TOGETHER AGAIN.

WITCHES GRAFFITI

**Shimada Humikane &
Projekt Kagonish**
illustrated by
Kyougoku Shin

Perrine-H.Clostermann

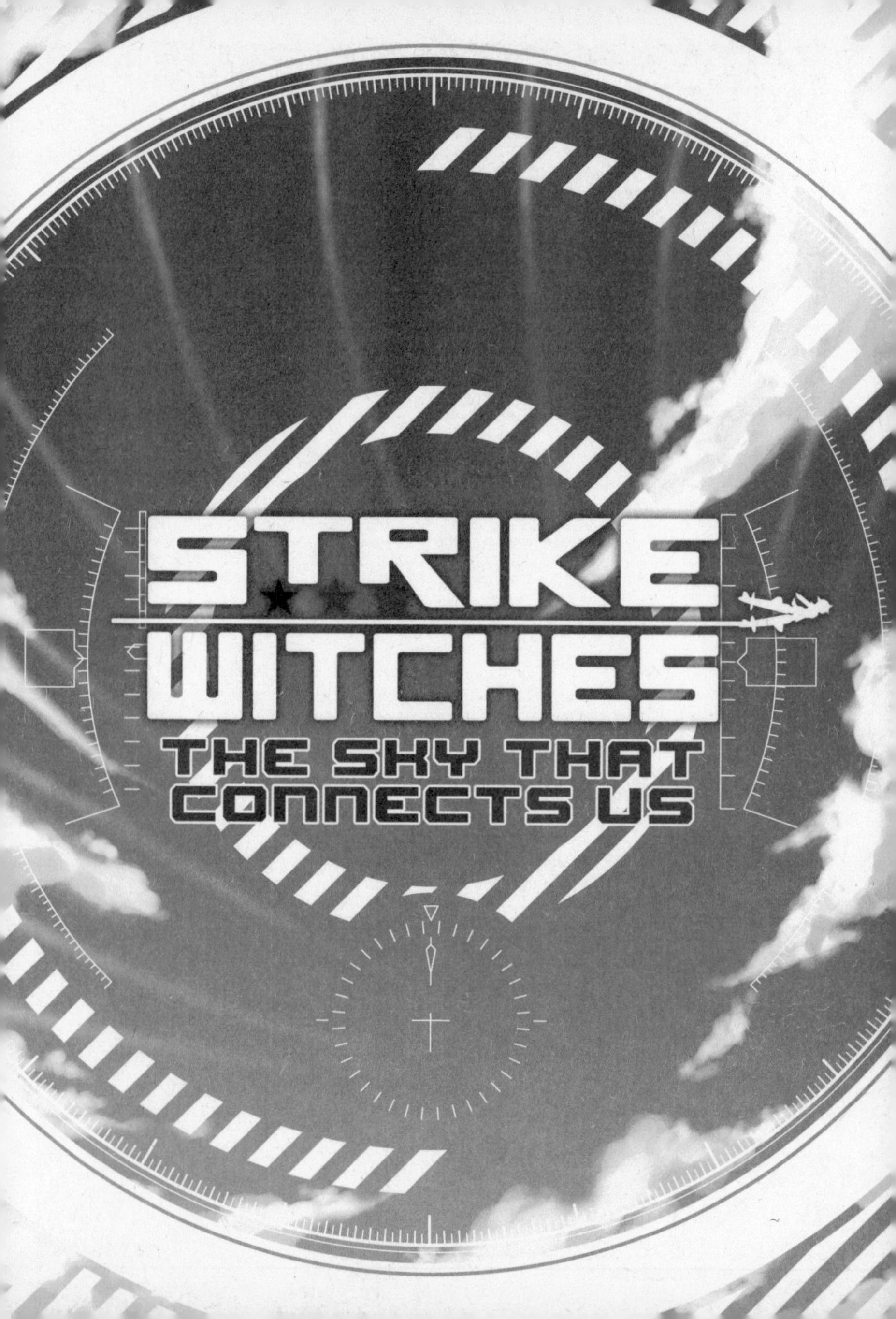
STRIKE WITCHES
THE SKY THAT CONNECTS US

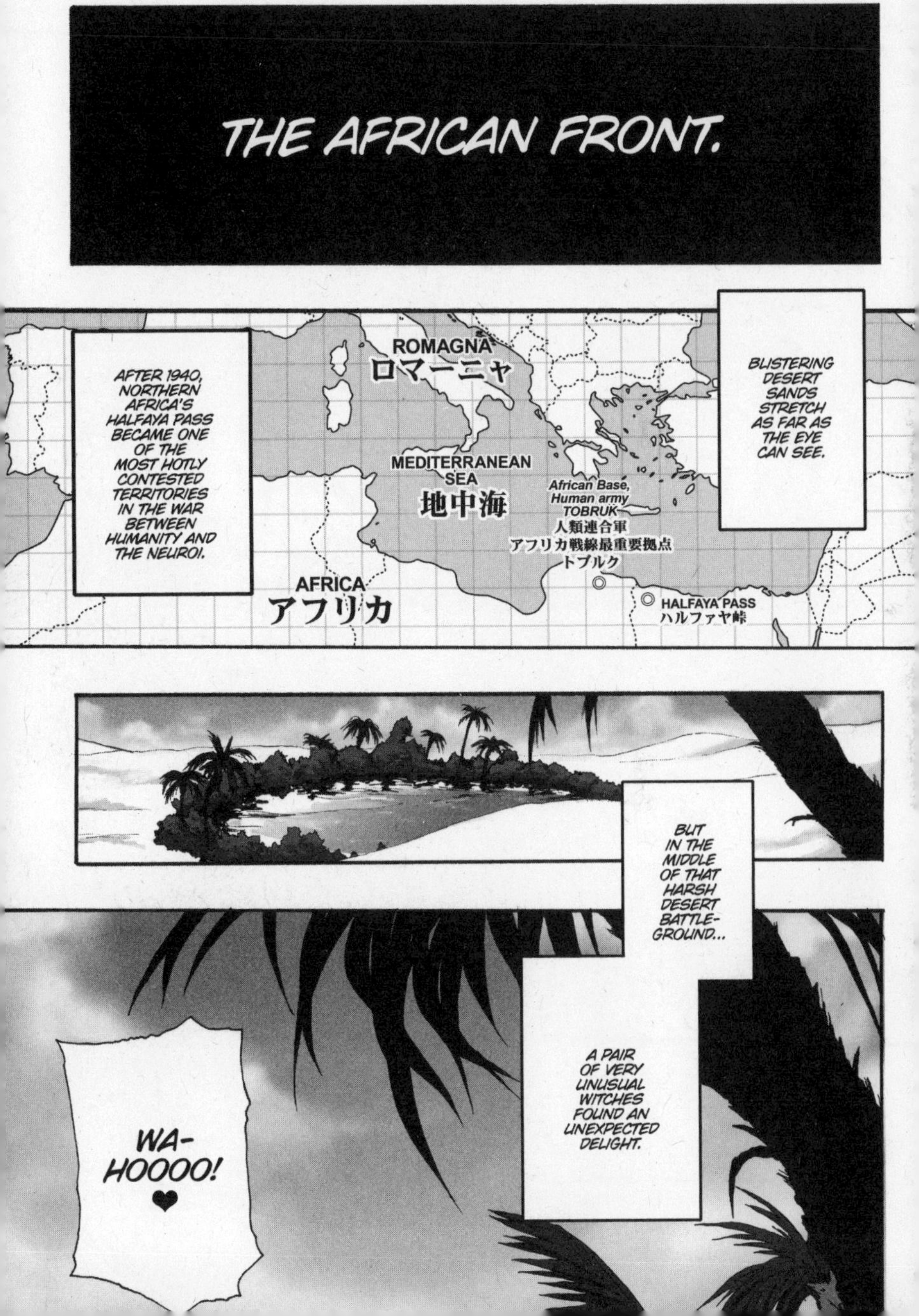
THE AFRICAN FRONT.
BLISTERING DESERT SANDS STRETCH AS FAR AS THE EYE CAN SEE.
ROMAGNA
ロマーニャ
MEDITERRANEAN SEA
地中海
African Base, Human army TOBRUK
人類連合軍
アフリカ戦線最重要拠点
トブルク
HALFAYA PASS
ハルファヤ峠
AFTER 1940, NORTHERN AFRICA'S HALFAYA PASS BECAME ONE OF THE MOST HOTLY CONTESTED TERRITORIES IN THE WAR BETWEEN HUMANITY AND THE NEUROI.
AFRICA
アフリカ
BUT IN THE MIDDLE OF THAT HARSH DESERT BATTLE-GROUND...
A PAIR OF VERY UNUSUAL WITCHES FOUND AN UNEXPECTED DELIGHT.
WA-HOOOO! ❤

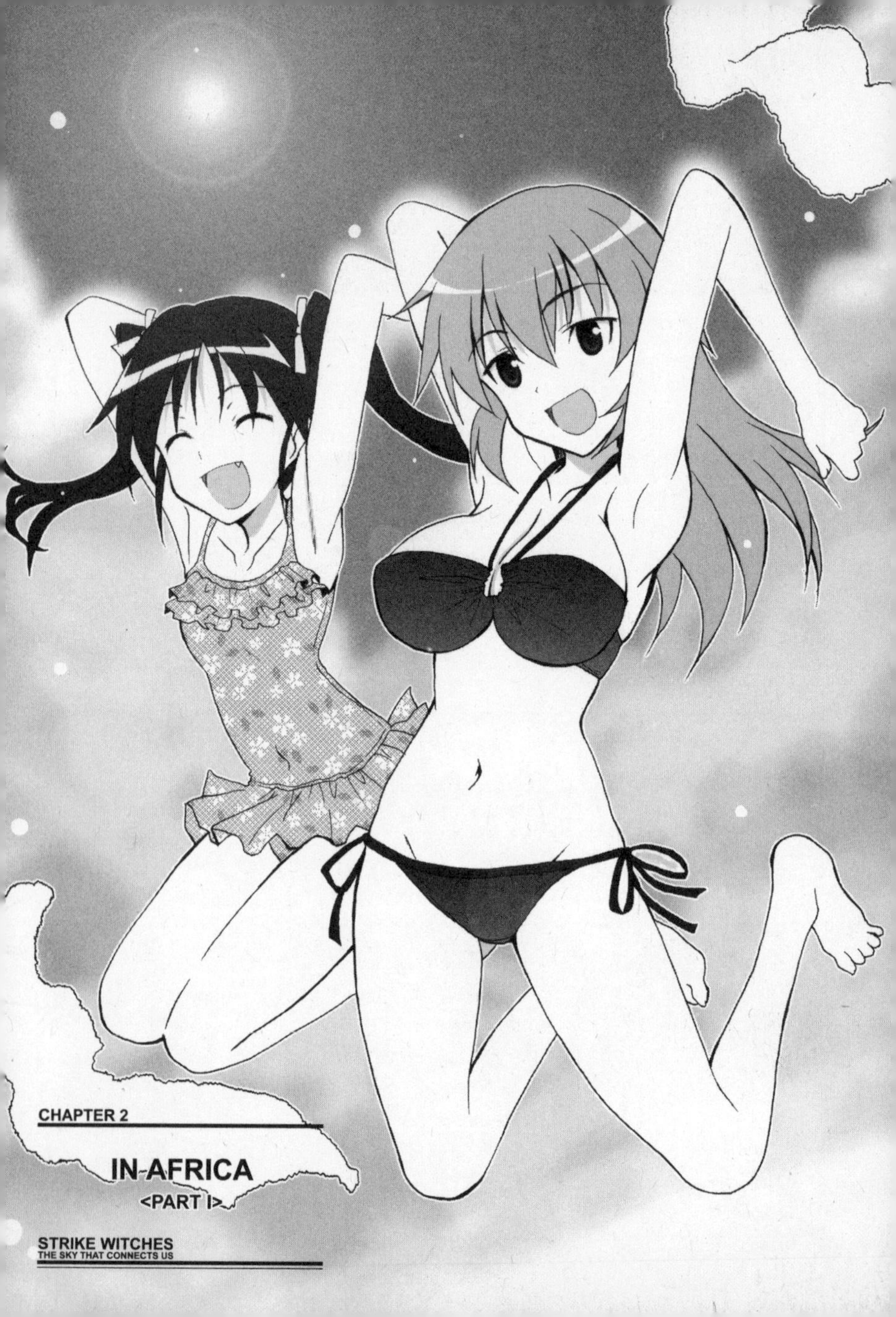

CHAPTER 2

IN AFRICA

<PART I>

STRIKE WITCHES
THE SKY THAT CONNECTS US

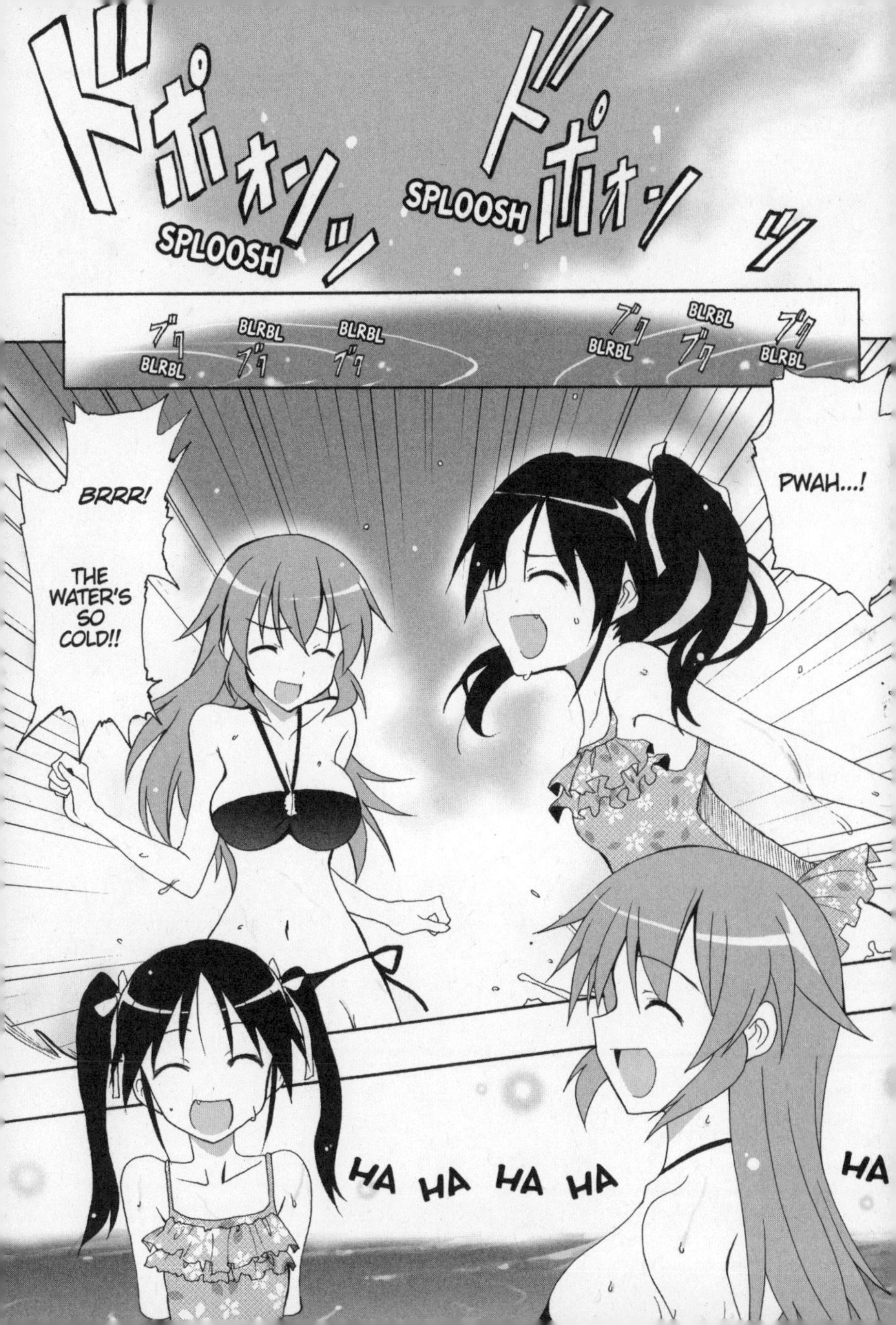
ドポォンッ
SPLOOSH
ドポォンッ
SPLOOSH
ブク
BLRBL
ブク
BLRBL
ブク
BLRBL
ブク
BLRBL
ブク
BLRBL
ブク
BLRBL
PWAH...!
BRRR!
THE WATER'S SO COLD!!
HA
HA HA HA HA

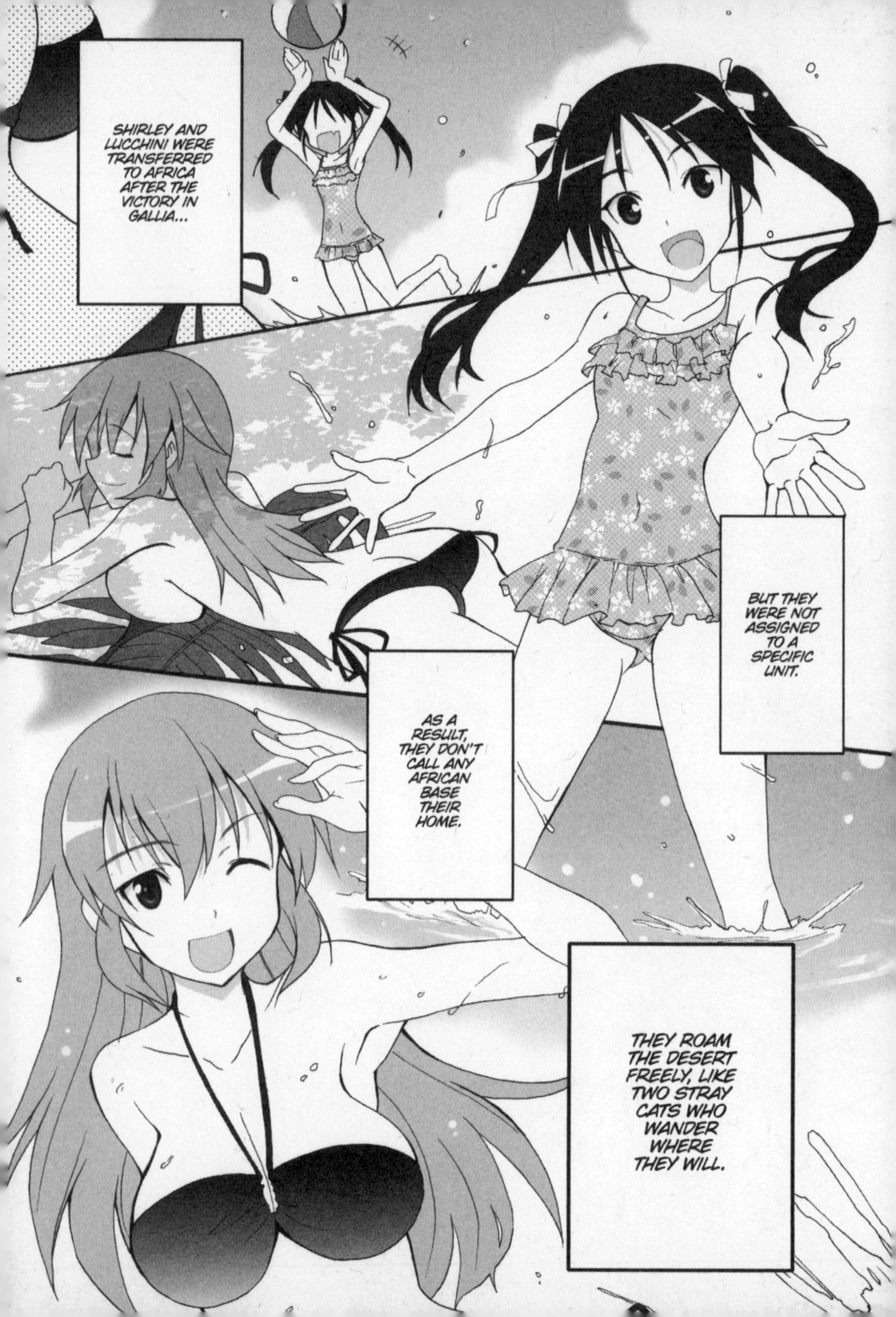
SHIRLEY AND LUCCHINI WERE TRANSFERRED TO AFRICA AFTER THE VICTORY IN GALLIA...
BUT THEY WERE NOT ASSIGNED TO A SPECIFIC UNIT.
AS A RESULT, THEY DON'T CALL ANY AFRICAN BASE THEIR HOME.
THEY ROAM THE DESERT FREELY, LIKE TWO STRAY CATS WHO WANDER WHERE THEY WILL.

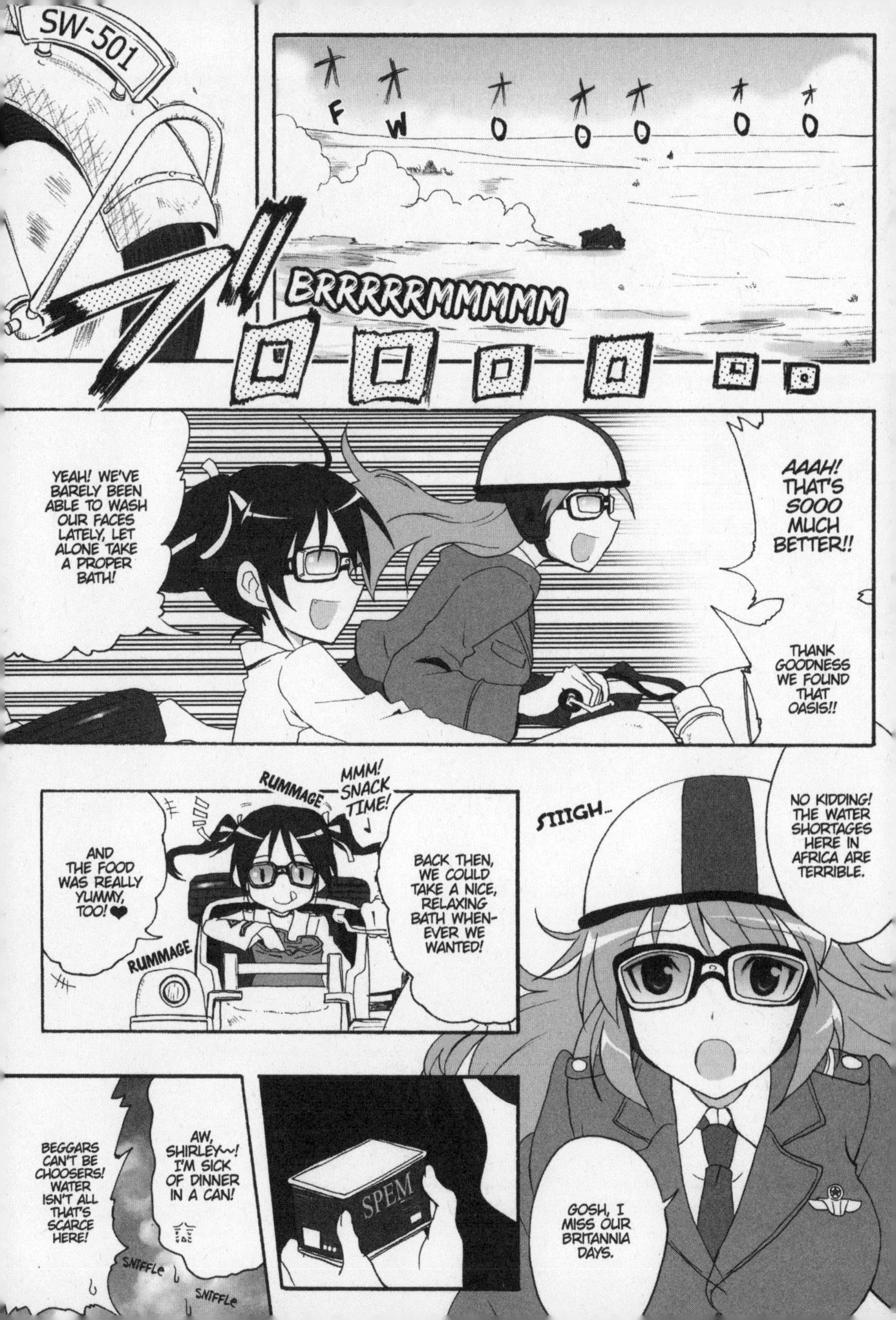
FWOOOOO
BRRRRRMMMMM
SW-501
AAAH! THAT'S SOOO MUCH BETTER!!
THANK GOODNESS WE FOUND THAT OASIS!!
YEAH! WE'VE BARELY BEEN ABLE TO WASH OUR FACES LATELY, LET ALONE TAKE A PROPER BATH!
NO KIDDING! THE WATER SHORTAGES HERE IN AFRICA ARE TERRIBLE.
STIIGH...
GOSH, I MISS OUR BRITANNIA DAYS.
MMM! SNACK TIME!
RUMMAGE
BACK THEN, WE COULD TAKE A NICE, RELAXING BATH WHENEVER WE WANTED!
AND THE FOOD WAS REALLY YUMMY, TOO! ❤
RUMMAGE
SPEM
AW, SHIRLEY~! I'M SICK OF DINNER IN A CAN!
BEGGARS CAN'T BE CHOOSERS! WATER ISN'T ALL THAT'S SCARCE HERE!
SNIFFLE
SNIFFLE

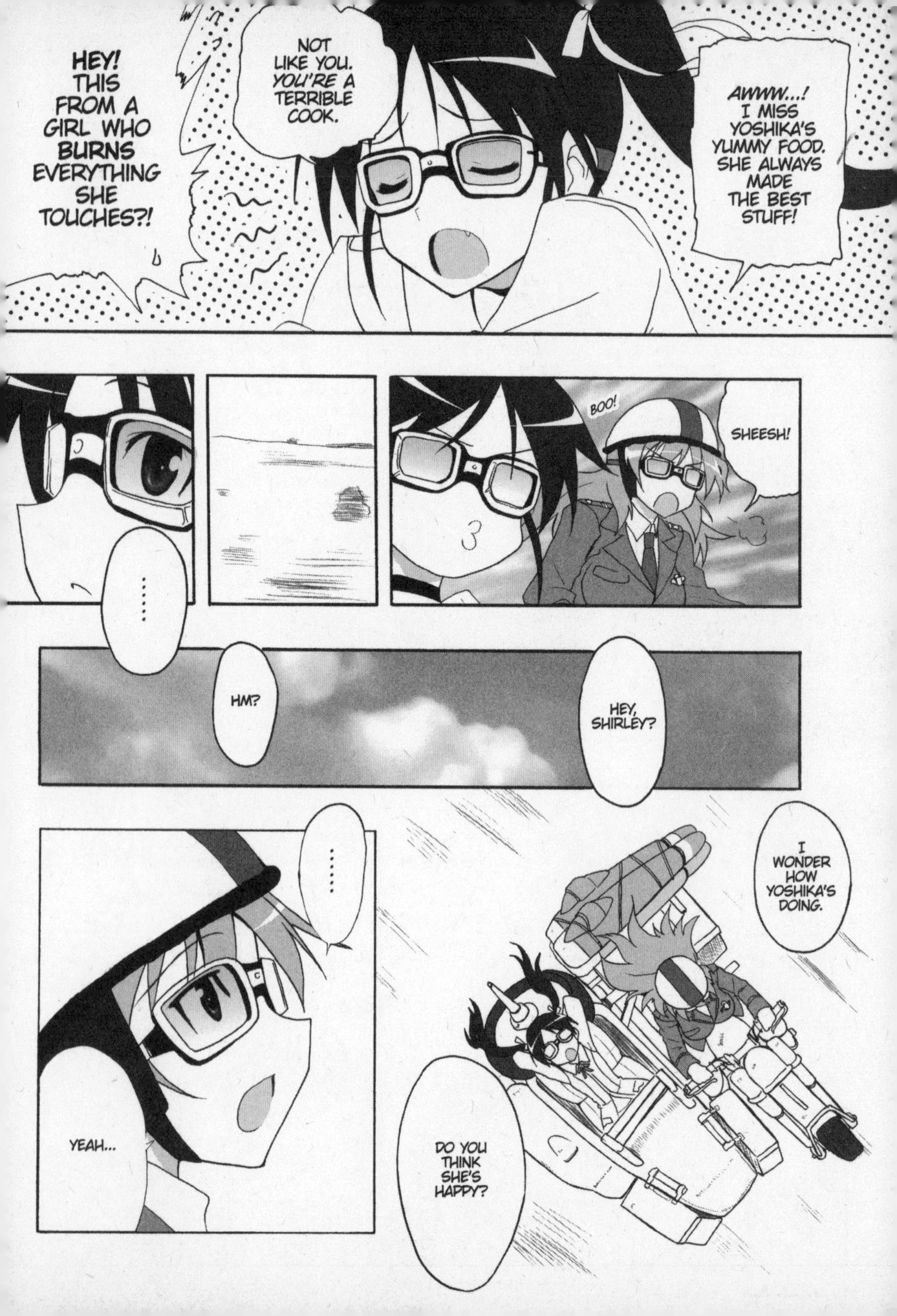
AWWW...! I MISS YOSHIKA'S YUMMY FOOD. SHE ALWAYS MADE THE BEST STUFF!
NOT LIKE YOU. YOU'RE A TERRIBLE COOK.
HEY! THIS FROM A GIRL WHO BURNS EVERYTHING SHE TOUCHES?!
SHEESH!
BOO!
......
HEY, SHIRLEY?
HM?
I WONDER HOW YOSHIKA'S DOING.
DO YOU THINK SHE'S HAPPY?
......
YEAH...

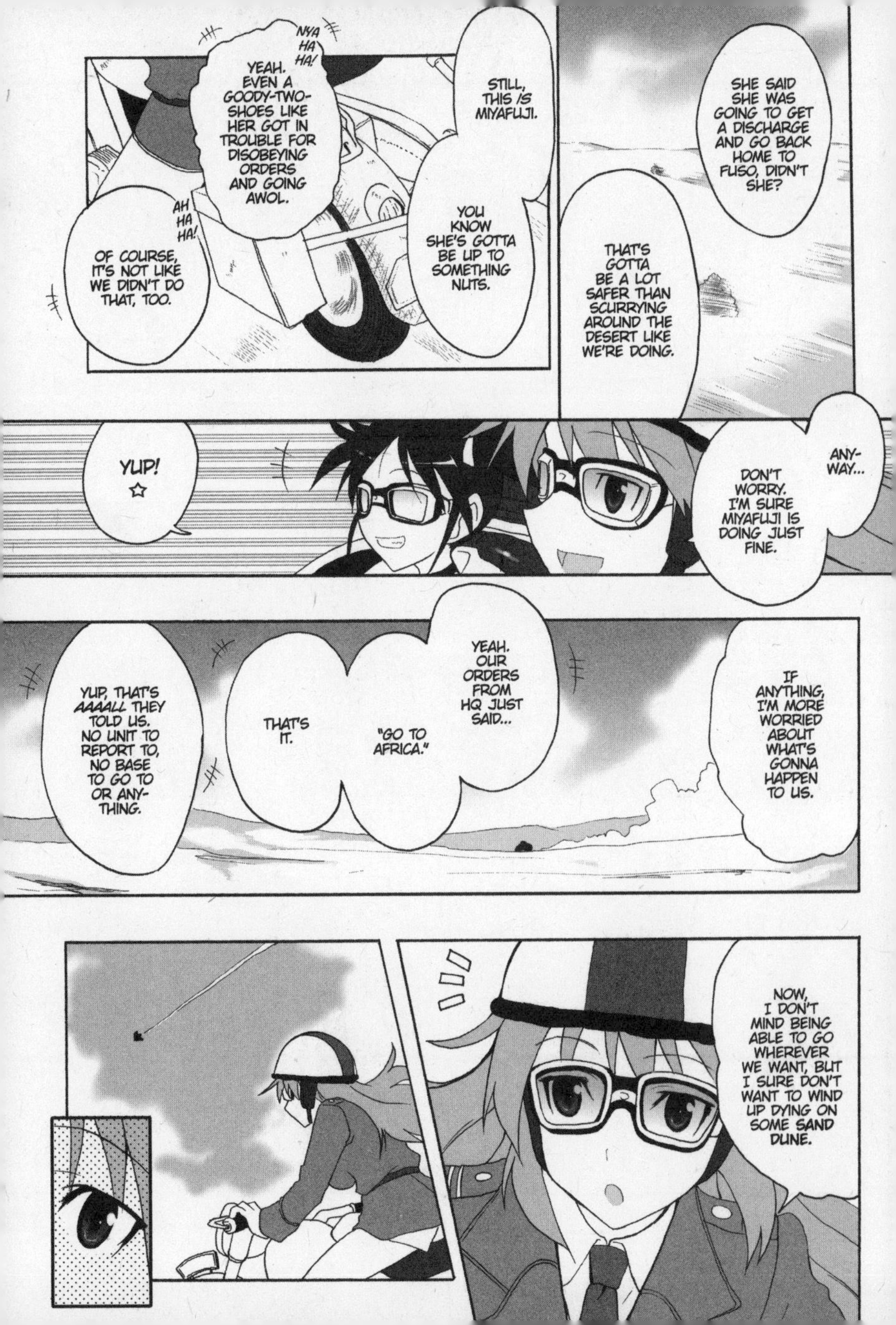
SHE SAID SHE WAS GOING TO GET A DISCHARGE AND GO BACK HOME TO FUSO, DIDN'T SHE?
THAT'S GOTTA BE A LOT SAFER THAN SCURRYING AROUND THE DESERT LIKE WE'RE DOING.
STILL, THIS *IS* MIYAFUJI.
YOU KNOW SHE'S GOTTA BE UP TO SOMETHING NUTS.
NYA HA HA!
YEAH. EVEN A GOODY-TWO-SHOES LIKE HER GOT IN TROUBLE FOR DISOBEYING ORDERS AND GOING AWOL.
AH HA HA!
OF COURSE, IT'S NOT LIKE WE DIDN'T DO THAT, TOO.
ANY-WAY...
DON'T WORRY. I'M SURE MIYAFUJI IS DOING JUST FINE.
YUP! ☆
IF ANYTHING, I'M MORE WORRIED ABOUT WHAT'S GONNA HAPPEN TO US.
YEAH. OUR ORDERS FROM HQ JUST SAID...
"GO TO AFRICA."
THAT'S IT.
YUP, THAT'S *AAAALL* THEY TOLD US. NO UNIT TO REPORT TO, NO BASE TO GO TO OR ANY-THING.
NOW, I DON'T MIND BEING ABLE TO GO WHEREVER WE WANT, BUT I SURE DON'T WANT TO WIND UP DYING ON SOME SAND DUNE.

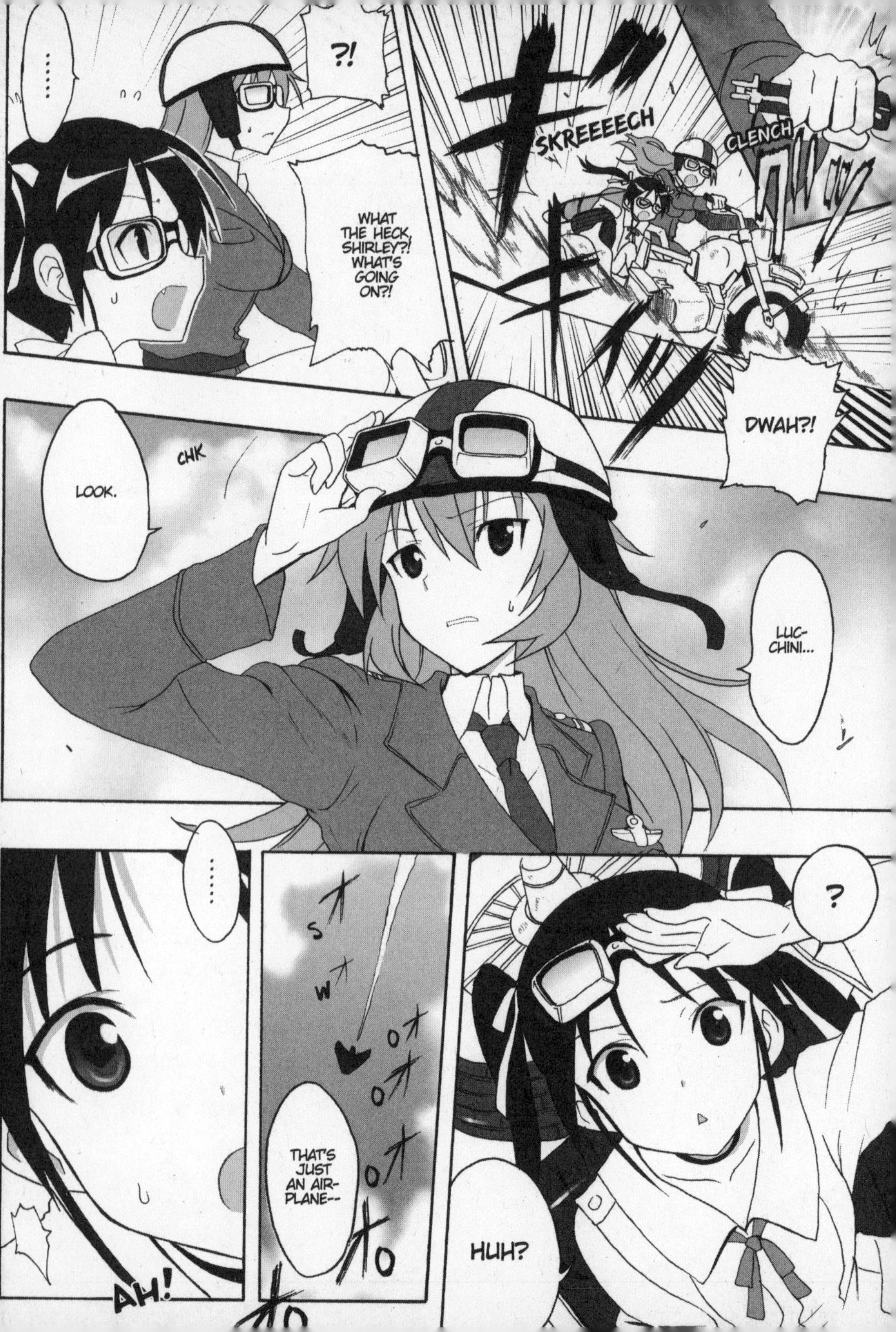
CLENCH
SKREEEECH
DWAH?!
?!
......
WHAT THE HECK, SHIRLEY?! WHAT'S GOING ON?!
LUC-CHINI...
CHK
LOOK.
?
HUH?
THAT'S JUST AN AIR-PLANE--
......
AH!

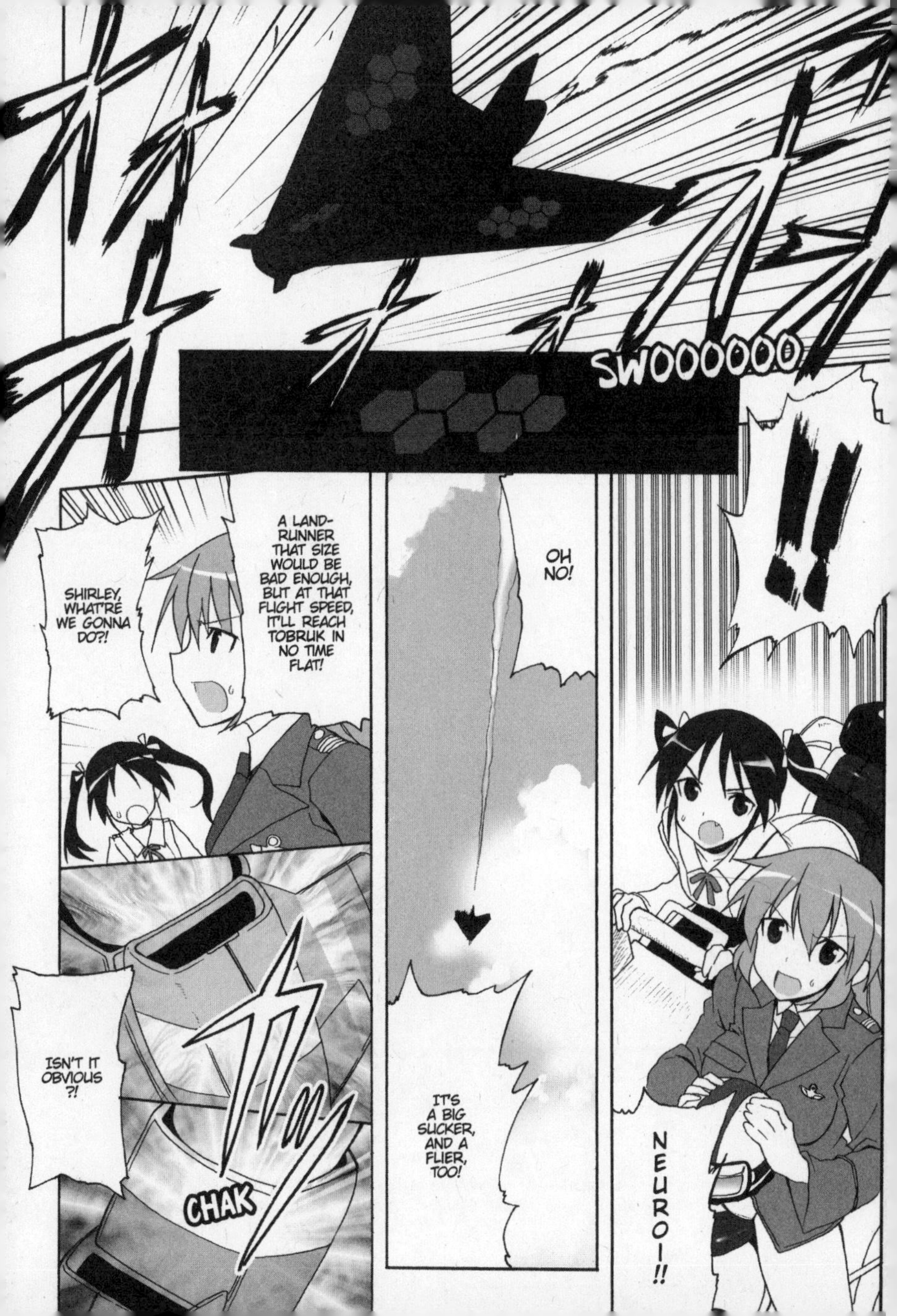
SWOOOOOO
!!
OH NO!
IT'S A BIG SUCKER, AND A FLIER, TOO!
NEUROI!!
A LAND-RUNNER THAT SIZE WOULD BE BAD ENOUGH, BUT AT THAT FLIGHT SPEED, IT'LL REACH TOBRUK IN NO TIME FLAT!
SHIRLEY, WHAT'RE WE GONNA DO?!
ISN'T IT OBVIOUS?!
CHAK

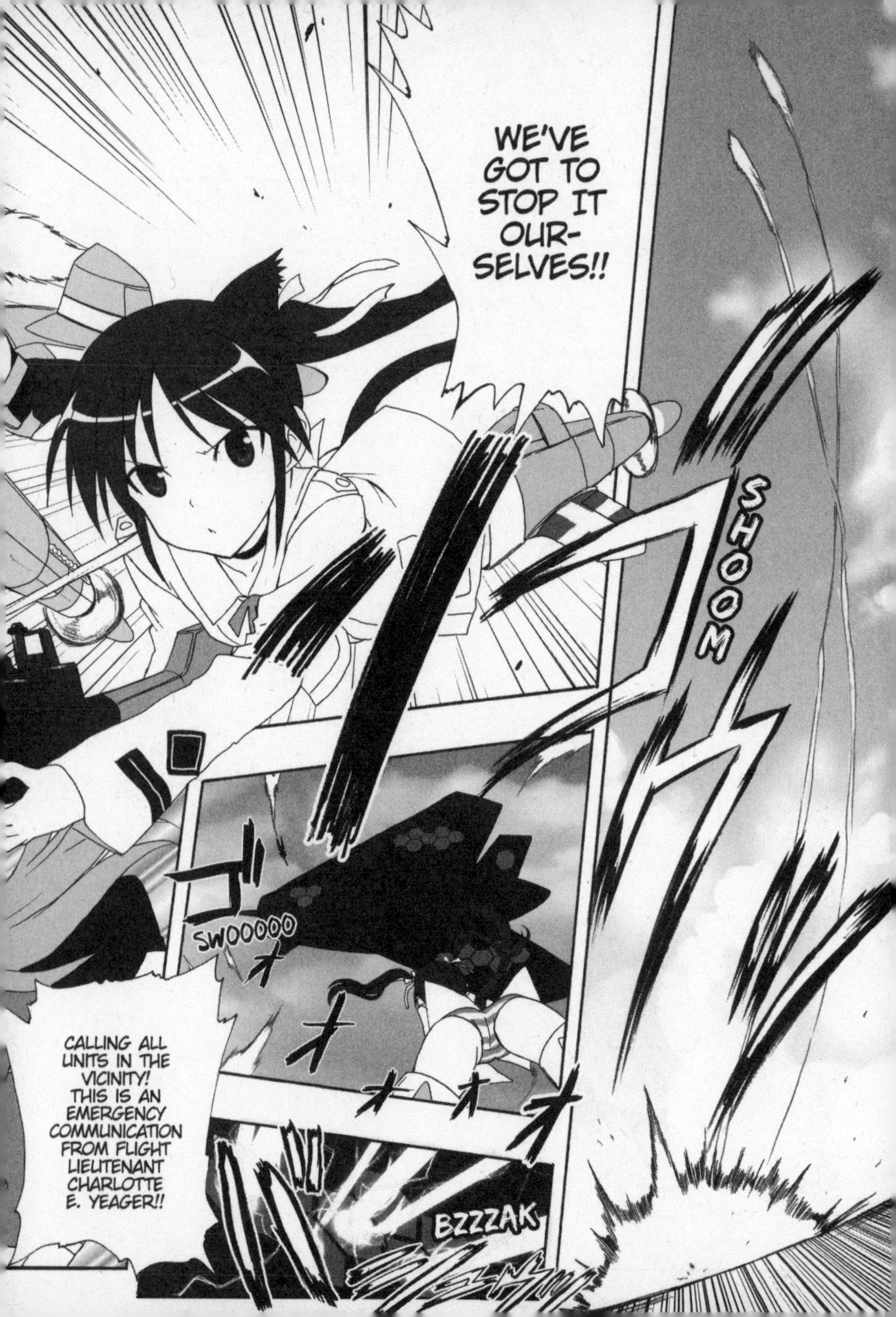
WE'VE GOT TO STOP IT OUR-SELVES!!
SHOOOM
SWOOOOO
CALLING ALL UNITS IN THE VICINITY! THIS IS AN EMERGENCY COMMUNICATION FROM FLIGHT LIEUTENANT CHARLOTTE E. YEAGER!!
BZZZAK

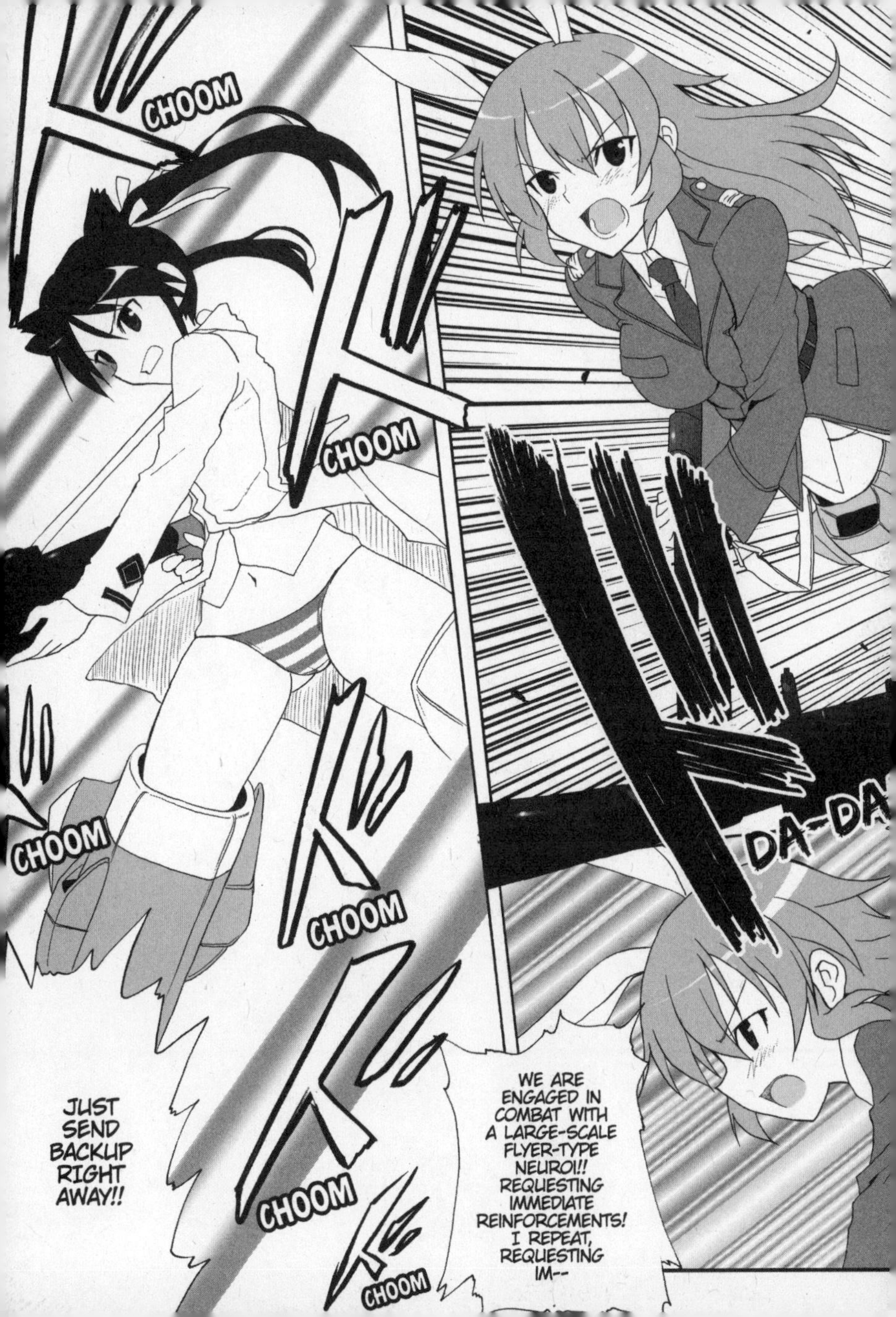
DA-DA
WE ARE ENGAGED IN COMBAT WITH A LARGE-SCALE FLYER-TYPE NEUROI!! REQUESTING IMMEDIATE REINFORCEMENTS! I REPEAT, REQUESTING IM--
CHOOM
CHOOM
CHOOM
CHOOM
CHOOM
CHOOM
JUST SEND BACKUP RIGHT AWAY!!
CHOOM

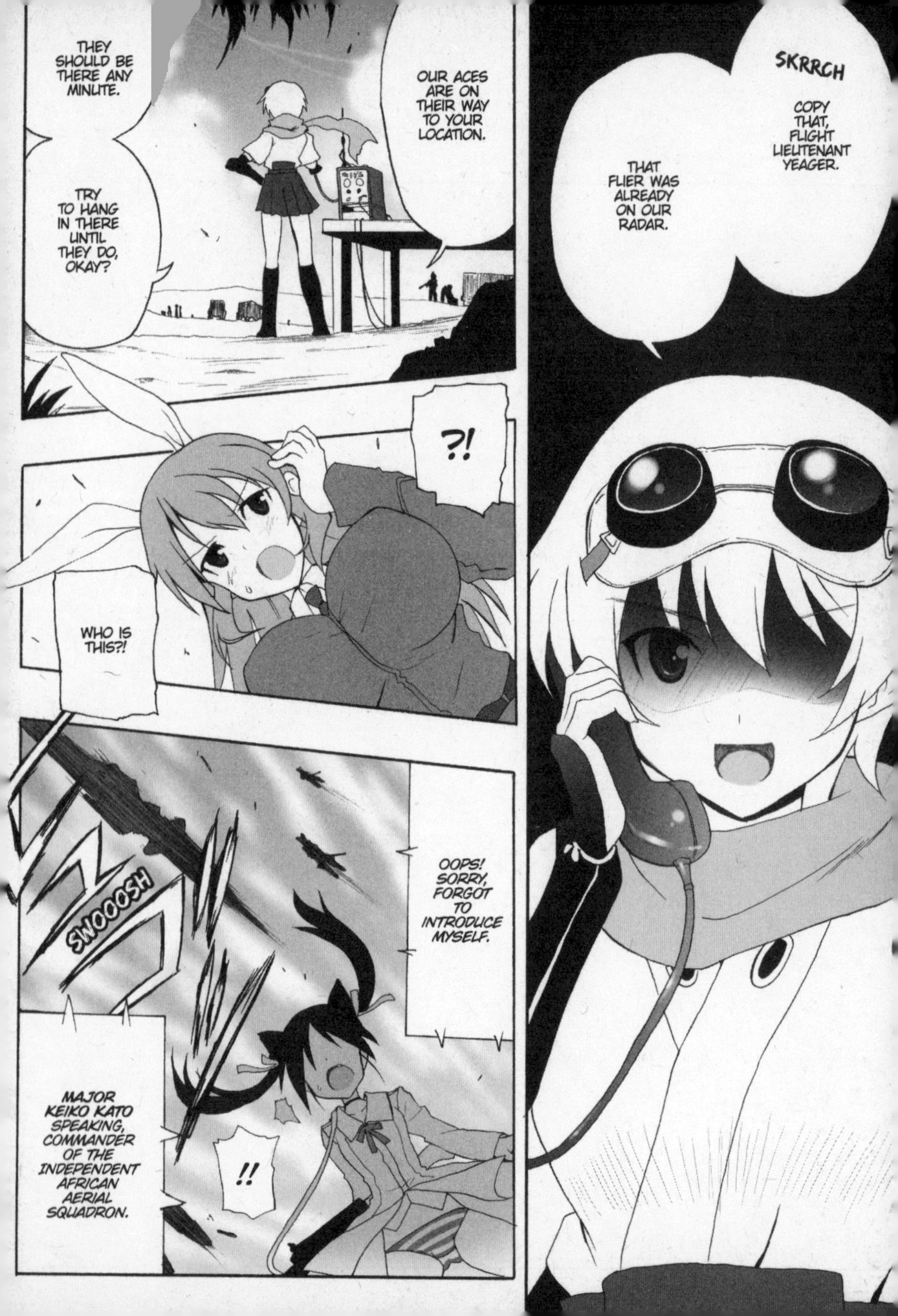
SKRRCH
COPY THAT, FLIGHT LIEUTENANT YEAGER.
THAT FLIER WAS ALREADY ON OUR RADAR.
OUR ACES ARE ON THEIR WAY TO YOUR LOCATION.
THEY SHOULD BE THERE ANY MINUTE.
TRY TO HANG IN THERE UNTIL THEY DO, OKAY?
?!
WHO IS THIS?!
OOPS! SORRY, FORGOT TO INTRODUCE MYSELF.
SWOOOSH
MAJOR KEIKO KATO SPEAKING, COMMANDER OF THE INDEPENDENT AFRICAN AERIAL SQUADRON.
!!

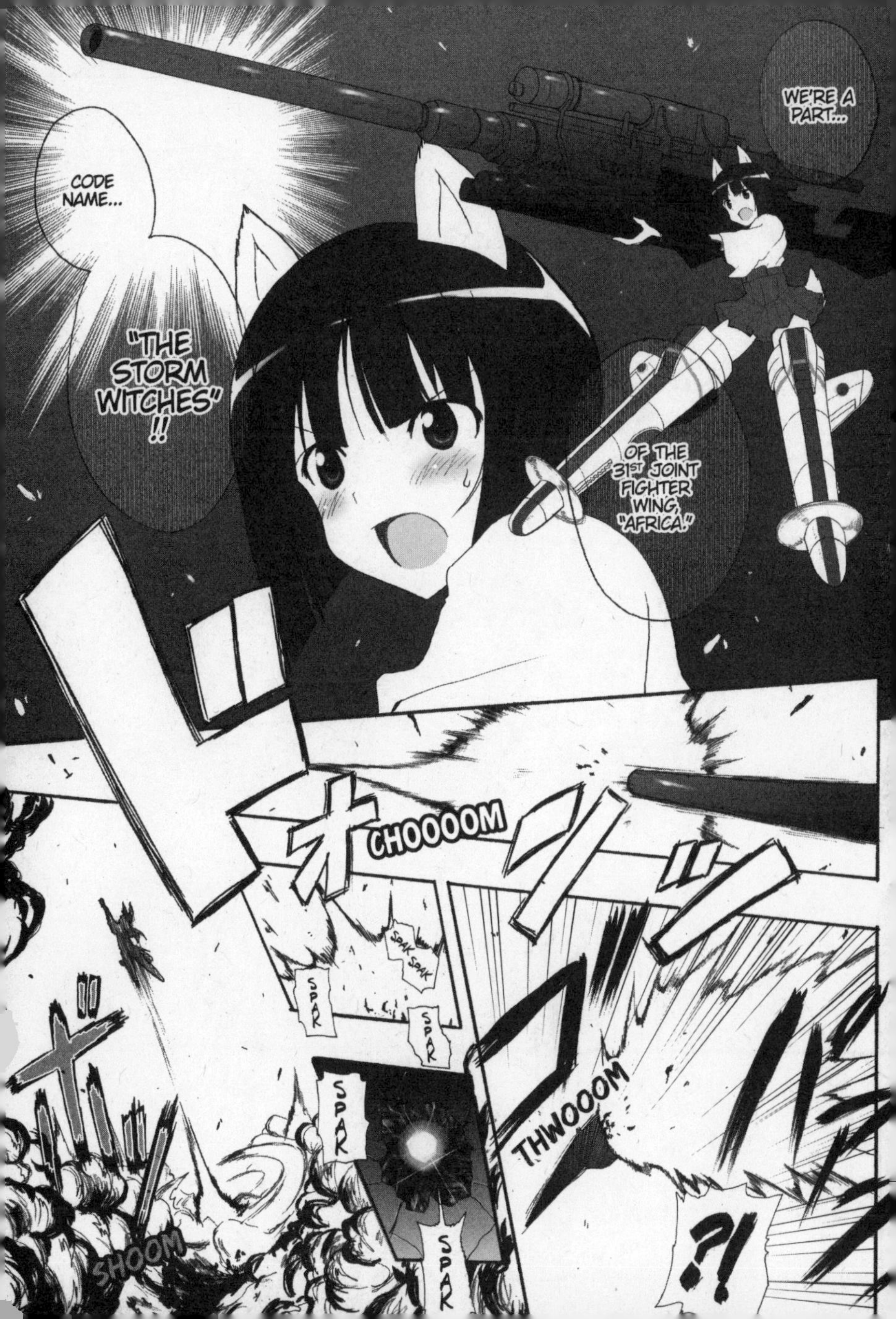
WE'RE A PART...
OF THE 31ST JOINT FIGHTER WING, "AFRICA."
CODE NAME...
"THE STORM WITCHES"!!
CHOOOOM
THWOOOM
?!
SPAK SPAK
SPAK
SPAK
SPAK
SPAK
SHOOM

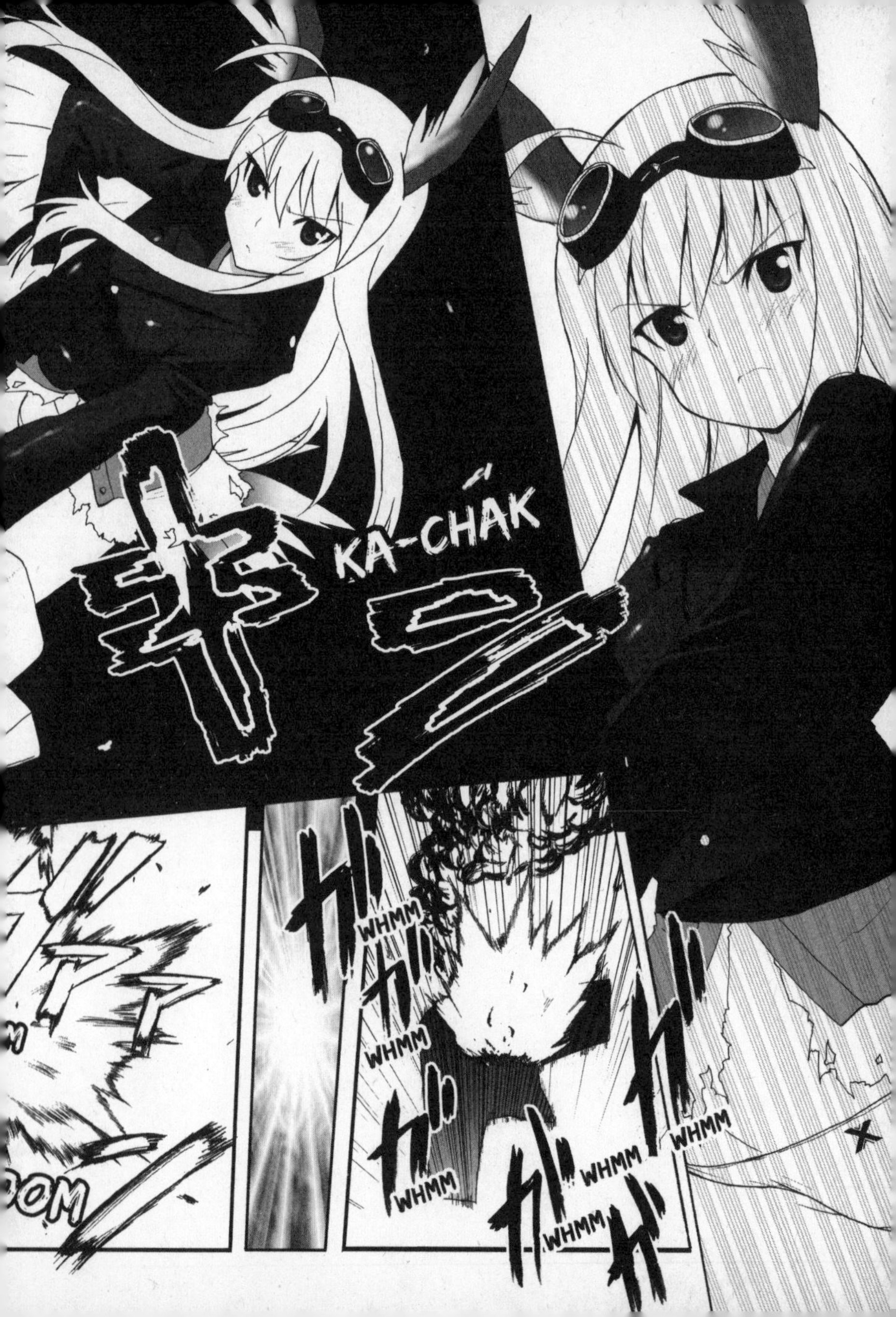
KA-CHAK
WHMM
WHMM
WHMM
WHMM
WHMM
WHMM
OOM

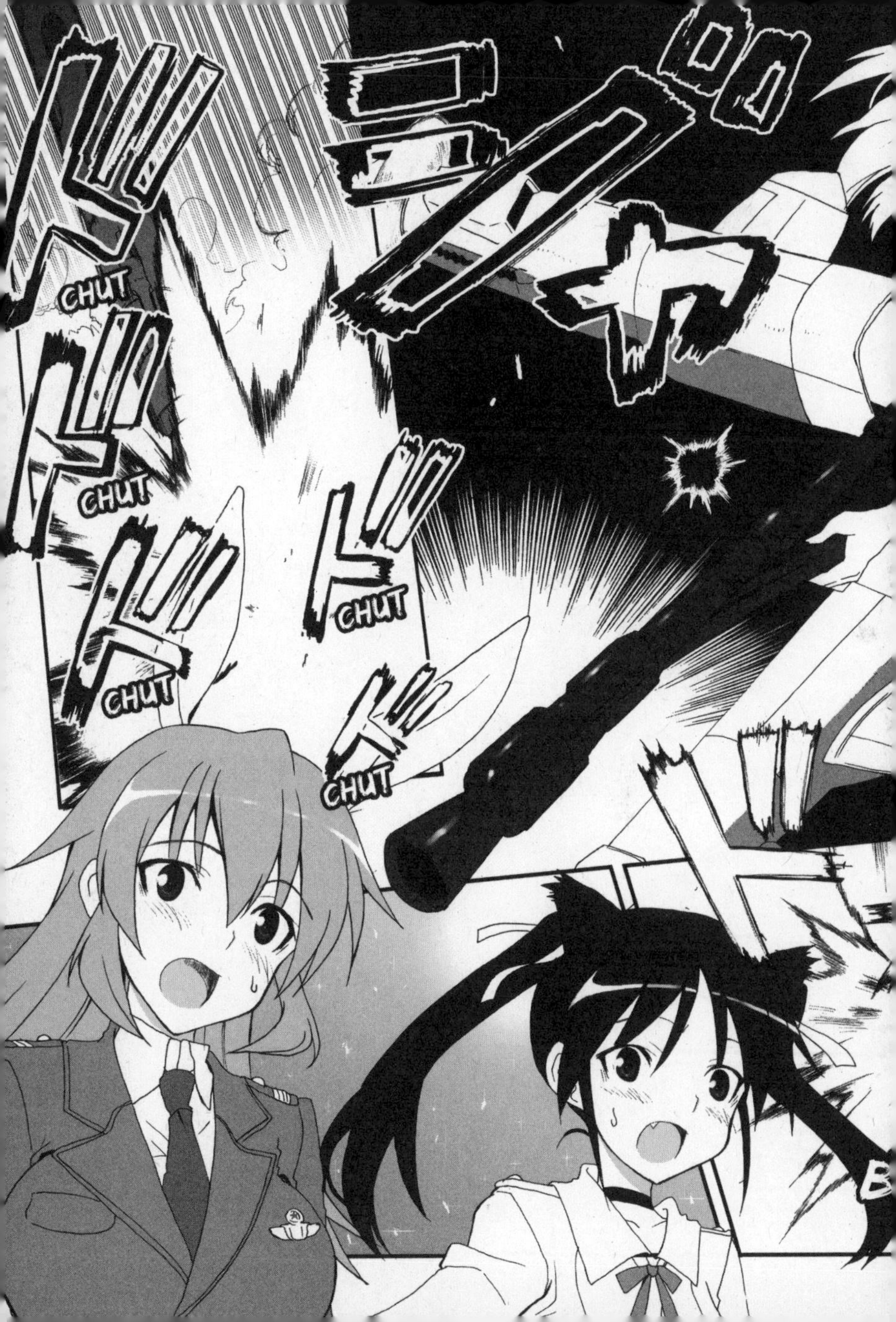
CHUT
CHUT
CHUT
CHUT
CHUT

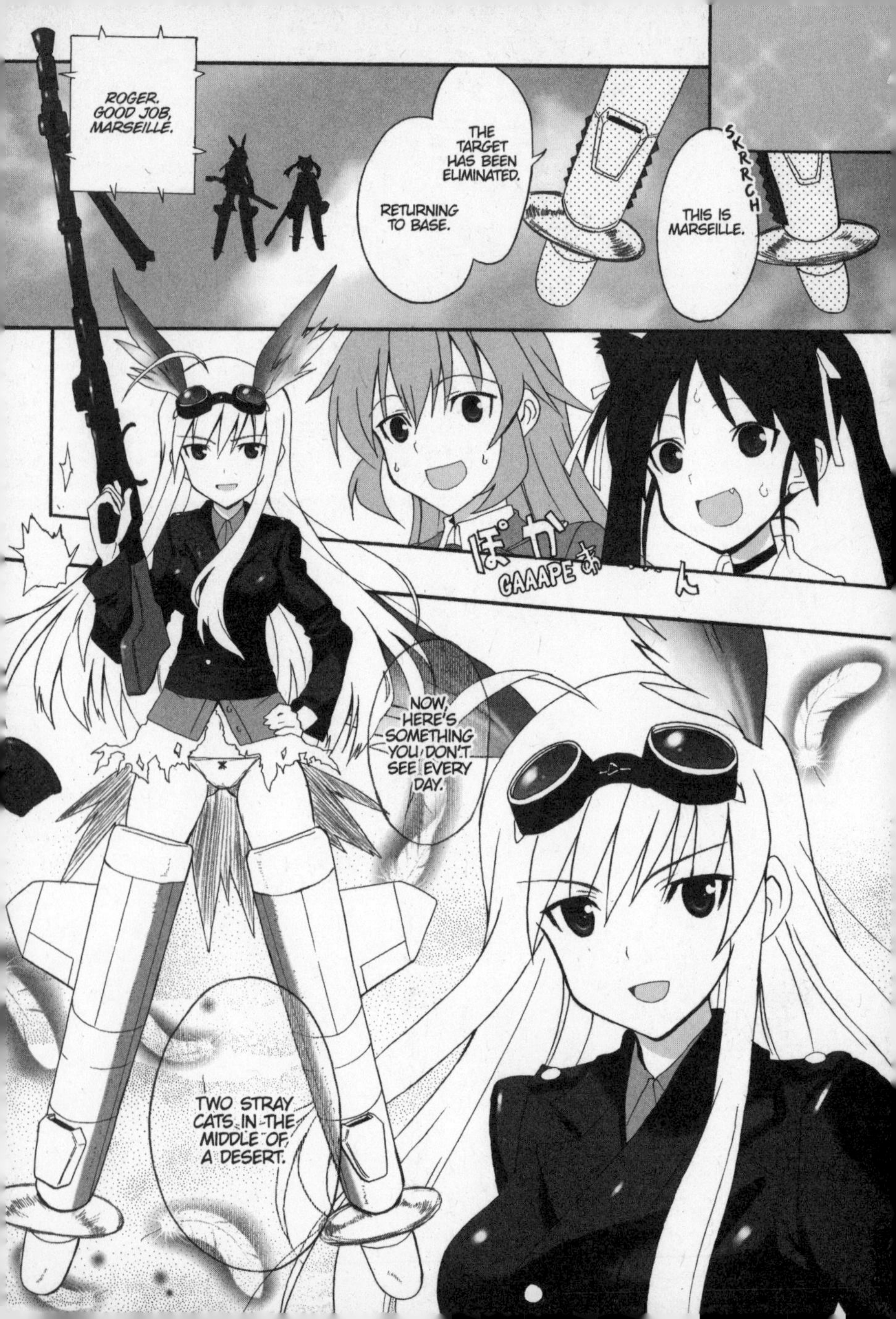
SKRRCH
THIS IS MARSEILLE.
THE TARGET HAS BEEN ELIMINATED.
RETURNING TO BASE.
ROGER. GOOD JOB, MARSEILLE.
ぽかあ…ん
GAAAPE
NOW, HERE'S SOMETHING YOU DON'T SEE EVERY DAY.
TWO STRAY CATS IN THE MIDDLE OF A DESERT.

WITCHES GRAFFITI

**Shimada Humikane &
Projekt Kagonish
illustrated by
Kyougoku Shin**

STREEETCH

Martina Crespi

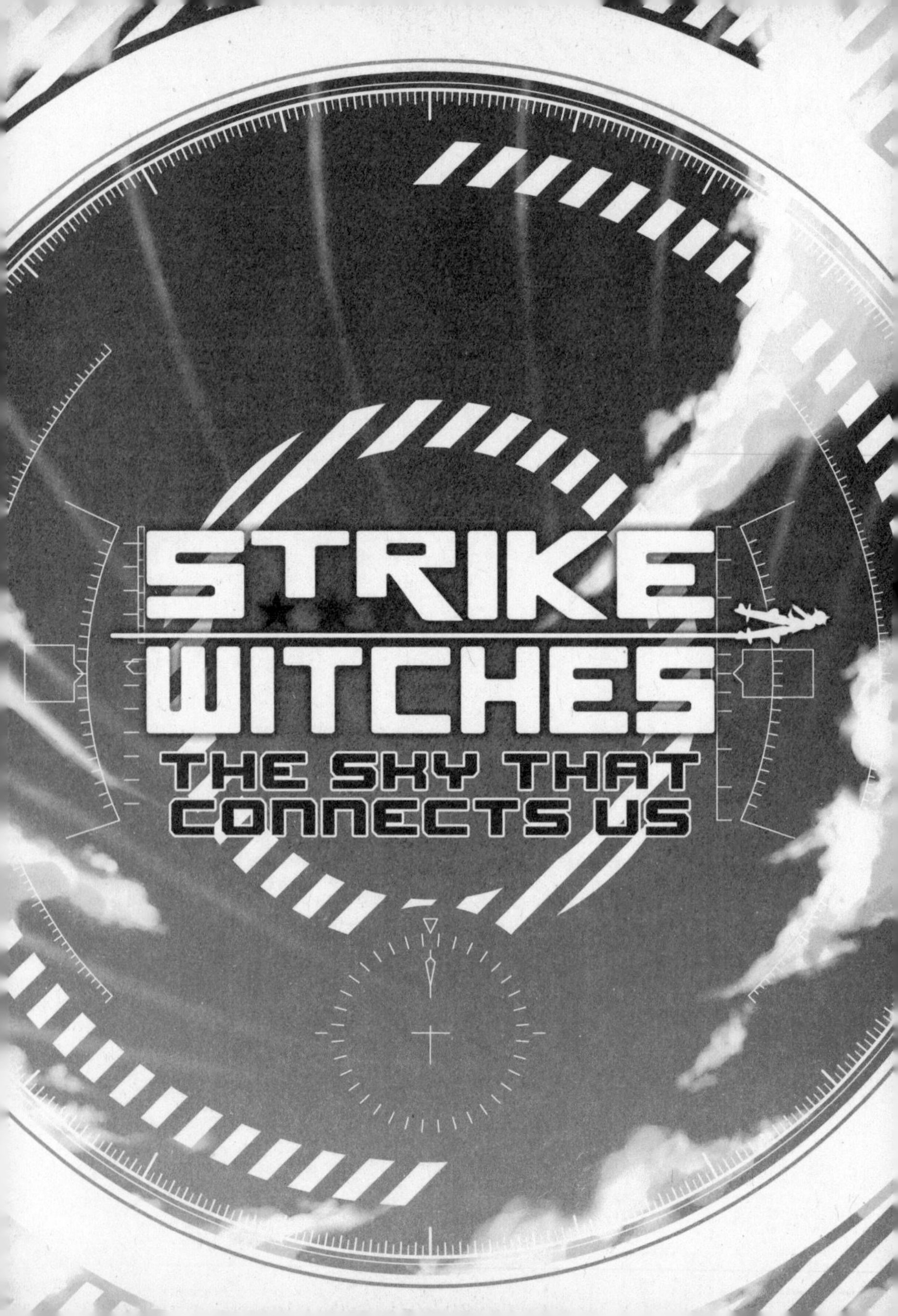
STRIKE WITCHES
THE SKY THAT CONNECTS US

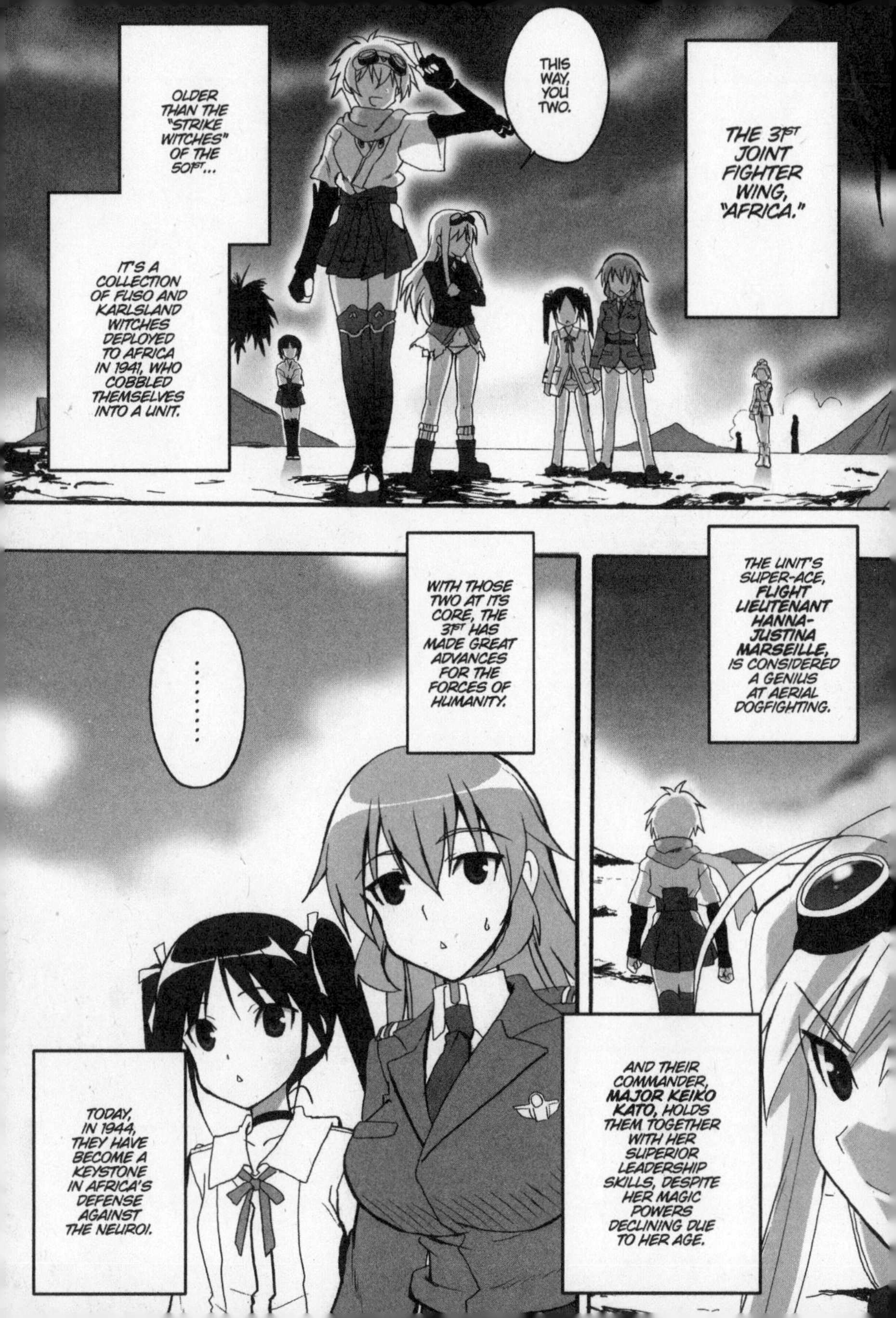
THE 31ST JOINT FIGHTER WING, "AFRICA."
THIS WAY, YOU TWO.
OLDER THAN THE "STRIKE WITCHES" OF THE 501ST...
IT'S A COLLECTION OF FUSO AND KARLSLAND WITCHES DEPLOYED TO AFRICA IN 1941, WHO COBBLED THEMSELVES INTO A UNIT.
THE UNIT'S SUPER-ACE, FLIGHT LIEUTENANT HANNA-JUSTINA MARSEILLE, IS CONSIDERED A GENIUS AT AERIAL DOGFIGHTING.
AND THEIR COMMANDER, MAJOR KEIKO KATO, HOLDS THEM TOGETHER WITH HER SUPERIOR LEADERSHIP SKILLS, DESPITE HER MAGIC POWERS DECLINING DUE TO HER AGE.
WITH THOSE TWO AT ITS CORE, THE 31ST HAS MADE GREAT ADVANCES FOR THE FORCES OF HUMANITY.
....
TODAY, IN 1944, THEY HAVE BECOME A KEYSTONE IN AFRICA'S DEFENSE AGAINST THE NEUROI.

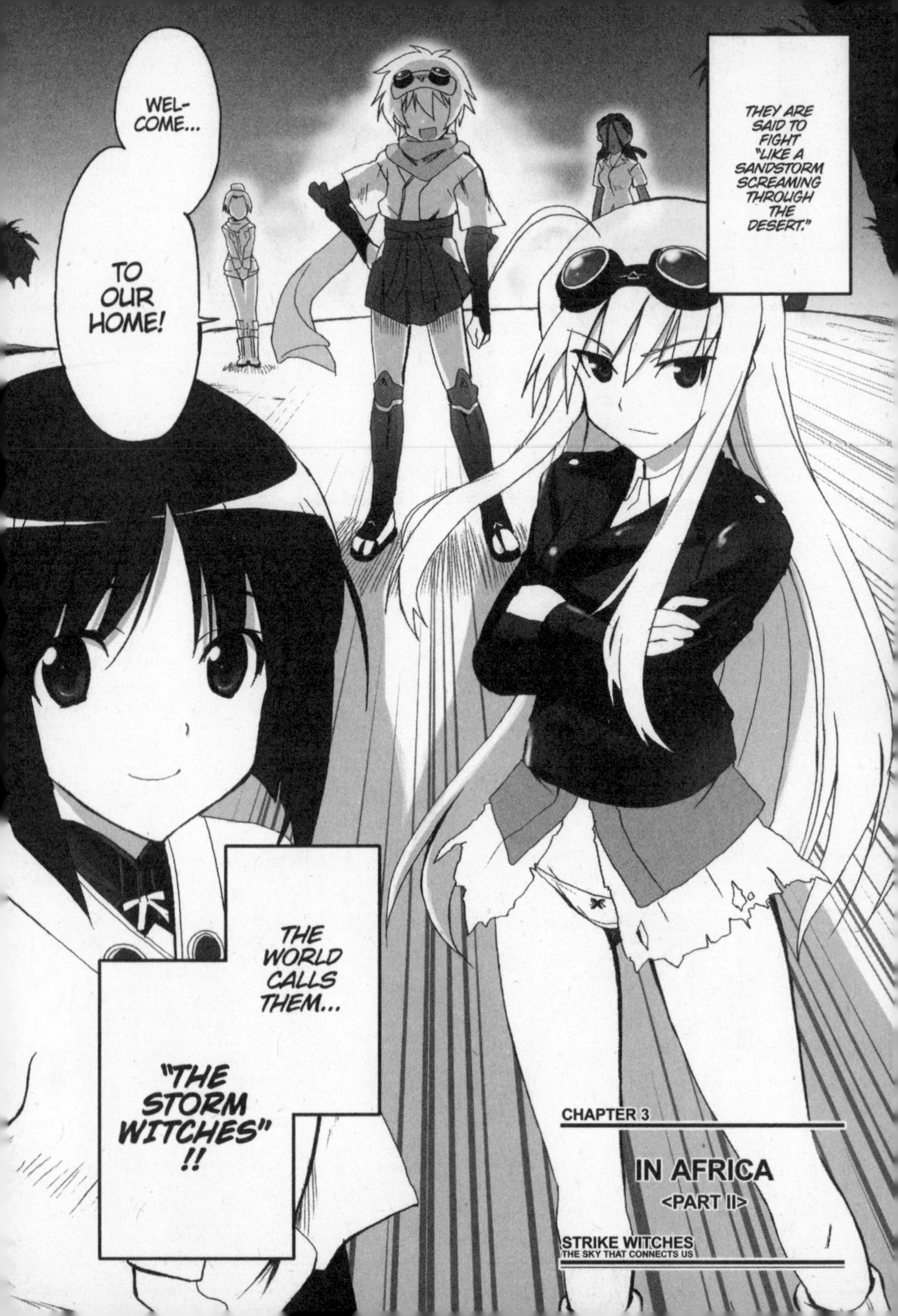
THEY ARE SAID TO FIGHT "LIKE A SANDSTORM SCREAMING THROUGH THE DESERT."
WEL-COME...
TO OUR HOME!
THE WORLD CALLS THEM...
"THE STORM WITCHES"!!
CHAPTER 3
IN AFRICA
<PART II>
STRIKE WITCHES
THE SKY THAT CONNECTS US

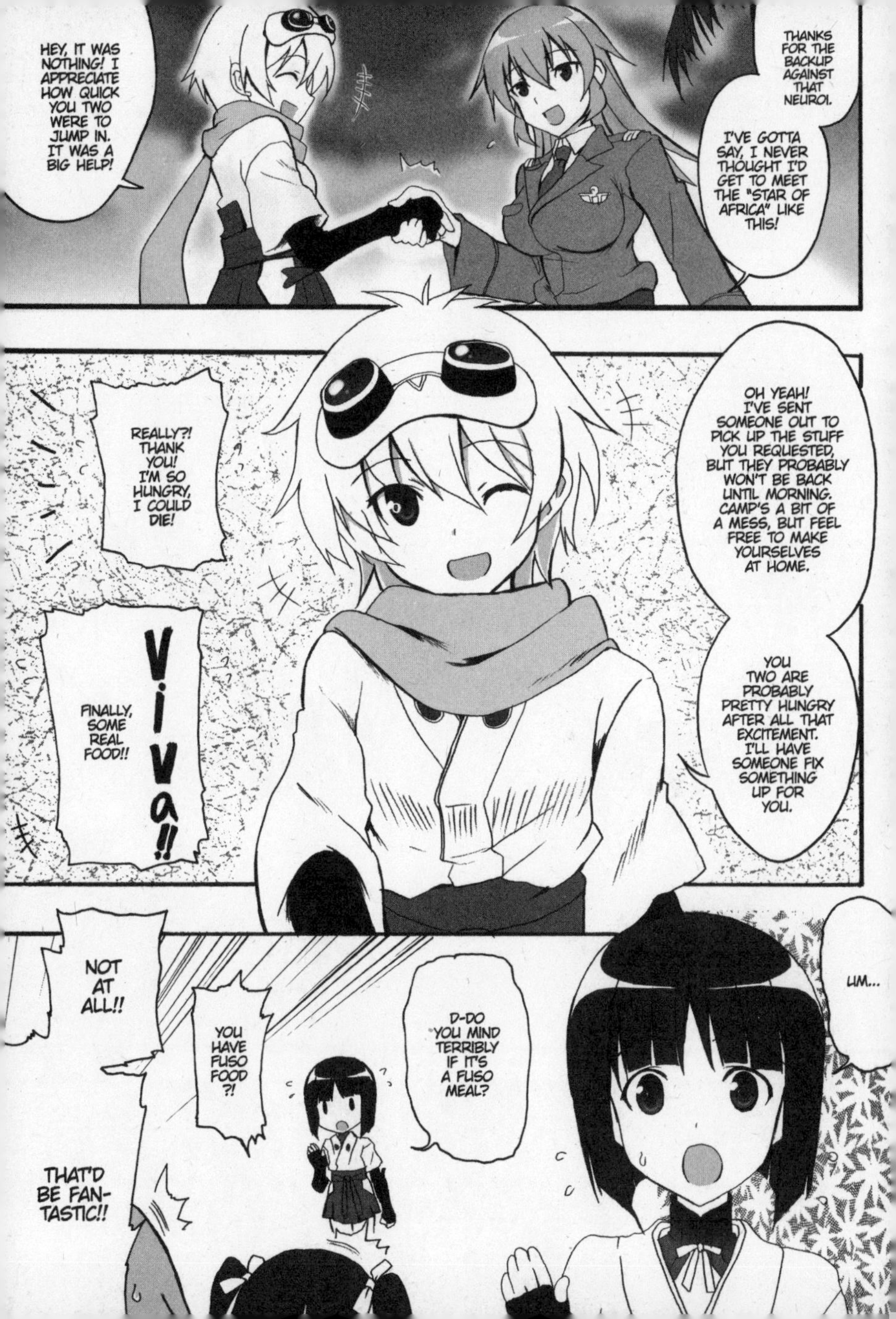
THANKS FOR THE BACKUP AGAINST THAT NEUROI.
I'VE GOTTA SAY, I NEVER THOUGHT I'D GET TO MEET THE "STAR OF AFRICA" LIKE THIS!
HEY, IT WAS NOTHING! I APPRECIATE HOW QUICK YOU TWO WERE TO JUMP IN. IT WAS A BIG HELP!
OH YEAH! I'VE SENT SOMEONE OUT TO PICK UP THE STUFF YOU REQUESTED, BUT THEY PROBABLY WON'T BE BACK UNTIL MORNING. CAMP'S A BIT OF A MESS, BUT FEEL FREE TO MAKE YOURSELVES AT HOME.
YOU TWO ARE PROBABLY PRETTY HUNGRY AFTER ALL THAT EXCITEMENT. I'LL HAVE SOMEONE FIX SOMETHING UP FOR YOU.
REALLY?! THANK YOU! I'M SO HUNGRY, I COULD DIE!
FINALLY, SOME REAL FOOD!!
Viva!!
UM...
D-DO YOU MIND TERRIBLY IF IT'S A FUSO MEAL?
YOU HAVE FUSO FOOD?!
NOT AT ALL!!
THAT'D BE FAN-TASTIC!!

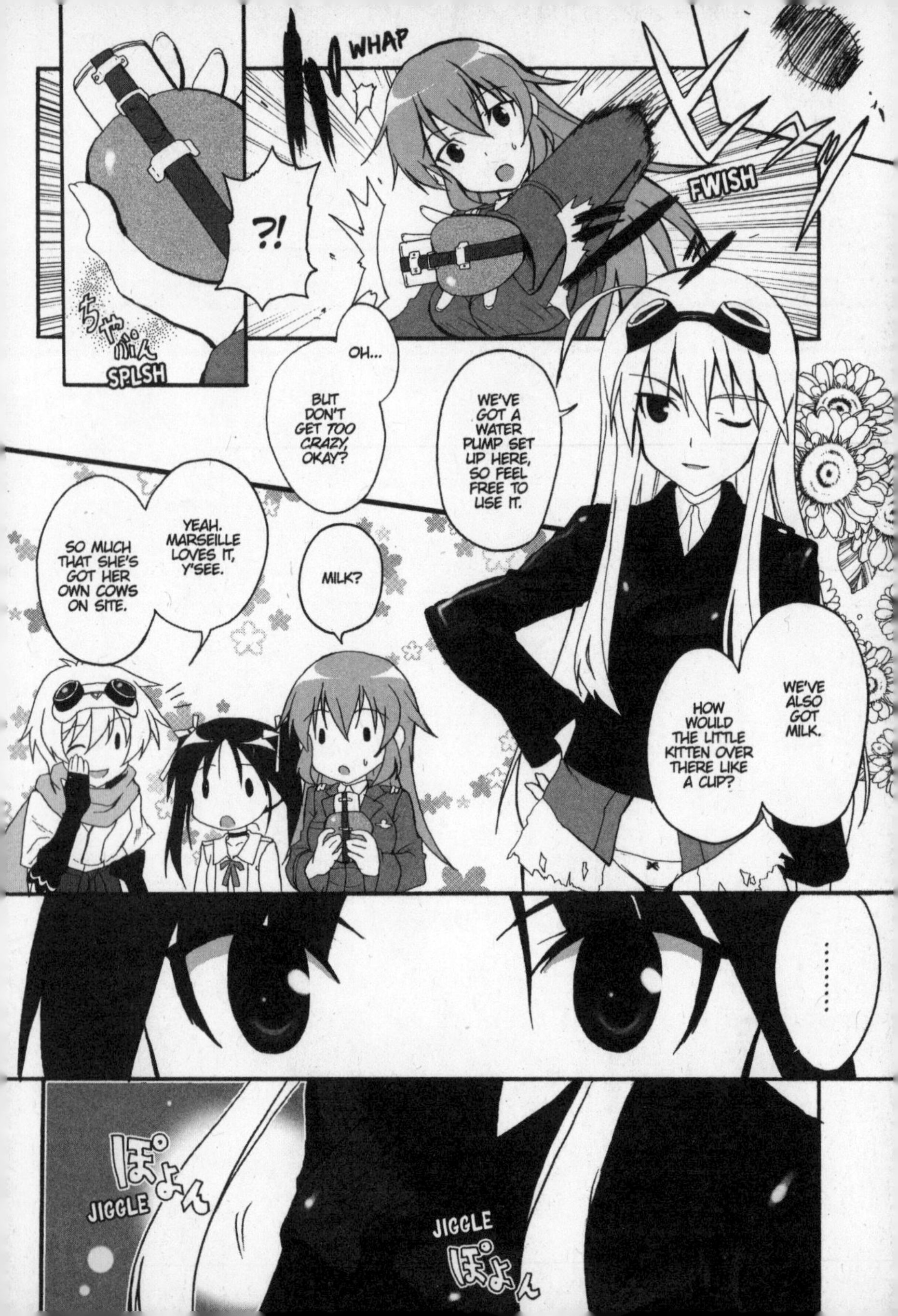
FWISH
WHAP
?!
ちゃぷん
SPLSH
WE'VE GOT A WATER PUMP SET UP HERE, SO FEEL FREE TO USE IT.
OH...
BUT DON'T GET *TOO* CRAZY, OKAY?
WE'VE ALSO GOT MILK.
HOW WOULD THE LITTLE KITTEN OVER THERE LIKE A CUP?
MILK?
YEAH. MARSEILLE LOVES IT, Y'SEE.
SO MUCH THAT SHE'S GOT HER OWN COWS ON SITE.
......
ぽよん
JIGGLE
JIGGLE
ぽよん

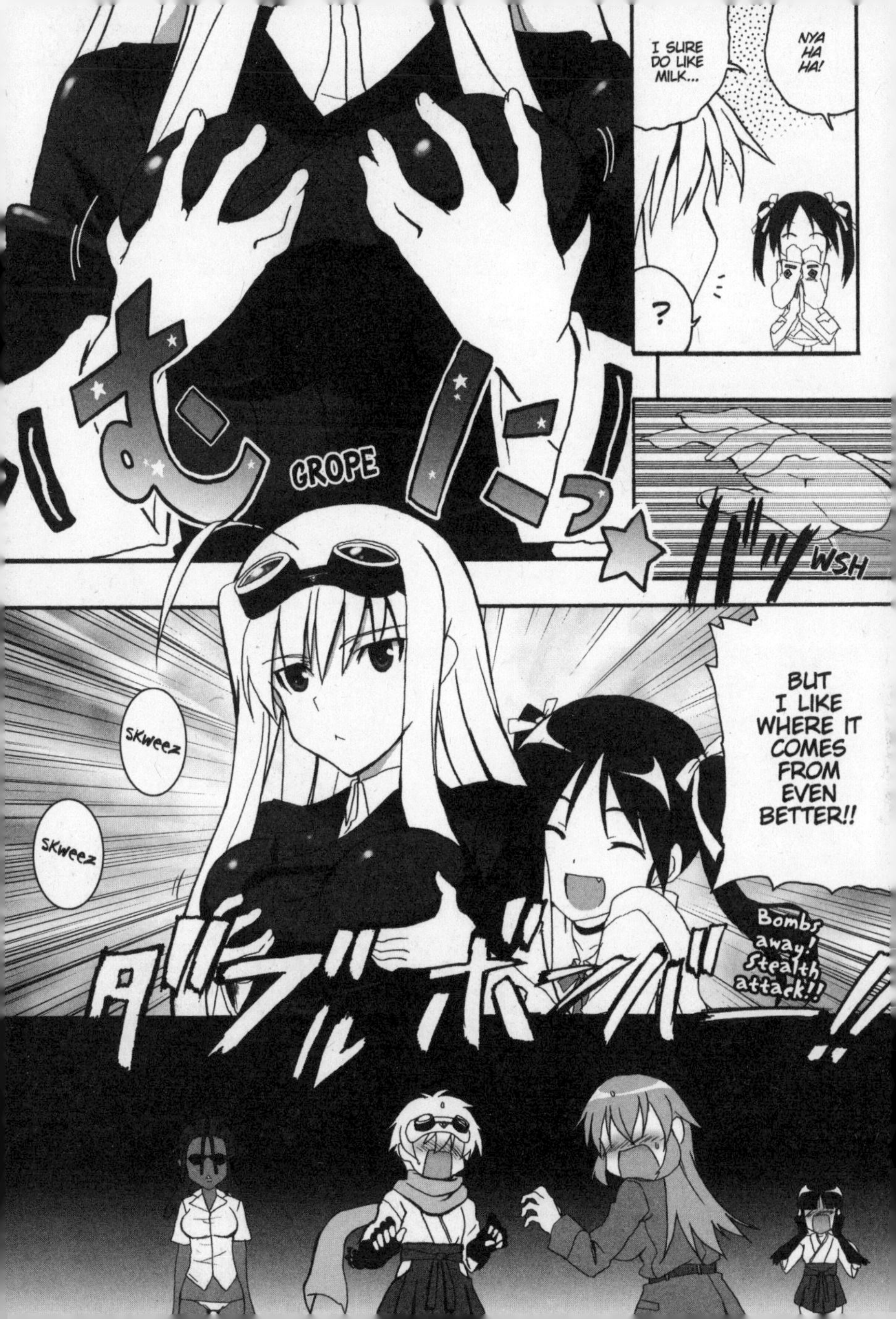
NYA HA HA!
I SURE DO LIKE MILK...
?
GROPE
WSH
BUT I LIKE WHERE IT COMES FROM EVEN BETTER!!
SKWEEZ
SKWEEZ
Bombs away! Stealth attack!!

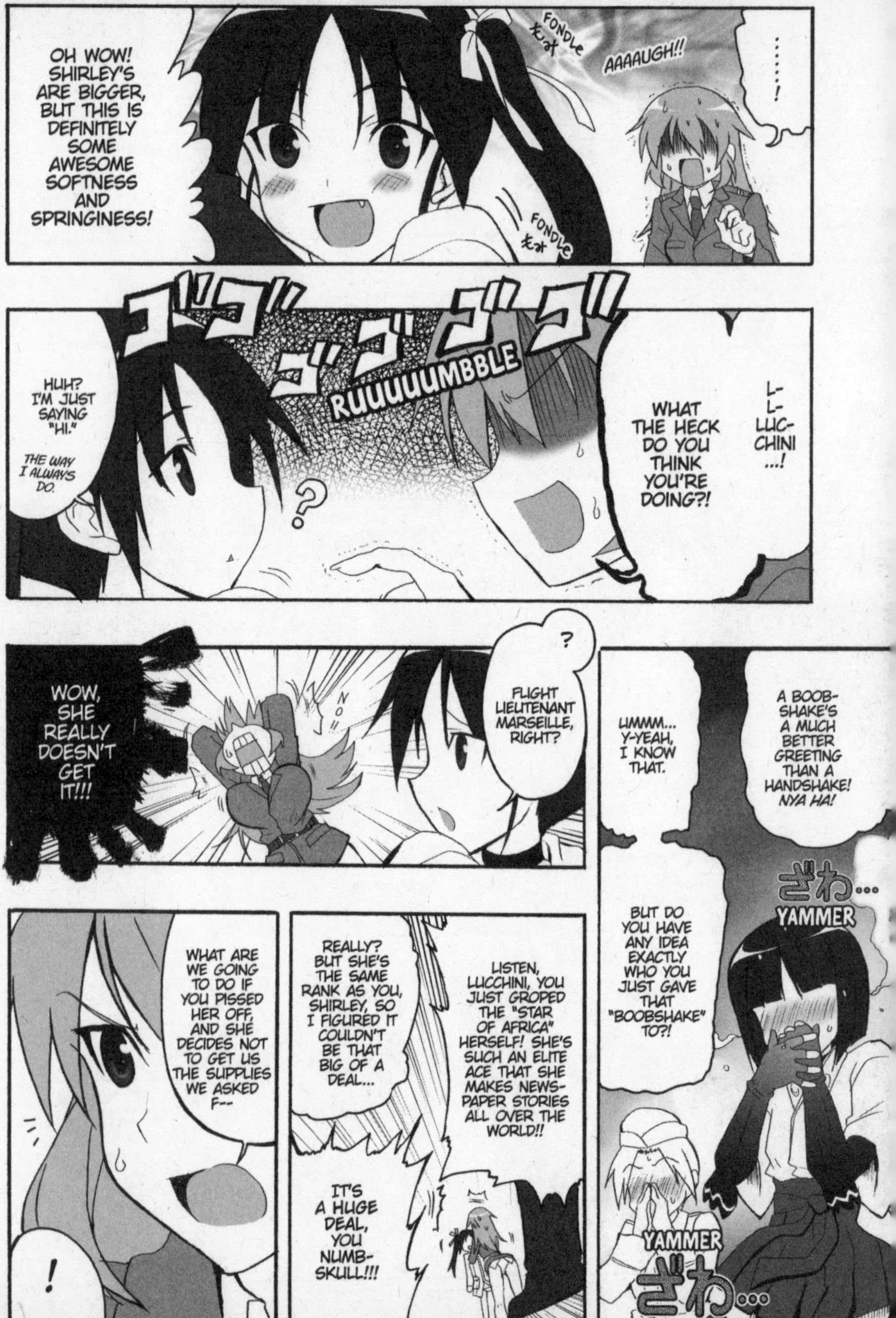

......!
AAAAUGH!!
FONDLE もみ
OH WOW! SHIRLEY'S ARE BIGGER, BUT THIS IS DEFINITELY SOME AWESOME SOFTNESS AND SPRINGINESS!
FONDLE もみ
ゴゴゴゴゴゴ
RUUUUUMBBLE
L- L- LUCCHINI ...!
WHAT THE HECK DO YOU THINK YOU'RE DOING?!
?
HUH? I'M JUST SAYING "HI."
THE WAY I ALWAYS DO.
A BOOB-SHAKE'S A MUCH BETTER GREETING THAN A HANDSHAKE! NYA HA!
UMMM... Y-YEAH, I KNOW THAT.
?
FLIGHT LIEUTENANT MARSEILLE, RIGHT?
NO!!
WOW, SHE REALLY DOESN'T GET IT!!!
ざわ... YAMMER
BUT DO YOU HAVE ANY IDEA EXACTLY WHO YOU JUST GAVE THAT "BOOBSHAKE" TO?!
YAMMER ざわ...
LISTEN, LUCCHINI, YOU JUST GROPED THE "STAR OF AFRICA" HERSELF! SHE'S SUCH AN ELITE ACE THAT SHE MAKES NEWS-PAPER STORIES ALL OVER THE WORLD!!
REALLY? BUT SHE'S THE SAME RANK AS YOU, SHIRLEY, SO I FIGURED IT COULDN'T BE THAT BIG OF A DEAL...
IT'S A HUGE DEAL, YOU NUMB-SKULL!!!
WHAT ARE WE GOING TO DO IF YOU PISSED HER OFF, AND SHE DECIDES NOT TO GET US THE SUPPLIES WE ASKED F--
!

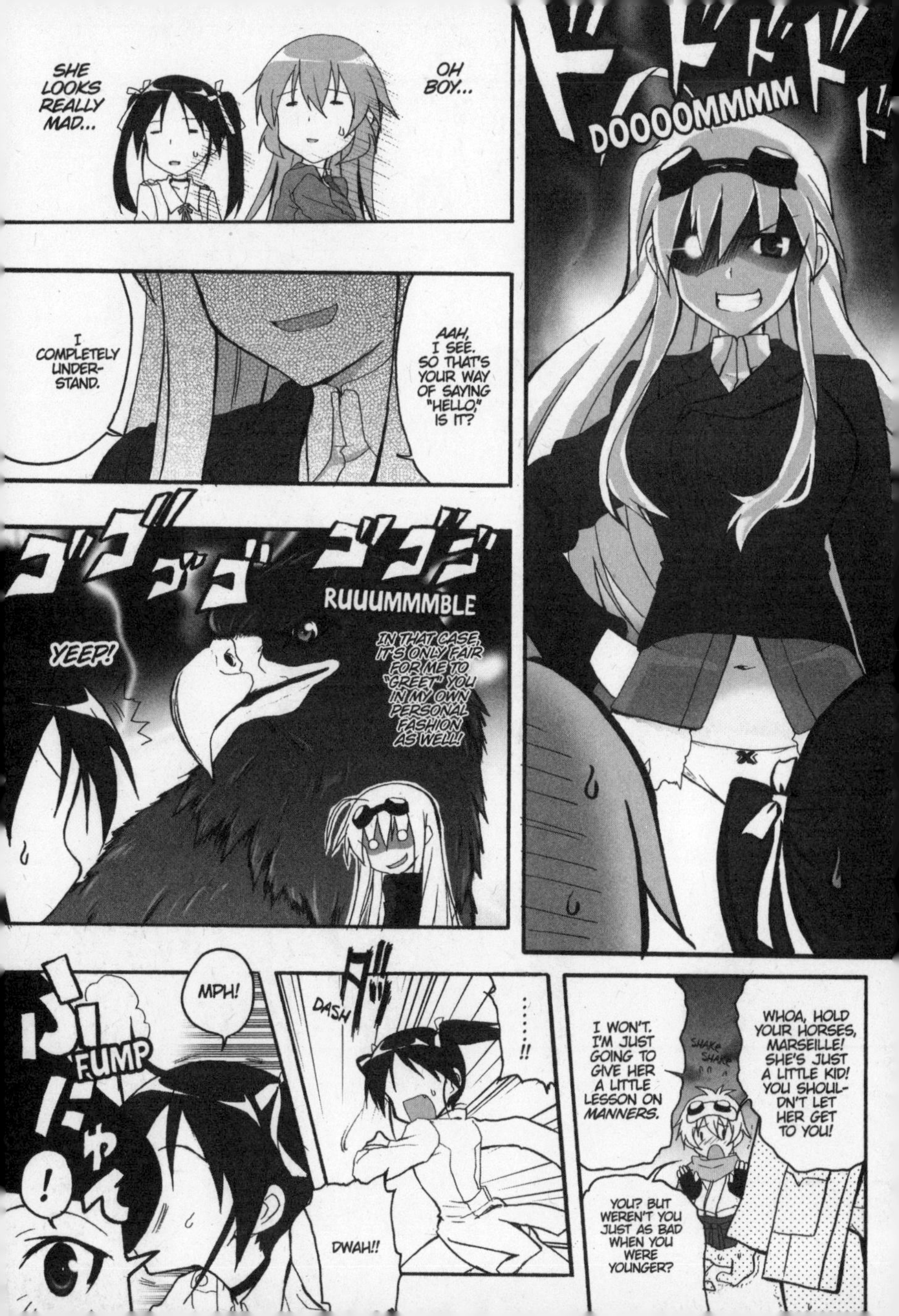
DOOOOMMMM
OH BOY...
SHE LOOKS REALLY MAD...
AAH, I SEE. SO THAT'S YOUR WAY OF SAYING "HELLO," IS IT?
I COMPLETELY UNDER-STAND.
RUUUMMMBLE
IN THAT CASE, IT'S ONLY FAIR FOR ME TO "GREET" YOU IN MY OWN PERSONAL FASHION AS WELL!
YEEP!
WHOA, HOLD YOUR HORSES, MARSEILLE! SHE'S JUST A LITTLE KID! YOU SHOUL-DN'T LET HER GET TO YOU!
SHAKE SHAKE
I WON'T. I'M JUST GOING TO GIVE HER A LITTLE LESSON ON MANNERS.
YOU? BUT WEREN'T YOU JUST AS BAD WHEN YOU WERE YOUNGER?
DASH
......!!
DWAH!!
MPH!
FUMP

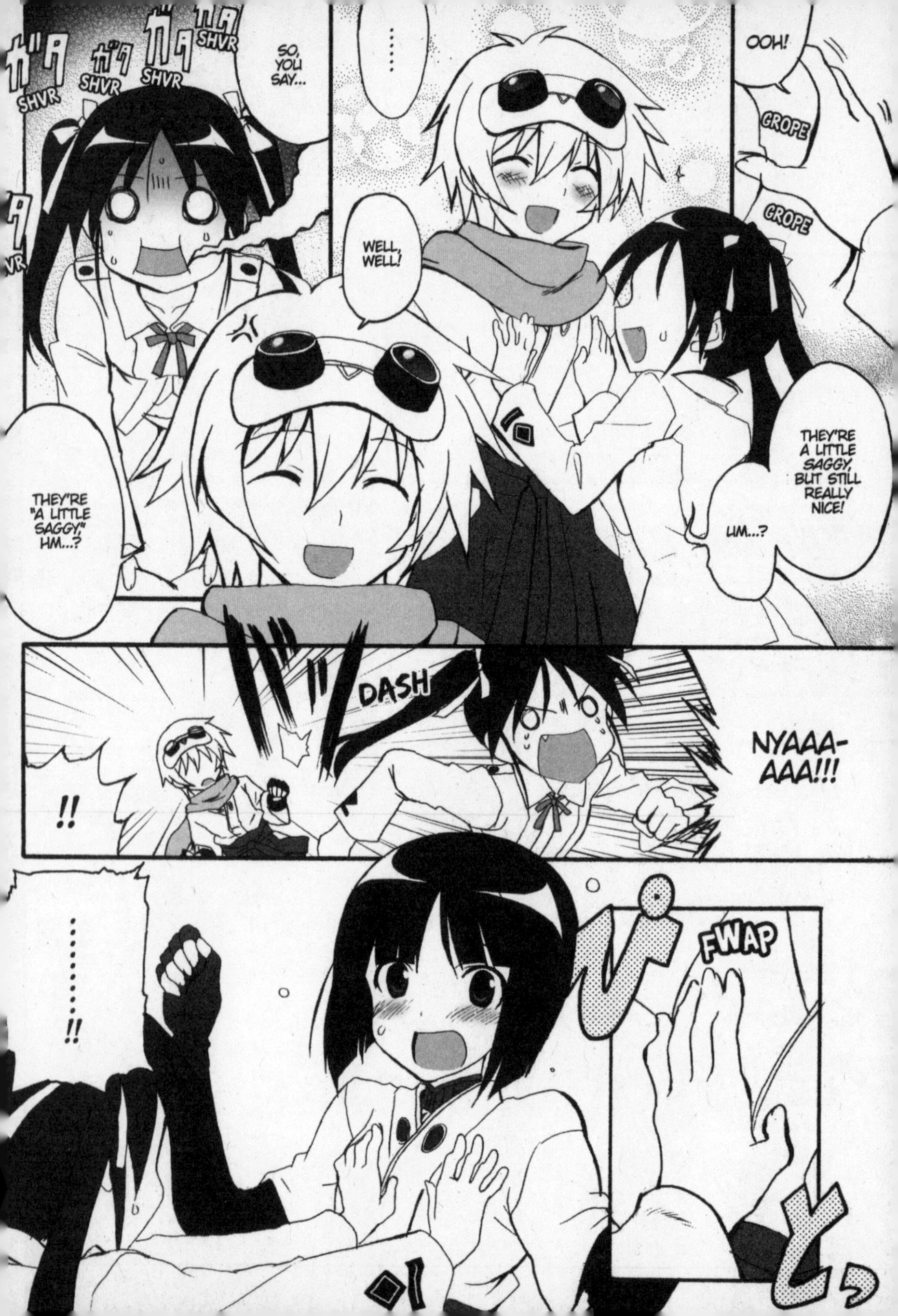
OOH!
GROPE
GROPE
THEY'RE A LITTLE SAGGY, BUT STILL REALLY NICE!
UM...?
......
WELL, WELL!
SHVR
SHVR
SHVR
SHVR
SO, YOU SAY...
THEY'RE "A LITTLE SAGGY," HM...?
NYAAA-AAA!!!
DASH
!!
FWAP
......!!

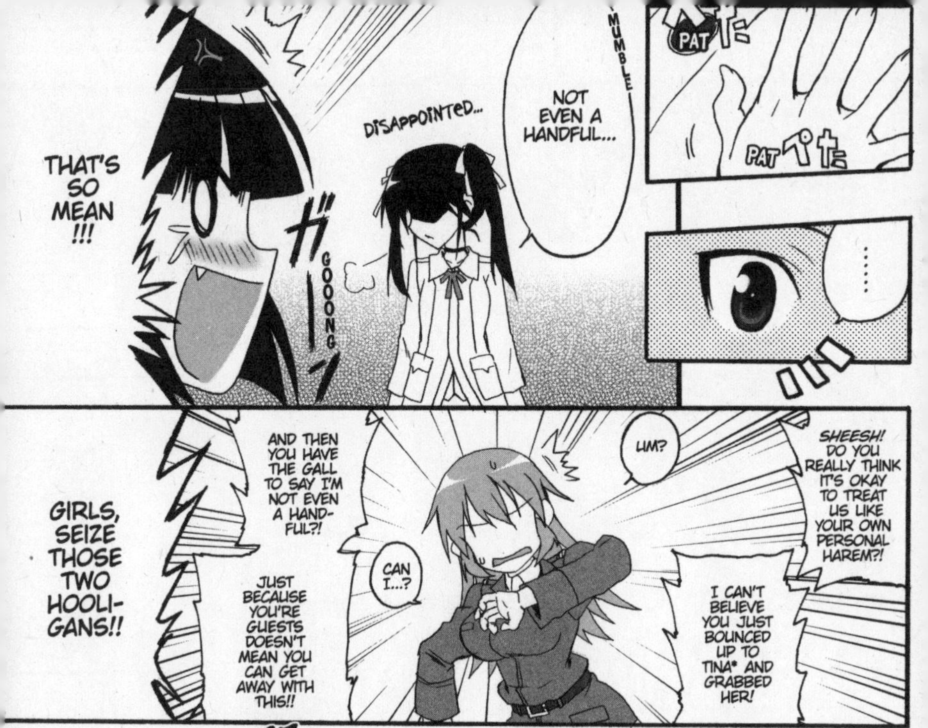
PAT
PAT
......
NOT EVEN A HANDFUL...
MUMBLE
DISAPPOINTED...
THAT'S SO MEAN!!!
GOOOONG
SHEESH! DO YOU REALLY THINK IT'S OKAY TO TREAT US LIKE YOUR OWN PERSONAL HAREM?!
UM?
AND THEN YOU HAVE THE GALL TO SAY I'M NOT EVEN A HAND-FUL?!
I CAN'T BELIEVE YOU JUST BOUNCED UP TO TINA* AND GRABBED HER!
CAN I...?
JUST BECAUSE YOU'RE GUESTS DOESN'T MEAN YOU CAN GET AWAY WITH THIS!!
GIRLS, SEIZE THOSE TWO HOOLI-GANS!!

*Hanna-Justina's nickname.

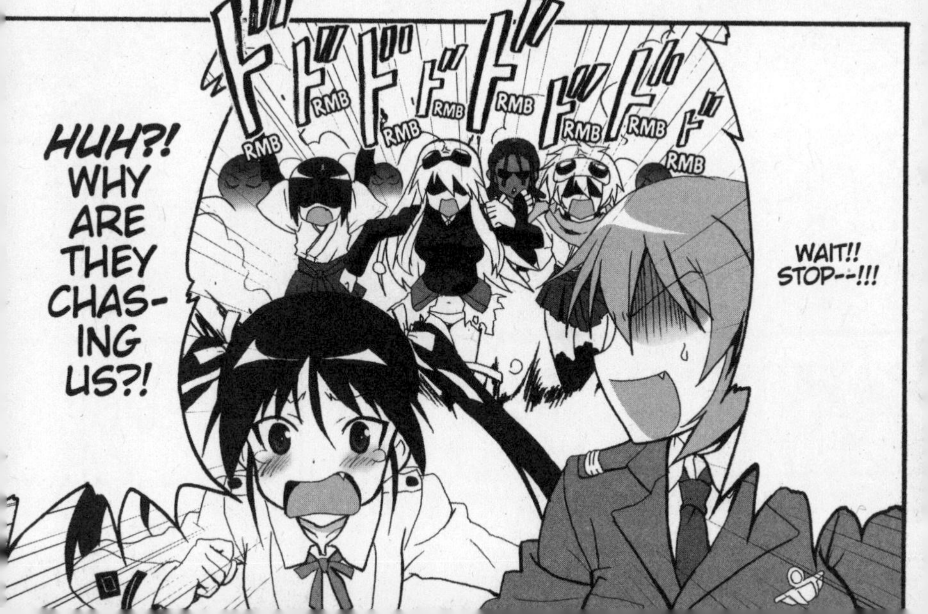
RMB
RMB
RMB
RMB
RMB
RMB
RMB
RMB
WAIT!! STOP--!!!
HUH?! WHY ARE THEY CHAS-ING US?!

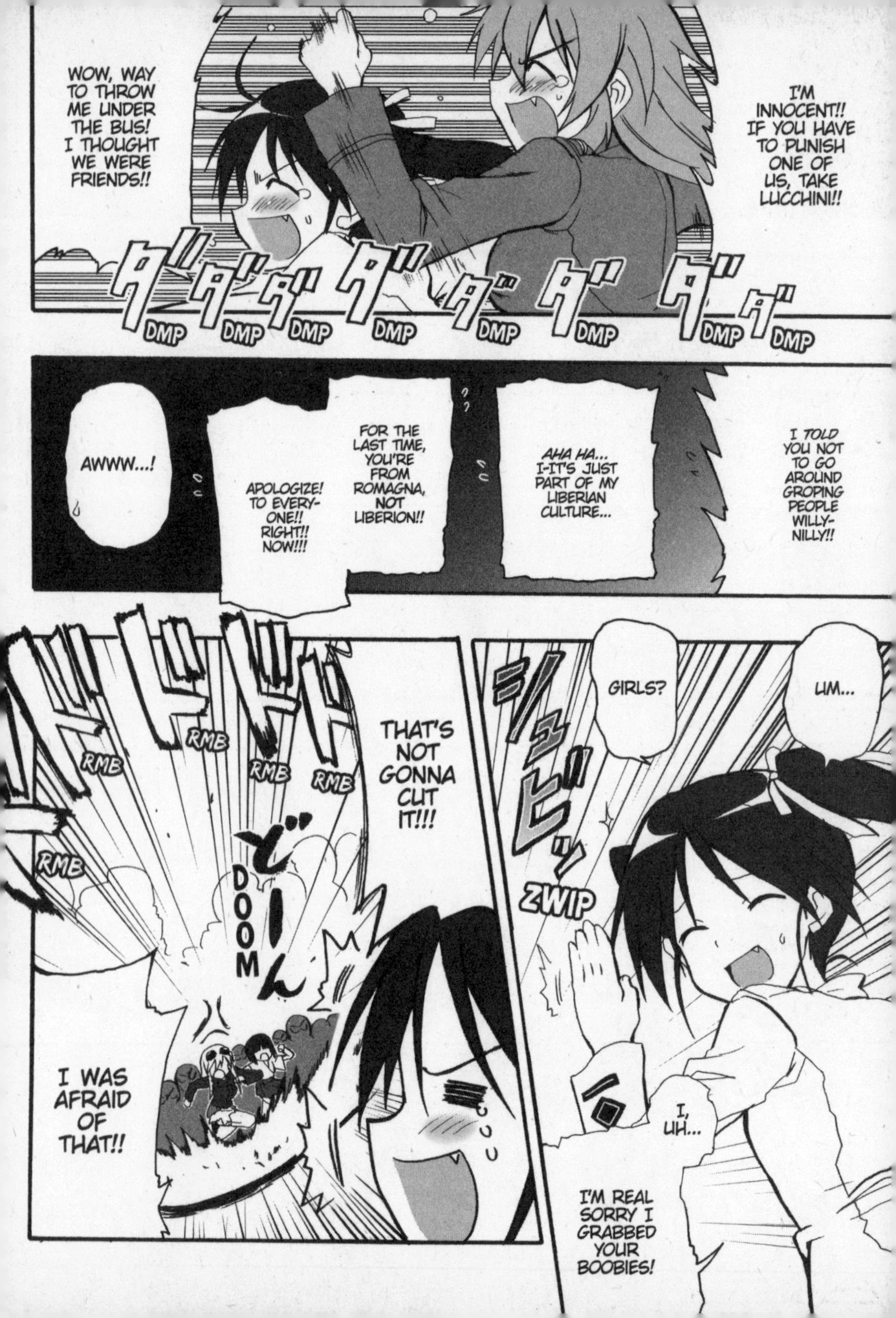

I'M INNOCENT!! IF YOU HAVE TO PUNISH ONE OF US, TAKE LUCCHINI!!
WOW, WAY TO THROW ME UNDER THE BUS! I THOUGHT WE WERE FRIENDS!!
DMP DMP DMP DMP DMP DMP DMP DMP
I TOLD YOU NOT TO GO AROUND GROPING PEOPLE WILLY-NILLY!!
AHA HA... I-IT'S JUST PART OF MY LIBERIAN CULTURE...
FOR THE LAST TIME, YOU'RE FROM ROMAGNA, NOT LIBERION!!
APOLOGIZE! TO EVERY-ONE!! RIGHT!! NOW!!!
AWWW...!
UM...
GIRLS?
ZWIP
I, UH...
I'M REAL SORRY I GRABBED YOUR BOOBIES!
THAT'S NOT GONNA CUT IT!!!
RMB RMB RMB RMB RMB
DOOM
I WAS AFRAID OF THAT!!

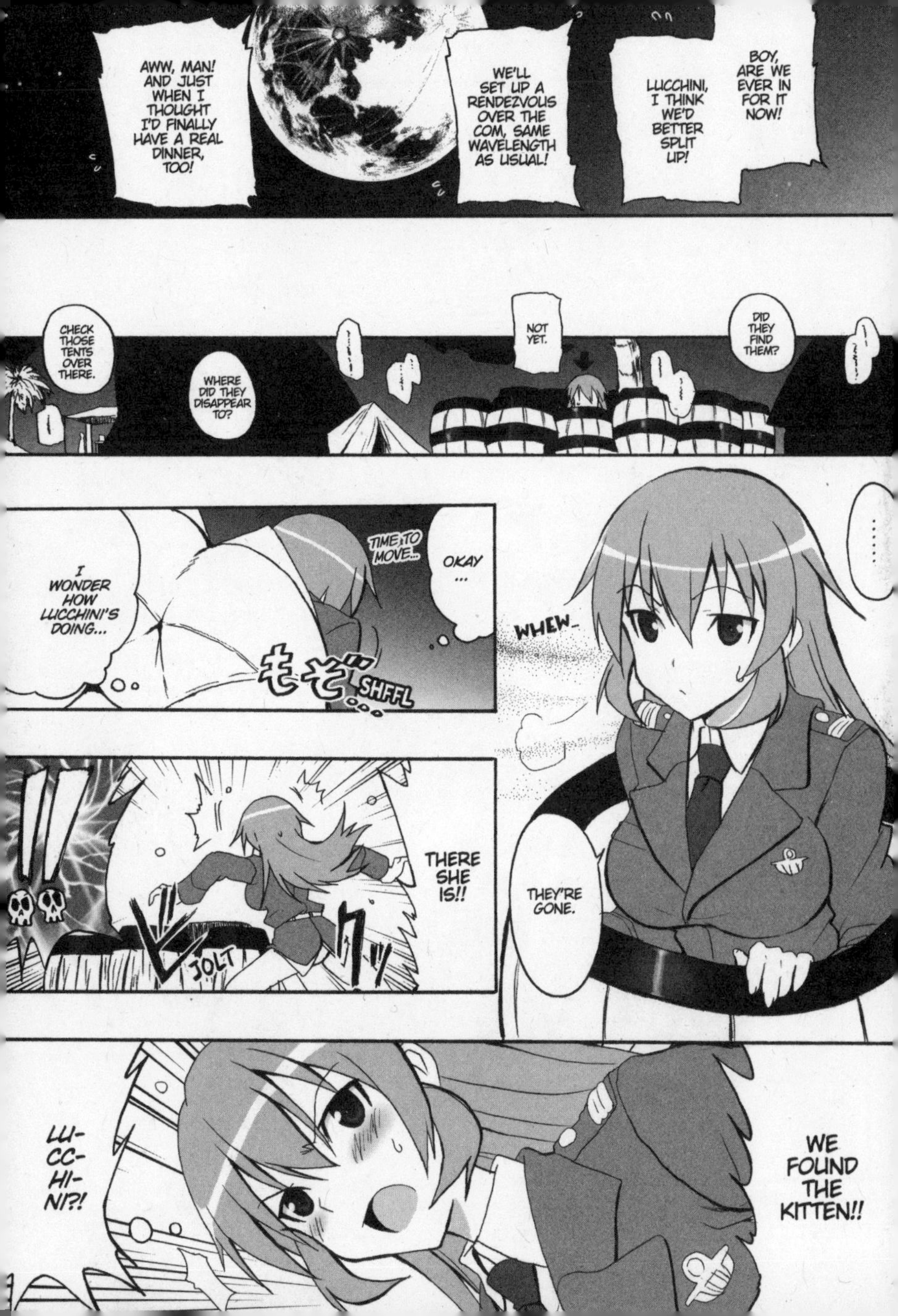

BOY, ARE WE EVER IN FOR IT NOW!
LUCCHINI, I THINK WE'D BETTER SPLIT UP!
WE'LL SET UP A RENDEZVOUS OVER THE COM, SAME WAVELENGTH AS USUAL!
AWW, MAN! AND JUST WHEN I THOUGHT I'D FINALLY HAVE A REAL DINNER, TOO!
DID THEY FIND THEM?
NOT YET.
WHERE DID THEY DISAPPEAR TO?
CHECK THOSE TENTS OVER THERE.
......
WHEW...
THEY'RE GONE.
OKAY...
TIME TO MOVE...
I WONDER HOW LUCCHINI'S DOING...
もぞ SHFFL
THERE SHE IS!!
ビクッ JOLT
!!
WE FOUND THE KITTEN!!
LU-CC-HI-NI?!

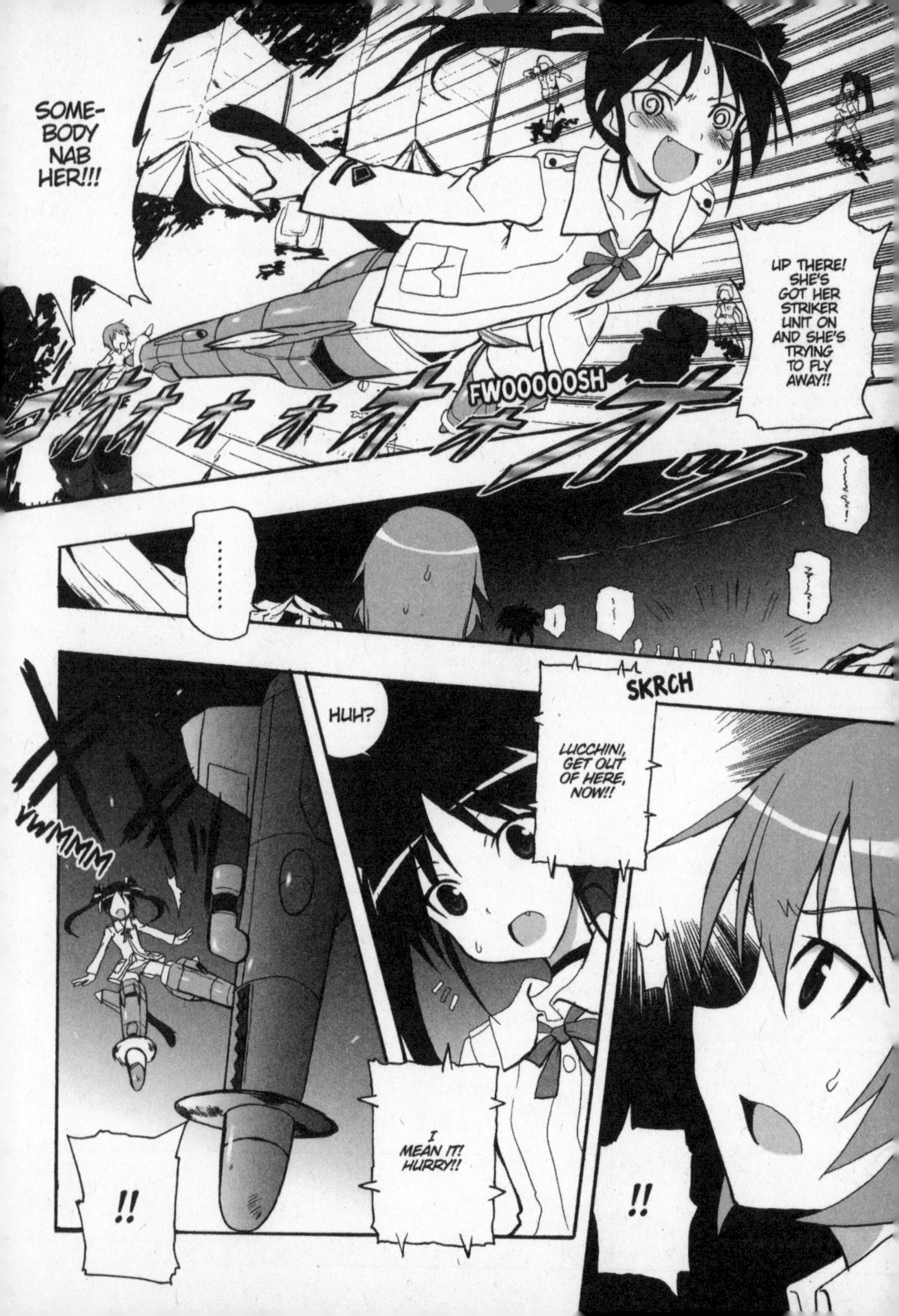
UP THERE! SHE'S GOT HER STRIKER UNIT ON AND SHE'S TRYING TO FLY AWAY!!
SOME-BODY NAB HER!!!
FWOOOOOSH
......
SKRCH
LUCCHINI, GET OUT OF HERE, NOW!!
!!
HUH?
I MEAN IT! HURRY!!
VWMMM
!!

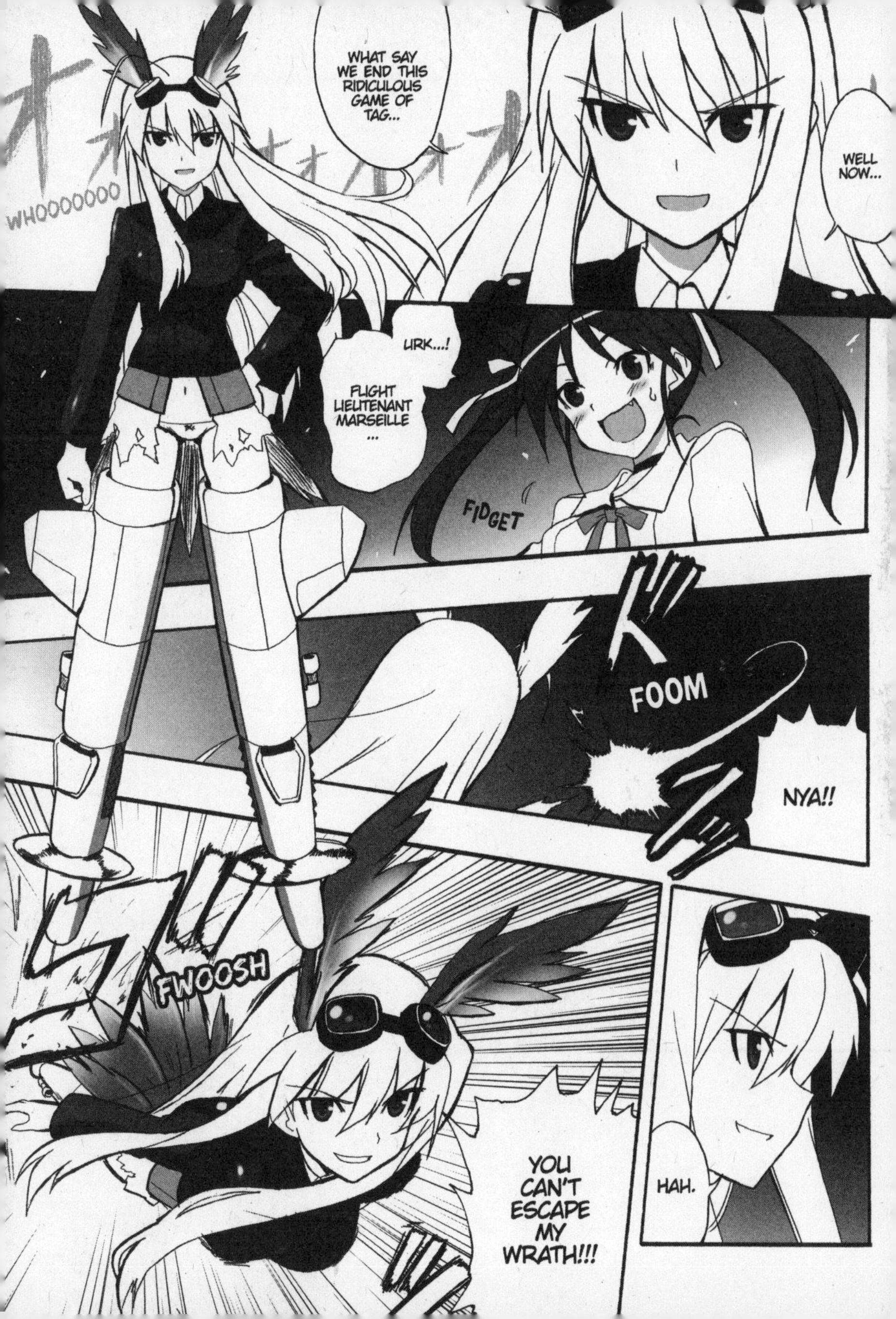
WELL NOW...
WHAT SAY WE END THIS RIDICULOUS GAME OF TAG...
URK...!
FLIGHT LIEUTENANT MARSEILLE ...
FIDGET
FOOM
NYA!!
WHOOOOOOO
HAH.
YOU CAN'T ESCAPE MY WRATH!!!
FWOOSH

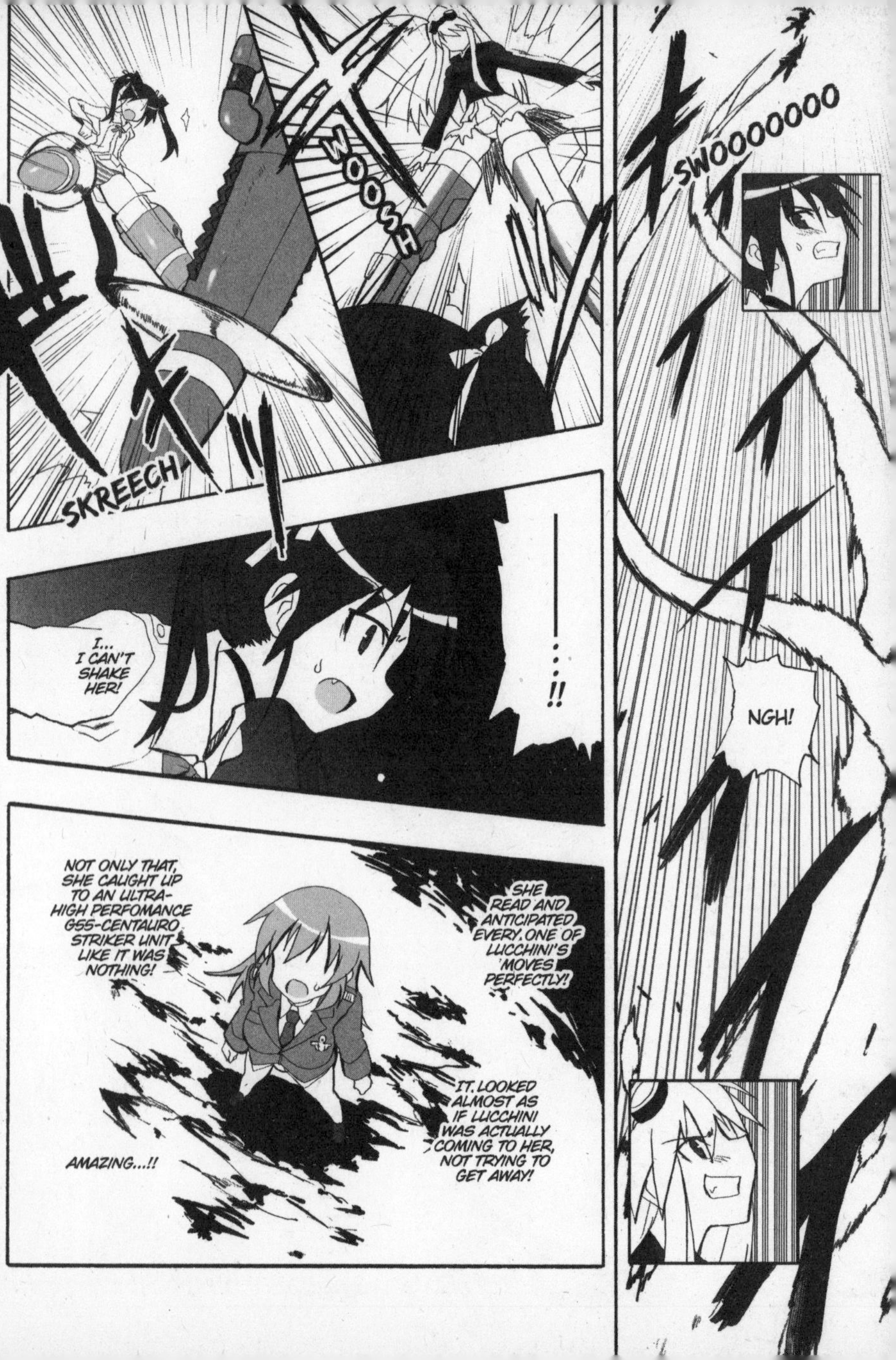
SWOOOOOOOO
NGH!
WOOOSH
SKREECH
——...!!
I... I CAN'T SHAKE HER!
SHE READ AND ANTICIPATED EVERY ONE OF LUCCHINI'S MOVES PERFECTLY!
NOT ONLY THAT, SHE CAUGHT UP TO AN ULTRA-HIGH PERFOMANCE G55-CENTAURO STRIKER UNIT LIKE IT WAS NOTHING!
IT LOOKED ALMOST AS IF LUCCHINI WAS ACTUALLY COMING TO HER, NOT TRYING TO GET AWAY!
AMAZING...!!

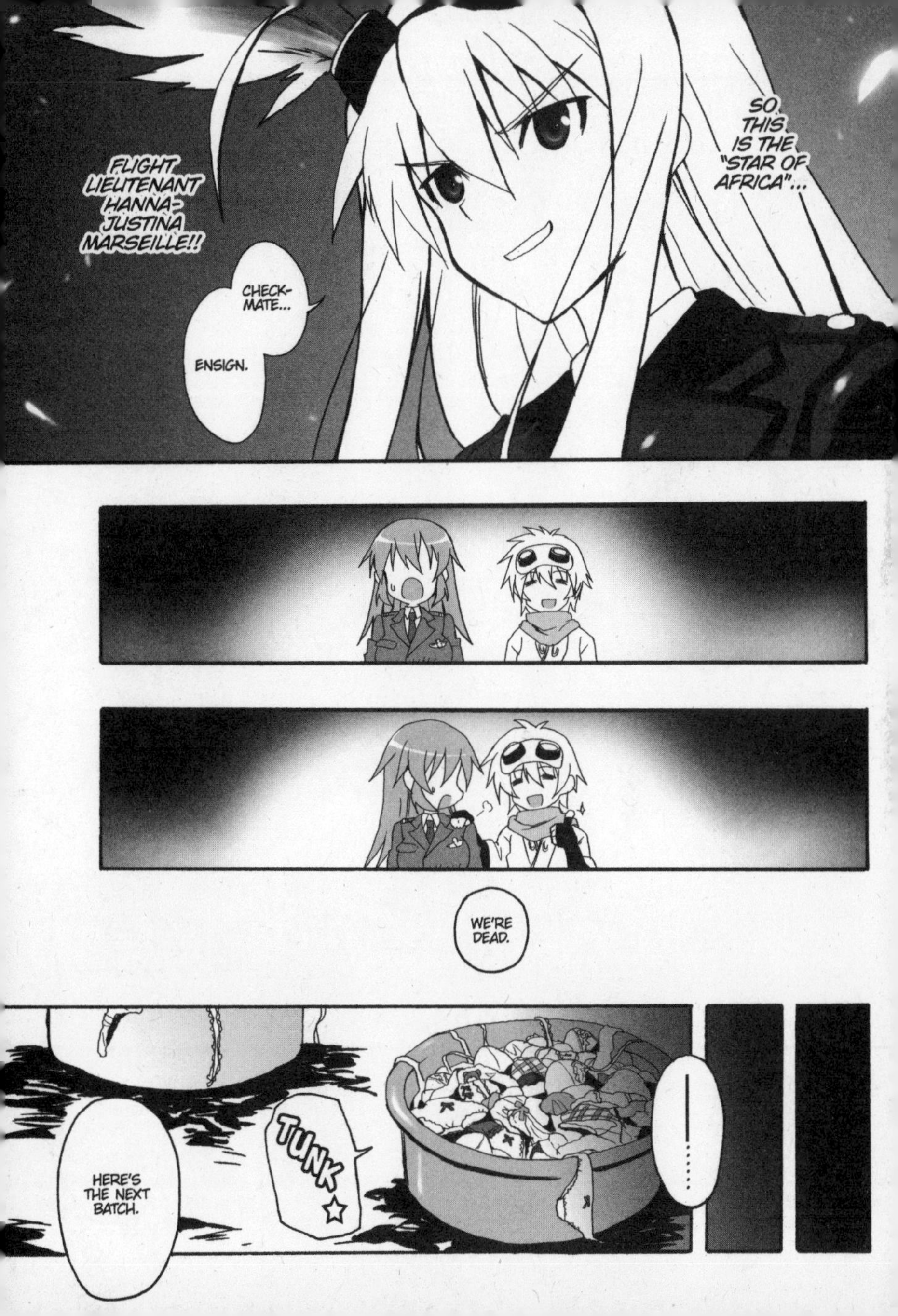
SO... THIS IS THE "STAR OF AFRICA"...
FLIGHT LIEUTENANT HANNA-JUSTINA MARSEILLE!!
CHECK-MATE...
ENSIGN.
WE'RE DEAD.
—......
TUNK
HERE'S THE NEXT BATCH.

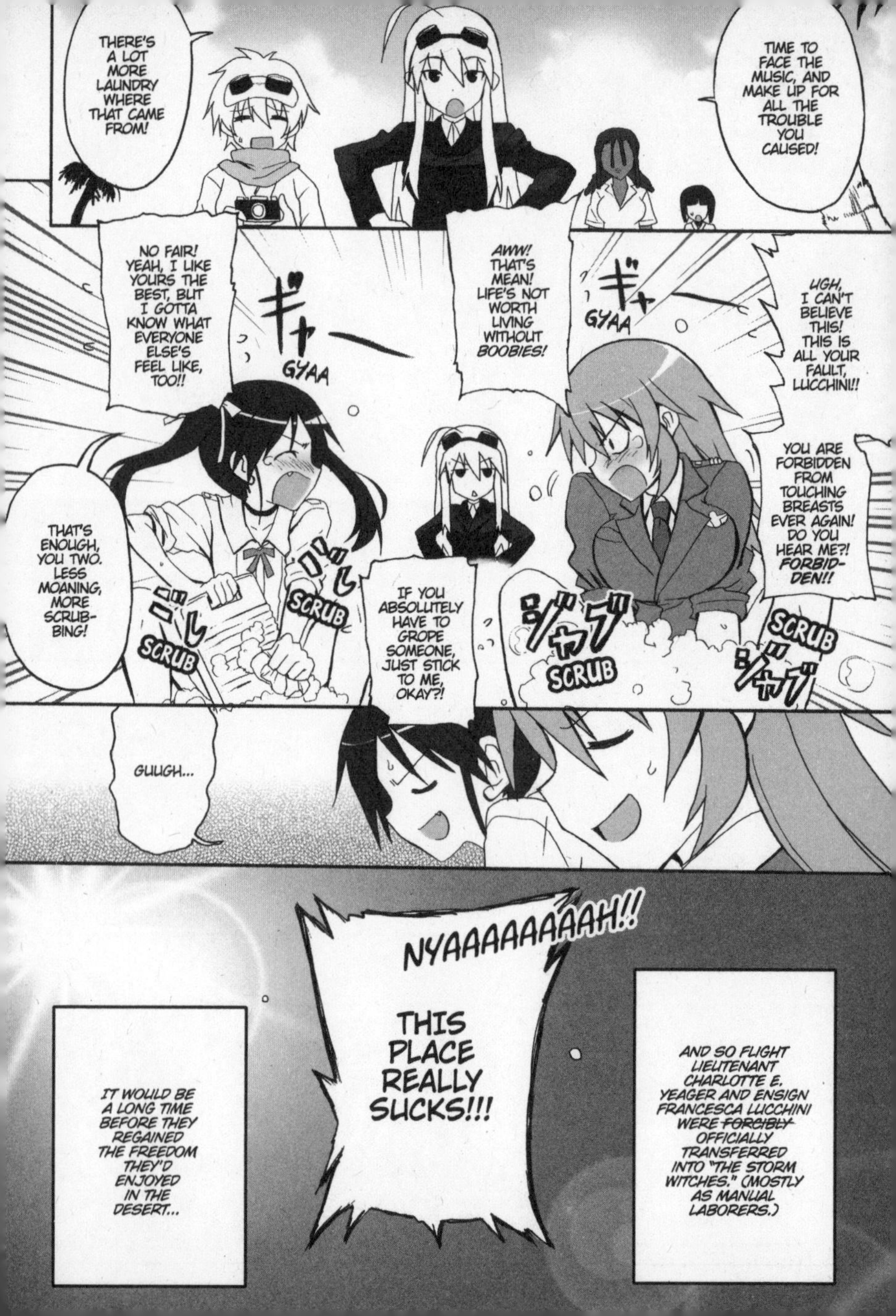

TIME TO FACE THE MUSIC, AND MAKE UP FOR ALL THE TROUBLE YOU CAUSED!
THERE'S A LOT MORE LAUNDRY WHERE THAT CAME FROM!
UGH, I CAN'T BELIEVE THIS! THIS IS ALL YOUR FAULT, LUCCHINI!!
GYAA
YOU ARE FORBIDDEN FROM TOUCHING BREASTS EVER AGAIN! DO YOU HEAR ME?! *FORBIDDEN!!*
AWW! THAT'S MEAN! LIFE'S NOT WORTH LIVING WITHOUT *BOOBIES!*
GYAA
NO FAIR! YEAH, I LIKE YOURS THE BEST, BUT I GOTTA KNOW WHAT EVERYONE ELSE'S FEEL LIKE, TOO!!
SCRUB
SCRUB
IF YOU ABSOLUTELY HAVE TO GROPE SOMEONE, JUST STICK TO ME, OKAY?!
SCRUB
SCRUB
THAT'S ENOUGH, YOU TWO. LESS MOANING, MORE SCRUBBING!
GUUGH...
NYAAAAAAAAH!!
THIS PLACE REALLY SUCKS!!!
AND SO FLIGHT LIEUTENANT CHARLOTTE E. YEAGER AND ENSIGN FRANCESCA LUCCHINI WERE ~~FORCIBLY~~ OFFICIALLY TRANSFERRED INTO "THE STORM WITCHES." (MOSTLY AS MANUAL LABORERS.)
IT WOULD BE A LONG TIME BEFORE THEY REGAINED THE FREEDOM THEY'D ENJOYED IN THE DESERT...

WITCHES GRAFFITI

**Shimada Humikane &
Projekt Kagonish**
illustrated by
Kyougoku Shin

Raysa Pettogen

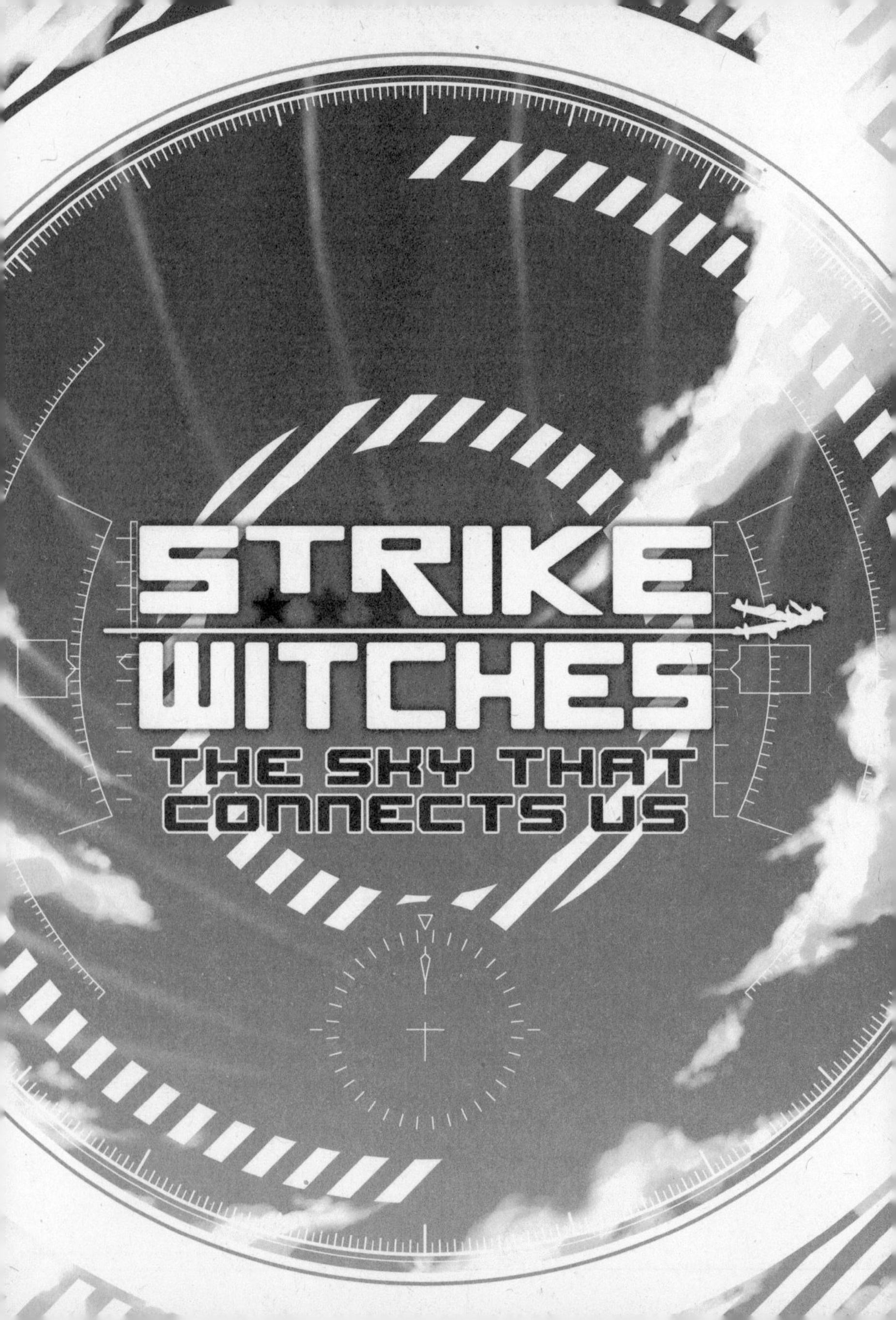
STRIKE
WITCHES
THE SKY THAT
CONNECTS US

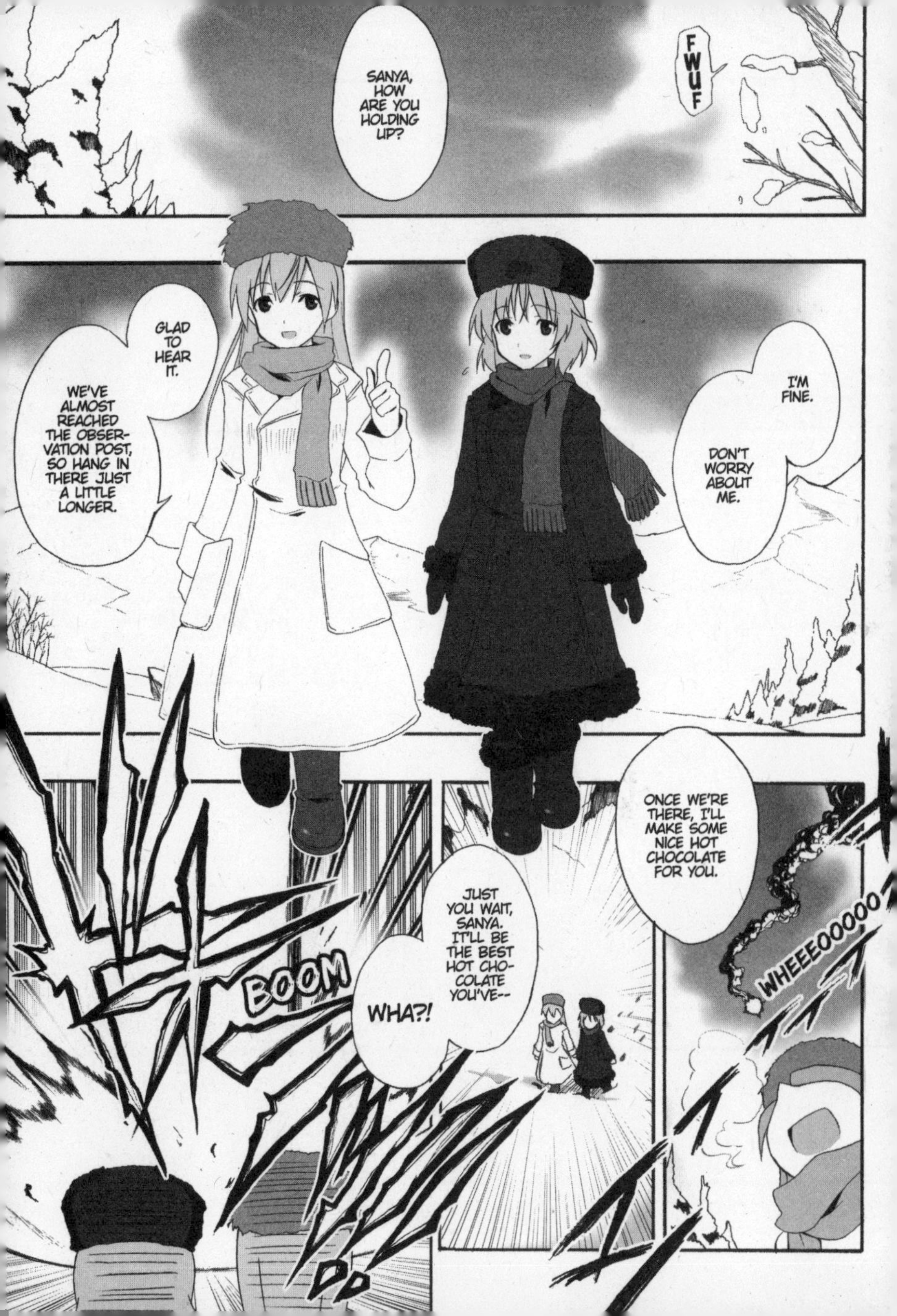
FWUF
SANYA, HOW ARE YOU HOLDING UP?
I'M FINE.
DON'T WORRY ABOUT ME.
GLAD TO HEAR IT.
WE'VE ALMOST REACHED THE OBSER-VATION POST, SO HANG IN THERE JUST A LITTLE LONGER.
WHEEEOOOOO
ONCE WE'RE THERE, I'LL MAKE SOME NICE HOT CHOCOLATE FOR YOU.
JUST YOU WAIT, SANYA. IT'LL BE THE BEST HOT CHO-COLATE YOU'VE--
WHA?!
BOOM
DD

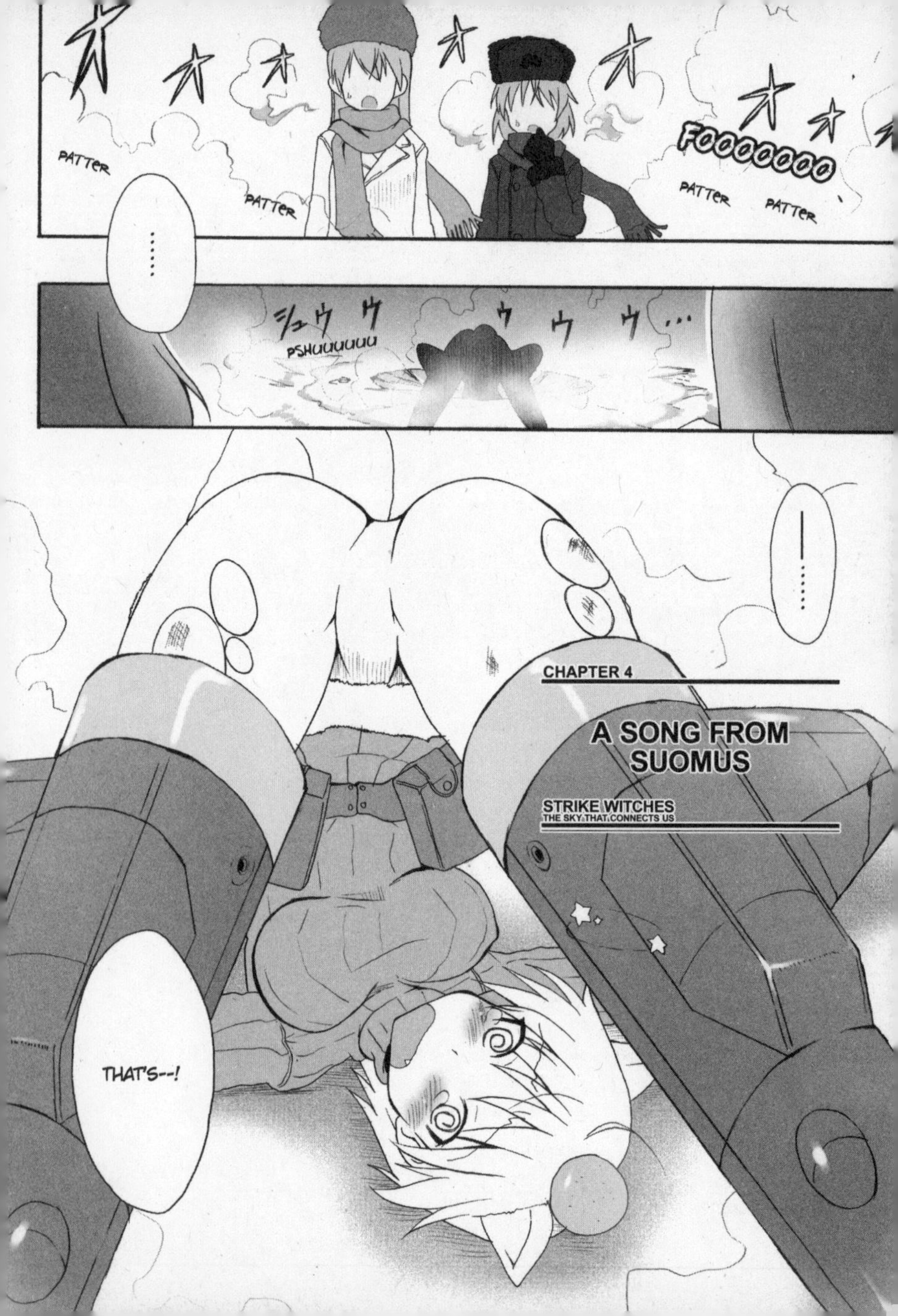

オオオオオオオオ
FOOOOOOOO
PATTER PATTER
PATTER PATTER
......
シュウウウウウ...
PSHUUUUUU
—......
CHAPTER 4
A SONG FROM SUOMUS
STRIKE WITCHES
THE SKY THAT CONNECTS US
THAT'S--!

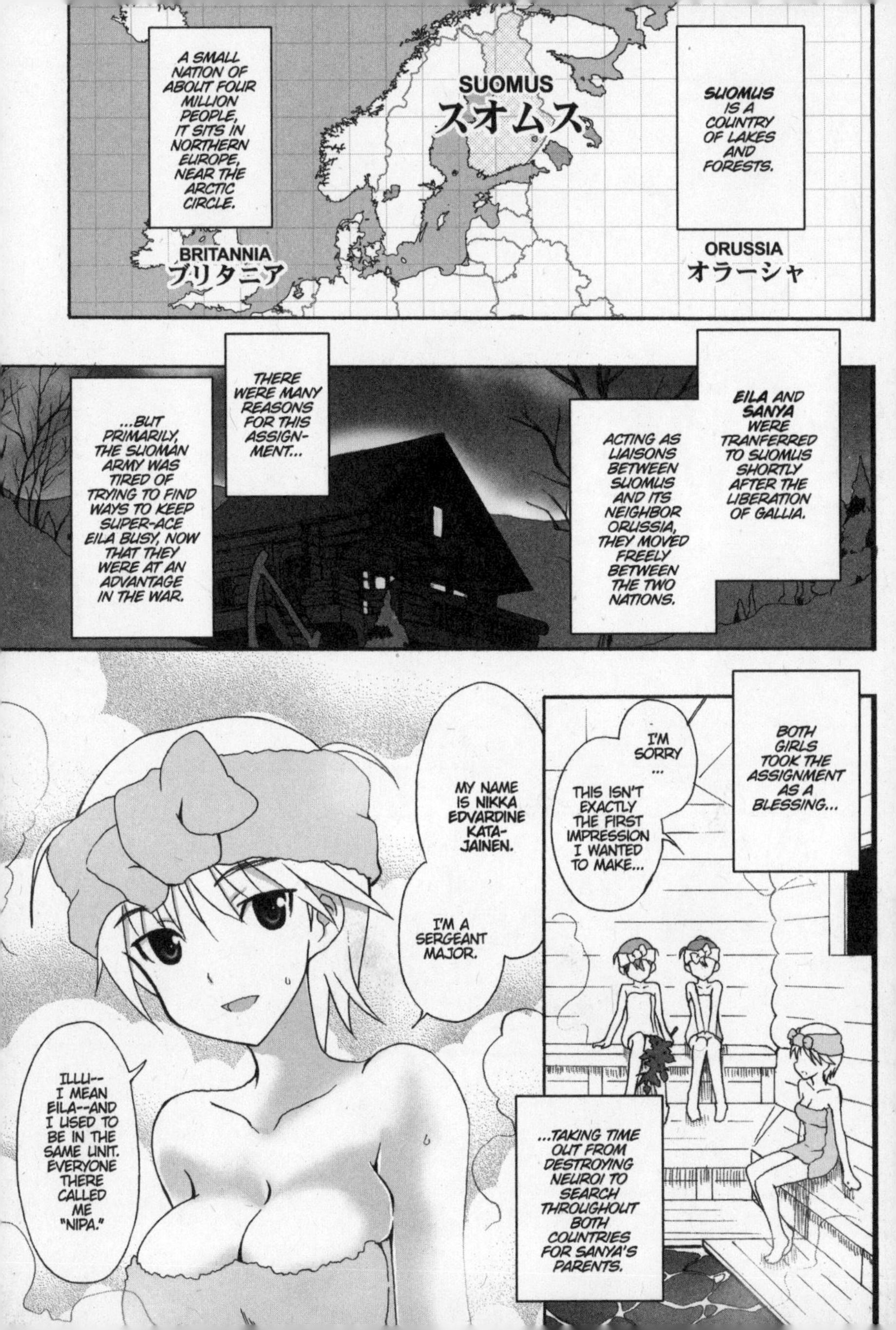
SUOMUS
スオムス
A SMALL NATION OF ABOUT FOUR MILLION PEOPLE, IT SITS IN NORTHERN EUROPE, NEAR THE ARCTIC CIRCLE.
SUOMUS IS A COUNTRY OF LAKES AND FORESTS.
ORUSSIA
オラーシャ
BRITANNIA
ブリタニア
EILA AND SANYA WERE TRANFERRED TO SUOMUS SHORTLY AFTER THE LIBERATION OF GALLIA.
ACTING AS LIAISONS BETWEEN SUOMUS AND ITS NEIGHBOR ORUSSIA, THEY MOVED FREELY BETWEEN THE TWO NATIONS.
THERE WERE MANY REASONS FOR THIS ASSIGN-MENT...
...BUT PRIMARILY, THE SUOMAN ARMY WAS TIRED OF TRYING TO FIND WAYS TO KEEP SUPER-ACE EILA BUSY, NOW THAT THEY WERE AT AN ADVANTAGE IN THE WAR.
BOTH GIRLS TOOK THE ASSIGNMENT AS A BLESSING...
I'M SORRY...
THIS ISN'T EXACTLY THE FIRST IMPRESSION I WANTED TO MAKE...
MY NAME IS NIKKA EDVARDINE KATA-JAINEN.
I'M A SERGEANT MAJOR.
ILLLI-- I MEAN EILA--AND I USED TO BE IN THE SAME UNIT. EVERYONE THERE CALLED ME "NIPA."
...TAKING TIME OUT FROM DESTROYING NEUROI TO SEARCH THROUGHOUT BOTH COUNTRIES FOR SANYA'S PARENTS.

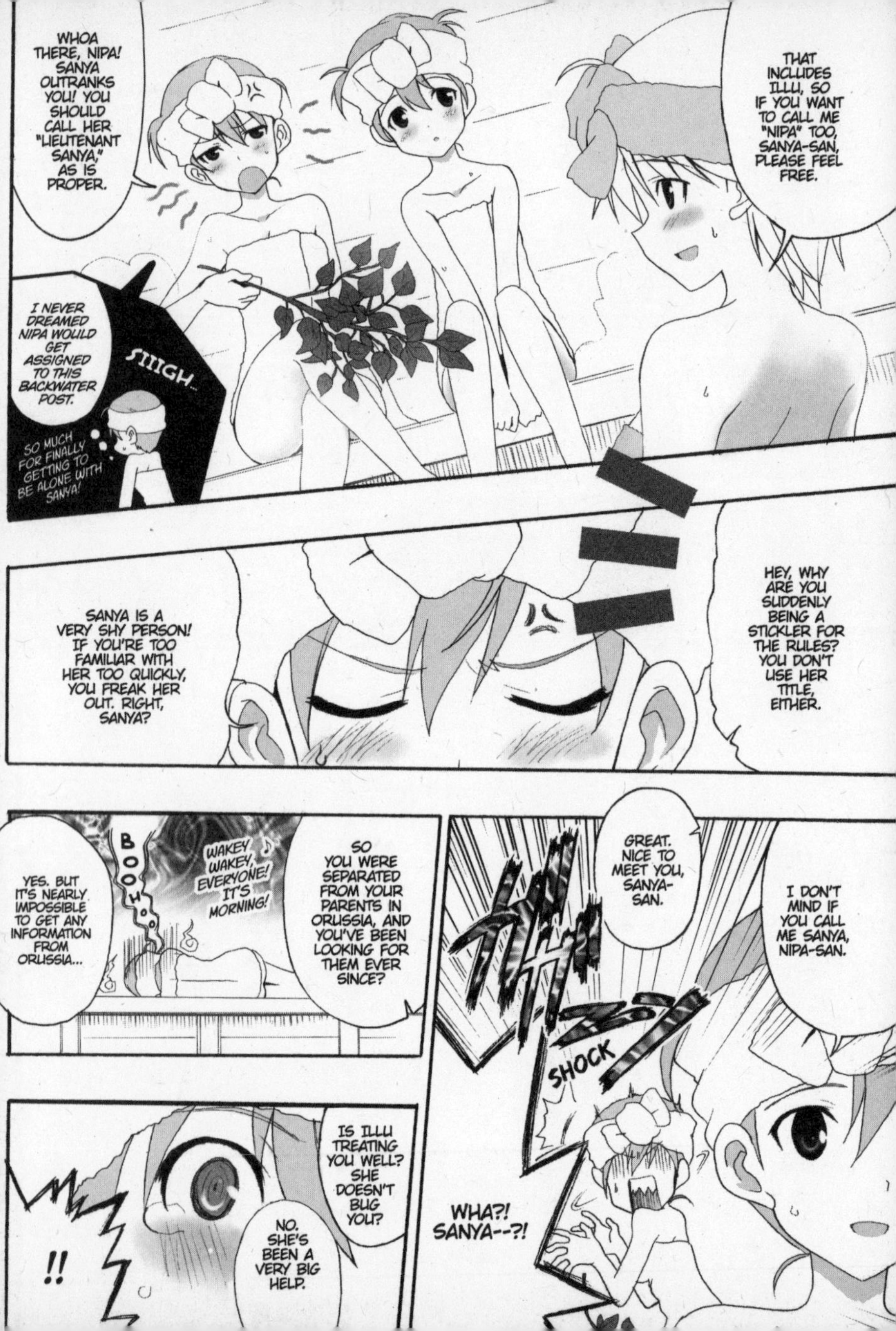
THAT INCLUDES ILLU, SO IF YOU WANT TO CALL ME "NIPA" TOO, SANYA-SAN, PLEASE FEEL FREE.
WHOA THERE, NIPA! SANYA OUTRANKS YOU! YOU SHOULD CALL HER "LIEUTENANT SANYA," AS IS PROPER.
I NEVER DREAMED NIPA WOULD GET ASSIGNED TO THIS BACKWATER POST.
SIIIGH...
SO MUCH FOR FINALLY GETTING TO BE ALONE WITH SANYA!
HEY, WHY ARE YOU SUDDENLY BEING A STICKLER FOR THE RULES? YOU DON'T USE HER TITLE, EITHER.
SANYA IS A VERY SHY PERSON! IF YOU'RE TOO FAMILIAR WITH HER TOO QUICKLY, YOU FREAK HER OUT. RIGHT, SANYA?
I DON'T MIND IF YOU CALL ME SANYA, NIPA-SAN.
GREAT. NICE TO MEET YOU, SANYA-SAN.
SHOCK
WHA?! SANYA--?!
SO YOU WERE SEPARATED FROM YOUR PARENTS IN ORUSSIA, AND YOU'VE BEEN LOOKING FOR THEM EVER SINCE?
WAKEY WAKEY, EVERYONE! IT'S MORNING! ♪
BOOHOO
YES. BUT IT'S NEARLY IMPOSSIBLE TO GET ANY INFORMATION FROM ORUSSIA...
IS ILLU TREATING YOU WELL? SHE DOESN'T BUG YOU?
NO. SHE'S BEEN A VERY BIG HELP.
!!

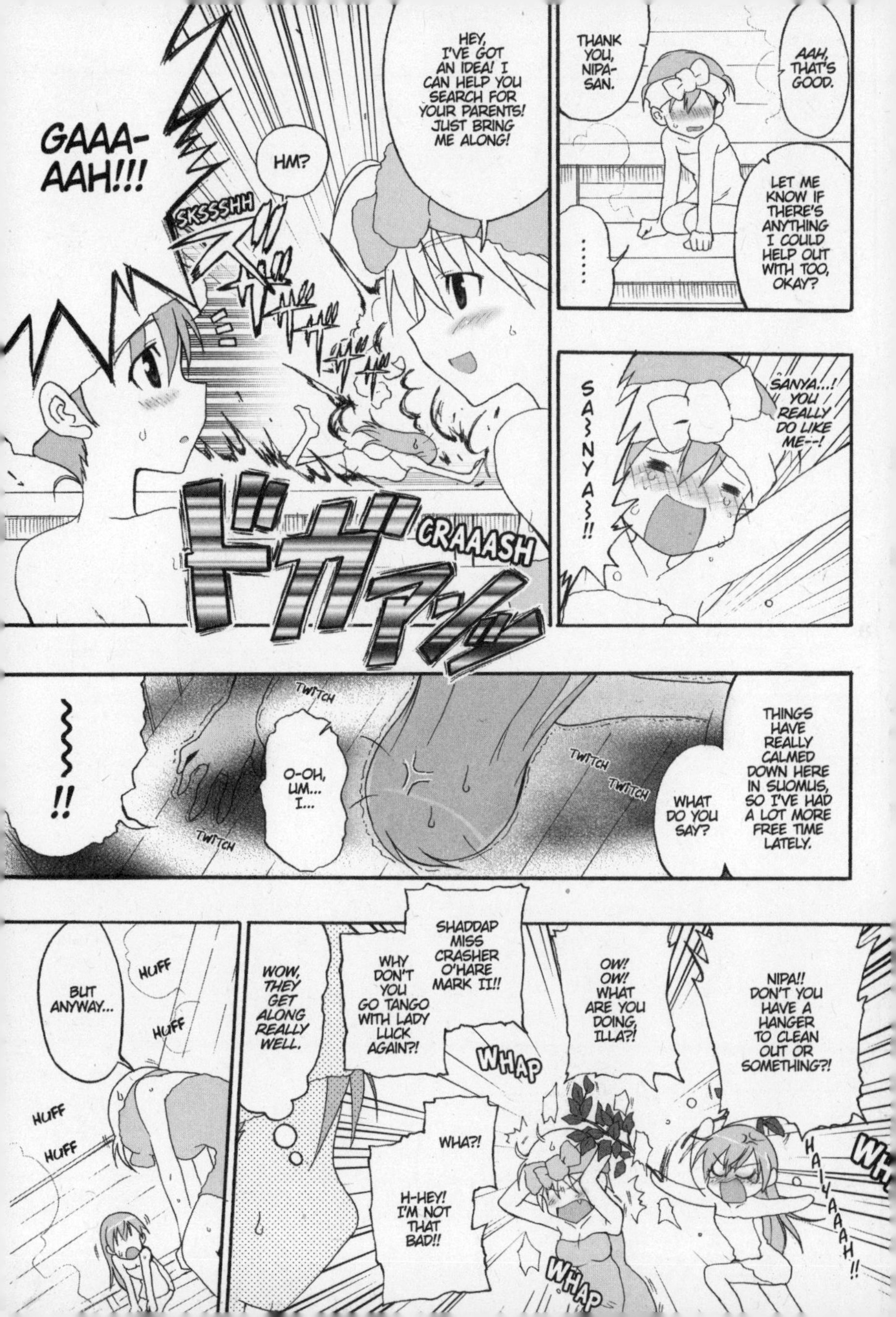
AAH, THAT'S GOOD.
THANK YOU, NIPA-SAN.
LET ME KNOW IF THERE'S ANYTHING I COULD HELP OUT WITH TOO, OKAY?
......
SANYA...! YOU REALLY DO LIKE ME--!
SA~NYA~!!
HEY, I'VE GOT AN IDEA! I CAN HELP YOU SEARCH FOR YOUR PARENTS! JUST BRING ME ALONG!
HM?
GAAAA-AAH!!!
SKSSSHH
CRAAASH
THINGS HAVE REALLY CALMED DOWN HERE IN SUOMUS, SO I'VE HAD A LOT MORE FREE TIME LATELY.
WHAT DO YOU SAY?
TWITCH
TWITCH
TWITCH
O-OH, UM... I...
TWITCH
~~~!!
NIPA!! DON'T YOU HAVE A HANGER TO CLEAN OUT OR SOMETHING?!
OW! OW! WHAT ARE YOU DOING, ILLA?!
SHADDAP MISS CRASHER O'HARE MARK II!!
WHY DON'T YOU GO TANGO WITH LADY LUCK AGAIN?!
WHAP
HAIYAAAH!!
WH
WHA?!
H-HEY! I'M NOT THAT BAD!!
WHAP
WOW, THEY GET ALONG REALLY WELL.
BUT ANYWAY...
HUFF
HUFF
HUFF
HUFF
~~~

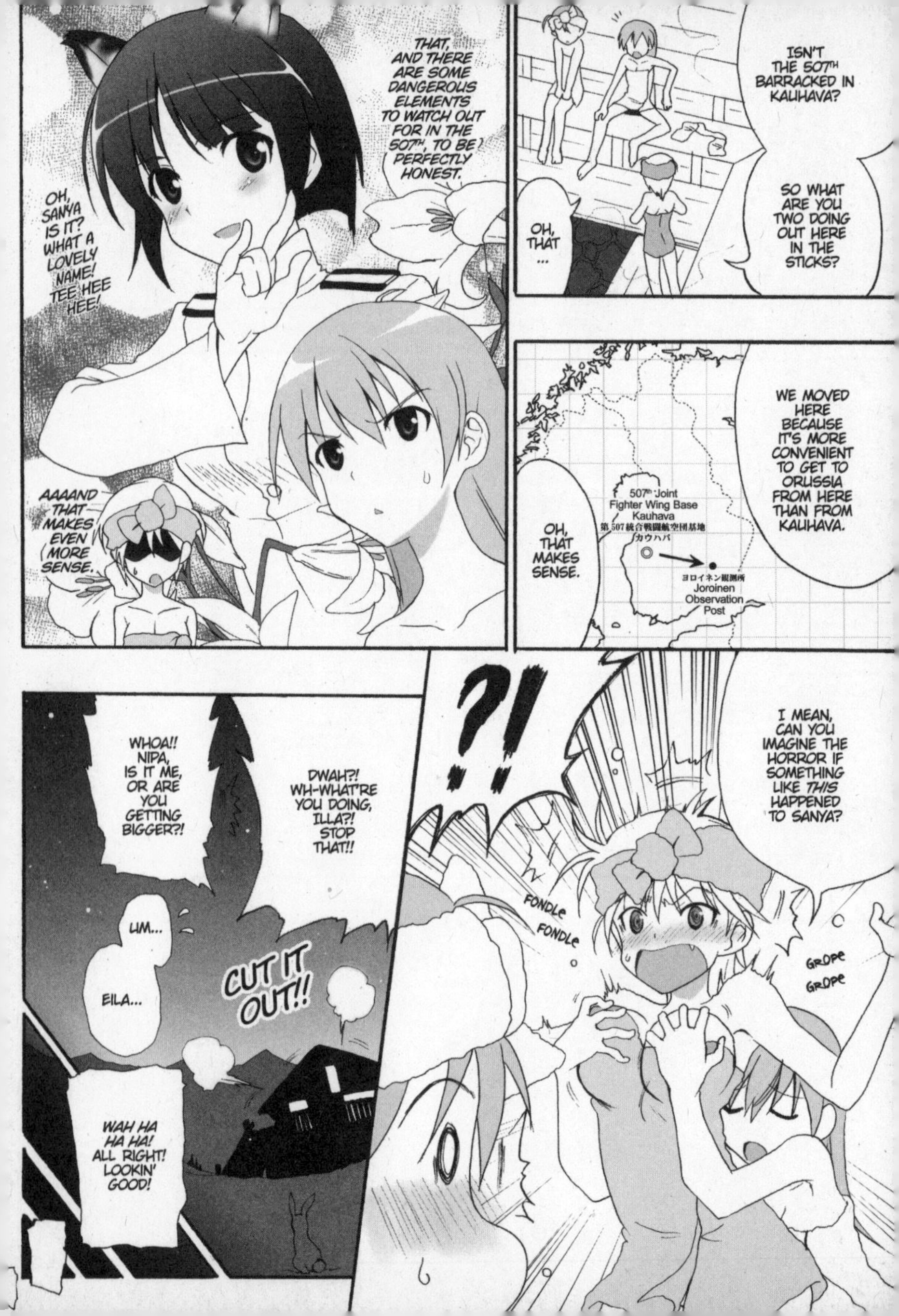
ISN'T THE 507TH BARRACKED IN KAUHAVA?
SO WHAT ARE YOU TWO DOING OUT HERE IN THE STICKS?
OH, THAT ...
WE MOVED HERE BECAUSE IT'S MORE CONVENIENT TO GET TO ORUSSIA FROM HERE THAN FROM KAUHAVA.
OH, THAT MAKES SENSE.
507th Joint Fighter Wing Base Kauhava
第507統合戦闘航空団基地 カウハバ
ヨロイネン観測所
Joroinen Observation Post
THAT, AND THERE ARE SOME DANGEROUS ELEMENTS TO WATCH OUT FOR IN THE 507TH, TO BE PERFECTLY HONEST.
OH, SANYA IS IT? WHAT A LOVELY NAME! TEE HEE HEE!
AAAAND THAT MAKES EVEN MORE SENSE.
?!
I MEAN, CAN YOU IMAGINE THE HORROR IF SOMETHING LIKE THIS HAPPENED TO SANYA?
FONDLE
FONDLE
GROPE
GROPE
WHOA!! NIPA, IS IT ME, OR ARE YOU GETTING BIGGER?!
DWAH?! WH-WHAT'RE YOU DOING, ILLA?! STOP THAT!!
UM...
EILA...
CUT IT OUT!!
WAH HA HA HA! ALL RIGHT! LOOKIN' GOOD!

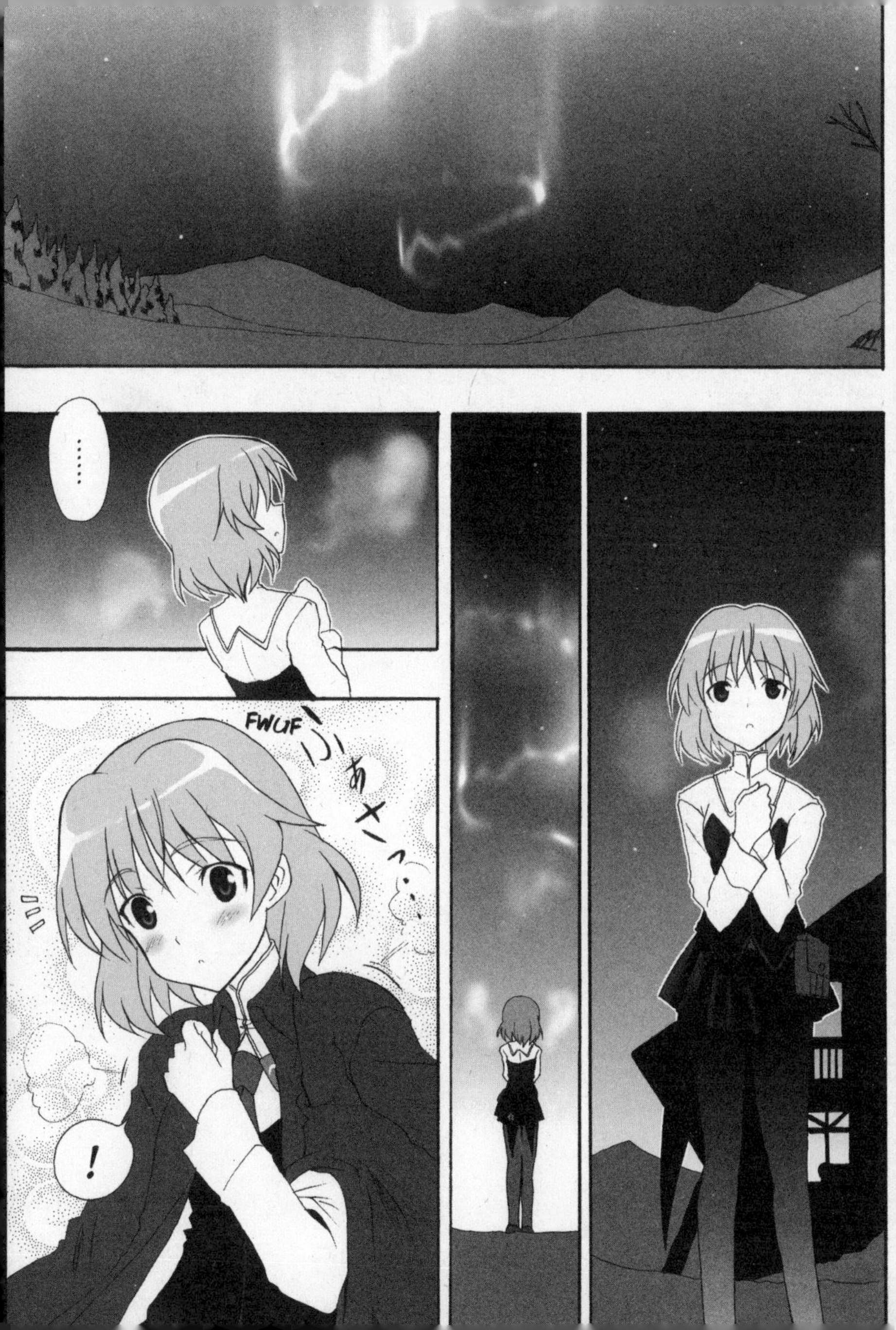
……
FWUF
!

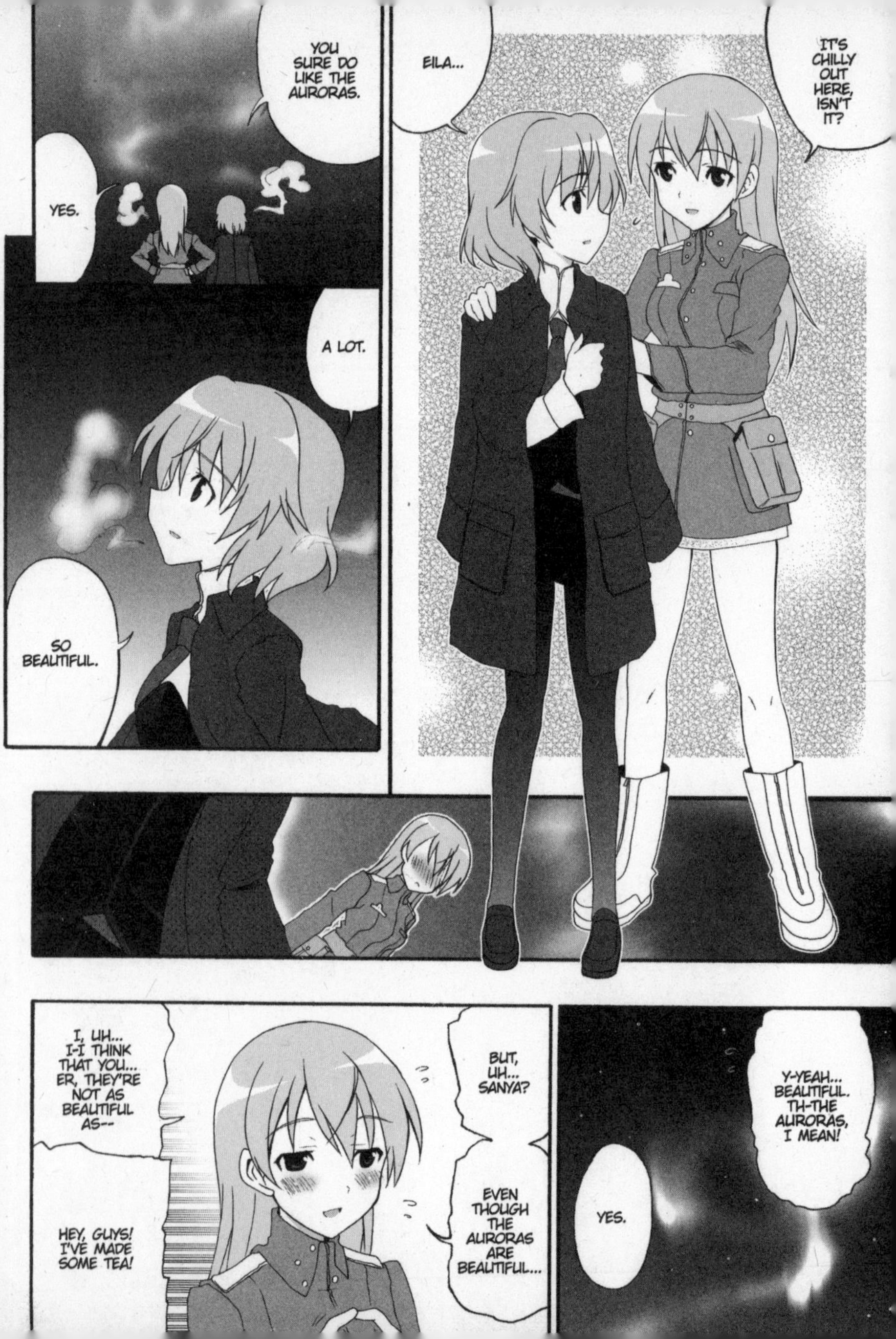
IT'S CHILLY OUT HERE, ISN'T IT?
EILA...
YOU SURE DO LIKE THE AURORAS.
YES.
A LOT.
SO BEAUTIFUL.
Y-YEAH... BEAUTIFUL. TH-THE AURORAS, I MEAN!
YES.
BUT, UH... SANYA?
EVEN THOUGH THE AURORAS ARE BEAUTIFUL...
I, UH... I-I THINK THAT YOU... ER, THEY'RE NOT AS BEAUTIFUL AS--
HEY, GUYS! I'VE MADE SOME TEA!

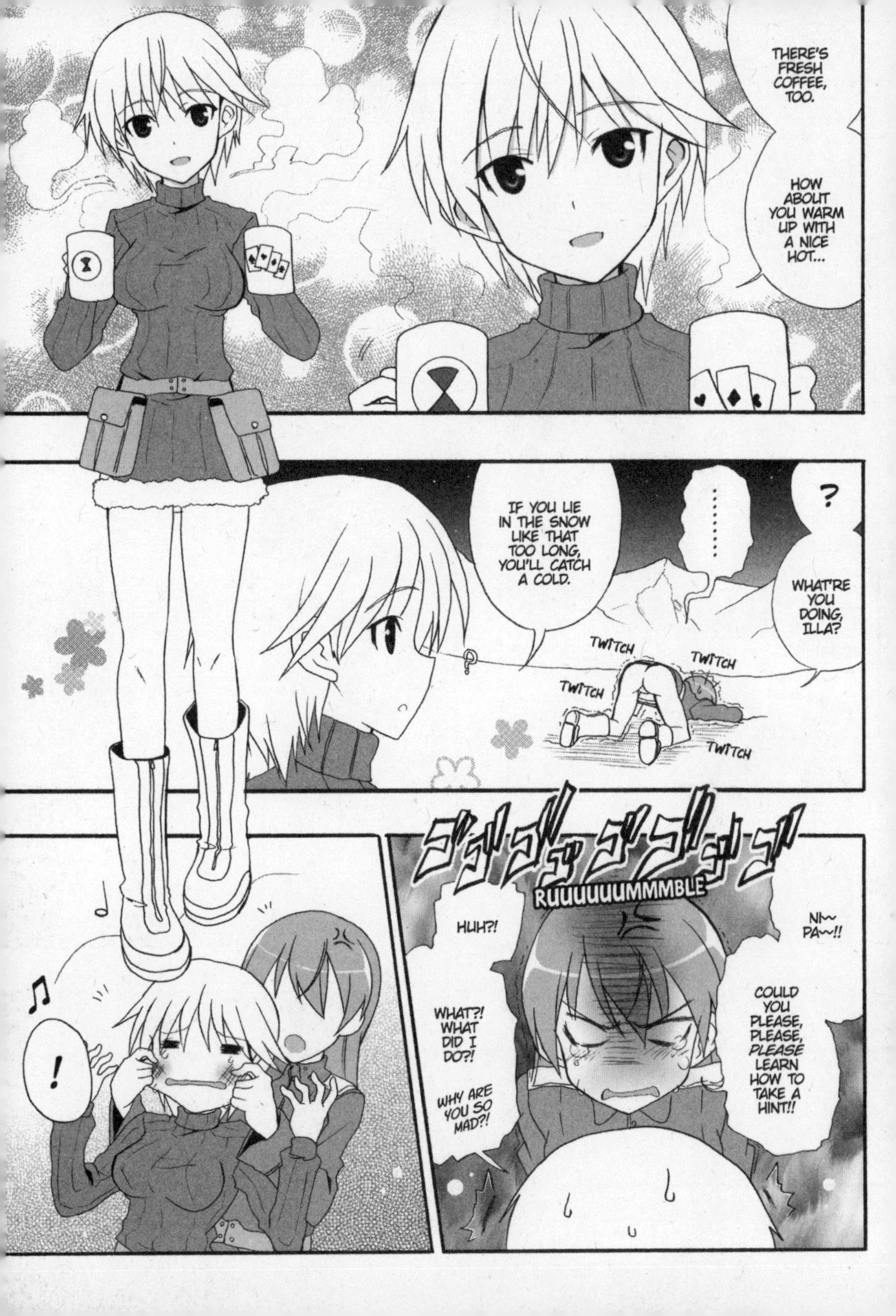
THERE'S FRESH COFFEE, TOO.
HOW ABOUT YOU WARM UP WITH A NICE HOT...
?
WHAT'RE YOU DOING, ILLA?
......
IF YOU LIE IN THE SNOW LIKE THAT TOO LONG, YOU'LL CATCH A COLD.
TWITCH
TWITCH
TWITCH
TWITCH
RUUUUUUMMMBLE
NI~ PA~!!
COULD YOU PLEASE, PLEASE, PLEASE LEARN HOW TO TAKE A HINT!!
HUH?!
WHAT?! WHAT DID I DO?!
WHY ARE YOU SO MAD?!
!

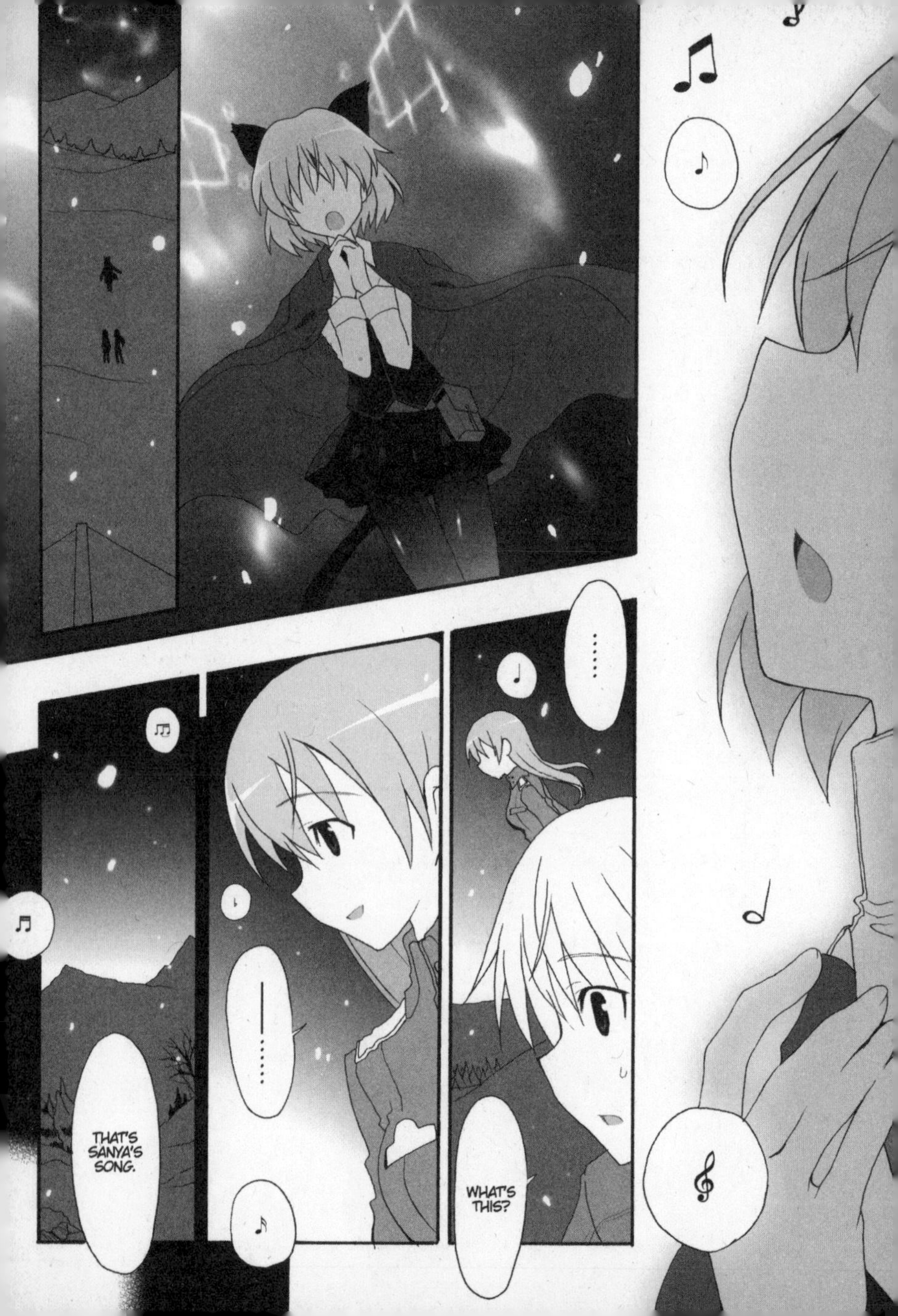
......
WHAT'S THIS?
—......
THAT'S SANYA'S SONG.

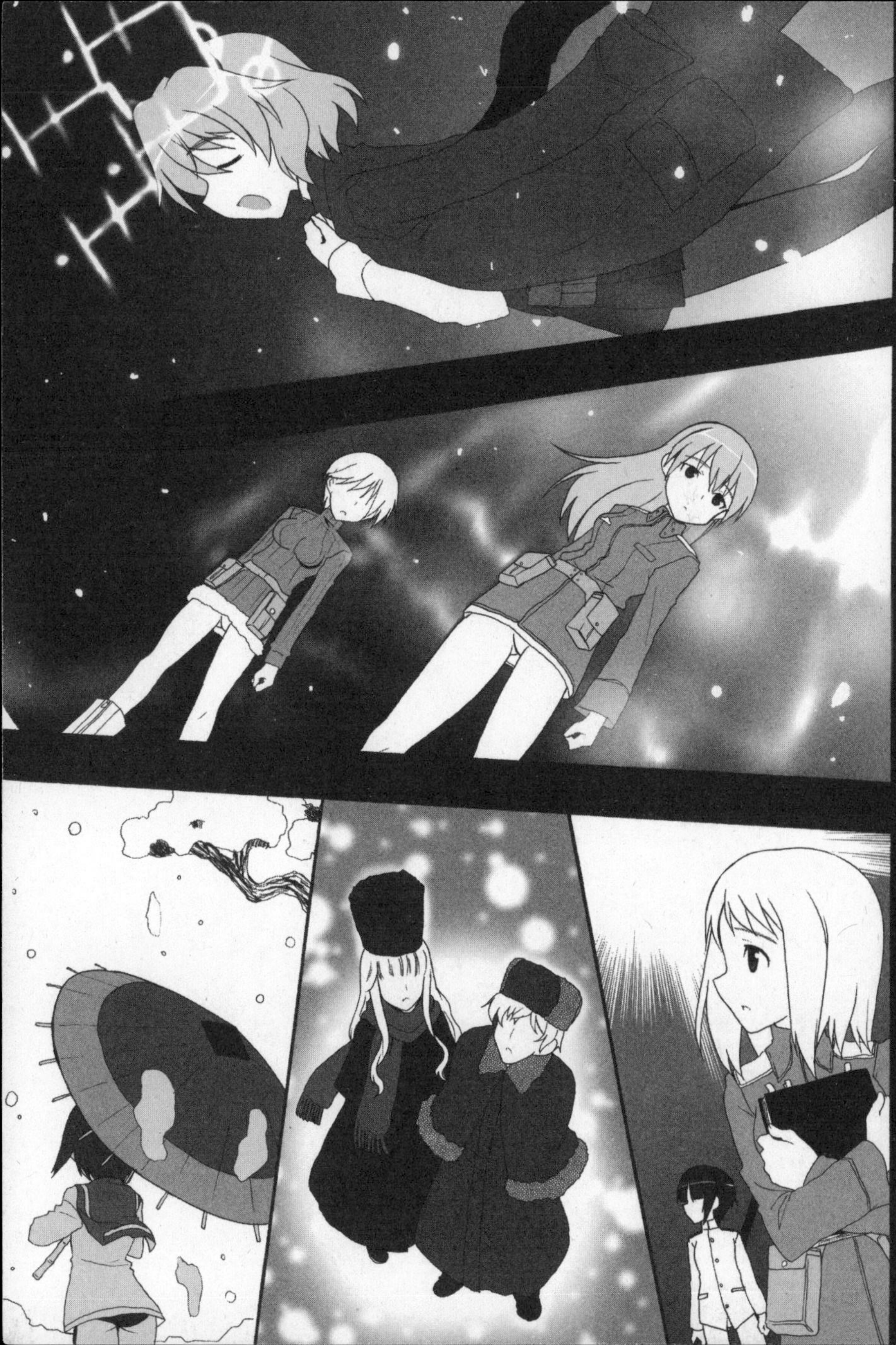

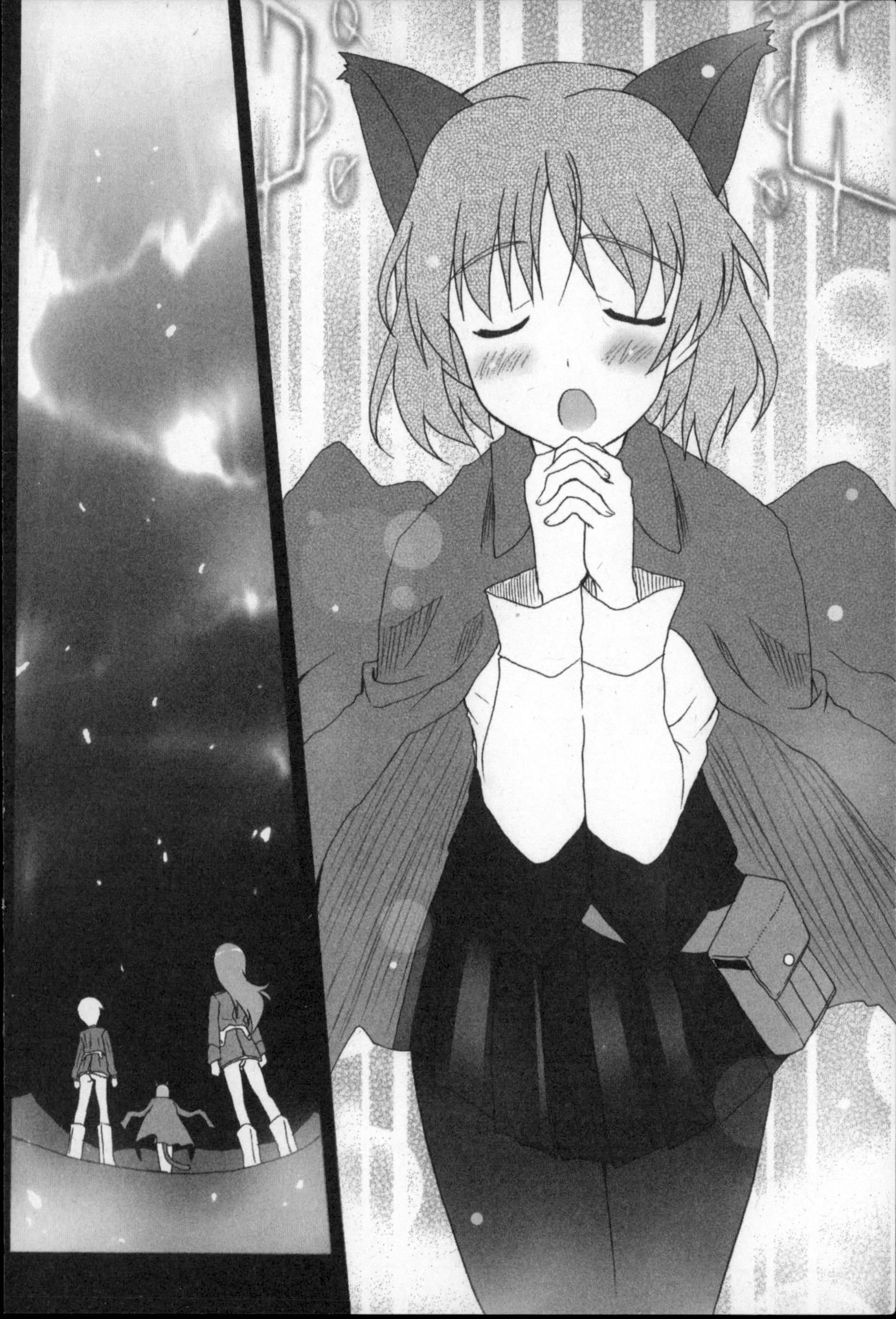

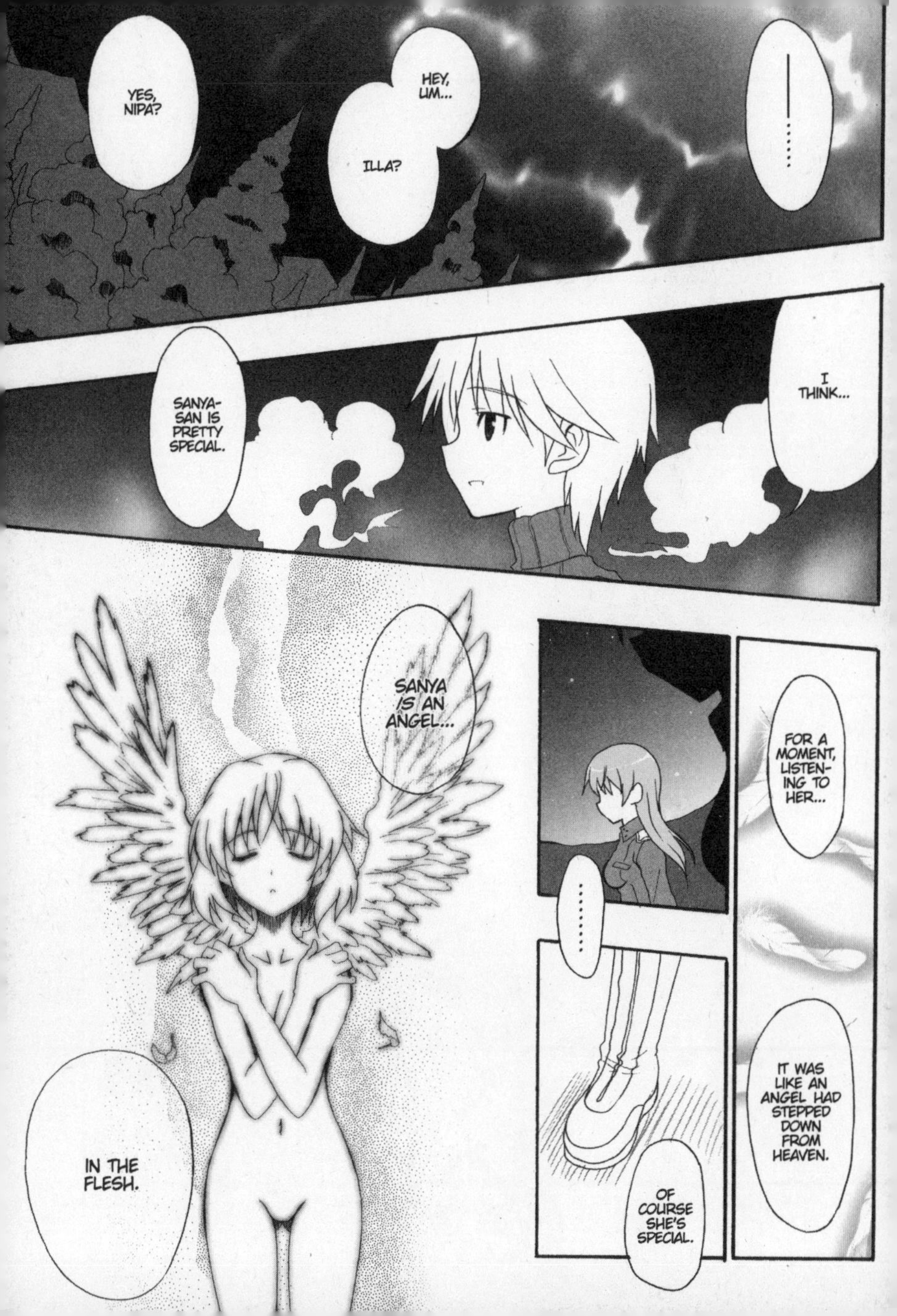
—......
HEY, UM... ILLA?
YES, NIPA?
I THINK...
SANYA-SAN IS PRETTY SPECIAL.
FOR A MOMENT, LISTENING TO HER...
IT WAS LIKE AN ANGEL HAD STEPPED DOWN FROM HEAVEN.
......
OF COURSE SHE'S SPECIAL.
SANYA IS AN ANGEL...
IN THE FLESH.

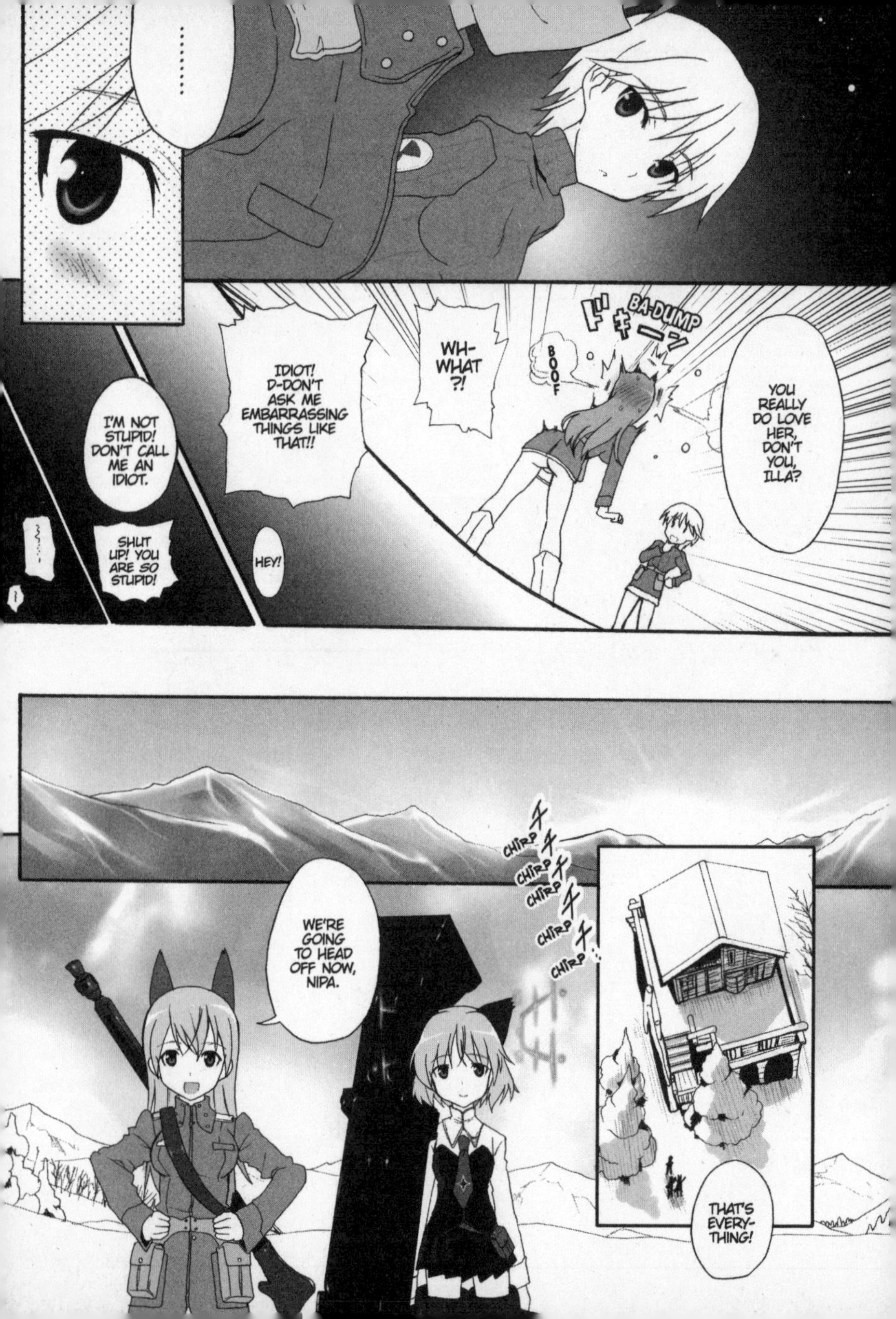
......
YOU REALLY DO LOVE HER, DON'T YOU, ILLA?
BA-DUMP
BOOF
WH-WHAT?!
IDIOT! D-DON'T ASK ME EMBARRASSING THINGS LIKE THAT!!
HEY!
I'M NOT STUPID! DON'T CALL ME AN IDIOT.
SHUT UP! YOU ARE SO STUPID!
CHIRP
CHIRP
CHIRP
CHIRP
CHIRP...
THAT'S EVERY-THING!
WE'RE GOING TO HEAD OFF NOW, NIPA.

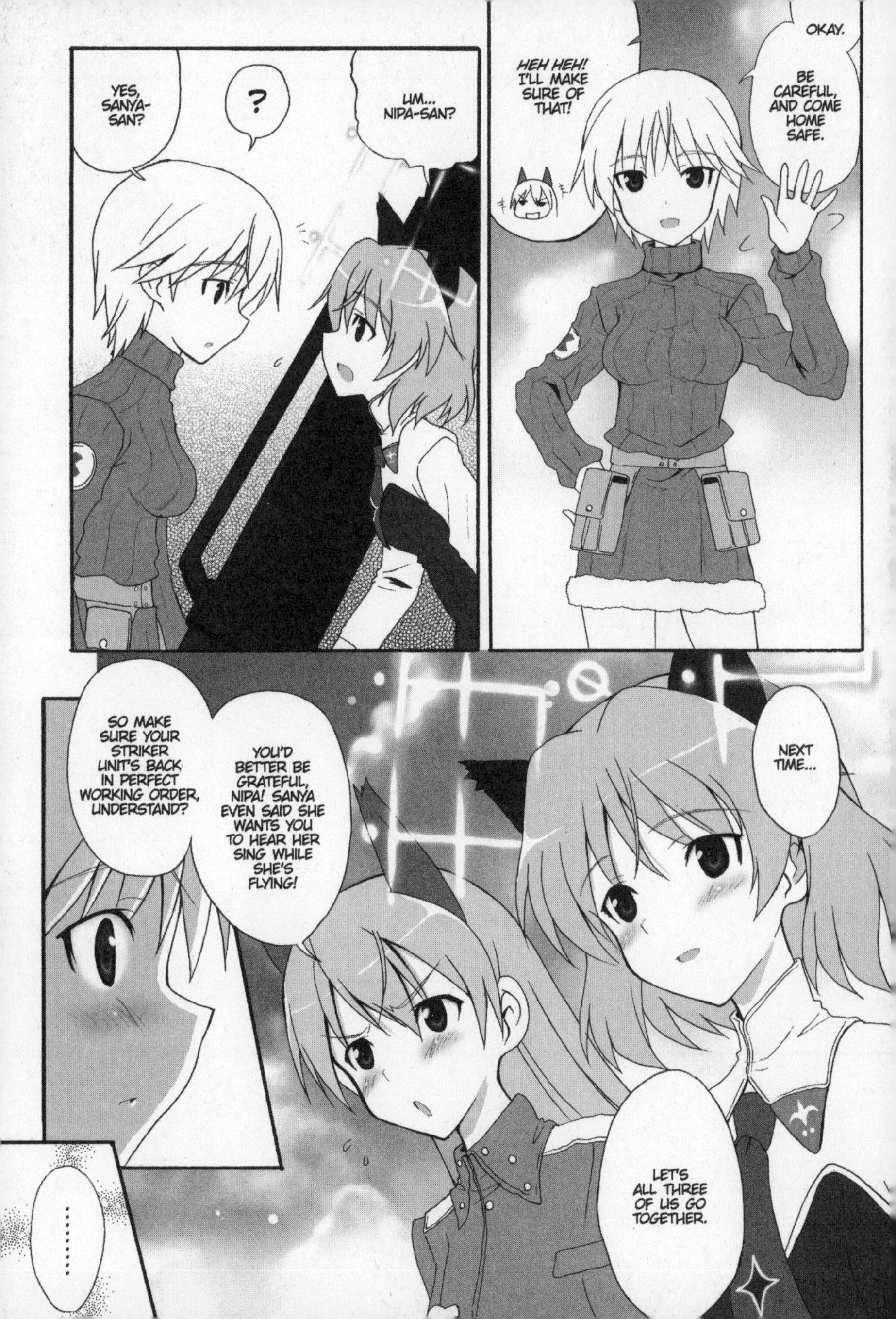
OKAY.
BE CAREFUL, AND COME HOME SAFE.
HEH HEH! I'LL MAKE SURE OF THAT!
UM... NIPA-SAN?
?
YES, SANYA-SAN?
NEXT TIME...
LET'S ALL THREE OF US GO TOGETHER.
YOU'D BETTER BE GRATEFUL, NIPA! SANYA EVEN SAID SHE WANTS YOU TO HEAR HER SING WHILE SHE'S FLYING!
SO MAKE SURE YOUR STRIKER UNIT'S BACK IN PERFECT WORKING ORDER, UNDERSTAND?
......

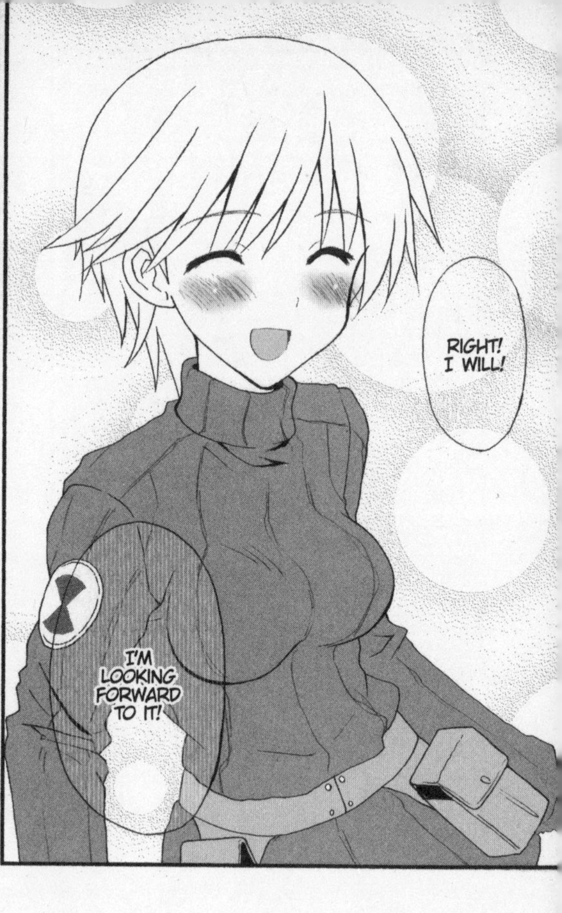
RIGHT! I WILL!
I'M LOOKING FORWARD TO IT!
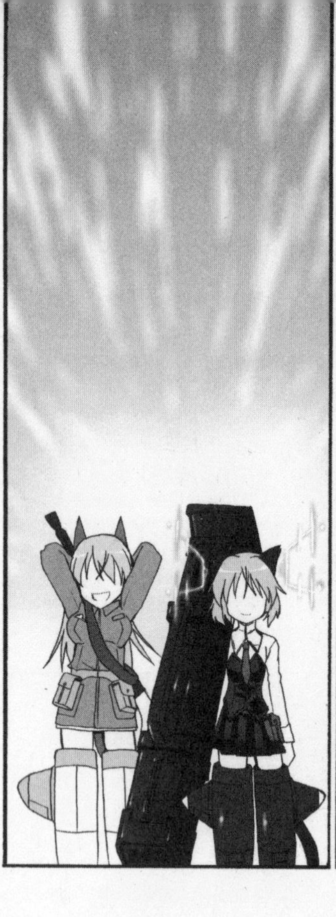
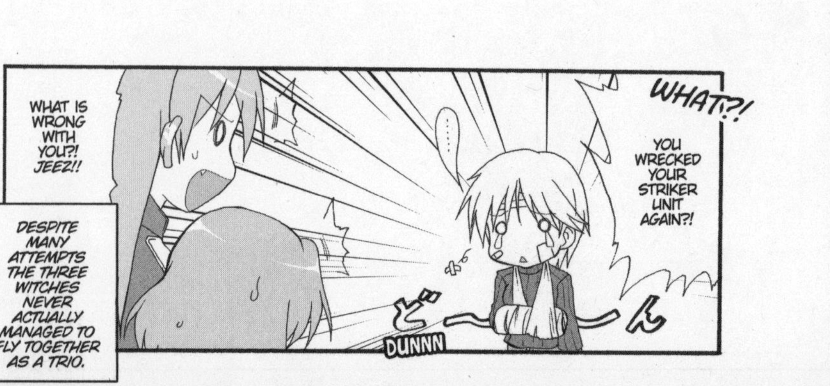
WHAT?!?!
YOU WRECKED YOUR STRIKER UNIT AGAIN?!
...
WHAT IS WRONG WITH YOU?! JEEZ!!
DUNNN
DESPITE MANY ATTEMPTS THE THREE WITCHES NEVER ACTUALLY MANAGED TO FLY TOGETHER AS A TRIO.

WITCHES
GRAFFITI

**Shimada Humikane &
Projekt Kagonish**
**illustrated by
Kyougoku Shin**

Erica Hartmann

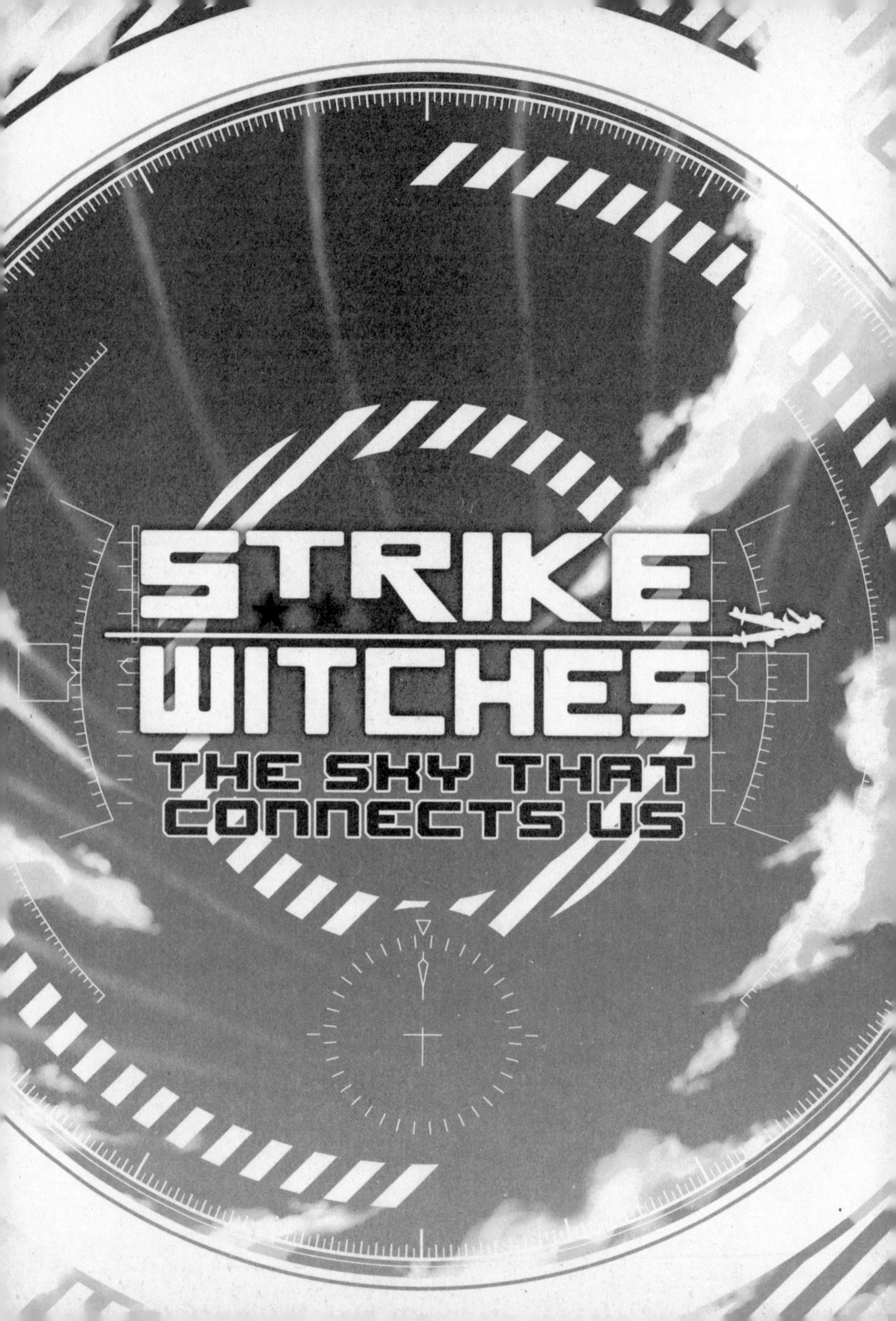
STRIKE WITCHES
THE SKY THAT CONNECTS US

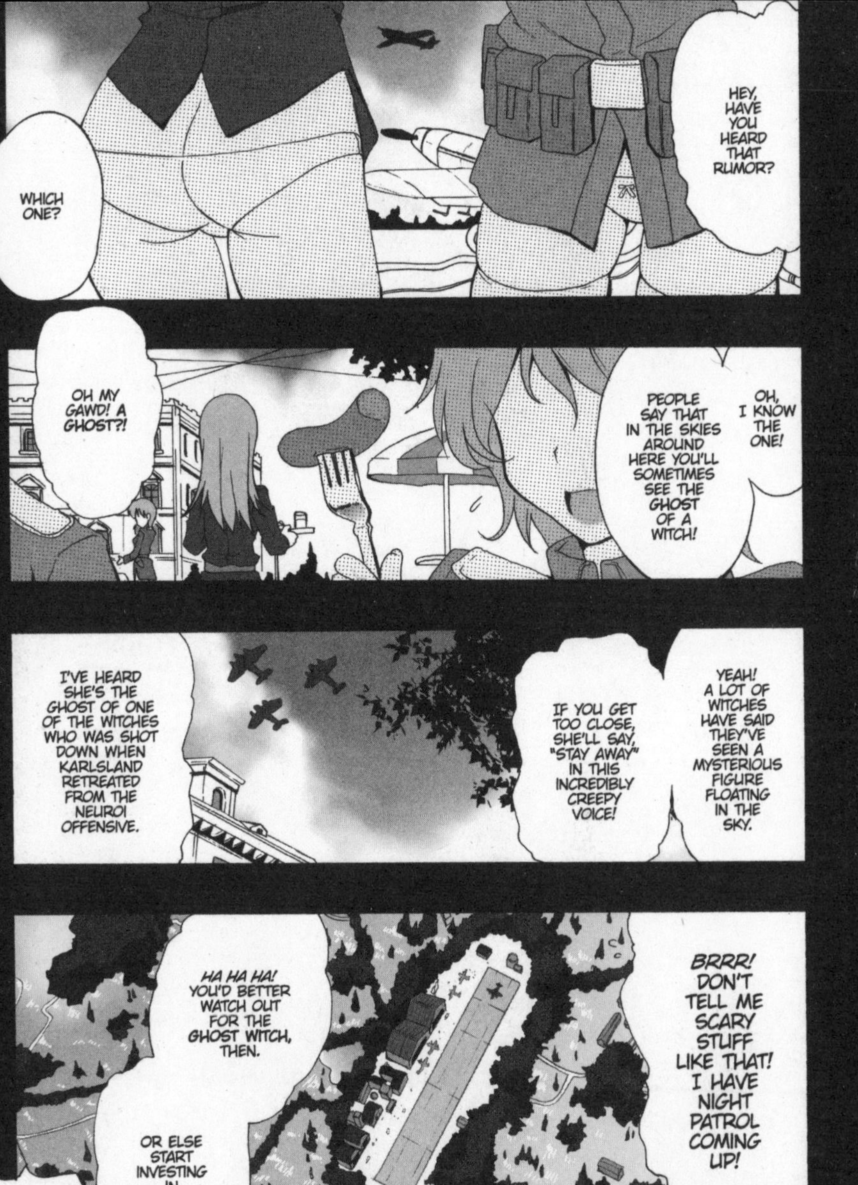
HEY, HAVE YOU HEARD THAT RUMOR?
WHICH ONE?
OH, I KNOW THE ONE!
PEOPLE SAY THAT IN THE SKIES AROUND HERE YOU'LL SOMETIMES SEE THE GHOST OF A WITCH!
OH MY GAWD! A GHOST?!
YEAH! A LOT OF WITCHES HAVE SAID THEY'VE SEEN A MYSTERIOUS FIGURE FLOATING IN THE SKY.
IF YOU GET TOO CLOSE, SHE'LL SAY, "STAY AWAY" IN THIS INCREDIBLY CREEPY VOICE!
I'VE HEARD SHE'S THE GHOST OF ONE OF THE WITCHES WHO WAS SHOT DOWN WHEN KARLSLAND RETREATED FROM THE NEUROI OFFENSIVE.
BRRR! DON'T TELL ME SCARY STUFF LIKE THAT! I HAVE NIGHT PATROL COMING UP!
HA HA HA! YOU'D BETTER WATCH OUT FOR THE GHOST WITCH, THEN.
OR ELSE START INVESTING IN DIAPERS!
C'MON, CUT IT OUT!

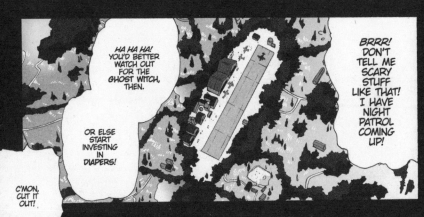

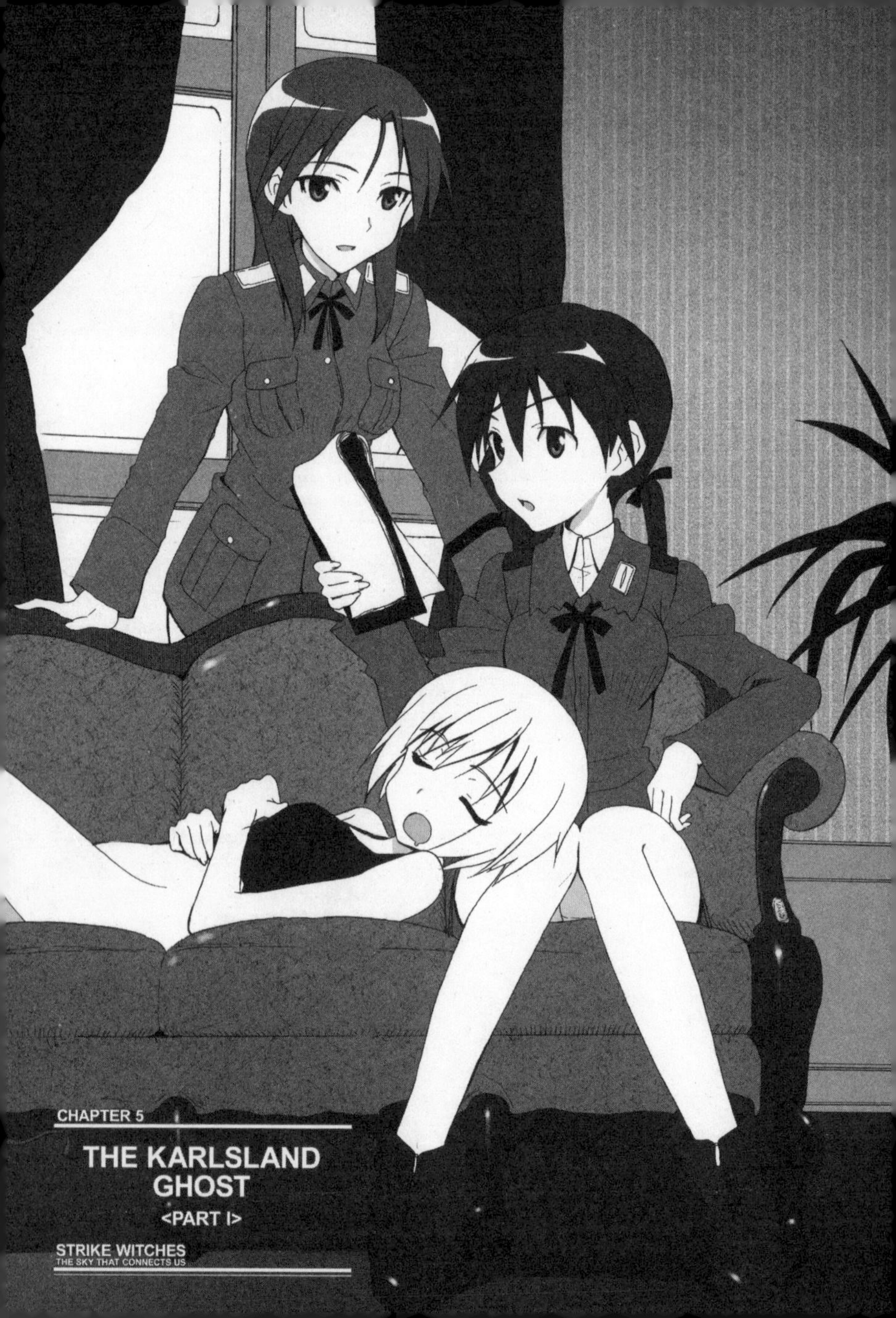

CHAPTER 5

THE KARLSLAND GHOST

<PART I>

STRIKE WITCHES
THE SKY THAT CONNECTS US

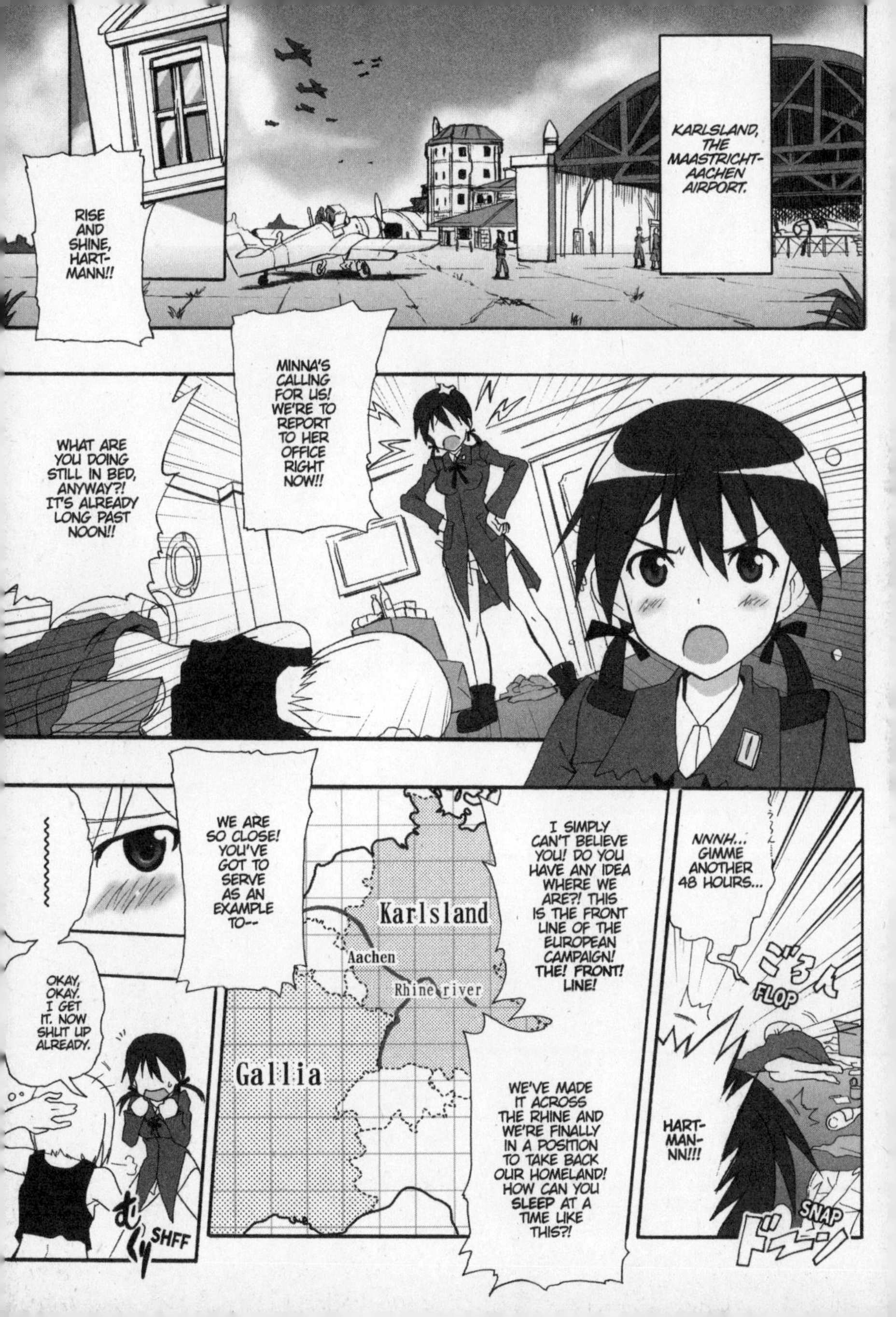
KARLSLAND, THE MAASTRICHT-AACHEN AIRPORT.
RISE AND SHINE, HART-MANN!!
MINNA'S CALLING FOR US! WE'RE TO REPORT TO HER OFFICE RIGHT NOW!!
WHAT ARE YOU DOING STILL IN BED, ANYWAY?! IT'S ALREADY LONG PAST NOON!!
NNNH... GIMME ANOTHER 48 HOURS...
FLOP
HART-MANN-NN!!!
SNAP
I SIMPLY CAN'T BELIEVE YOU! DO YOU HAVE ANY IDEA WHERE WE ARE?! THIS IS THE FRONT LINE OF THE EUROPEAN CAMPAIGN! THE! FRONT! LINE!
WE'VE MADE IT ACROSS THE RHINE AND WE'RE FINALLY IN A POSITION TO TAKE BACK OUR HOMELAND! HOW CAN YOU SLEEP AT A TIME LIKE THIS?!
Karlsland
Aachen
Rhine river
Gallia
WE ARE SO CLOSE! YOU'VE GOT TO SERVE AS AN EXAMPLE TO--
OKAY, OKAY. I GET IT. NOW SHUT UP ALREADY.
SHFF

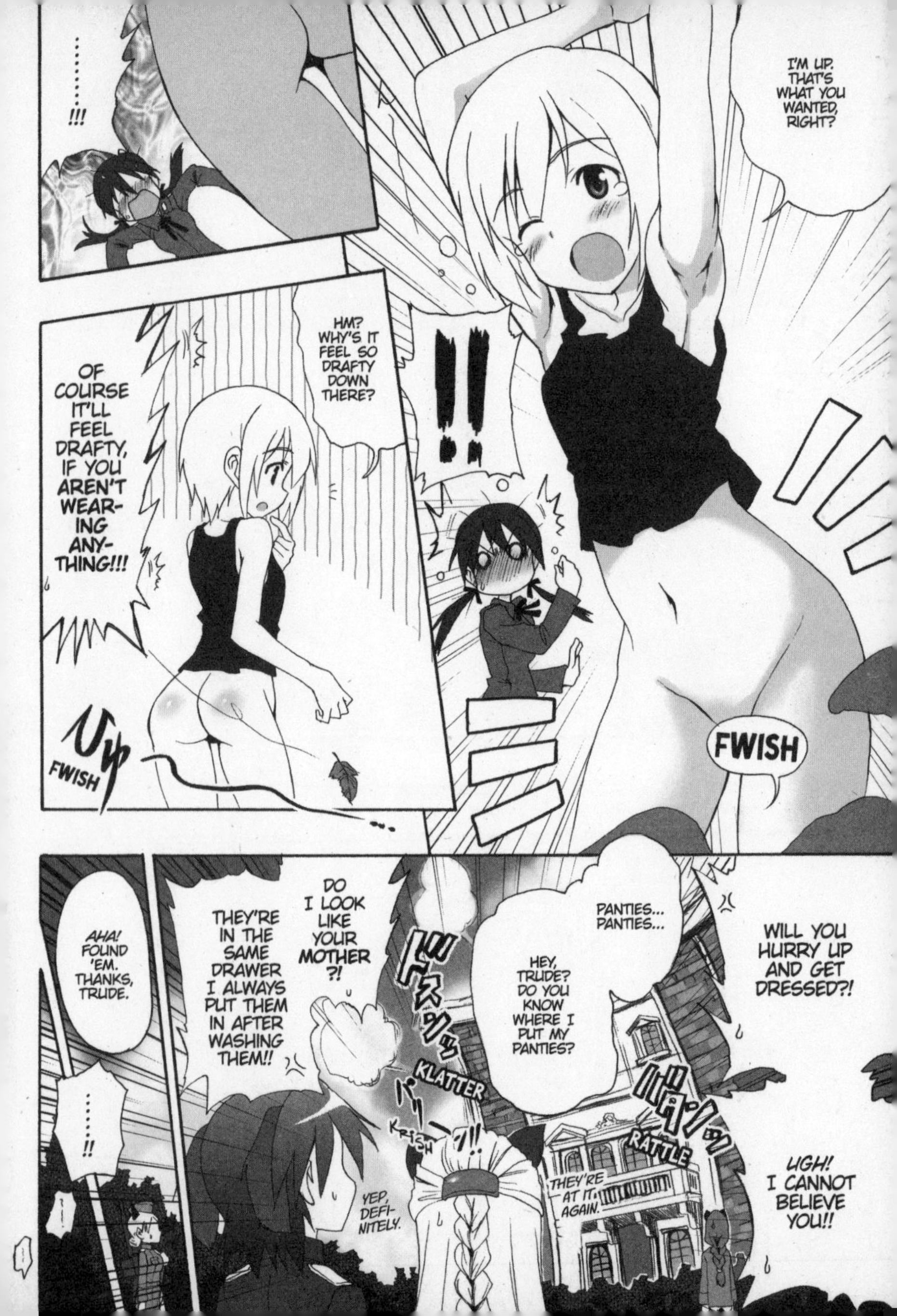
I'M UP. THAT'S WHAT YOU WANTED, RIGHT?
!!
FWISH
......!!!
HM? WHY'S IT FEEL SO DRAFTY DOWN THERE?
OF COURSE IT'LL FEEL DRAFTY, IF YOU AREN'T WEARING ANYTHING!!!
FWISH
WILL YOU HURRY UP AND GET DRESSED?!
PANTIES... PANTIES...
HEY, TRUDE? DO YOU KNOW WHERE I PUT MY PANTIES?
DO I LOOK LIKE YOUR MOTHER?!
THEY'RE IN THE SAME DRAWER I ALWAYS PUT THEM IN AFTER WASHING THEM!!
RATTLE
KLATTER
KRISH
UGH! I CANNOT BELIEVE YOU!!
THEY'RE AT IT. AGAIN.
YEP, DEFINITELY.
AHA! FOUND 'EM. THANKS, TRUDE.
......!!

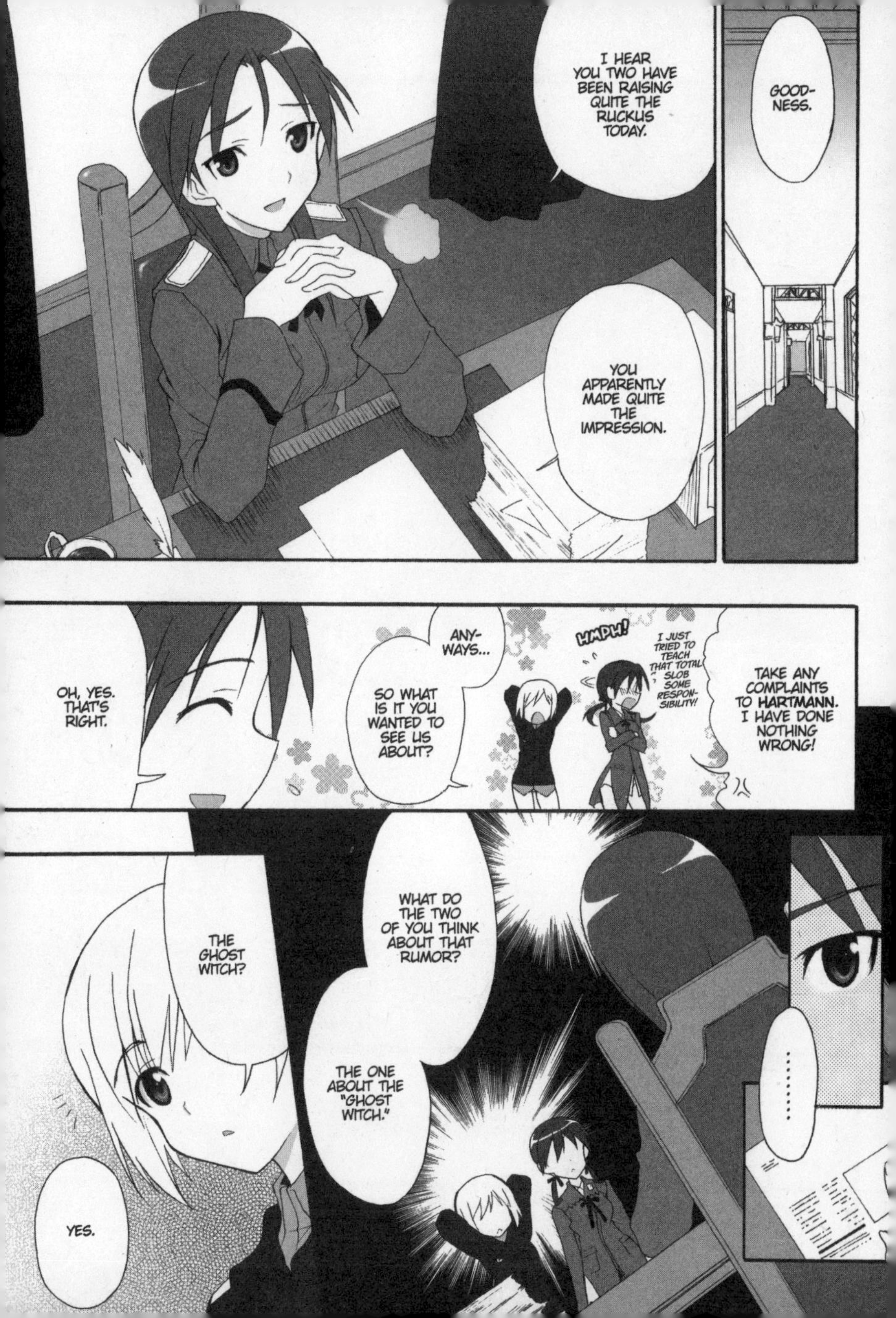
GOODNESS.
I HEAR YOU TWO HAVE BEEN RAISING QUITE THE RUCKUS TODAY.
YOU APPARENTLY MADE QUITE THE IMPRESSION.
TAKE ANY COMPLAINTS TO HARTMANN. I HAVE DONE NOTHING WRONG!
I JUST TRIED TO TEACH THAT TOTAL SLOB SOME RESPONSIBILITY!
HMPH!
ANYWAYS...
SO WHAT IS IT YOU WANTED TO SEE US ABOUT?
OH, YES. THAT'S RIGHT.
......
WHAT DO THE TWO OF YOU THINK ABOUT THAT RUMOR?
THE ONE ABOUT THE "GHOST WITCH."
THE GHOST WITCH?
YES.

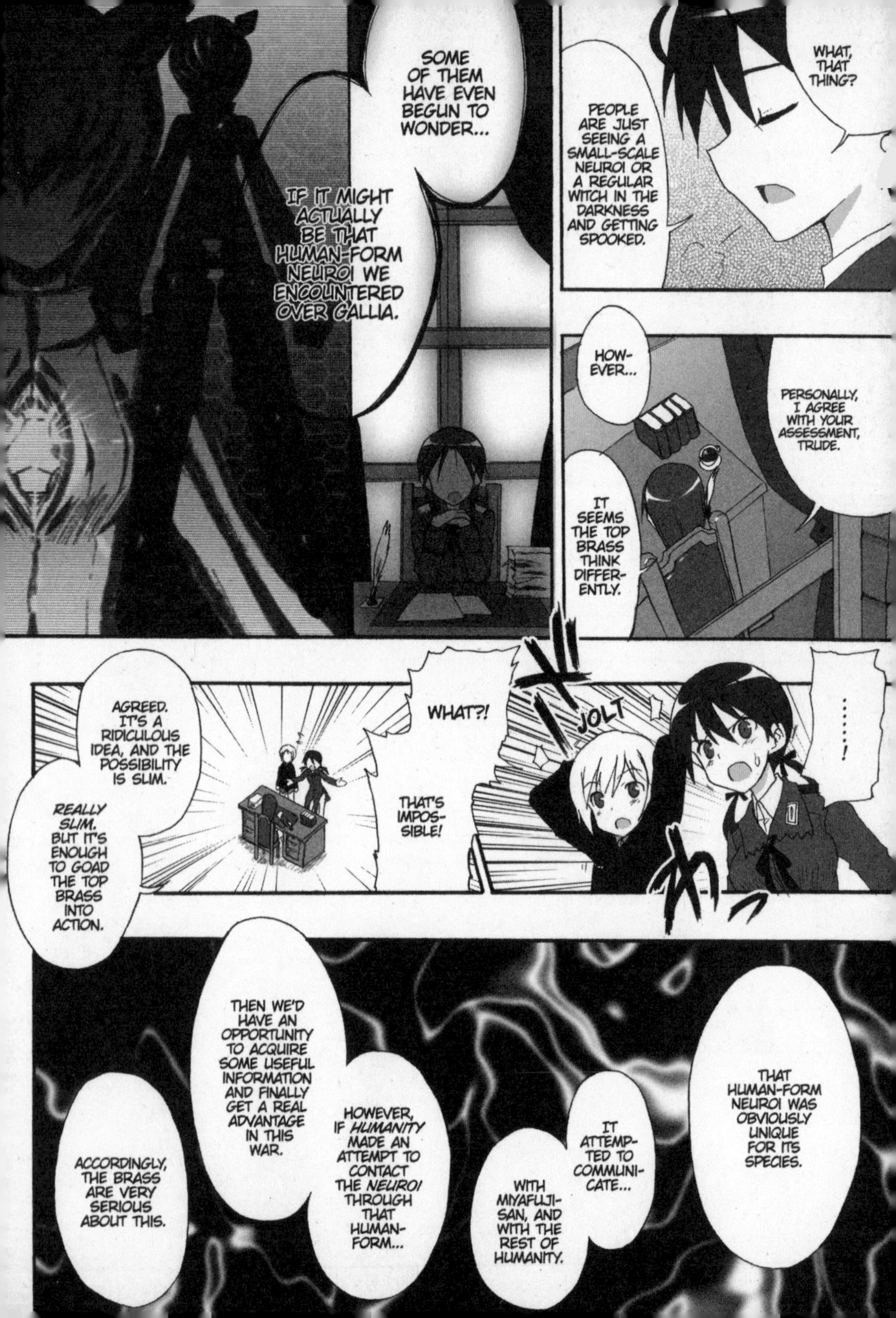
WHAT, THAT THING?
PEOPLE ARE JUST SEEING A SMALL-SCALE NEUROI OR A REGULAR WITCH IN THE DARKNESS AND GETTING SPOOKED.
PERSONALLY, I AGREE WITH YOUR ASSESSMENT, TRUDE.
HOW-EVER...
IT SEEMS THE TOP BRASS THINK DIFFER-ENTLY.
SOME OF THEM HAVE EVEN BEGUN TO WONDER...
IF IT MIGHT ACTUALLY BE THAT HUMAN-FORM NEUROI WE ENCOUNTERED OVER GALLIA.
......!
JOLT
WHAT?!
THAT'S IMPOS-SIBLE!
AGREED. IT'S A RIDICULOUS IDEA, AND THE POSSIBILITY IS SLIM.
REALLY SLIM. BUT IT'S ENOUGH TO GOAD THE TOP BRASS INTO ACTION.
THAT HUMAN-FORM NEUROI WAS OBVIOUSLY UNIQUE FOR ITS SPECIES.
IT ATTEMP-TED TO COMMUNI-CATE...
WITH MIYAFUJI-SAN, AND WITH THE REST OF HUMANITY.
HOWEVER, IF *HUMANITY* MADE AN ATTEMPT TO CONTACT THE *NEUROI* THROUGH THAT HUMAN-FORM...
THEN WE'D HAVE AN OPPORTUNITY TO ACQUIRE SOME USEFUL INFORMATION AND FINALLY GET A REAL ADVANTAGE IN THIS WAR.
ACCORDINGLY, THE BRASS ARE VERY SERIOUS ABOUT THIS.

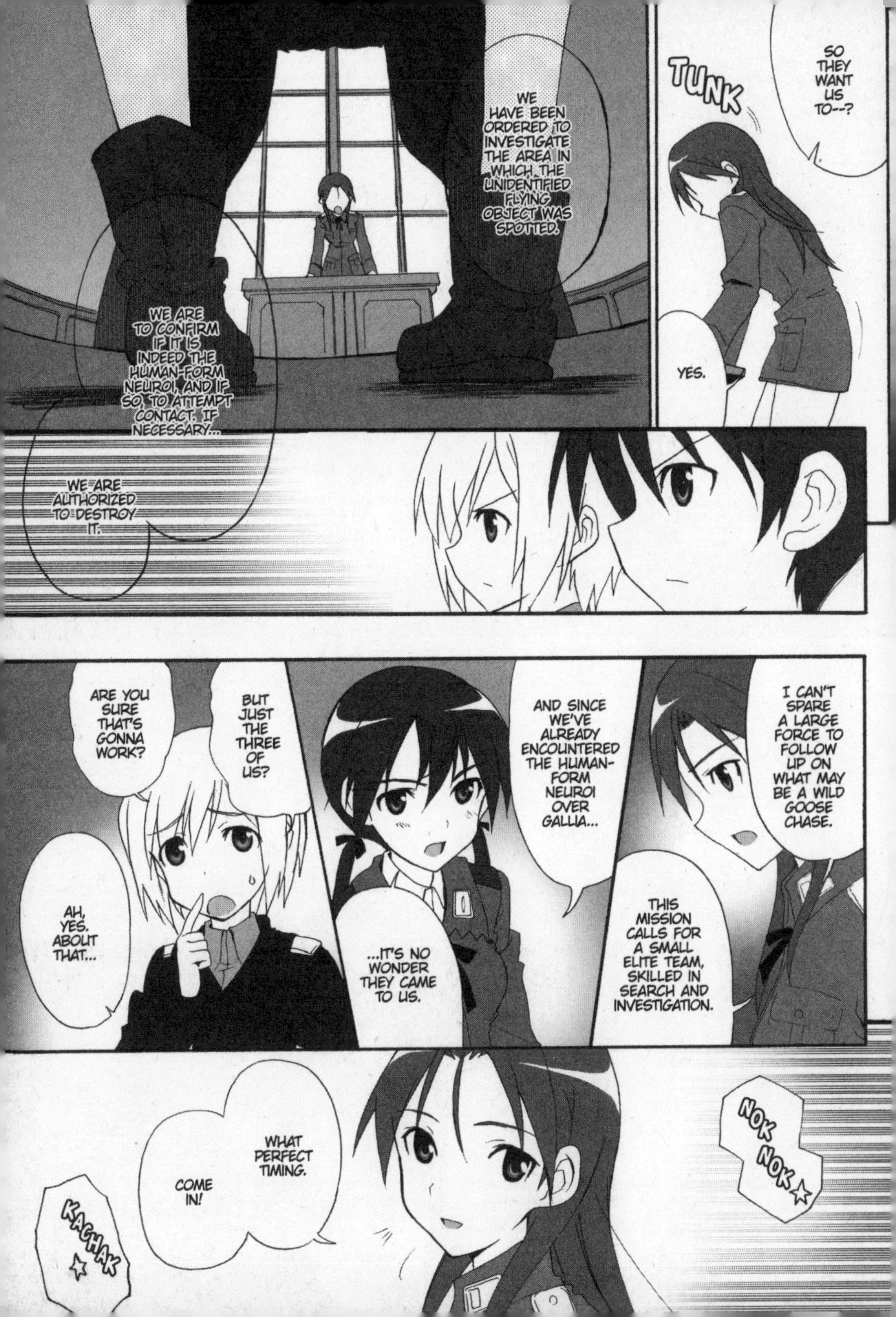
SO THEY WANT US TO--?
TUNK
YES.
WE HAVE BEEN ORDERED TO INVESTIGATE THE AREA IN WHICH THE UNIDENTIFIED FLYING OBJECT WAS SPOTTED.
WE ARE TO CONFIRM IF IT IS INDEED THE HUMAN-FORM NEUROI, AND IF SO, TO ATTEMPT CONTACT. IF NECESSARY...
WE ARE AUTHORIZED TO DESTROY IT.
I CAN'T SPARE A LARGE FORCE TO FOLLOW UP ON WHAT MAY BE A WILD GOOSE CHASE.
THIS MISSION CALLS FOR A SMALL ELITE TEAM, SKILLED IN SEARCH AND INVESTIGATION.
AND SINCE WE'VE ALREADY ENCOUNTERED THE HUMAN-FORM NEUROI OVER GALLIA...
...IT'S NO WONDER THEY CAME TO US.
BUT JUST THE THREE OF US?
ARE YOU SURE THAT'S GONNA WORK?
AH, YES. ABOUT THAT...
NOK NOK☆
WHAT PERFECT TIMING.
COME IN!
KACHAK☆

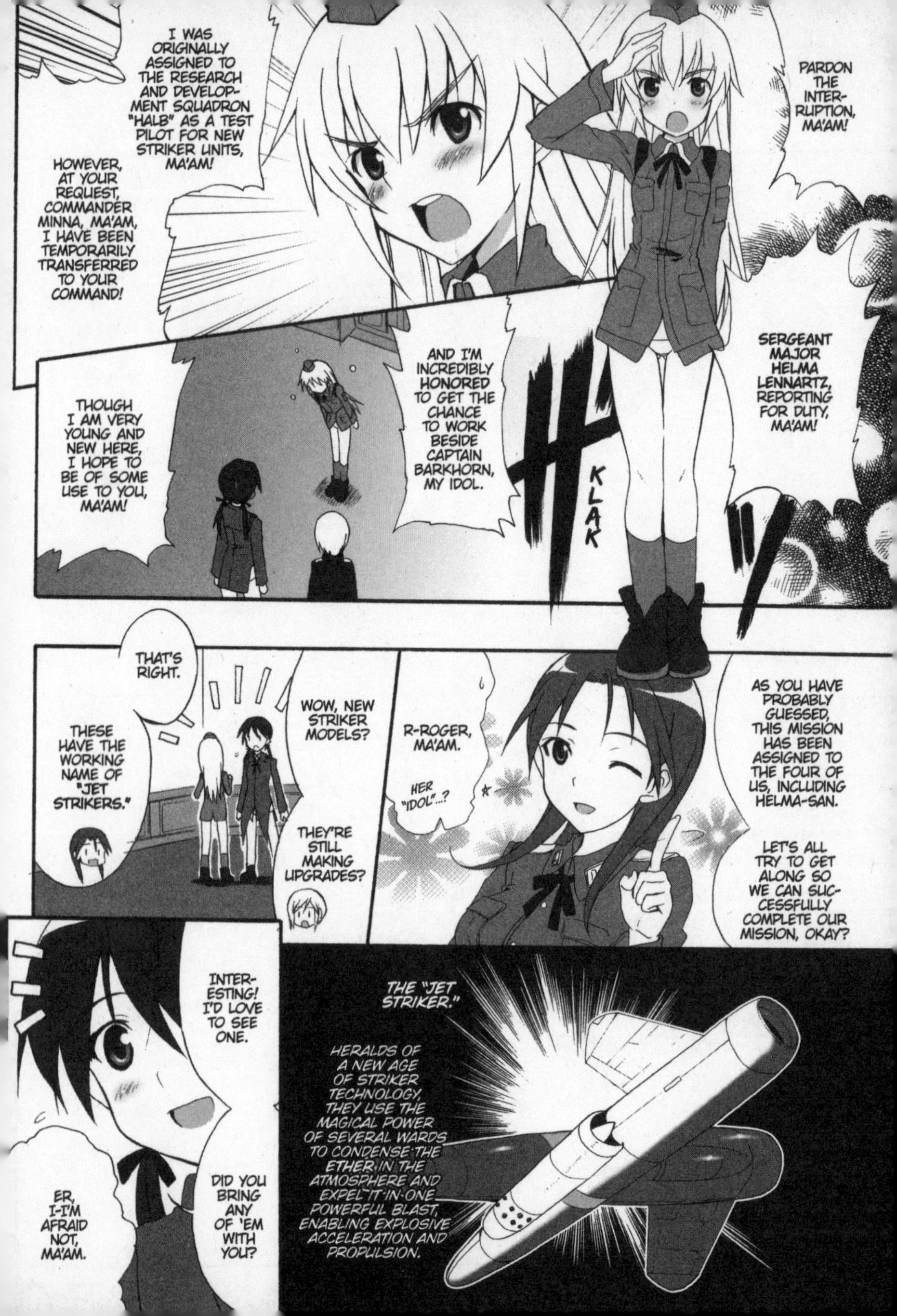
PARDON THE INTERRUPTION, MA'AM!
SERGEANT MAJOR HELMA LENNARTZ, REPORTING FOR DUTY, MA'AM!
KLAK
I WAS ORIGINALLY ASSIGNED TO THE RESEARCH AND DEVELOPMENT SQUADRON "HALB" AS A TEST PILOT FOR NEW STRIKER UNITS, MA'AM!
HOWEVER, AT YOUR REQUEST, COMMANDER MINNA, MA'AM, I HAVE BEEN TEMPORARILY TRANSFERRED TO YOUR COMMAND!
AND I'M INCREDIBLY HONORED TO GET THE CHANCE TO WORK BESIDE CAPTAIN BARKHORN, MY IDOL.
THOUGH I AM VERY YOUNG AND NEW HERE, I HOPE TO BE OF SOME USE TO YOU, MA'AM!
AS YOU HAVE PROBABLY GUESSED, THIS MISSION HAS BEEN ASSIGNED TO THE FOUR OF US, INCLUDING HELMA-SAN.
LET'S ALL TRY TO GET ALONG SO WE CAN SUCCESSFULLY COMPLETE OUR MISSION, OKAY?
R-ROGER, MA'AM.
HER "IDOL"...?
WOW, NEW STRIKER MODELS?
THEY'RE STILL MAKING UPGRADES?
THAT'S RIGHT.
THESE HAVE THE WORKING NAME OF "JET STRIKERS."
THE "JET STRIKER."
HERALDS OF A NEW AGE OF STRIKER TECHNOLOGY, THEY USE THE MAGICAL POWER OF SEVERAL WARDS TO CONDENSE THE ETHER IN THE ATMOSPHERE AND EXPEL IT IN ONE POWERFUL BLAST, ENABLING EXPLOSIVE ACCELERATION AND PROPULSION.
INTERESTING! I'D LOVE TO SEE ONE.
DID YOU BRING ANY OF 'EM WITH YOU?
ER, I-I'M AFRAID NOT, MA'AM.

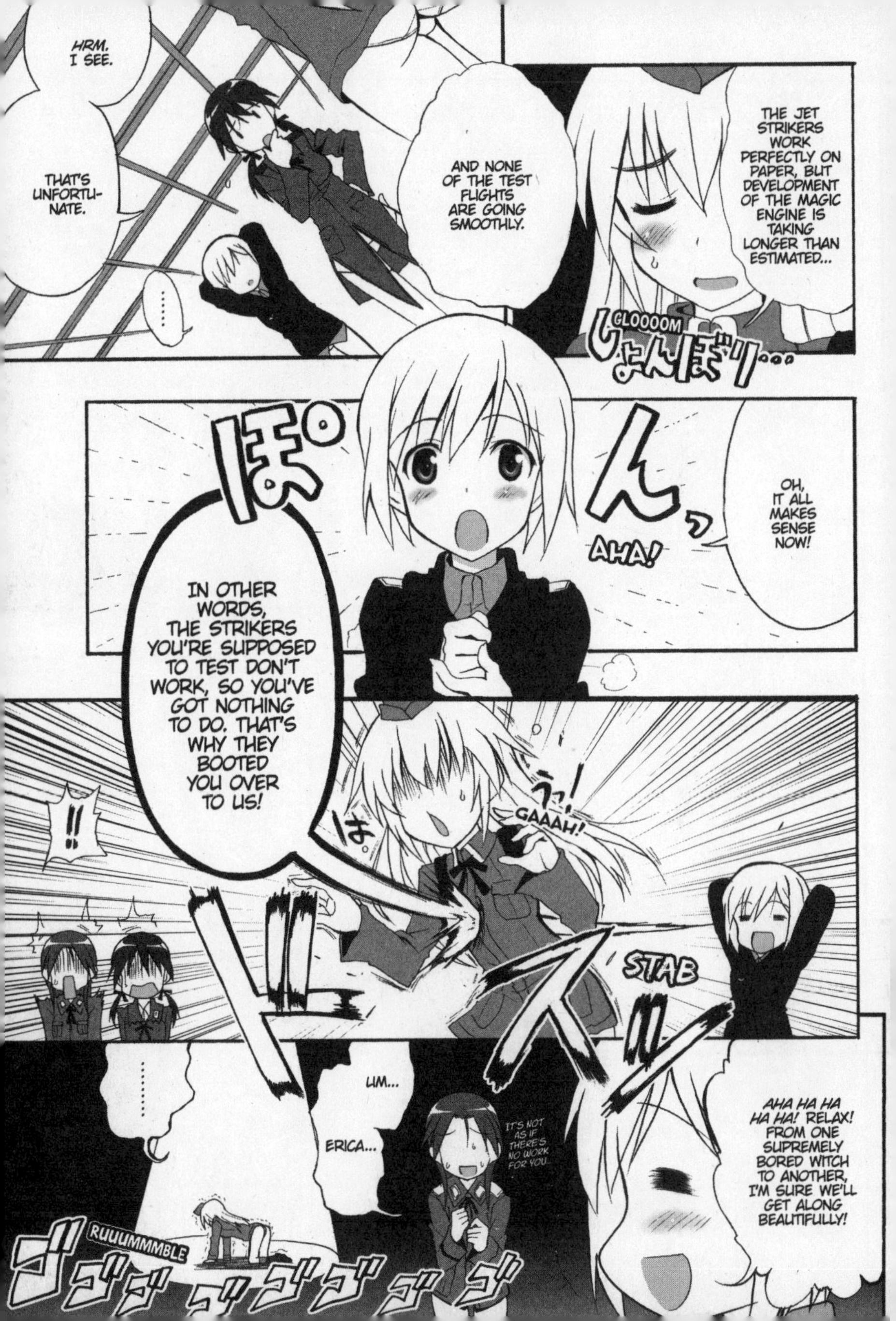
THE JET STRIKERS WORK PERFECTLY ON PAPER, BUT DEVELOPMENT OF THE MAGIC ENGINE IS TAKING LONGER THAN ESTIMATED...
AND NONE OF THE TEST FLIGHTS ARE GOING SMOOTHLY.
GLOOOOM
しょんぼり…
HRM. I SEE.
THAT'S UNFORTU-NATE.
......
OH, IT ALL MAKES SENSE NOW!
ぽんっ
AHA!
IN OTHER WORDS, THE STRIKERS YOU'RE SUPPOSED TO TEST DON'T WORK, SO YOU'VE GOT NOTHING TO DO. THAT'S WHY THEY BOOTED YOU OVER TO US!
STAB
うっ!
GAAAH!
は。
!!
AHA HA HA HA HA! RELAX! FROM ONE SUPREMELY BORED WITCH TO ANOTHER, I'M SURE WE'LL GET ALONG BEAUTIFULLY!
UM...
ERICA...
IT'S NOT AS IF THERE'S NO WORK FOR YOU...
......
RUUUMMMBLE

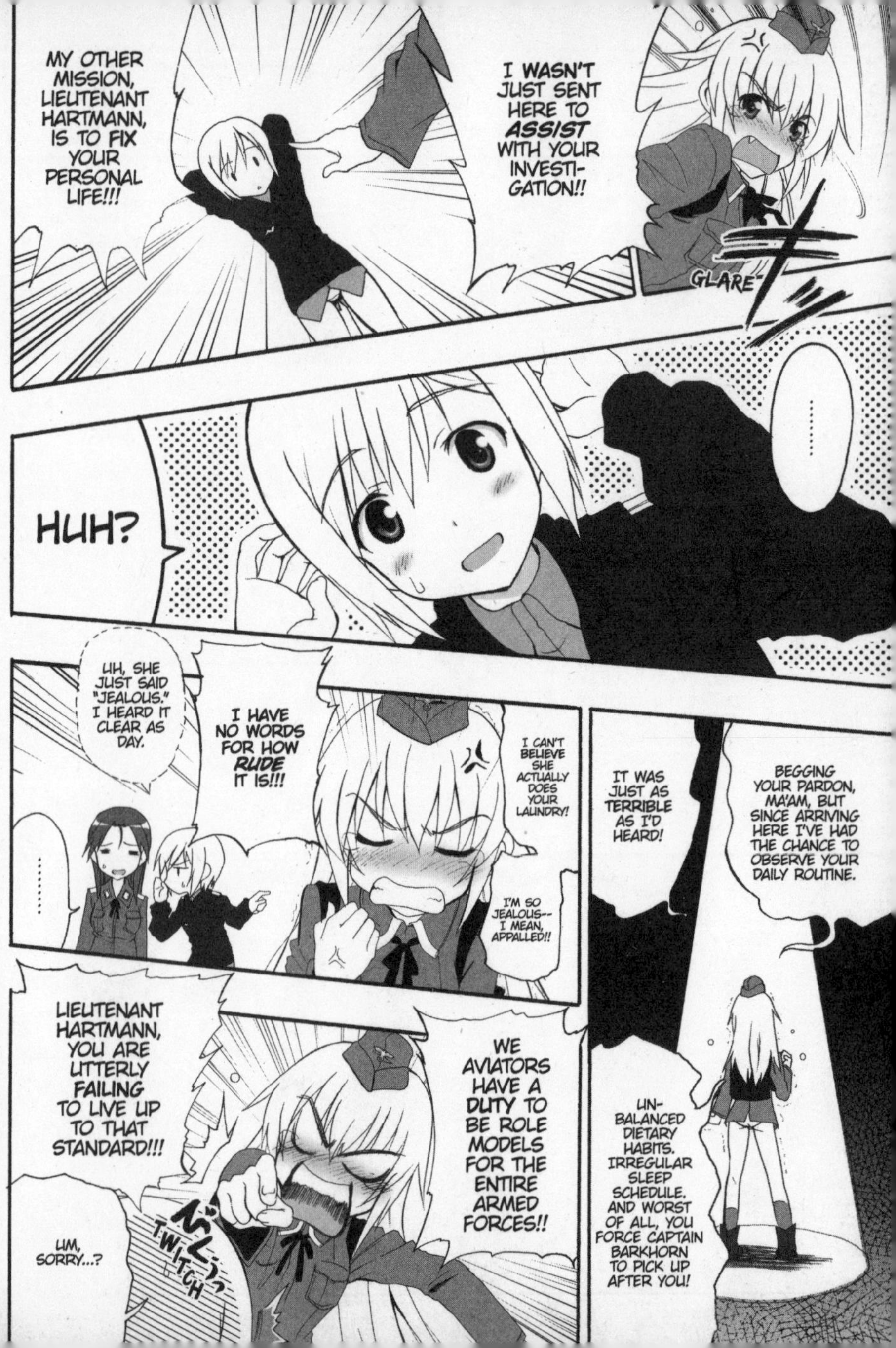
I WASN'T JUST SENT HERE TO ASSIST WITH YOUR INVESTIGATION!!
GLARE
MY OTHER MISSION, LIEUTENANT HARTMANN, IS TO FIX YOUR PERSONAL LIFE!!!
......
HUH?
BEGGING YOUR PARDON, MA'AM, BUT SINCE ARRIVING HERE I'VE HAD THE CHANCE TO OBSERVE YOUR DAILY ROUTINE.
UN-BALANCED DIETARY HABITS. IRREGULAR SLEEP SCHEDULE. AND WORST OF ALL, YOU FORCE CAPTAIN BARKHORN TO PICK UP AFTER YOU!
IT WAS JUST AS TERRIBLE AS I'D HEARD!
I CAN'T BELIEVE SHE ACTUALLY DOES YOUR LAUNDRY!
I'M SO JEALOUS-- I MEAN, APPALLED!!
I HAVE NO WORDS FOR HOW RUDE IT IS!!!
UH, SHE JUST SAID "JEALOUS." I HEARD IT CLEAR AS DAY.
......
WE AVIATORS HAVE A DUTY TO BE ROLE MODELS FOR THE ENTIRE ARMED FORCES!!
LIEUTENANT HARTMANN, YOU ARE UTTERLY FAILING TO LIVE UP TO THAT STANDARD!!!
TWITCH
UM, SORRY...?

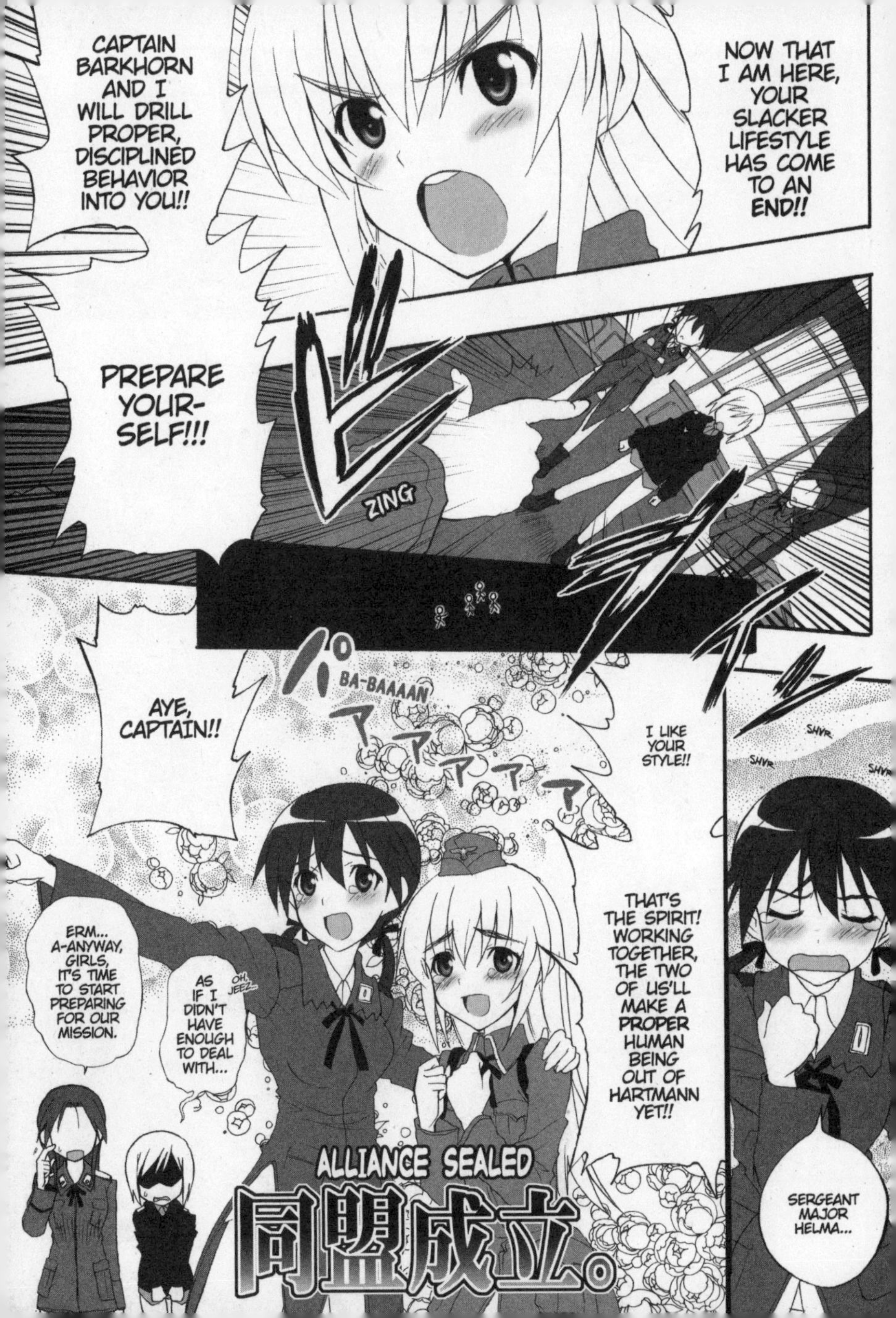
NOW THAT I AM HERE, YOUR SLACKER LIFESTYLE HAS COME TO AN END!!
CAPTAIN BARKHORN AND I WILL DRILL PROPER, DISCIPLINED BEHAVIOR INTO YOU!!
PREPARE YOUR-SELF!!!
ZING
SHVR
SHVR
SHVR
SERGEANT MAJOR HELMA...
I LIKE YOUR STYLE!!
BA-BAAAAAN
AYE, CAPTAIN!!
THAT'S THE SPIRIT! WORKING TOGETHER, THE TWO OF US'LL MAKE A PROPER HUMAN BEING OUT OF HARTMANN YET!!
OH, JEEZ...
AS IF I DIDN'T HAVE ENOUGH TO DEAL WITH...
ERM... A-ANYWAY, GIRLS, IT'S TIME TO START PREPARING FOR OUR MISSION.
ALLIANCE SEALED
同盟成立。

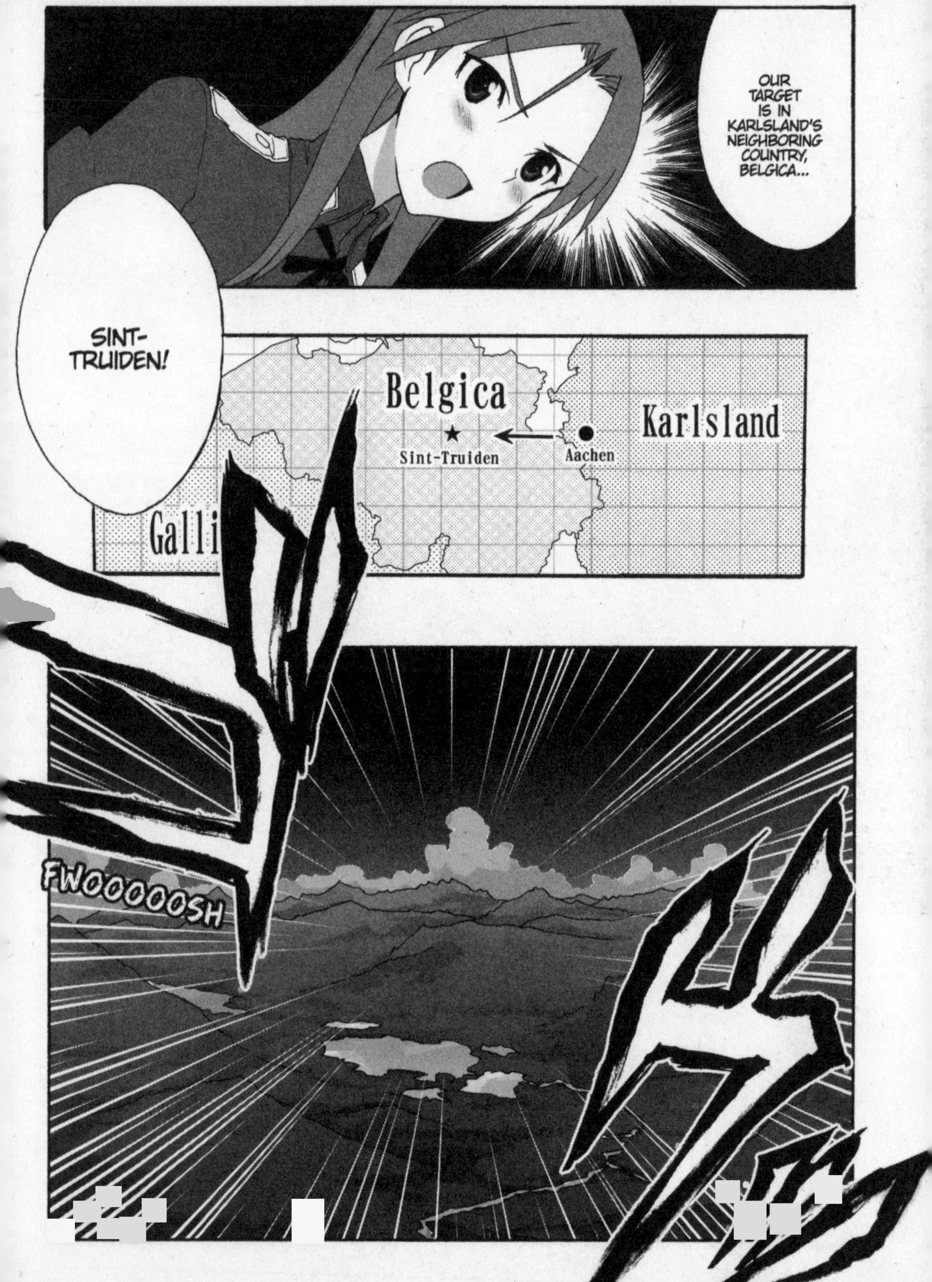
OUR TARGET IS IN KARLSLAND'S NEIGHBORING COUNTRY, BELGICA...
SINT-TRUIDEN!
Belgica
Karlsland
Sint-Truiden
Aachen
Galli
FWOOOOOOSH

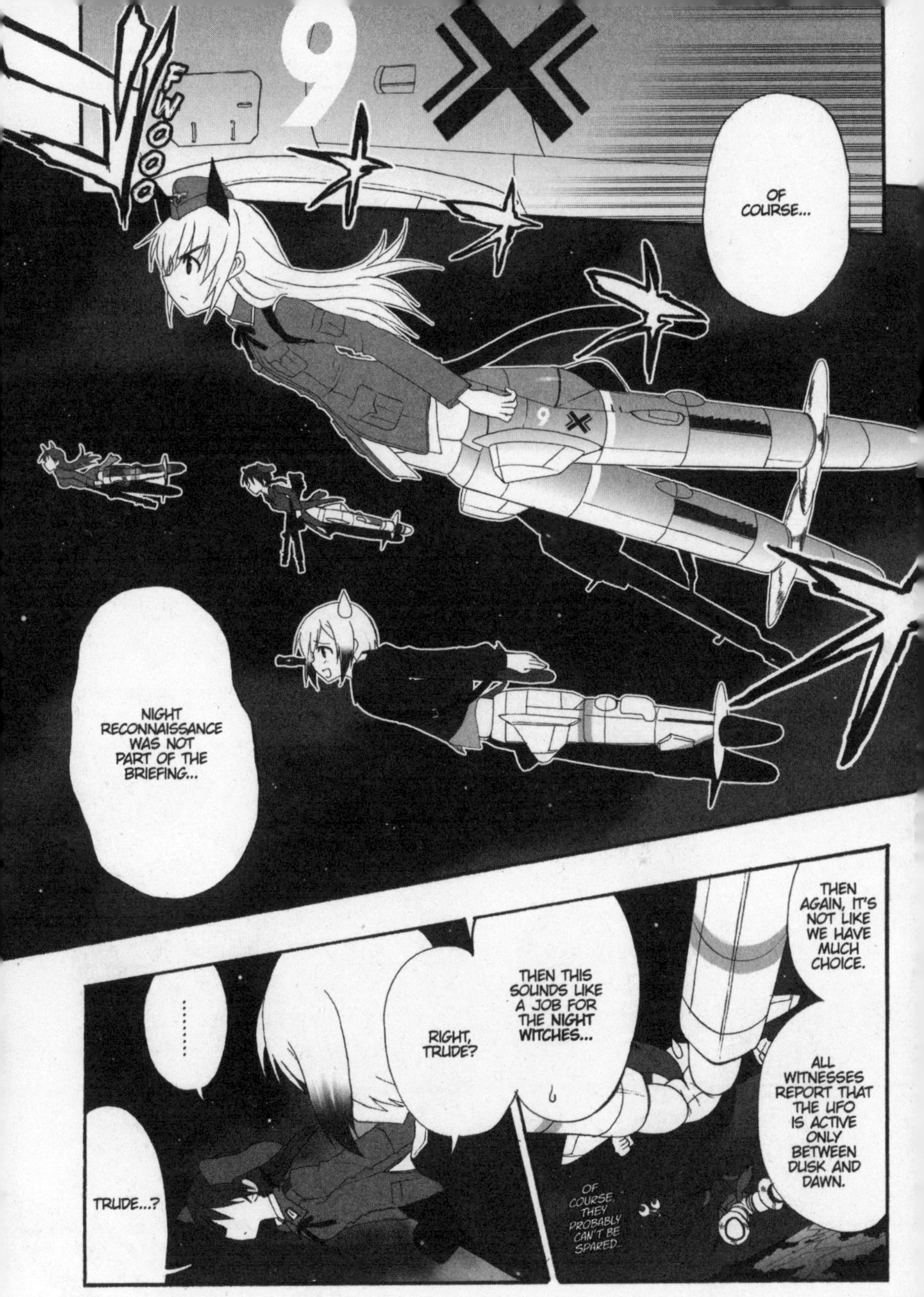
OF COURSE...
FWOOOO
NIGHT RECONNAISSANCE WAS NOT PART OF THE BRIEFING...
THEN AGAIN, IT'S NOT LIKE WE HAVE MUCH CHOICE.
ALL WITNESSES REPORT THAT THE UFO IS ACTIVE ONLY BETWEEN DUSK AND DAWN.
THEN THIS SOUNDS LIKE A JOB FOR THE NIGHT WITCHES...
RIGHT, TRUDE?
OF COURSE, THEY PROBABLY CAN'T BE SPARED...
....
TRUDE...?

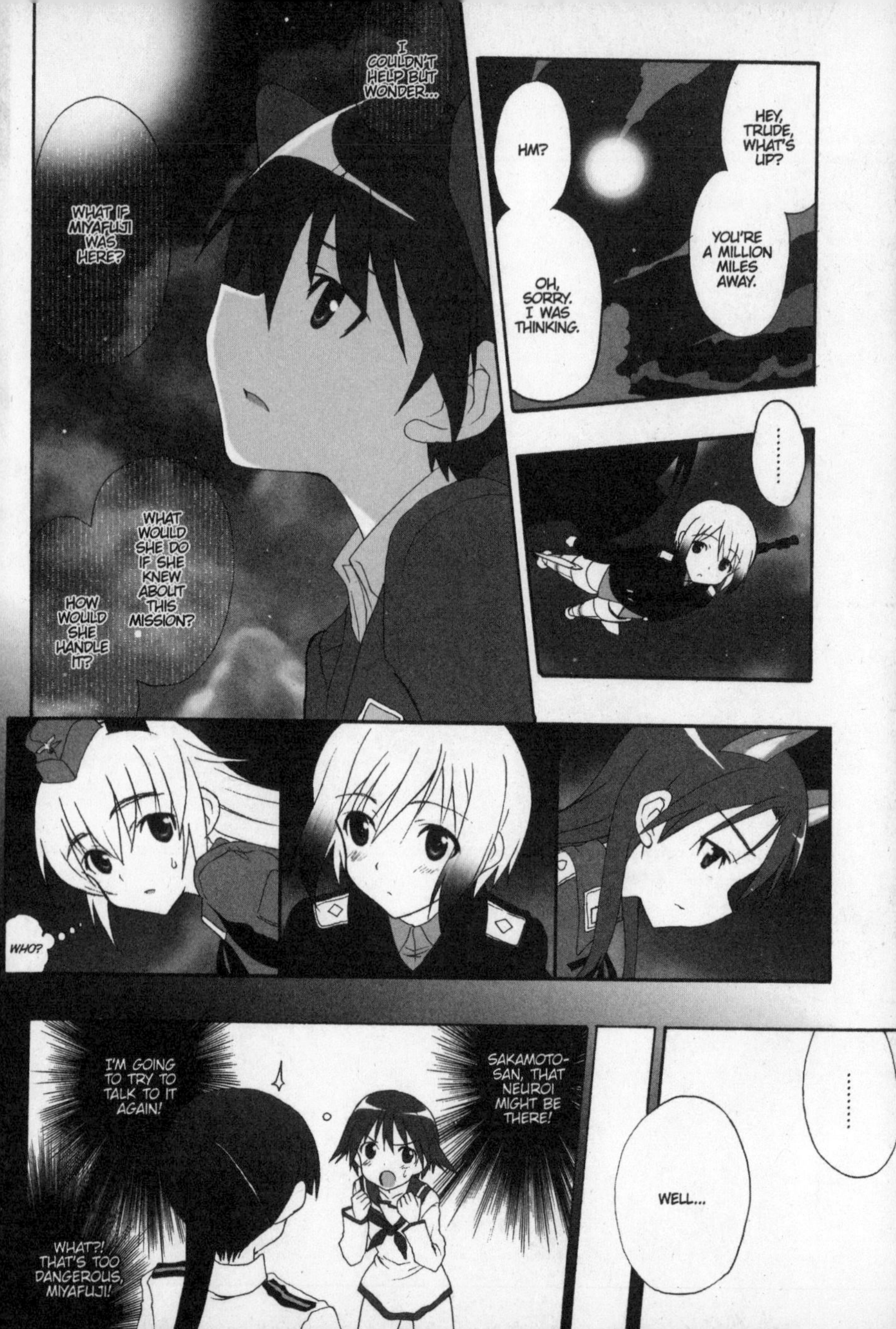
HEY, TRUDE, WHAT'S UP?
YOU'RE A MILLION MILES AWAY.
HM?
OH, SORRY. I WAS THINKING.
......
I COULDN'T HELP BUT WONDER...
WHAT IF MIYAFUJI WAS HERE?
WHAT WOULD SHE DO IF SHE KNEW ABOUT THIS MISSION?
HOW WOULD SHE HANDLE IT?
WHO?
......
WELL...
SAKAMOTO-SAN, THAT NEUROI MIGHT BE THERE!
I'M GOING TO TRY TO TALK TO IT AGAIN!
WHAT?! THAT'S TOO DANGEROUS, MIYAFUJI!

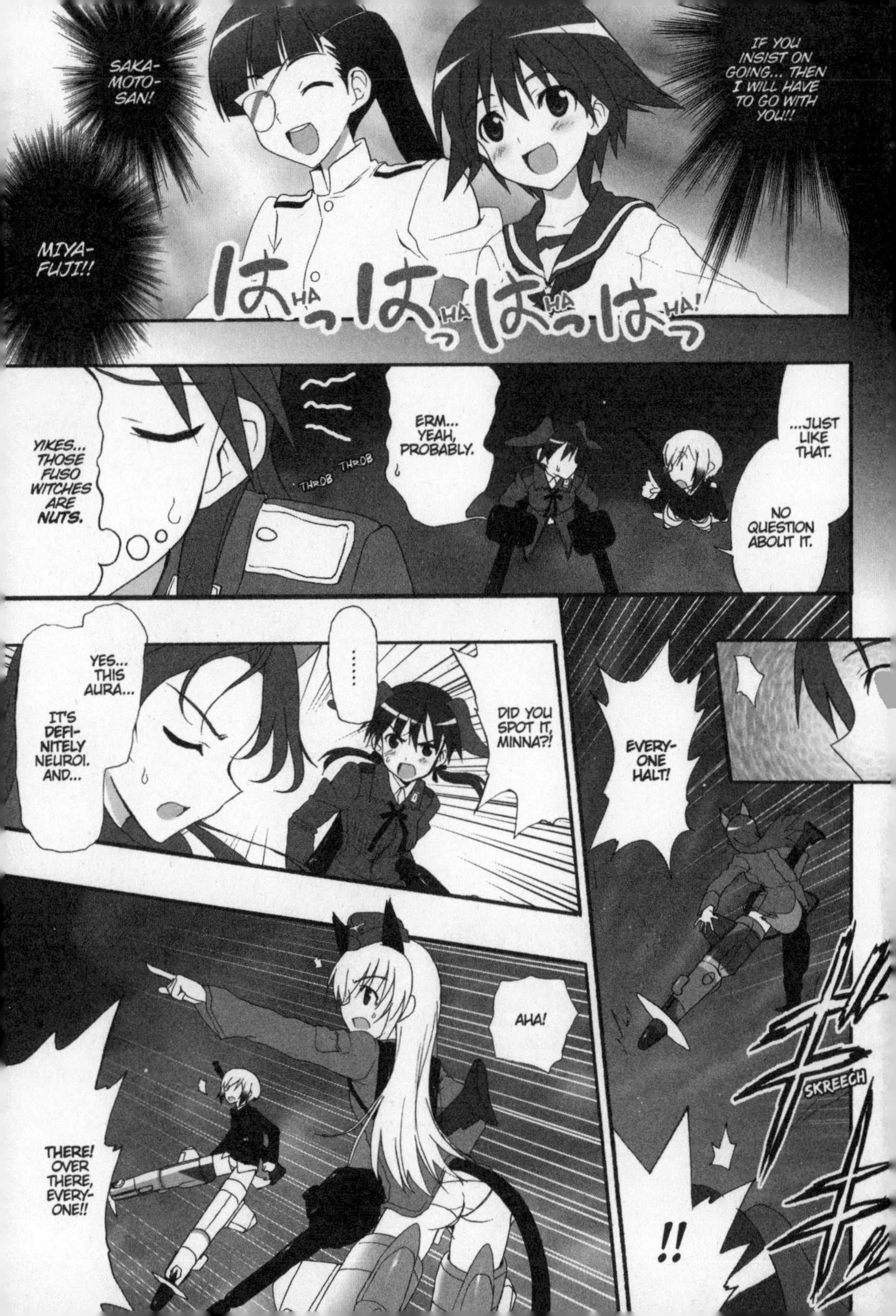
IF YOU INSIST ON GOING... THEN I WILL HAVE TO GO WITH YOU!!
SAKA-MOTO-SAN!
MIYA-FUJI!!
はっ HA はっ HA はっ HA はっ HA!
...JUST LIKE THAT.
NO QUESTION ABOUT IT.
ERM... YEAH, PROBABLY.
THROB THROB
YIKES... THOSE FUSO WITCHES ARE NUTS.
EVERY-ONE HALT!
SKREECH
!!
DID YOU SPOT IT, MINNA?!
......
YES... THIS AURA...
IT'S DEFI-NITELY NEUROI. AND...
AHA!
THERE! OVER THERE, EVERY-ONE!!

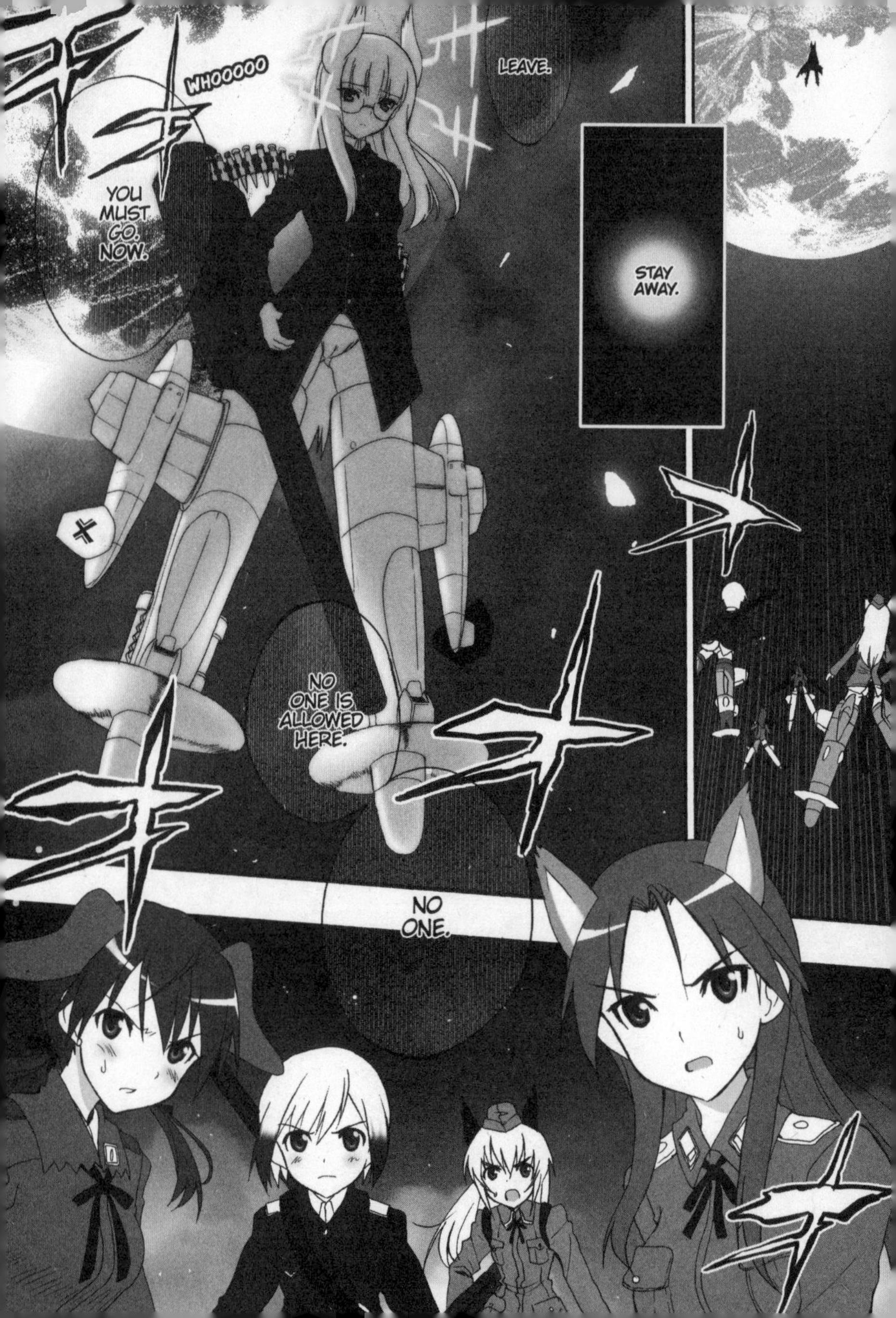
STAY AWAY.
LEAVE.
WHOOOOO
YOU MUST GO. NOW.
NO ONE IS ALLOWED HERE.
NO ONE.

WITCHES GRAFFITI

Shimada Humikane &
Projekt Kagonish
illustrated by
Kyougoku Shin

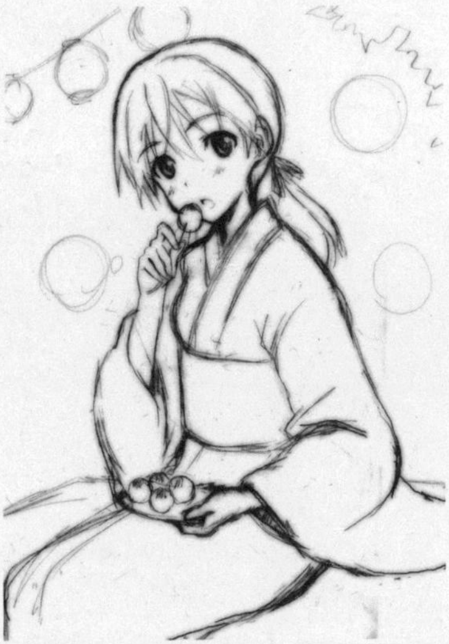

Gertrud Barkhorn

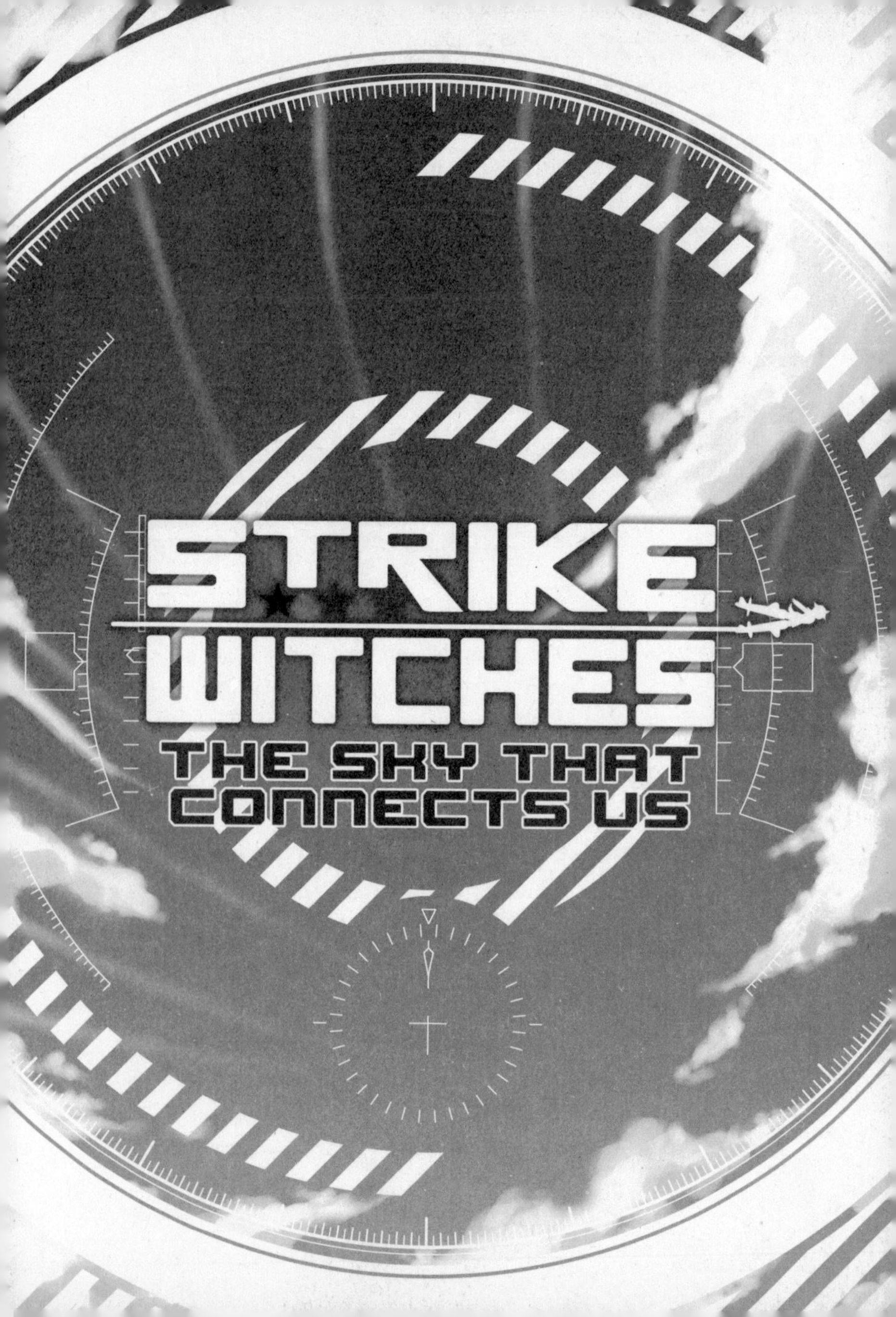
STRIKE WITCHES
THE SKY THAT CONNECTS US

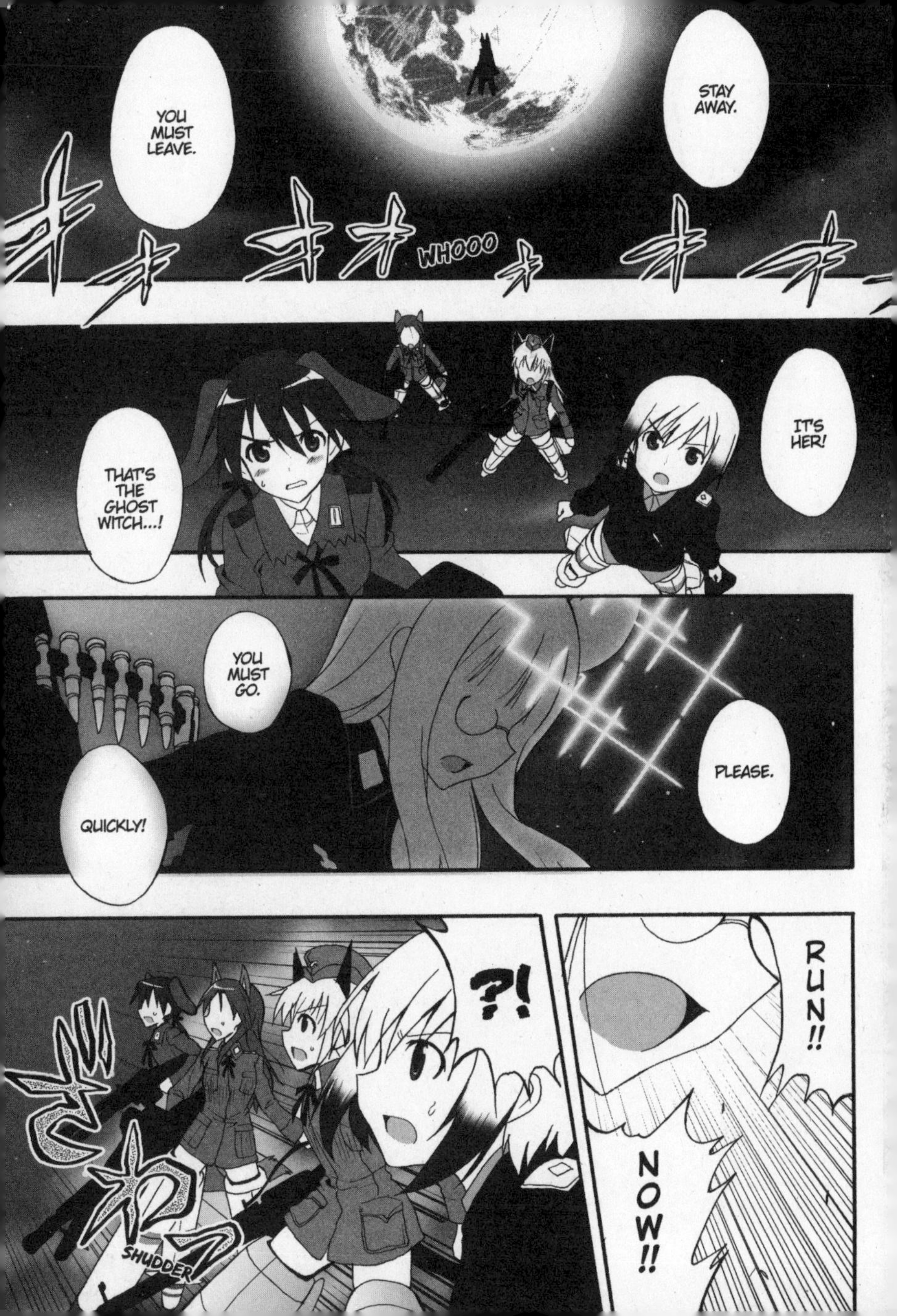
STAY AWAY.
YOU MUST LEAVE.
WHOOO
IT'S HER!
THAT'S THE GHOST WITCH...!
YOU MUST GO.
PLEASE.
QUICKLY!
RUN NOW!!
?!
SHUDDER

CHAPTER 6

THE KARLSLAND GHOST

<PART II>

STRIKE WITCHES
THE SKY THAT CONNECTS US

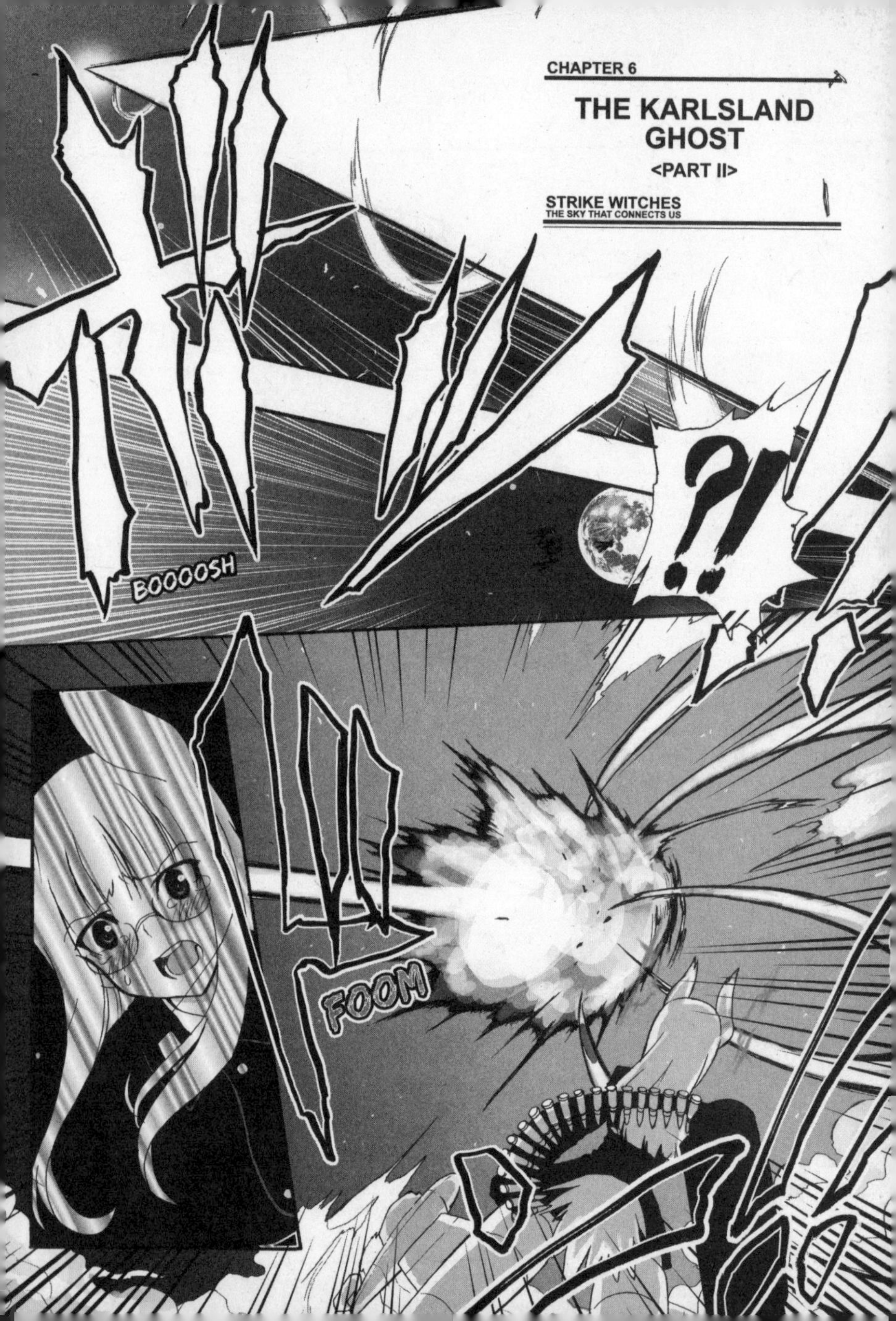
?!
BOOOOSH
FOOM

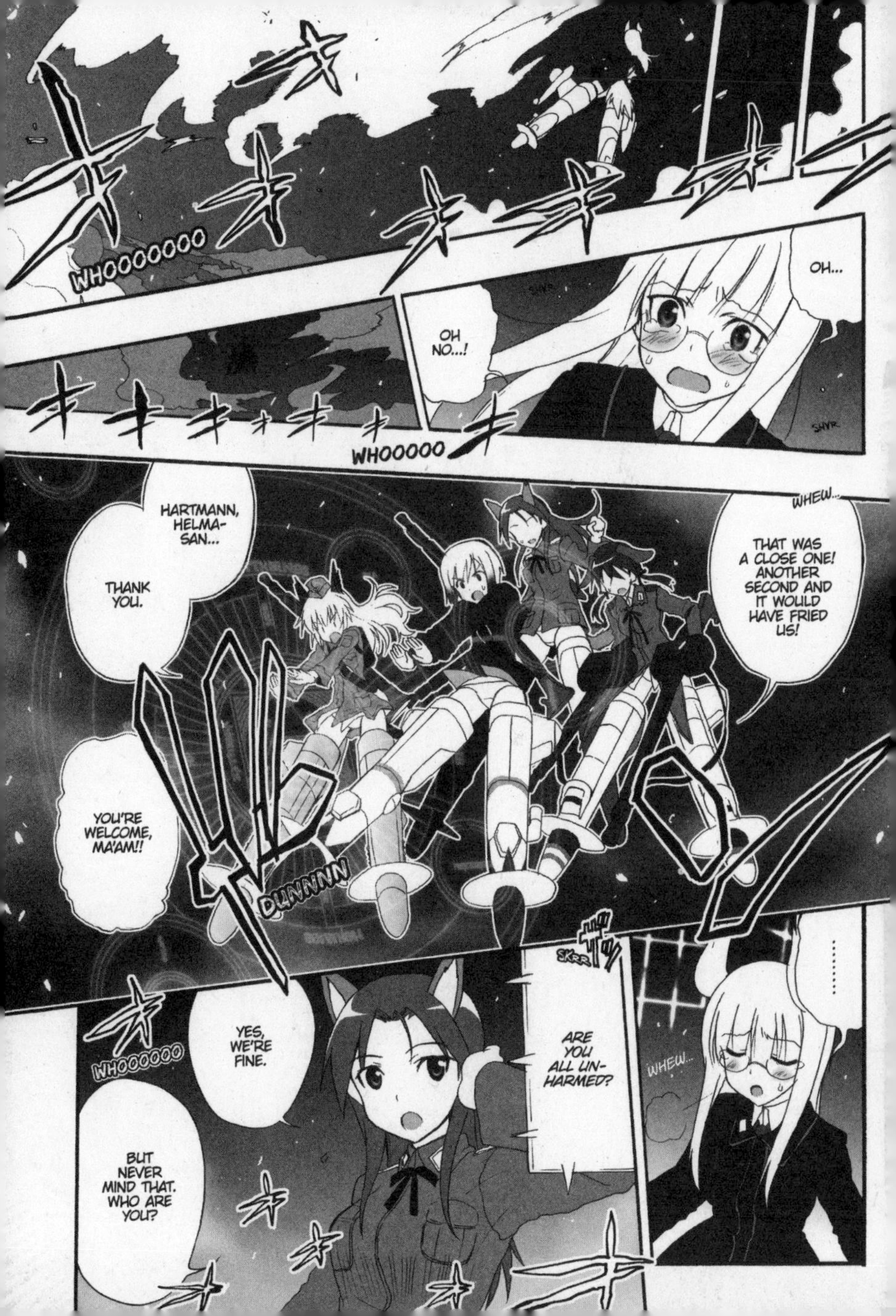
WHOOOOOOOO
OH...
SHYR
OH NO...!
SHYR
WHOOOOO
WHEW...
THAT WAS A CLOSE ONE! ANOTHER SECOND AND IT WOULD HAVE FRIED US!
HARTMANN, HELMA-SAN...
THANK YOU.
YOU'RE WELCOME, MA'AM!!
DUNNNNN
......
WHEW...
SKRR
ARE YOU ALL UN-HARMED?
YES, WE'RE FINE.
BUT NEVER MIND THAT. WHO ARE YOU?
WHOOOOOOO

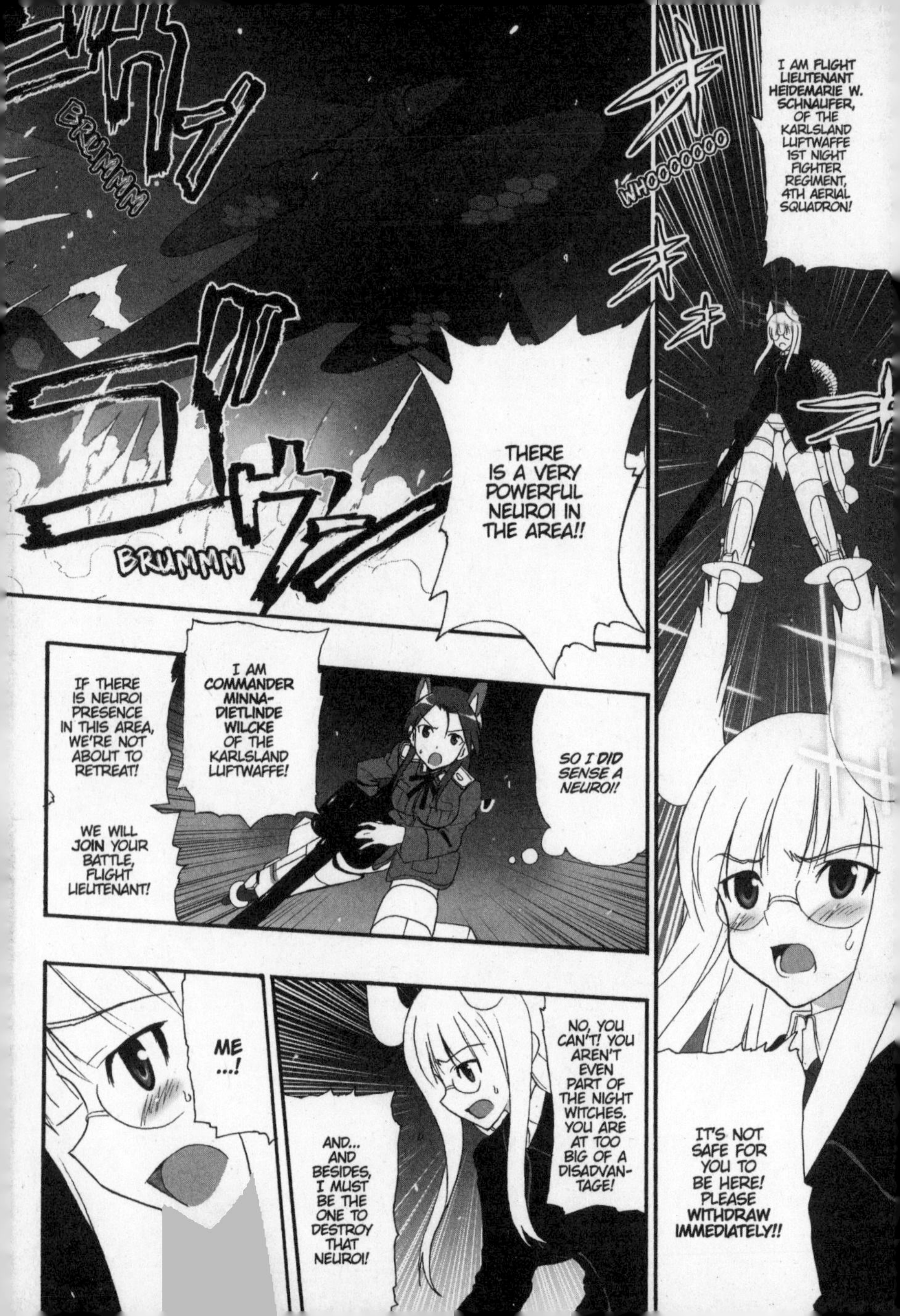
I AM FLIGHT LIEUTENANT HEIDEMARIE W. SCHNAUFER, OF THE KARLSLAND LUFTWAFFE 1ST NIGHT FIGHTER REGIMENT, 4TH AERIAL SQUADRON!
WHOOOOOOO
IT'S NOT SAFE FOR YOU TO BE HERE! PLEASE WITHDRAW IMMEDIATELY!!
THERE IS A VERY POWERFUL NEUROI IN THE AREA!!
BRUMMM
BRUMMM
SO I DID SENSE A NEUROI!
I AM COMMANDER MINNA-DIETLINDE WILCKE OF THE KARLSLAND LUFTWAFFE!
IF THERE IS NEUROI PRESENCE IN THIS AREA, WE'RE NOT ABOUT TO RETREAT!
WE WILL JOIN YOUR BATTLE, FLIGHT LIEUTENANT!
NO, YOU CAN'T! YOU AREN'T EVEN PART OF THE NIGHT WITCHES. YOU ARE AT TOO BIG OF A DISADVAN-TAGE!
AND... AND BESIDES, I MUST BE THE ONE TO DESTROY THAT NEUROI!
ME ...!

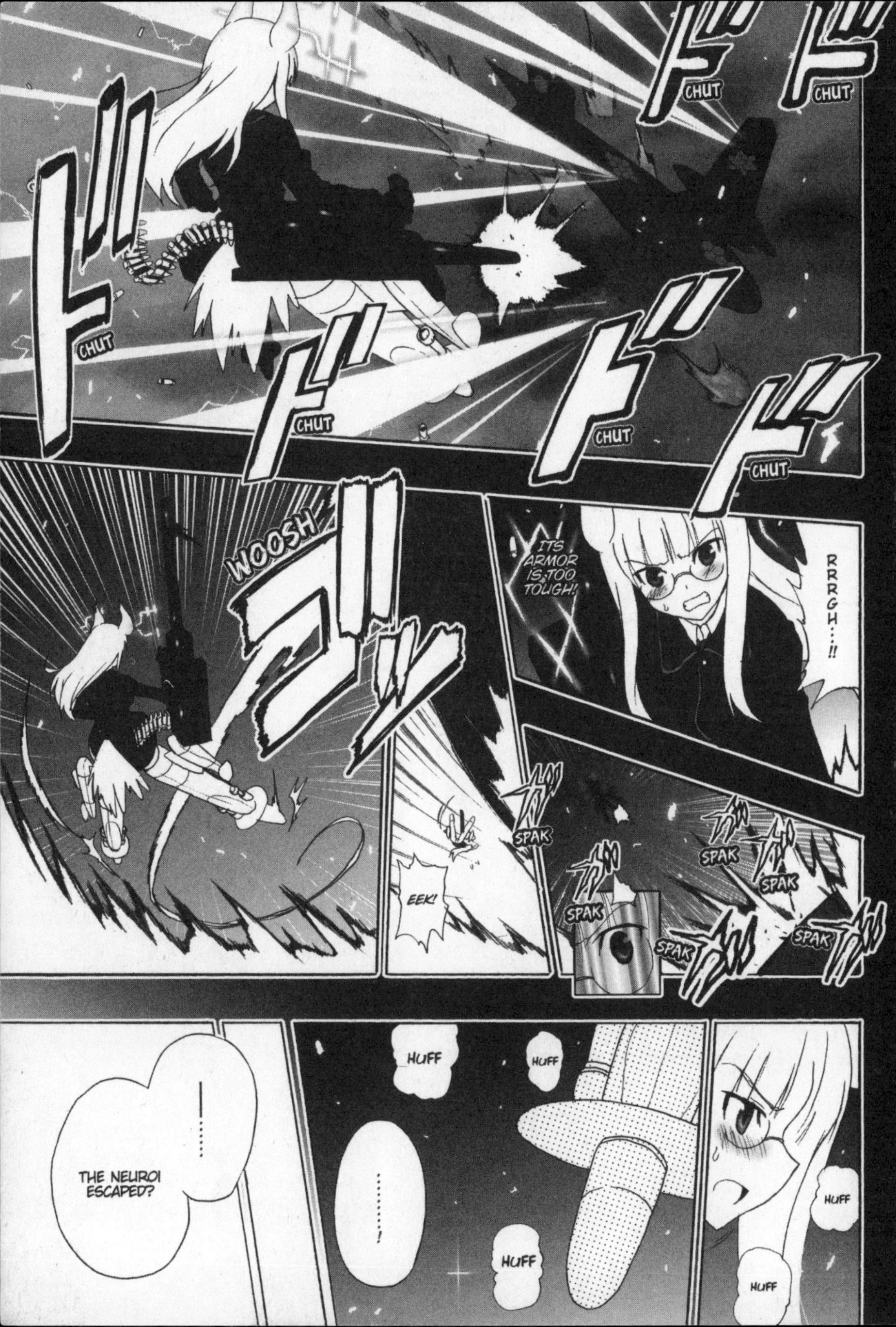
CHUT
CHUT
CHUT
CHUT
CHUT
CHUT
RRRGH...!!
ITS ARMOR IS TOO TOUGH!
SPAK
SPAK
SPAK
SPAK
SPAK
SPAK
EEK!
SPAK
WOOSH
HUFF
HUFF
HUFF
HUFF
HUFF
HUFF
......!
......
THE NEUROI ESCAPED?

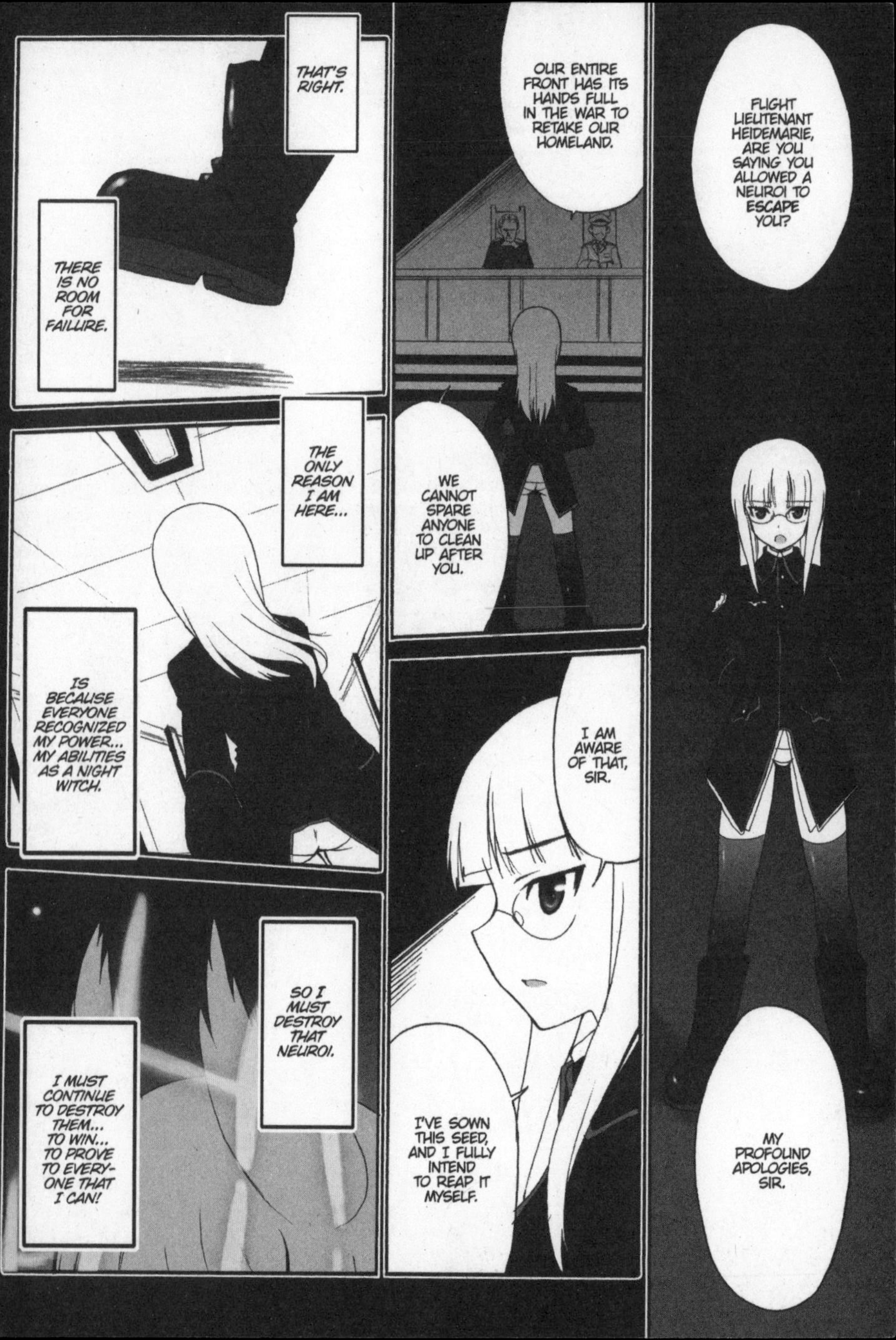
FLIGHT LIEUTENANT HEIDEMARIE, ARE YOU SAYING YOU ALLOWED A NEUROI TO ESCAPE YOU?
MY PROFOUND APOLOGIES, SIR.
OUR ENTIRE FRONT HAS ITS HANDS FULL IN THE WAR TO RETAKE OUR HOMELAND.
WE CANNOT SPARE ANYONE TO CLEAN UP AFTER YOU.
I AM AWARE OF THAT, SIR.
I'VE SOWN THIS SEED, AND I FULLY INTEND TO REAP IT MYSELF.
THAT'S RIGHT.
THERE IS NO ROOM FOR FAILURE.
THE ONLY REASON I AM HERE...
IS BECAUSE EVERYONE RECOGNIZED MY POWER... MY ABILITIES AS A NIGHT WITCH.
SO I MUST DESTROY THAT NEUROI.
I MUST CONTINUE TO DESTROY THEM... TO WIN... TO PROVE TO EVERY-ONE THAT I CAN!

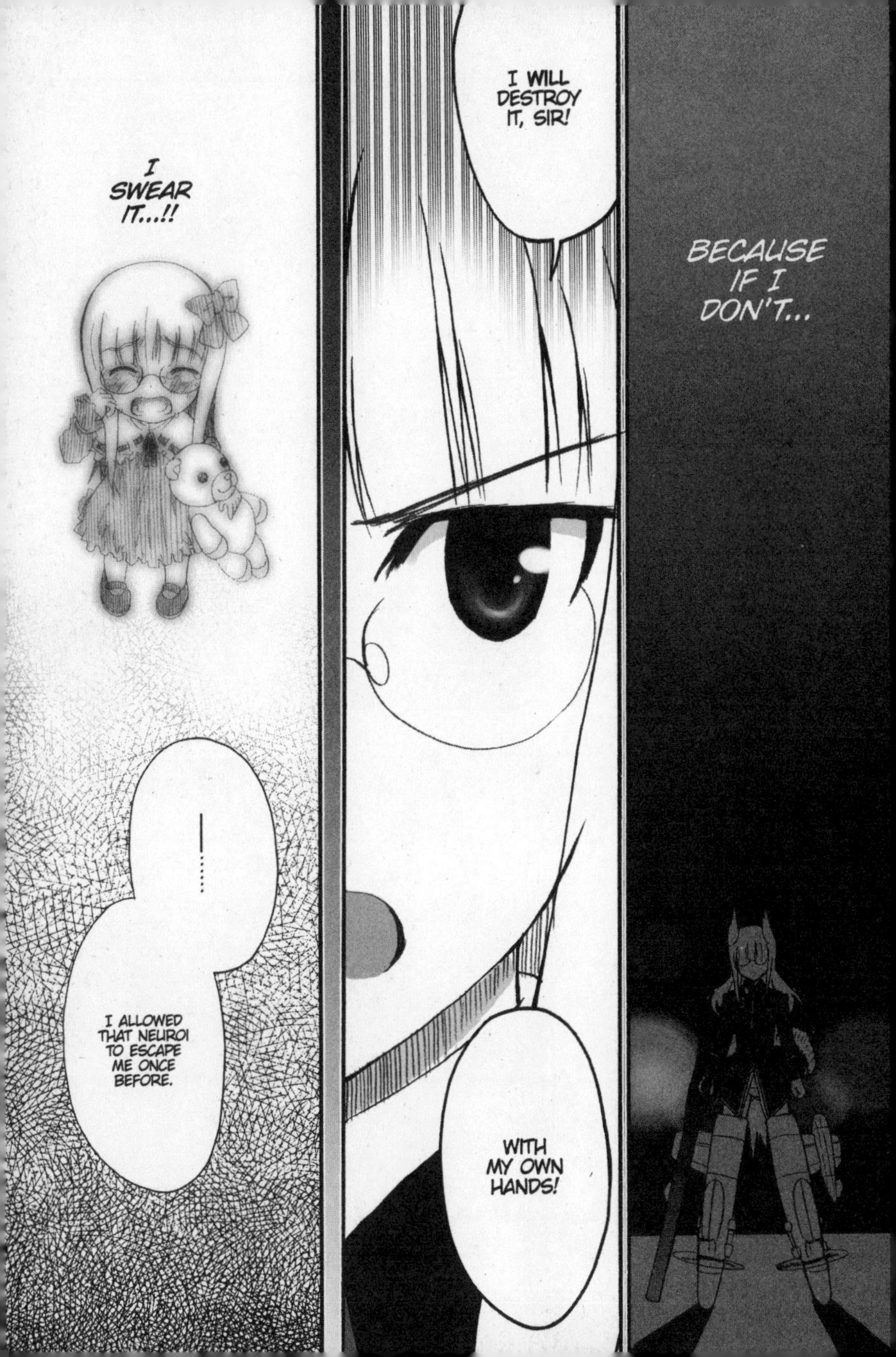
BECAUSE IF I DON'T...
I WILL DESTROY IT, SIR!
WITH MY OWN HANDS!
I SWEAR IT...!!
—......
I ALLOWED THAT NEUROI TO ESCAPE ME ONCE BEFORE.

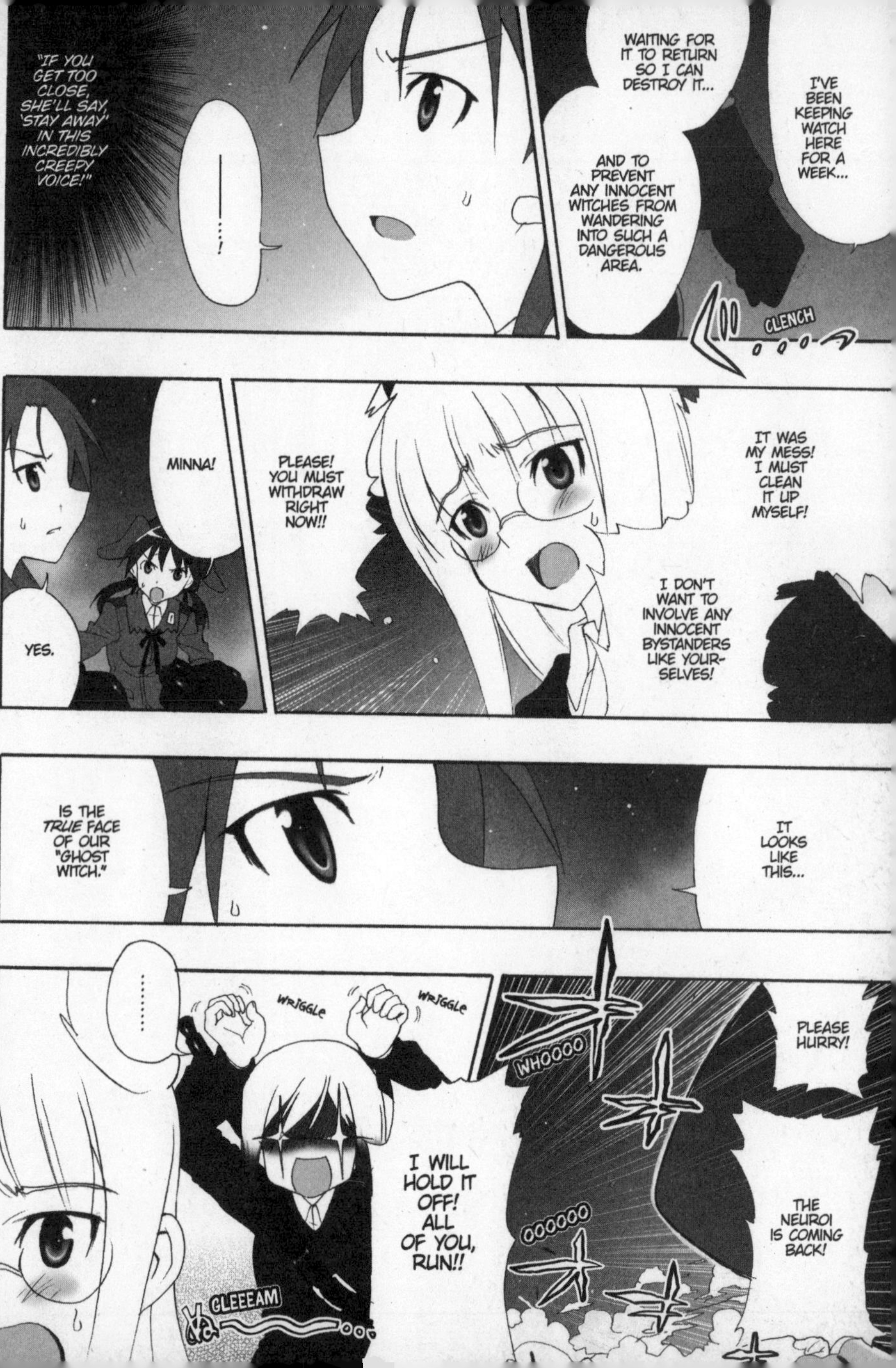
I'VE BEEN KEEPING WATCH HERE FOR A WEEK...
WAITING FOR IT TO RETURN SO I CAN DESTROY IT...
AND TO PREVENT ANY INNOCENT WITCHES FROM WANDERING INTO SUCH A DANGEROUS AREA.
CLENCH
—...!
"IF YOU GET TOO CLOSE, SHE'LL SAY, 'STAY AWAY' IN THIS INCREDIBLY CREEPY VOICE!"
IT WAS MY MESS! I MUST CLEAN IT UP MYSELF!
PLEASE! YOU MUST WITHDRAW RIGHT NOW!!
I DON'T WANT TO INVOLVE ANY INNOCENT BYSTANDERS LIKE YOURSELVES!
MINNA!
YES.
IT LOOKS LIKE THIS...
IS THE TRUE FACE OF OUR "GHOST WITCH."
PLEASE HURRY!
WHOOOO
THE NEUROI IS COMING BACK!
OOOOOO
I WILL HOLD IT OFF! ALL OF YOU, RUN!!
wriggle
wriggle
......
GLEEEAM

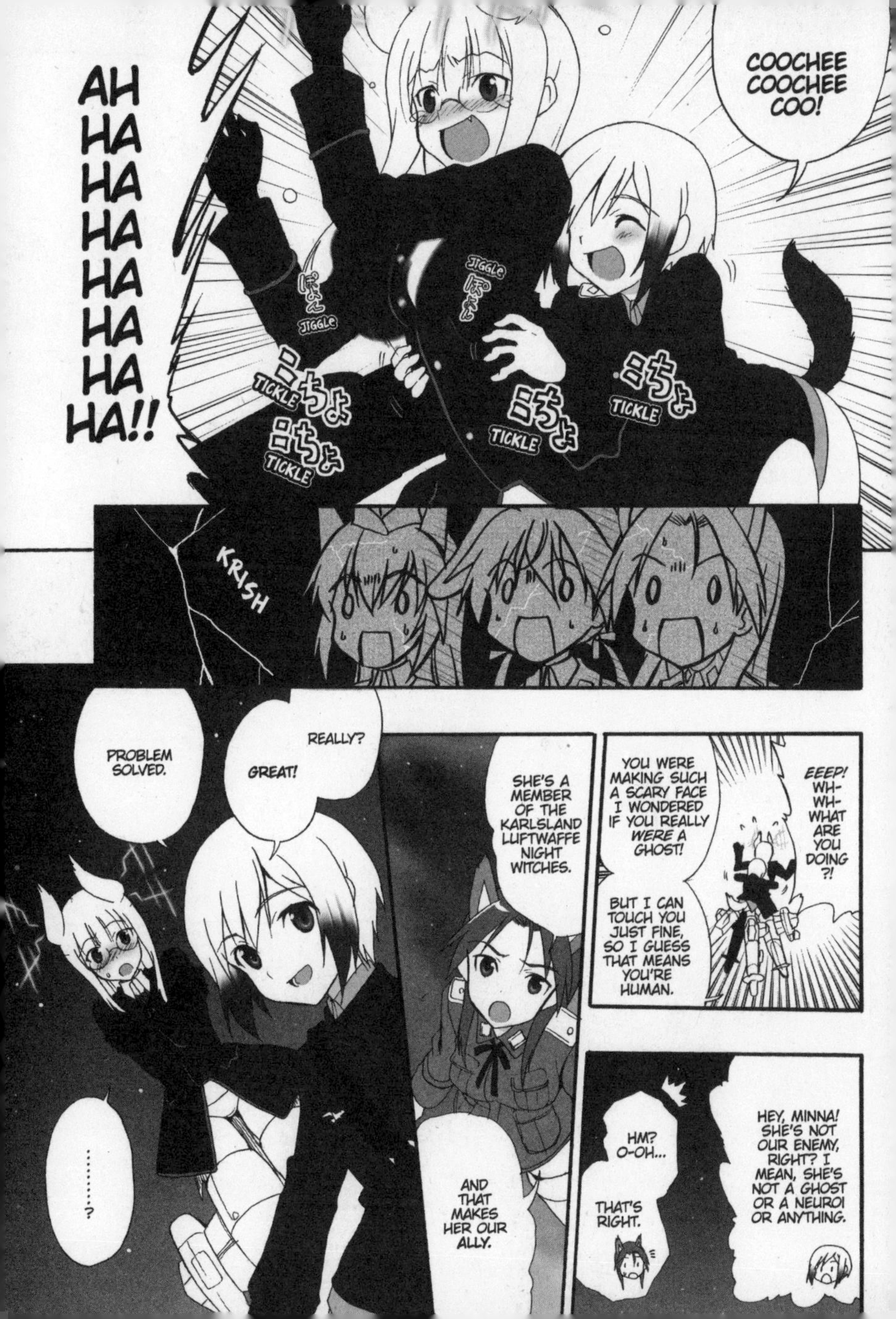
COOCHEE COOCHEE COO!
ぽよん JIGGLE
ぽよん JIGGLE
こちょ TICKLE
こちょ TICKLE
こちょ TICKLE
こちょ TICKLE
AH HA HA HA HA HA HA HA HA!!
KRISH
EEEP! WH-WH-WHAT ARE YOU DOING?!
YOU WERE MAKING SUCH A SCARY FACE I WONDERED IF YOU REALLY *WERE* A GHOST!
BUT I CAN TOUCH YOU JUST FINE, SO I GUESS THAT MEANS YOU'RE HUMAN.
HEY, MINNA! SHE'S NOT OUR ENEMY, RIGHT? I MEAN, SHE'S NOT A GHOST OR A NEUROI OR ANYTHING.
HM? O-OH...
THAT'S RIGHT.
SHE'S A MEMBER OF THE KARLSLAND LUFTWAFFE NIGHT WITCHES.
AND THAT MAKES HER OUR ALLY.
REALLY? GREAT!
PROBLEM SOLVED.
.......?

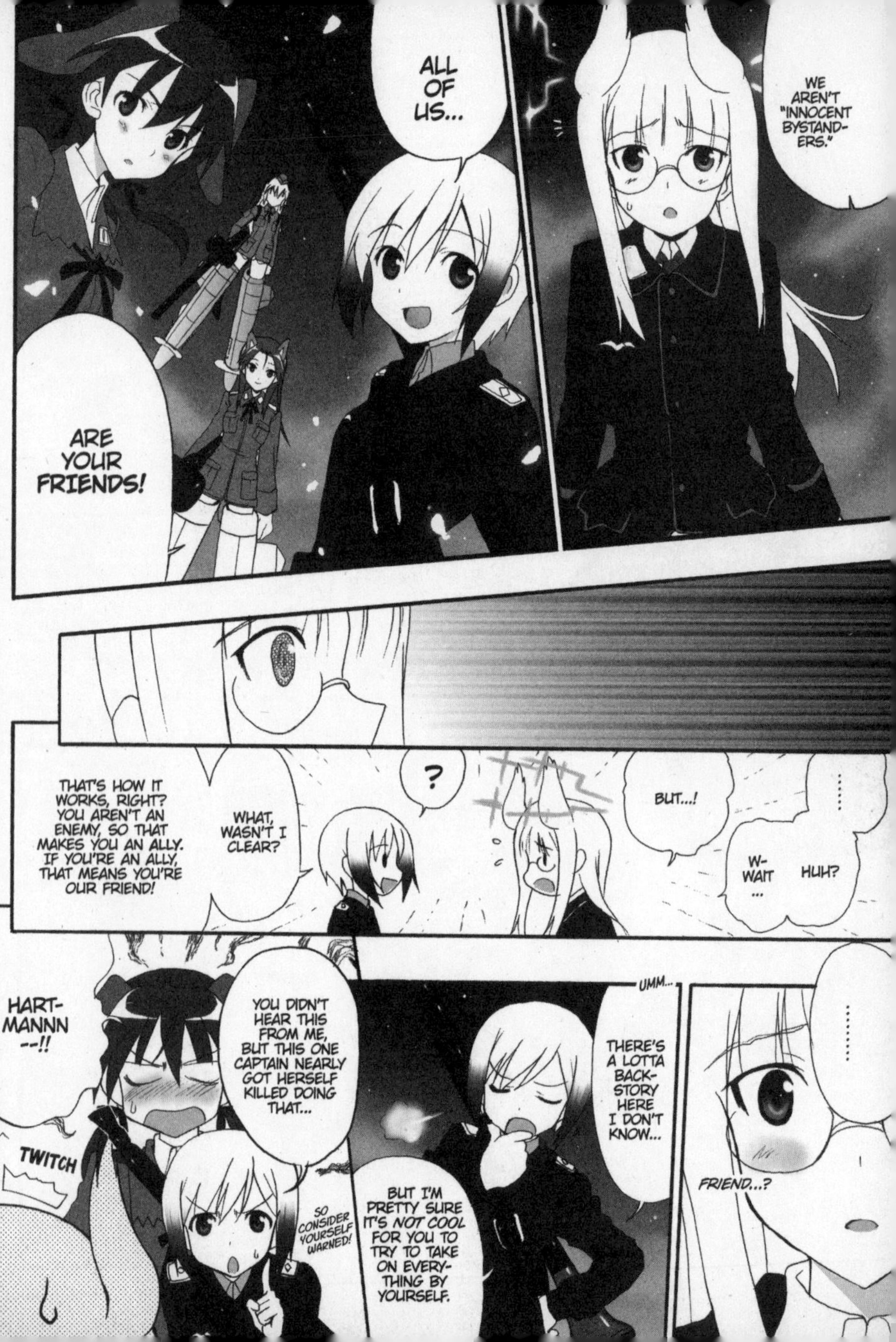

WE AREN'T "INNOCENT BYSTANDERS."
ALL OF US...
ARE YOUR FRIENDS!
......
BUT...!
HUH?
W-WAIT...
?
WHAT, WASN'T I CLEAR?
THAT'S HOW IT WORKS, RIGHT? YOU AREN'T AN ENEMY, SO THAT MAKES YOU AN ALLY. IF YOU'RE AN ALLY, THAT MEANS YOU'RE OUR FRIEND!
......
FRIEND...?
UMM...
THERE'S A LOTTA BACKSTORY HERE I DON'T KNOW...
BUT I'M PRETTY SURE IT'S NOT COOL FOR YOU TO TRY TO TAKE ON EVERYTHING BY YOURSELF.
YOU DIDN'T HEAR THIS FROM ME, BUT THIS ONE CAPTAIN NEARLY GOT HERSELF KILLED DOING THAT...
SO CONSIDER YOURSELF WARNED!
HARTMANNN--!!
TWITCH

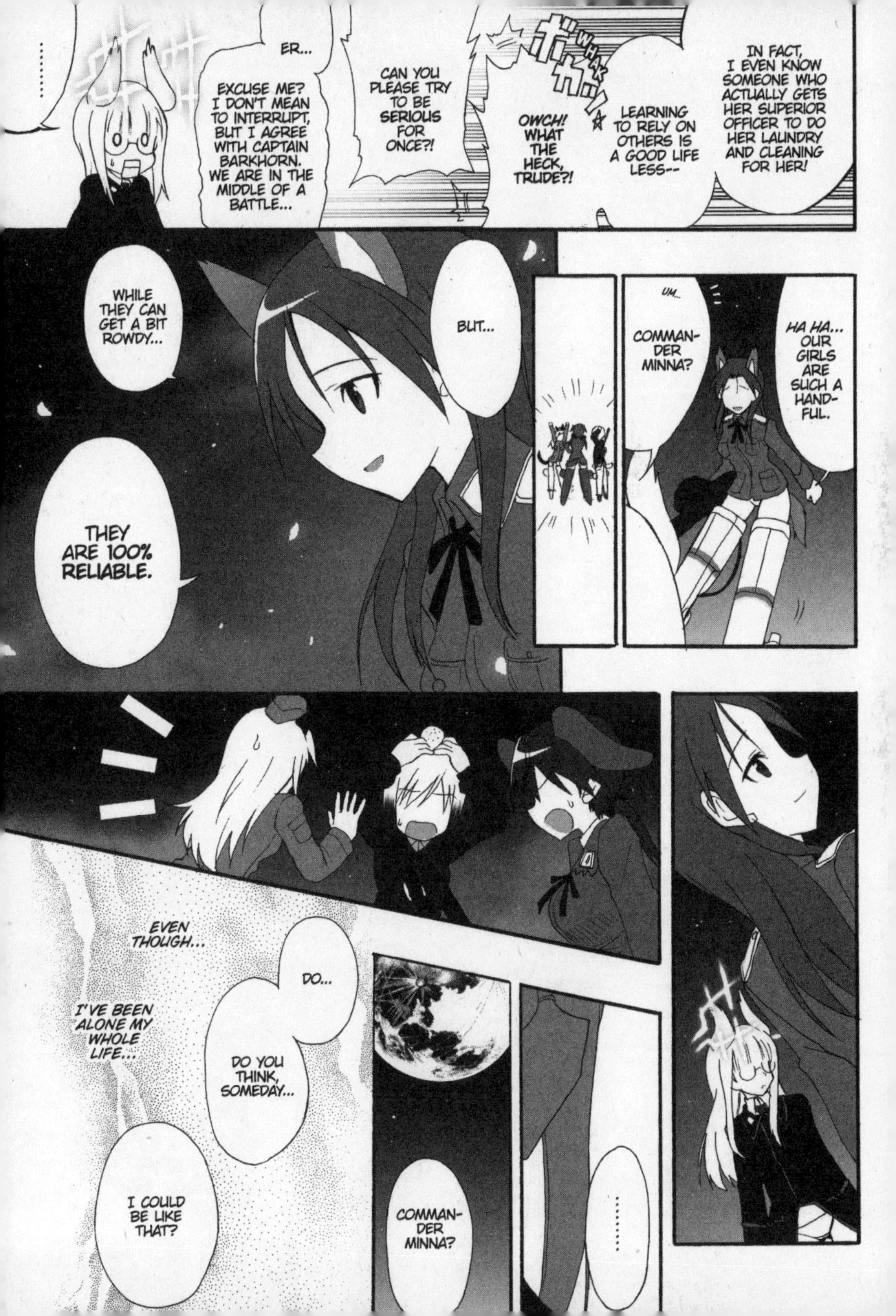
IN FACT, I EVEN KNOW SOMEONE WHO ACTUALLY GETS HER SUPERIOR OFFICER TO DO HER LAUNDRY AND CLEANING FOR HER!
LEARNING TO RELY ON OTHERS IS A GOOD LIFE LESS--
WHAK
OWCH! WHAT THE HECK, TRUDE?!
CAN YOU PLEASE TRY TO BE SERIOUS FOR ONCE?!
ER...
EXCUSE ME? I DON'T MEAN TO INTERRUPT, BUT I AGREE WITH CAPTAIN BARKHORN. WE ARE IN THE MIDDLE OF A BATTLE...
......
HA HA... OUR GIRLS ARE SUCH A HANDFUL.
UM...
COMMANDER MINNA?
BUT...
WHILE THEY CAN GET A BIT ROWDY...
THEY ARE 100% RELIABLE.
......
COMMANDER MINNA?
DO...
DO YOU THINK, SOMEDAY...
EVEN THOUGH...
I'VE BEEN ALONE MY WHOLE LIFE...
I COULD BE LIKE THAT?

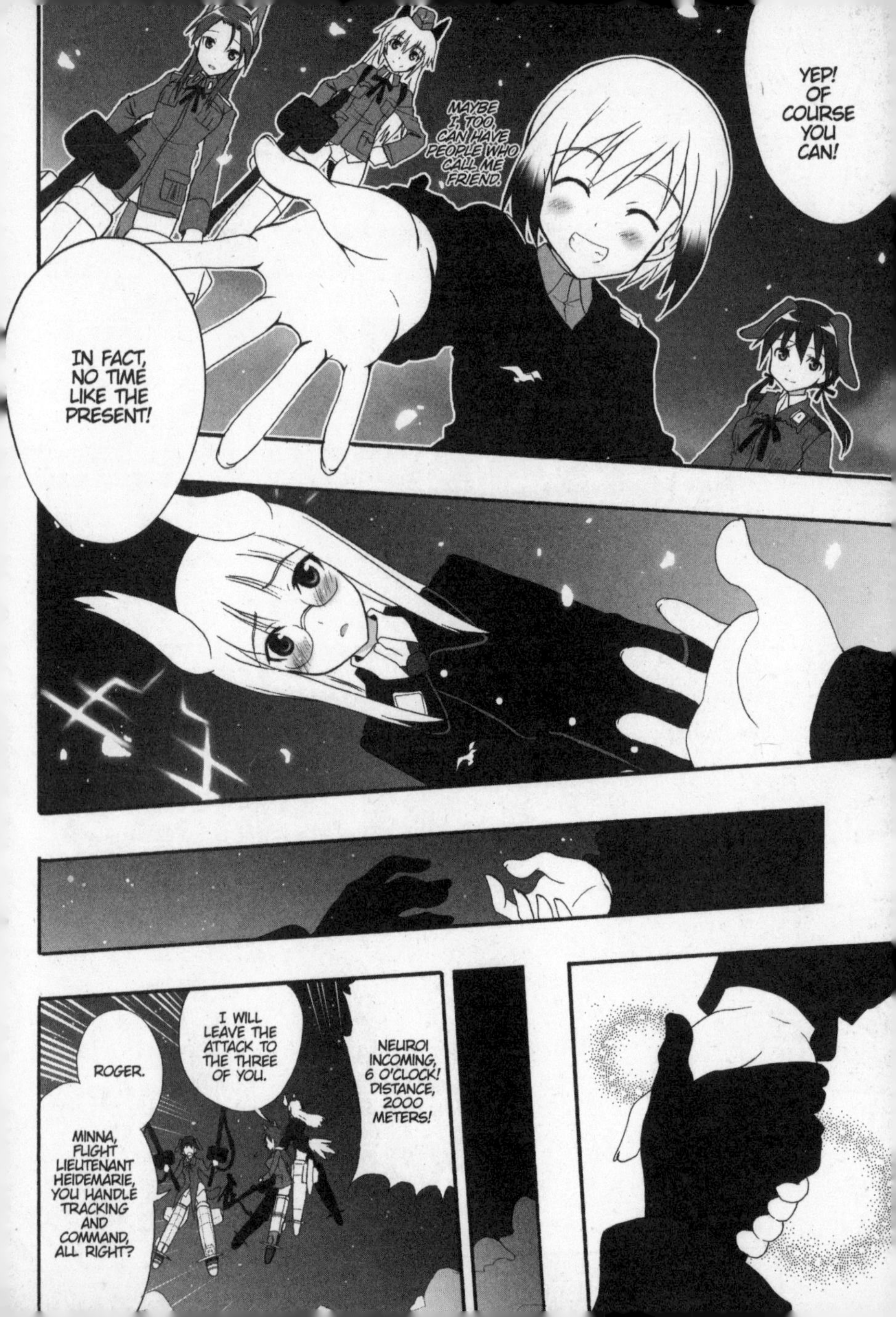
YEP! OF COURSE YOU CAN!
MAYBE I, TOO, CAN HAVE PEOPLE WHO CALL ME FRIEND.
IN FACT, NO TIME LIKE THE PRESENT!
NEUROI INCOMING, 6 O'CLOCK! DISTANCE, 2000 METERS!
I WILL LEAVE THE ATTACK TO THE THREE OF YOU.
ROGER.
MINNA, FLIGHT LIEUTENANT HEIDEMARIE, YOU HANDLE TRACKING AND COMMAND, ALL RIGHT?

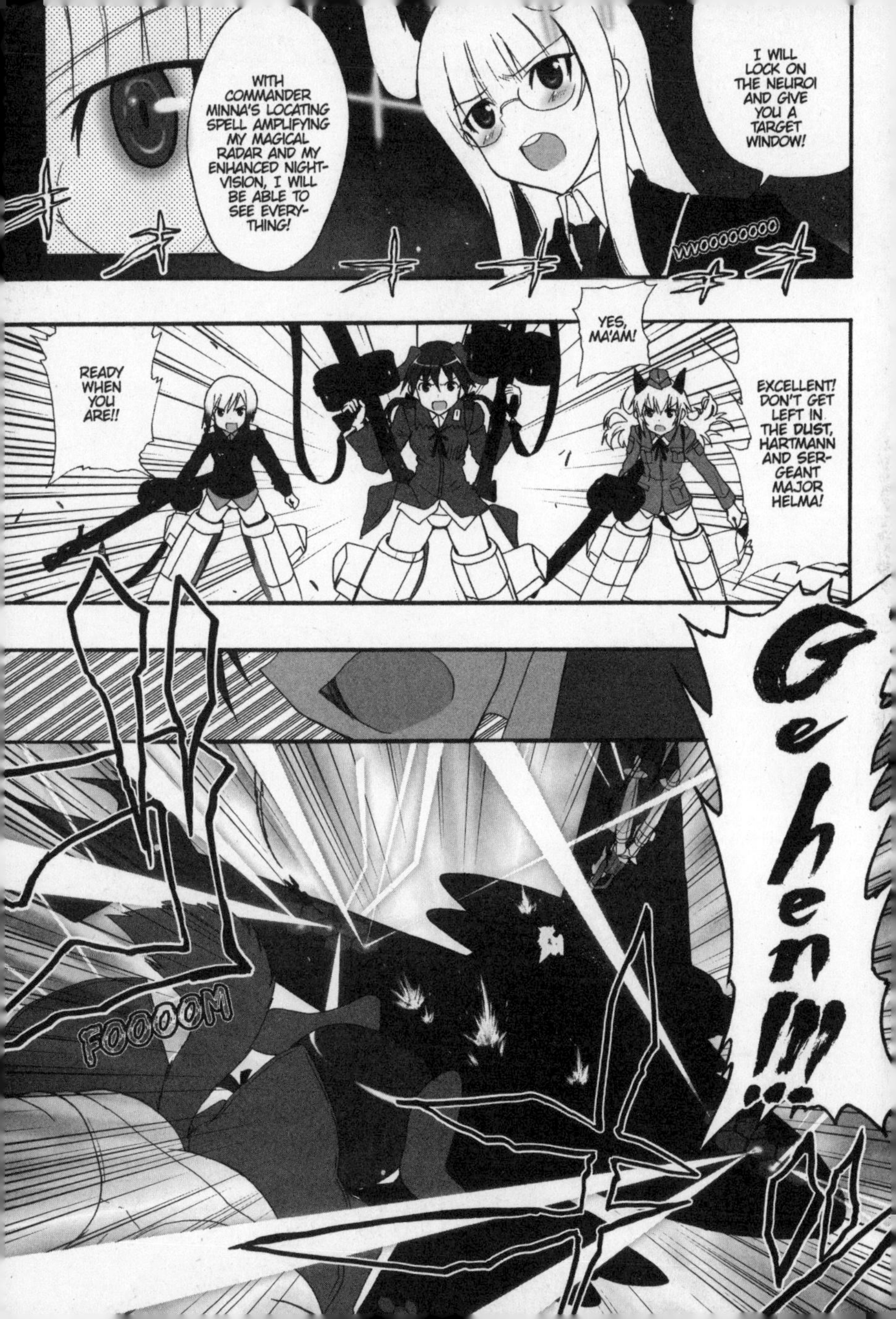
I WILL LOCK ON THE NEUROI AND GIVE YOU A TARGET WINDOW!
WITH COMMANDER MINNA'S LOCATING SPELL AMPLIFYING MY MAGICAL RADAR AND MY ENHANCED NIGHT-VISION, I WILL BE ABLE TO SEE EVERY-THING!
VVVOOOOOOOOO
EXCELLENT! DON'T GET LEFT IN THE DUST, HARTMANN AND SER-GEANT MAJOR HELMA!
YES, MA'AM!
READY WHEN YOU ARE!!
Gehenn!!...!
FOOOOM

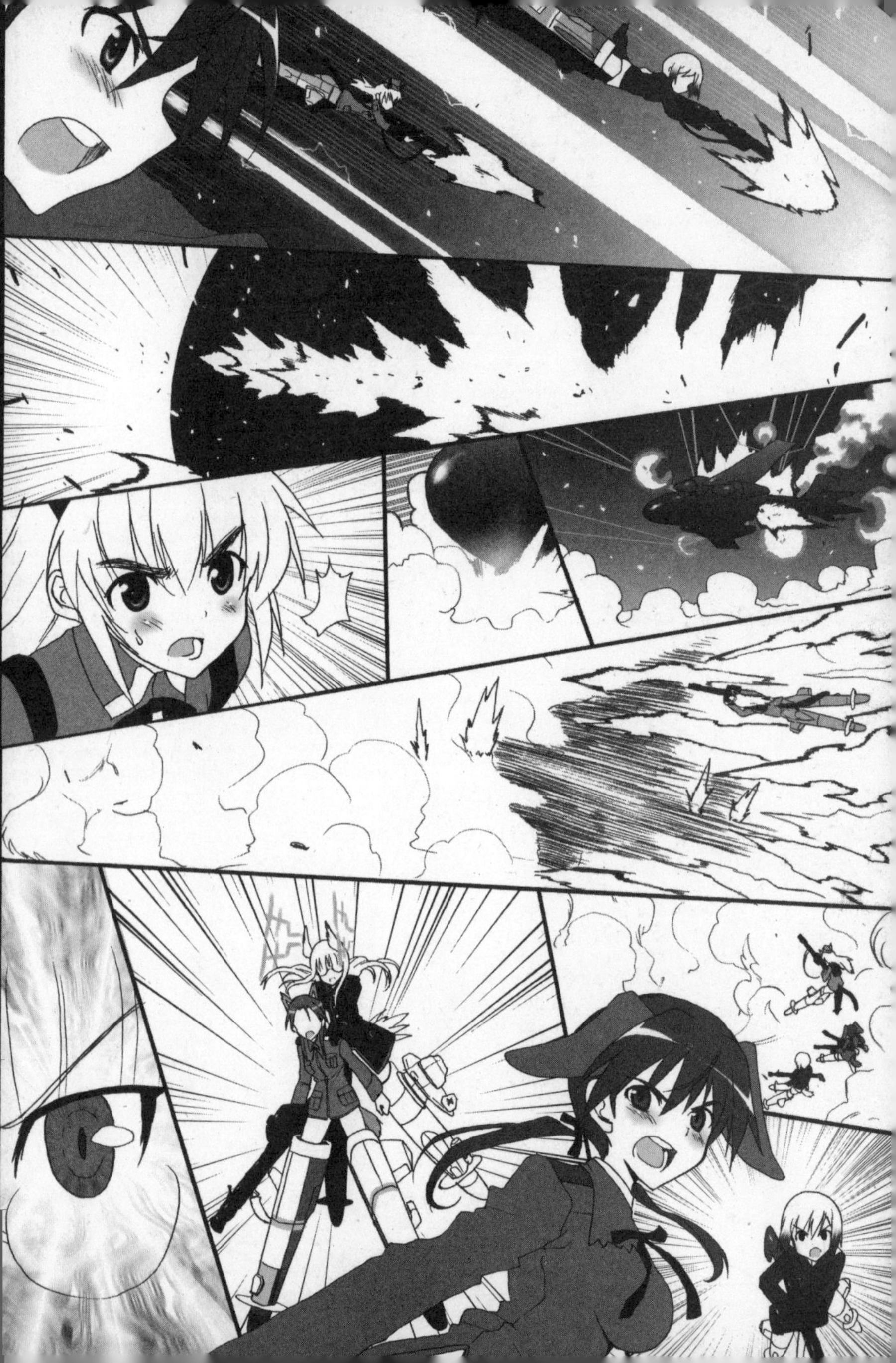

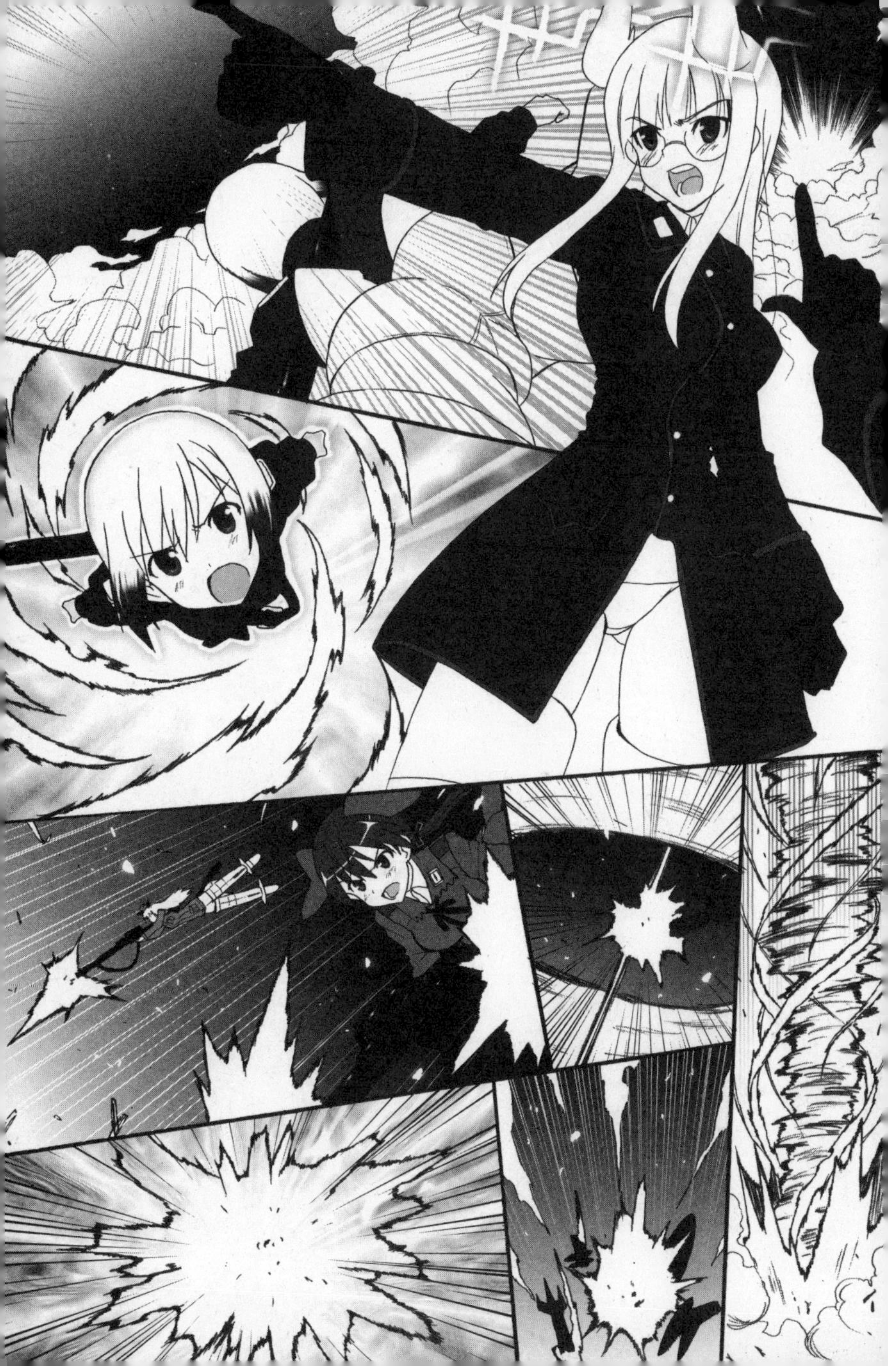

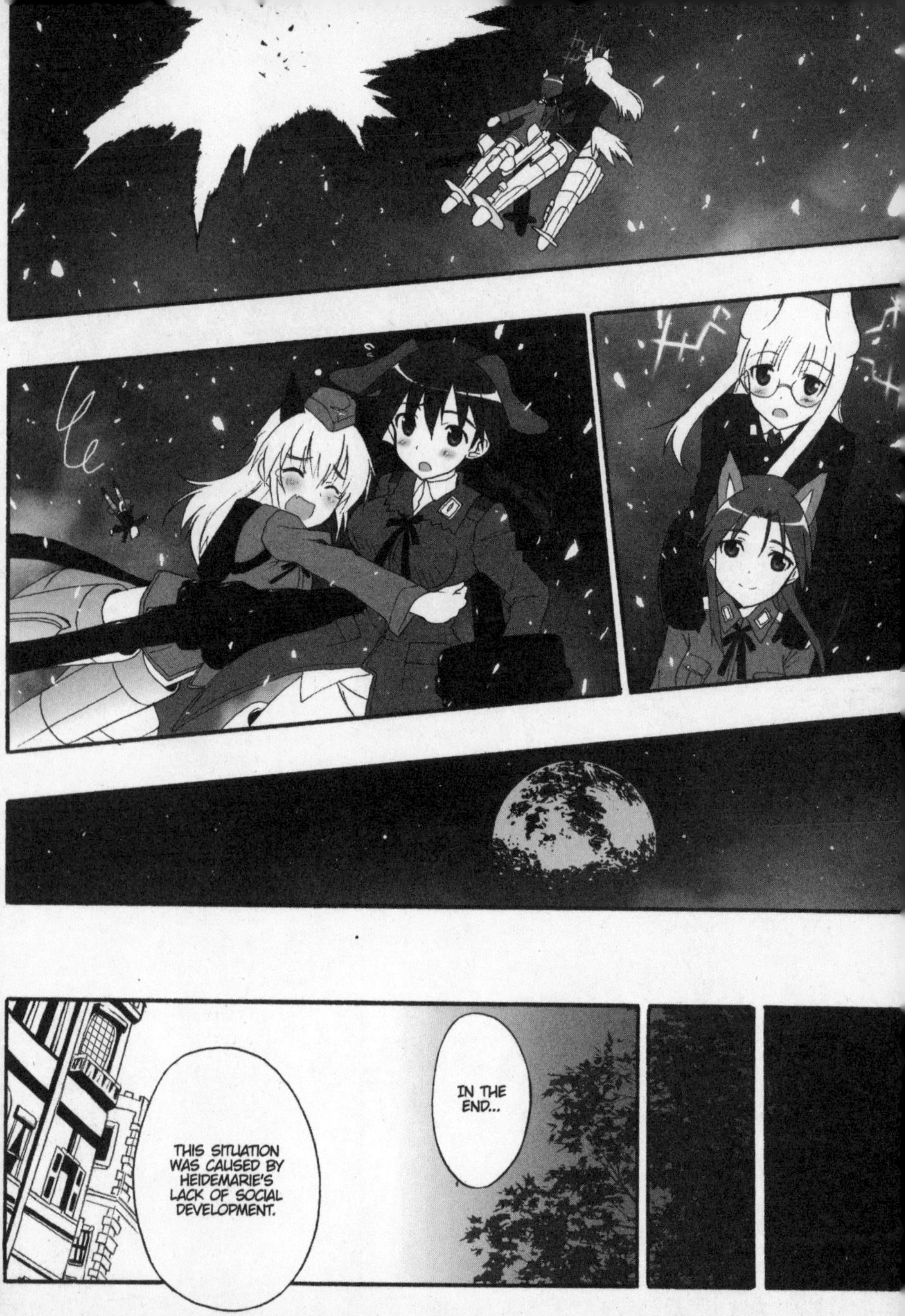
IN THE END...
THIS SITUATION WAS CAUSED BY HEIDEMARIE'S LACK OF SOCIAL DEVELOPMENT.

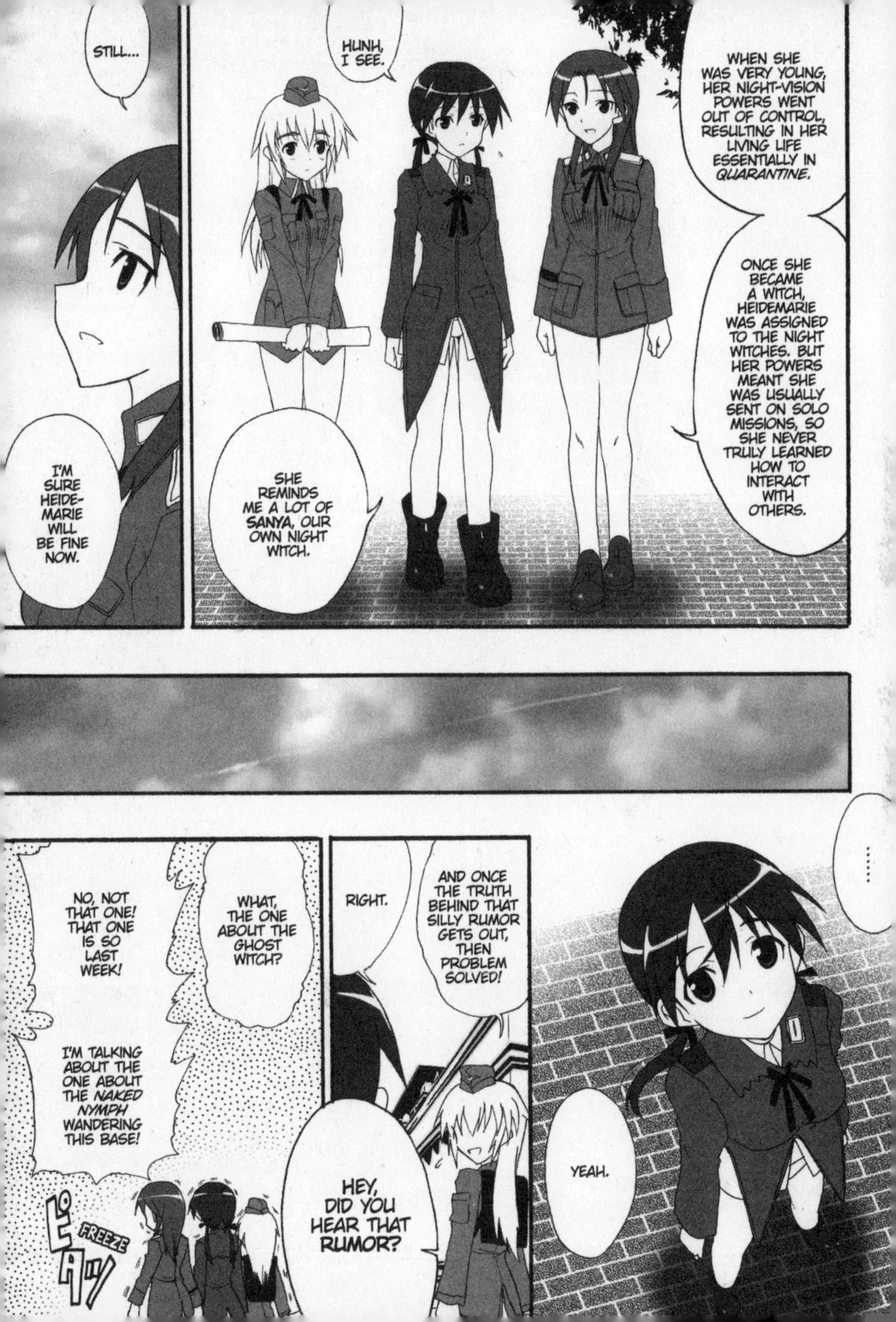

WHEN SHE WAS VERY YOUNG, HER NIGHT-VISION POWERS WENT OUT OF CONTROL, RESULTING IN HER LIVING LIFE ESSENTIALLY IN *QUARANTINE*.
ONCE SHE BECAME A WITCH, HEIDEMARIE WAS ASSIGNED TO THE NIGHT WITCHES. BUT HER POWERS MEANT SHE WAS USUALLY SENT ON SOLO MISSIONS, SO SHE NEVER TRULY LEARNED HOW TO INTERACT WITH OTHERS.
HUNH, I SEE.
SHE REMINDS ME A LOT OF SANYA, OUR OWN NIGHT WITCH.
STILL...
I'M SURE HEIDEMARIE WILL BE FINE NOW.
......
YEAH.
AND ONCE THE TRUTH BEHIND THAT SILLY RUMOR GETS OUT, THEN PROBLEM SOLVED!
RIGHT.
HEY, DID YOU HEAR THAT RUMOR?
WHAT, THE ONE ABOUT THE GHOST WITCH?
NO, NOT THAT ONE! THAT ONE IS SO LAST WEEK!
I'M TALKING ABOUT THE ONE ABOUT THE *NAKED NYMPH* WANDERING THIS BASE!
FREEZE

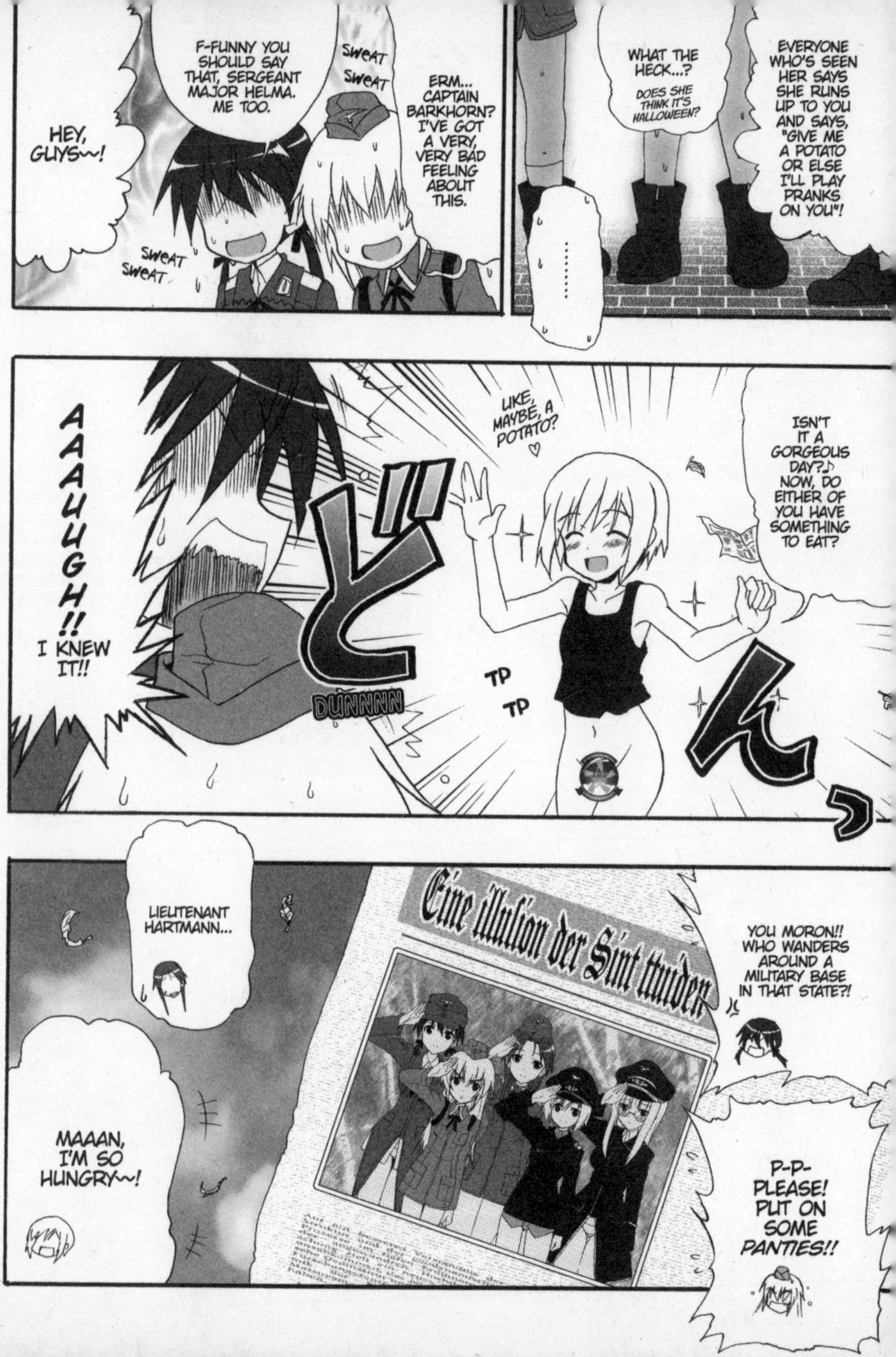
EVERYONE WHO'S SEEN HER SAYS SHE RUNS UP TO YOU AND SAYS, "GIVE ME A POTATO OR ELSE I'LL PLAY PRANKS ON YOU"!
WHAT THE HECK...?
DOES SHE THINK IT'S HALLOWEEN?
......
SWEAT SWEAT
ERM... CAPTAIN BARKHORN? I'VE GOT A VERY, VERY BAD FEELING ABOUT THIS.
F-FUNNY YOU SHOULD SAY THAT, SERGEANT MAJOR HELMA. ME TOO.
HEY, GUYS~~!
SWEAT SWEAT
ISN'T IT A GORGEOUS DAY?♪ NOW, DO EITHER OF YOU HAVE SOMETHING TO EAT?
LIKE, MAYBE, A POTATO?♡
ん
TP TP
ど
DUNNNNN
AAAAUUGH!! I KNEW IT!!
YOU MORON!! WHO WANDERS AROUND A MILITARY BASE IN THAT STATE?!
P-P-PLEASE! PUT ON SOME PANTIES!!
Eine illusion der Sint ttuden
LIEUTENANT HARTMANN...
MAAAN, I'M SO HUNGRY~~!

WITCHES GRAFFITI

Shimada Humikane &
Projekt Kagonish
illustrated by
Kyougoku Shin

Mio Sakamoto

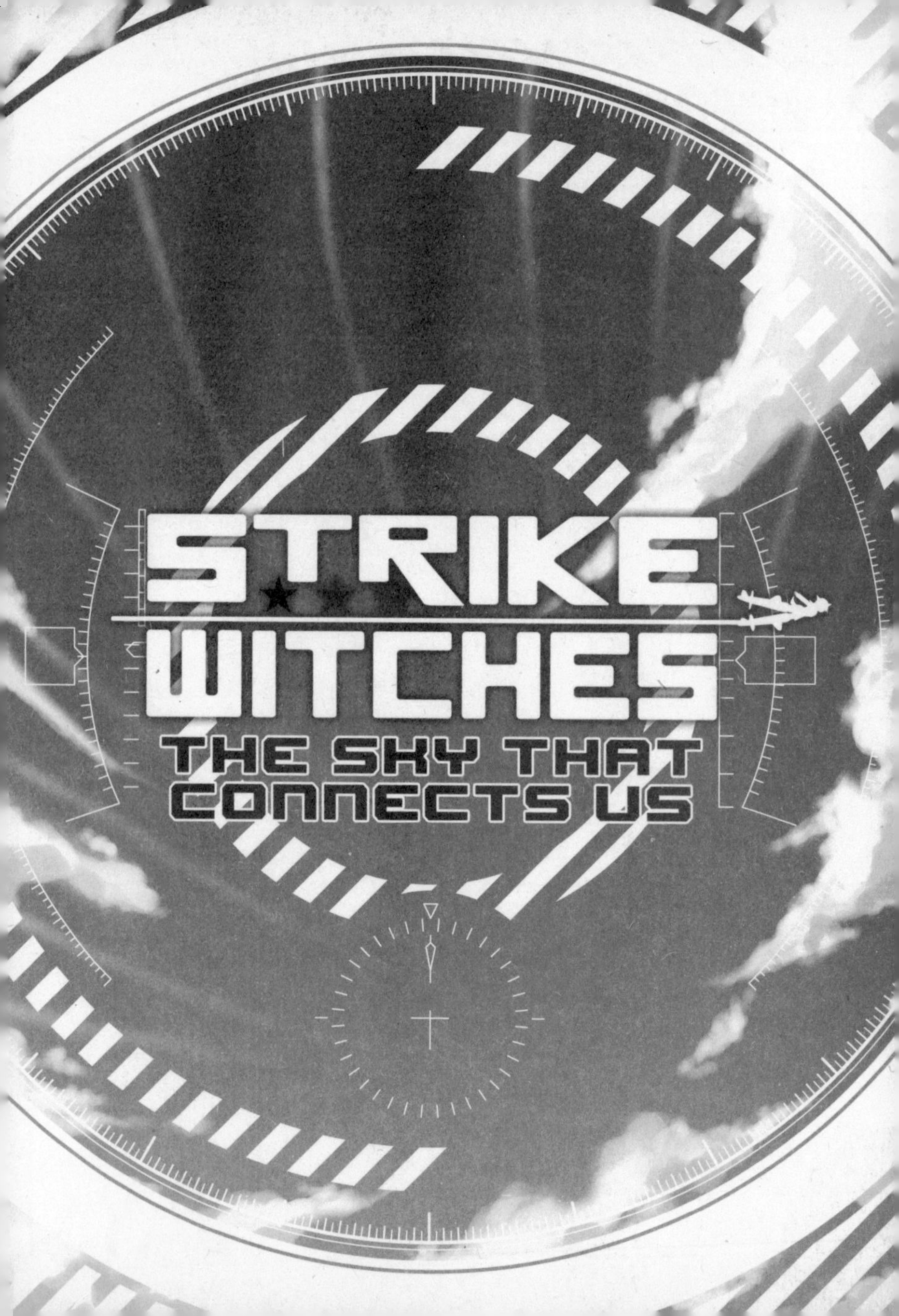
STRIKE WITCHES
THE SKY THAT CONNECTS US

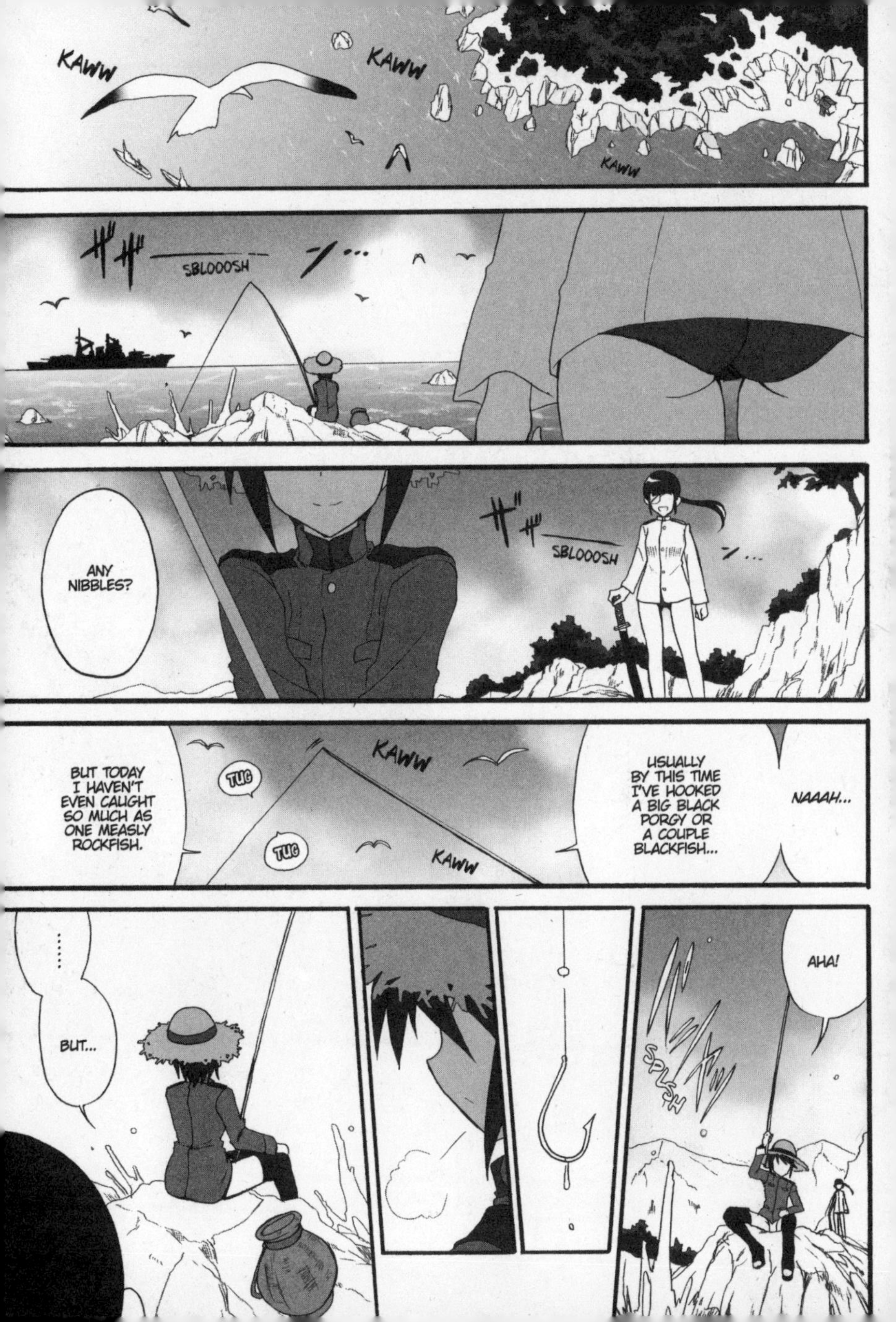
KAWW
KAWW
KAWW
SBLOOOSH
SBLOOOSH
ANY NIBBLES?
NAAAH...
USUALLY BY THIS TIME I'VE HOOKED A BIG BLACK PORGY OR A COUPLE BLACKFISH...
KAWW
TUG
TUG
KAWW
BUT TODAY I HAVEN'T EVEN CAUGHT SO MUCH AS ONE MEASLY ROCKFISH.
AHA!
SPLSH
......
BUT...

CHAPTER 7

A BATTLE IN FUSO

STRIKE WITCHES
THE SKY THAT CONNECTS US

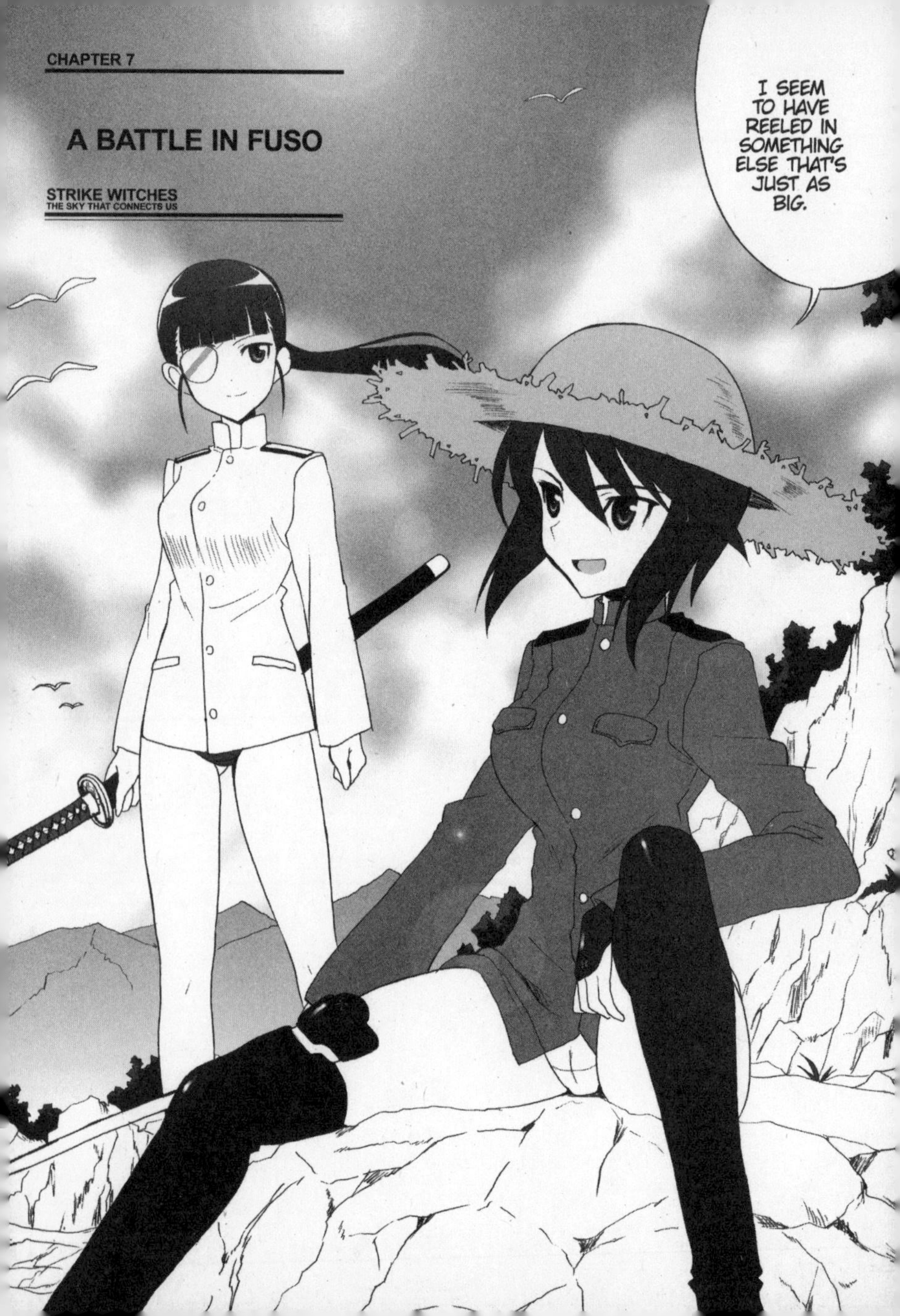
I SEEM TO HAVE REELED IN SOMETHING ELSE THAT'S JUST AS BIG.

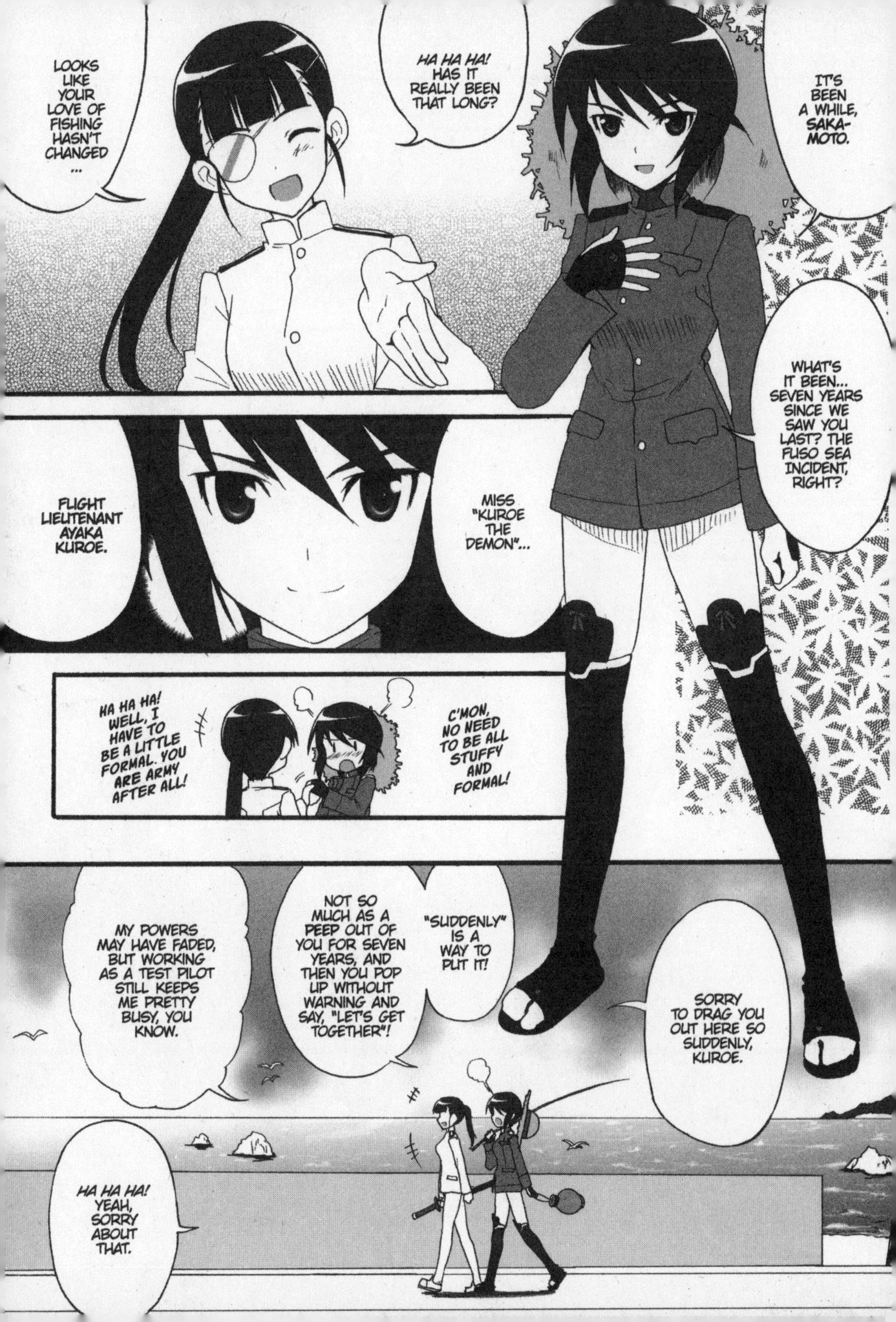
IT'S BEEN A WHILE, SAKAMOTO.
HA HA HA! HAS IT REALLY BEEN THAT LONG?
LOOKS LIKE YOUR LOVE OF FISHING HASN'T CHANGED ...
WHAT'S IT BEEN... SEVEN YEARS SINCE WE SAW YOU LAST? THE FUSO SEA INCIDENT, RIGHT?
MISS "KUROE THE DEMON"...
FLIGHT LIEUTENANT AYAKA KUROE.
C'MON, NO NEED TO BE ALL STUFFY AND FORMAL!
HA HA HA! WELL, I HAVE TO BE A LITTLE FORMAL. YOU ARE ARMY AFTER ALL!
SORRY TO DRAG YOU OUT HERE SO SUDDENLY, KUROE.
"SUDDENLY" IS A WAY TO PUT IT!
NOT SO MUCH AS A PEEP OUT OF YOU FOR SEVEN YEARS, AND THEN YOU POP UP WITHOUT WARNING AND SAY, "LET'S GET TOGETHER"!
MY POWERS MAY HAVE FADED, BUT WORKING AS A TEST PILOT STILL KEEPS ME PRETTY BUSY, YOU KNOW.
HA HA HA! YEAH, SORRY ABOUT THAT.

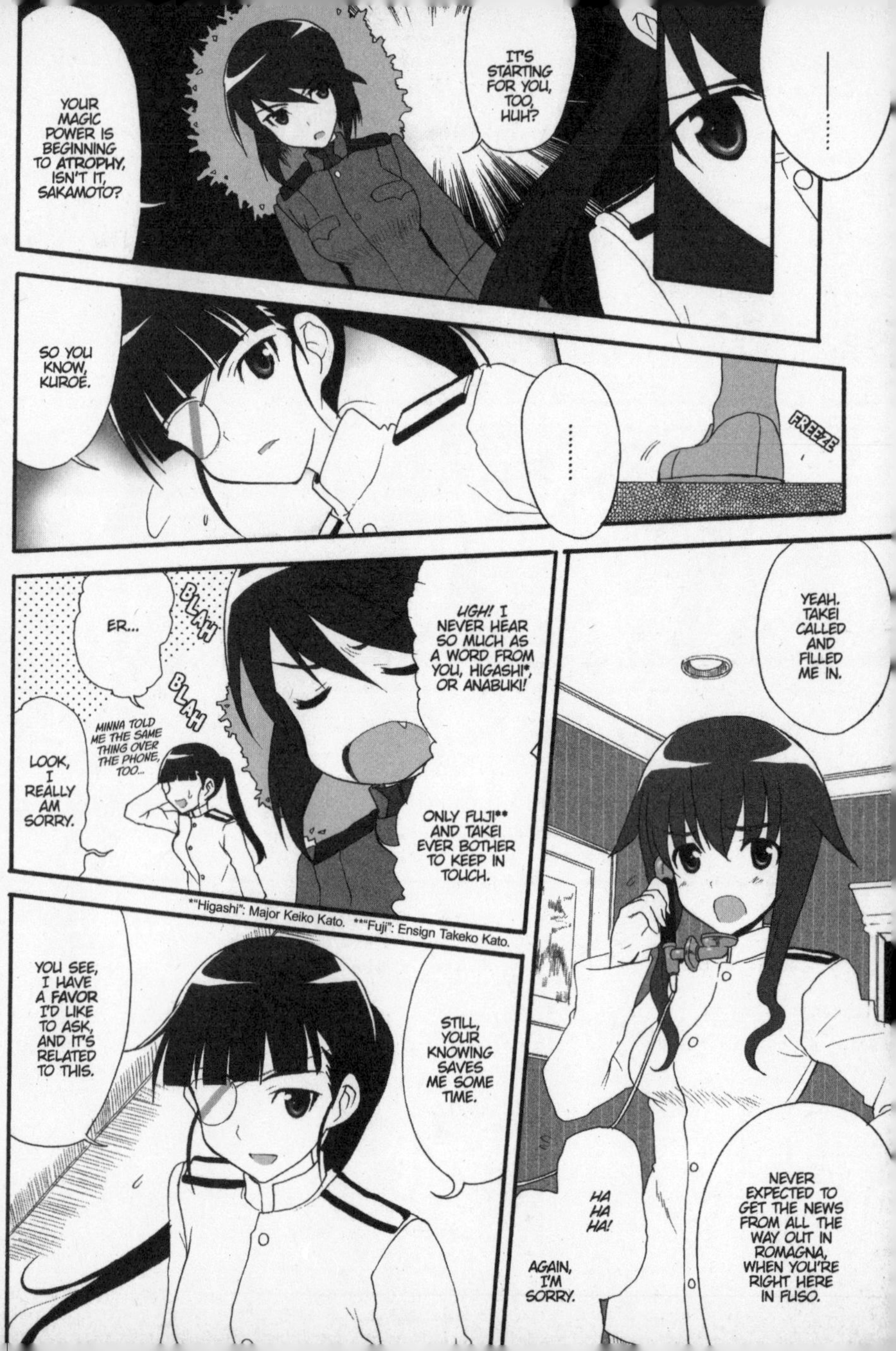
……
IT'S STARTING FOR YOU, TOO, HUH?
YOUR MAGIC POWER IS BEGINNING TO ATROPHY, ISN'T IT, SAKAMOTO?
FREEZE
……
SO YOU KNOW, KUROE.
YEAH. TAKEI CALLED AND FILLED ME IN.
NEVER EXPECTED TO GET THE NEWS FROM ALL THE WAY OUT IN ROMAGNA, WHEN YOU'RE RIGHT HERE IN FUSO.
HA HA HA!
AGAIN, I'M SORRY.
UGH! I NEVER HEAR SO MUCH AS A WORD FROM YOU, HIGASHI*, OR ANABUKI!
ONLY FUJI** AND TAKEI EVER BOTHER TO KEEP IN TOUCH.
BLAH
BLAH
ER...
MINNA TOLD ME THE SAME THING OVER THE PHONE, TOO...
LOOK, I REALLY AM SORRY.
STILL, YOUR KNOWING SAVES ME SOME TIME.
YOU SEE, I HAVE A FAVOR I'D LIKE TO ASK, AND IT'S RELATED TO THIS.

*"Higashi": Major Keiko Kato. **"Fuji": Ensign Takeko Kato.

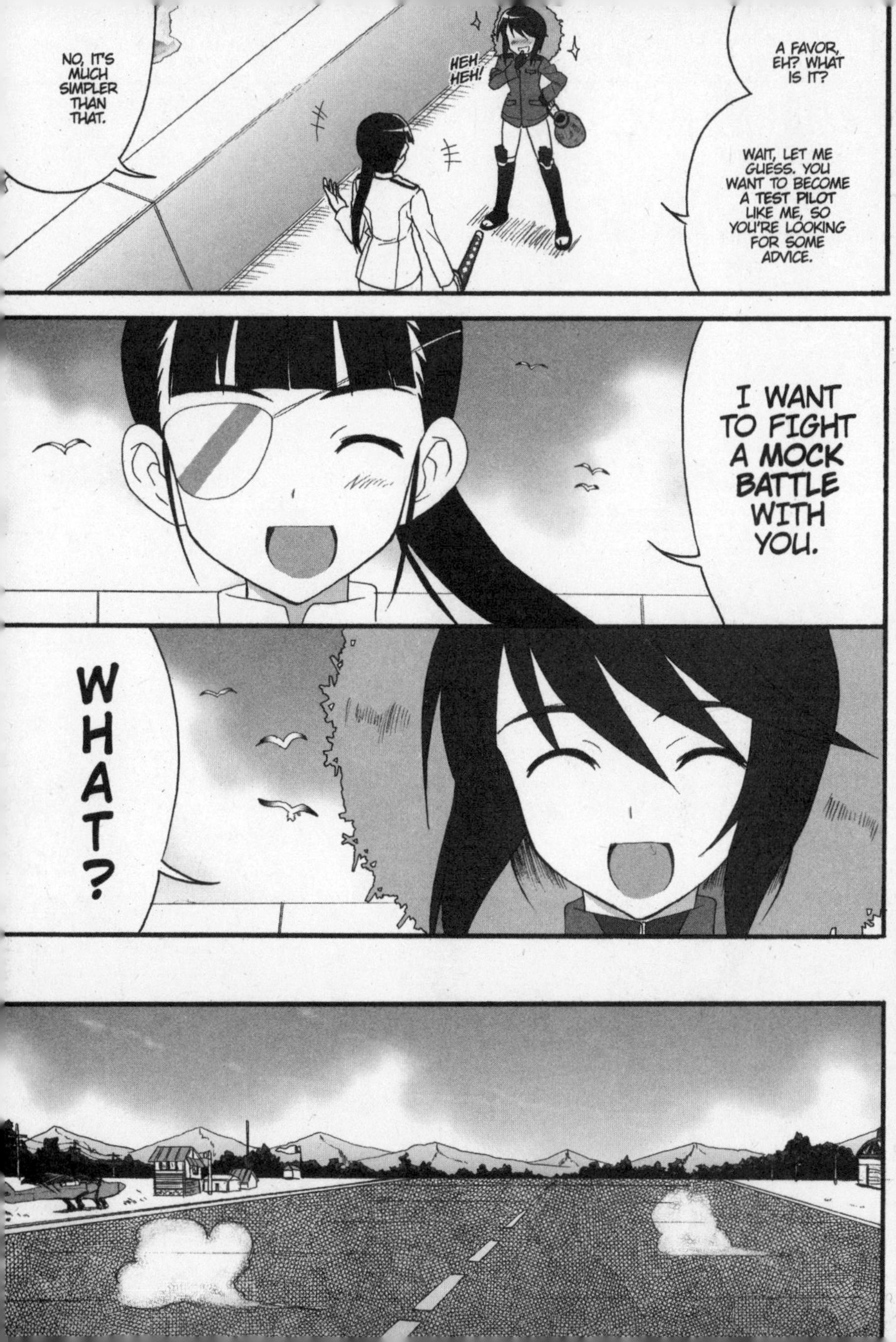
A FAVOR, EH? WHAT IS IT?
HEH HEH!
WAIT, LET ME GUESS. YOU WANT TO BECOME A TEST PILOT LIKE ME, SO YOU'RE LOOKING FOR SOME ADVICE.
NO, IT'S MUCH SIMPLER THAN THAT.
I WANT TO FIGHT A MOCK BATTLE WITH YOU.
WHAT?

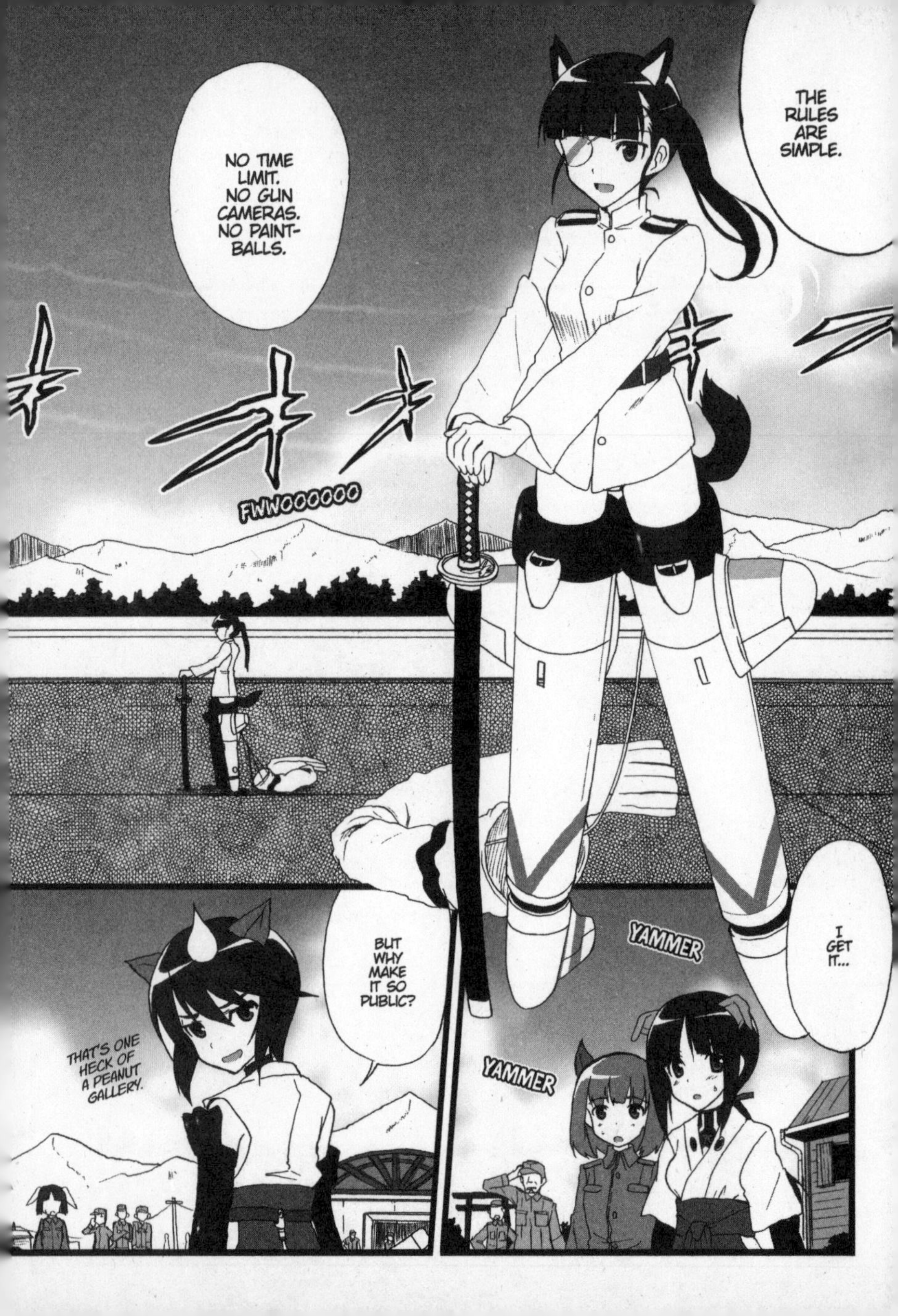
THE RULES ARE SIMPLE.
NO TIME LIMIT. NO GUN CAMERAS. NO PAINT-BALLS.
FWWOOOOOO
YAMMER
I GET IT...
YAMMER
BUT WHY MAKE IT SO PUBLIC?
THAT'S ONE HECK OF A PEANUT GALLERY.

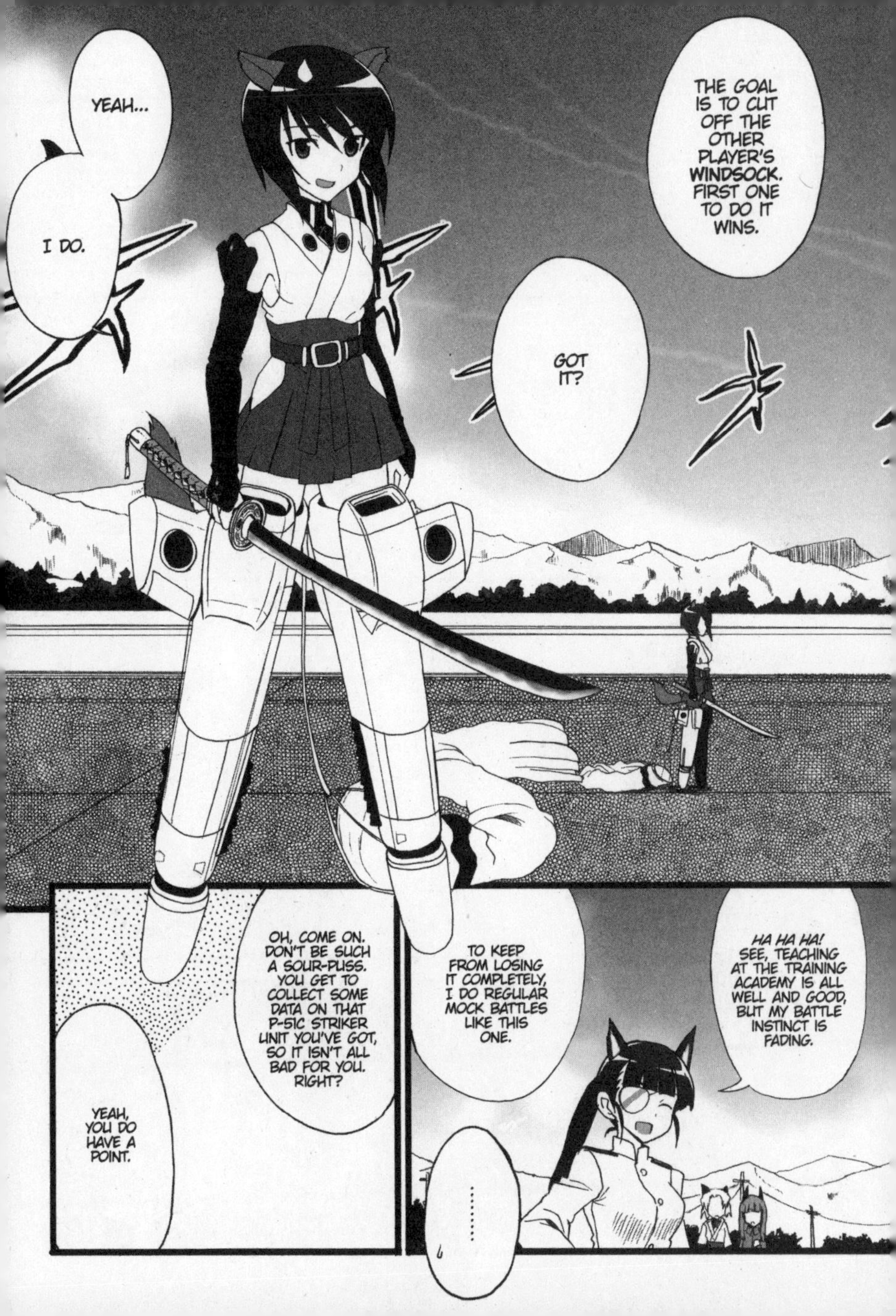
THE GOAL IS TO CUT OFF THE OTHER PLAYER'S WINDSOCK. FIRST ONE TO DO IT WINS.
GOT IT?
YEAH...
I DO.
HA HA HA! SEE, TEACHING AT THE TRAINING ACADEMY IS ALL WELL AND GOOD, BUT MY BATTLE INSTINCT IS FADING.
TO KEEP FROM LOSING IT COMPLETELY, I DO REGULAR MOCK BATTLES LIKE THIS ONE.
......
OH, COME ON. DON'T BE SUCH A SOUR-PUSS. YOU GET TO COLLECT SOME DATA ON THAT P-51C STRIKER UNIT YOU'VE GOT, SO IT ISN'T ALL BAD FOR YOU. RIGHT?
YEAH, YOU DO HAVE A POINT.

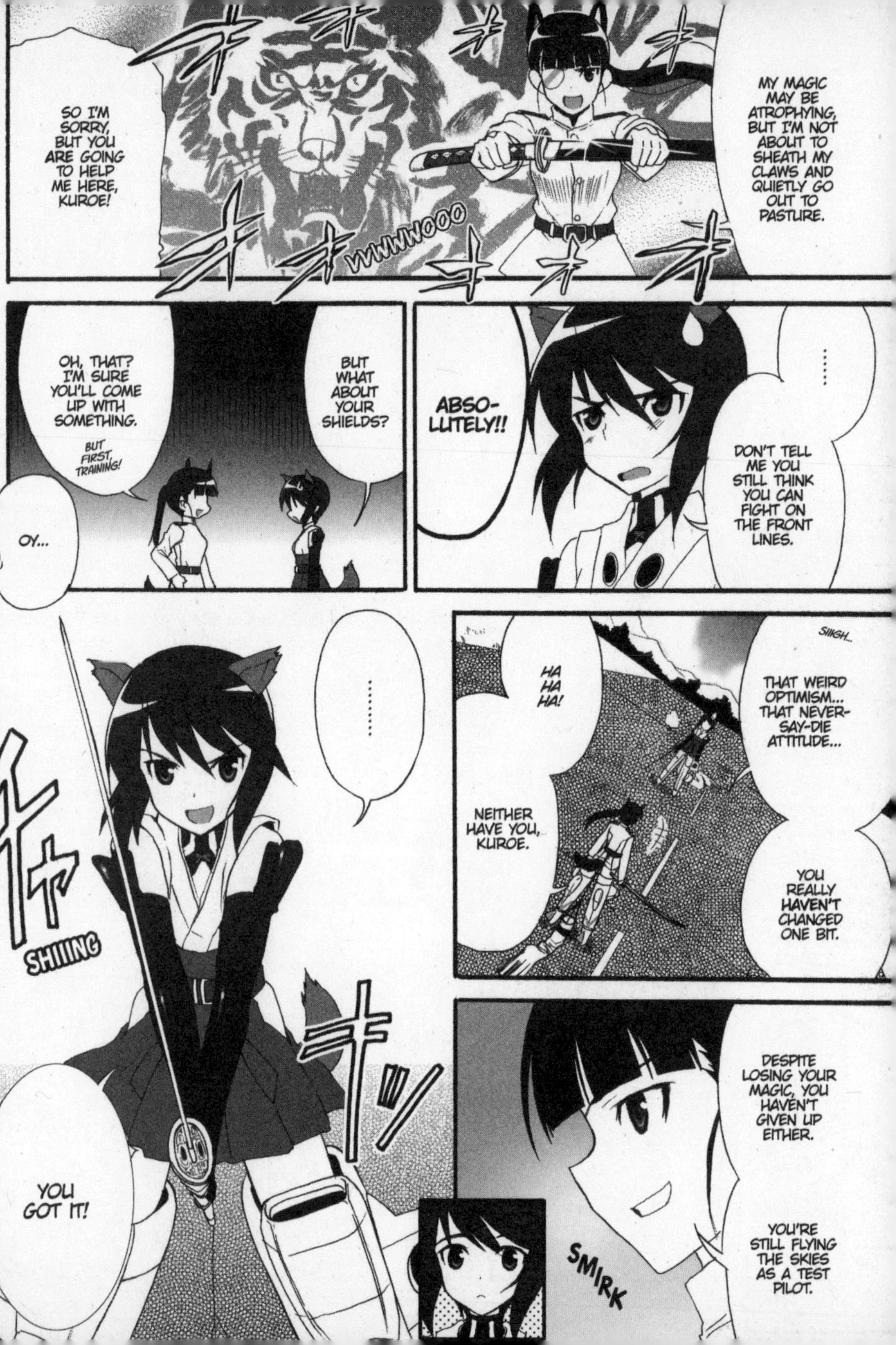
MY MAGIC MAY BE ATROPHYING, BUT I'M NOT ABOUT TO SHEATH MY CLAWS AND QUIETLY GO OUT TO PASTURE.
SO I'M SORRY, BUT YOU ARE GOING TO HELP ME HERE, KUROE!
WWWWOOO
......
DON'T TELL ME YOU STILL THINK YOU CAN FIGHT ON THE FRONT LINES.
ABSO-LUTELY!!
BUT WHAT ABOUT YOUR SHIELDS?
OH, THAT? I'M SURE YOU'LL COME UP WITH SOMETHING.
BUT FIRST, TRAINING!
OY...
SIIIGH...
THAT WEIRD OPTIMISM... THAT NEVER-SAY-DIE ATTITUDE...
YOU REALLY HAVEN'T CHANGED ONE BIT.
HA HA HA!
NEITHER HAVE YOU, KUROE.
DESPITE LOSING YOUR MAGIC, YOU HAVEN'T GIVEN UP EITHER.
YOU'RE STILL FLYING THE SKIES AS A TEST PILOT.
SMIRK
......
SHIIING
YOU GOT IT!

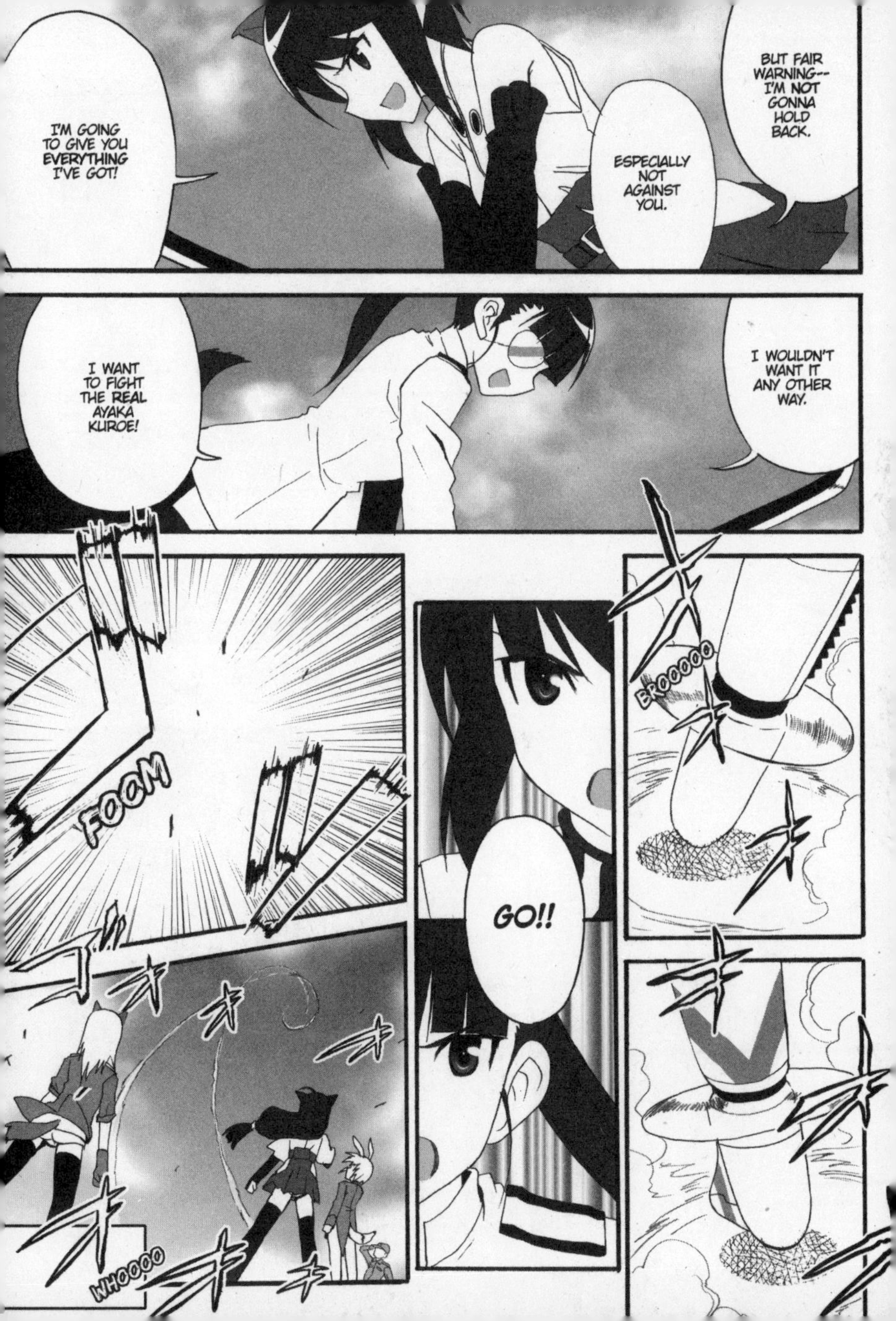
BUT FAIR WARNING-- I'M NOT GONNA HOLD BACK.
ESPECIALLY NOT AGAINST YOU.
I'M GOING TO GIVE YOU EVERYTHING I'VE GOT!
I WOULDN'T WANT IT ANY OTHER WAY.
I WANT TO FIGHT THE REAL AYAKA KUROE!
BROOOOO
GO!!
FOOM
WHOOOO

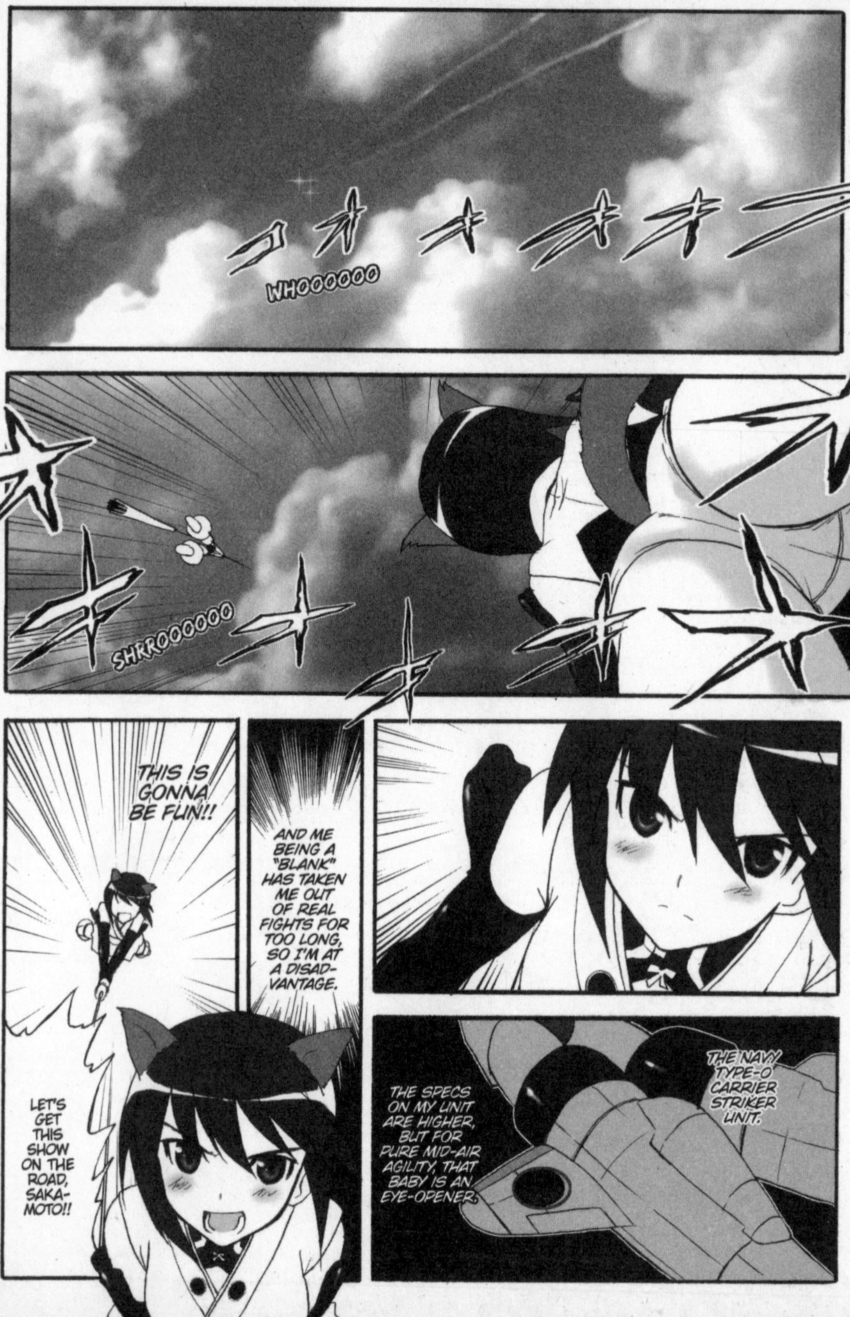
WHOOOOOO
SHRROOOOOO
THE NAVY TYPE-0 CARRIER STRIKER UNIT.
THE SPECS ON MY UNIT ARE HIGHER, BUT FOR PURE MID-AIR AGILITY, THAT BABY IS AN EYE-OPENER.
AND ME BEING A "BLANK" HAS TAKEN ME OUT OF REAL FIGHTS FOR TOO LONG, SO I'M AT A DISAD-VANTAGE.
THIS IS GONNA BE FUN!!
LET'S GET THIS SHOW ON THE ROAD, SAKA-MOTO!!

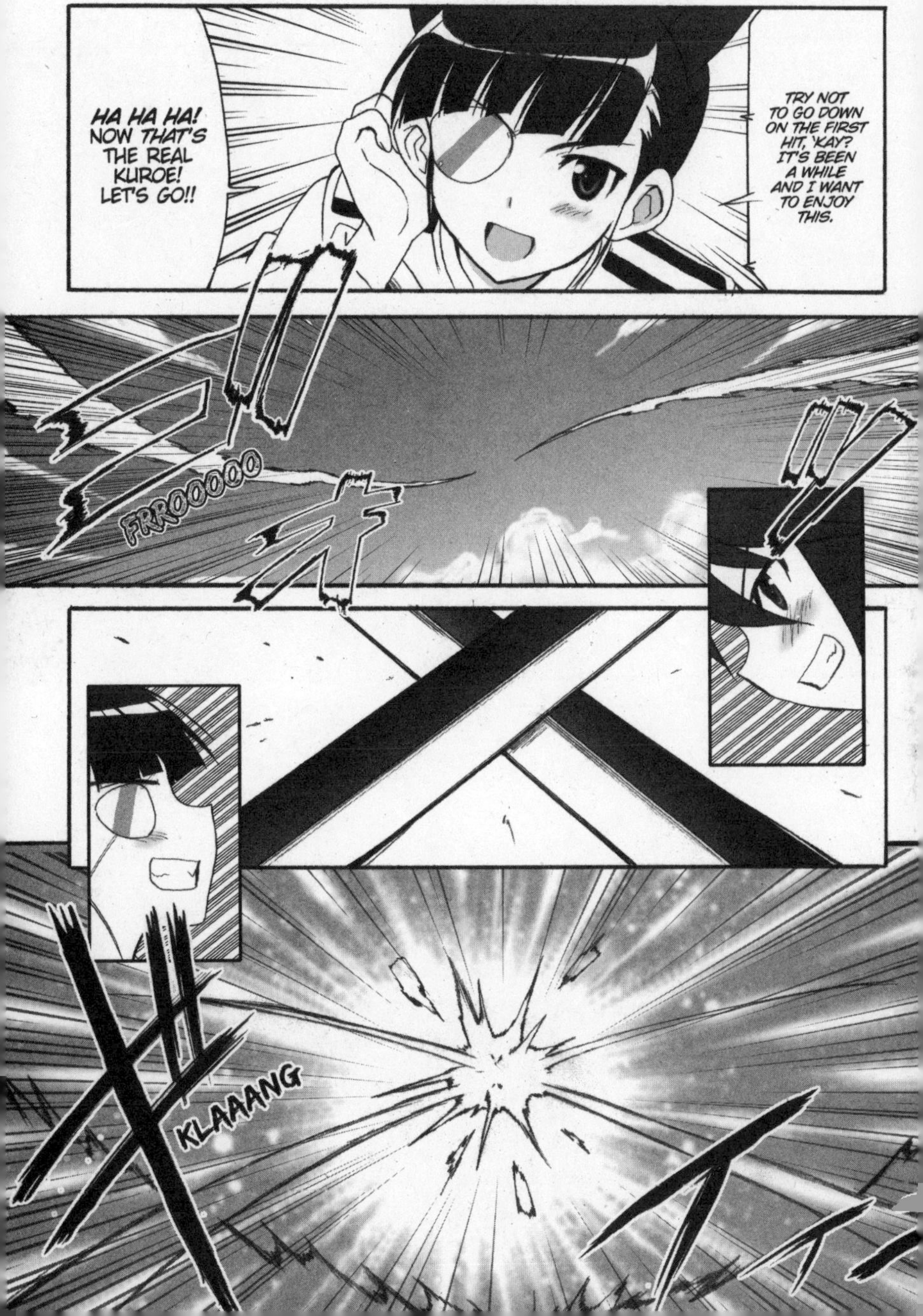
TRY NOT TO GO DOWN ON THE FIRST HIT, 'KAY? IT'S BEEN A WHILE AND I WANT TO ENJOY THIS.
HA HA HA! NOW THAT'S THE REAL KUROE! LET'S GO!!
FRROOOOO
KLAAANG

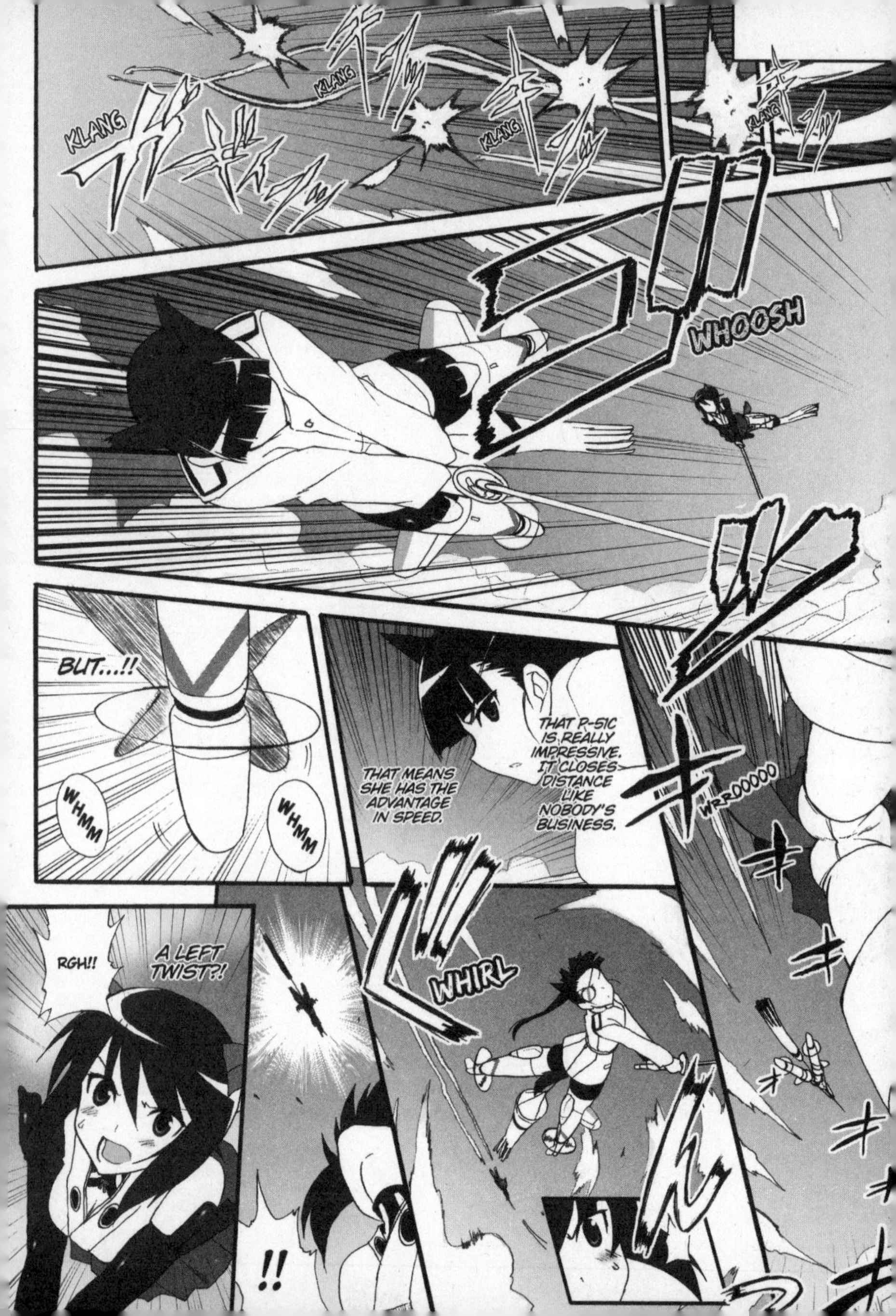
KLANG
KLANG
KLANG
KLANG
KLANG
WHOOSH
WRROOOOO
THAT P-51C IS REALLY IMPRESSIVE. IT CLOSES DISTANCE LIKE NOBODY'S BUSINESS.
THAT MEANS SHE HAS THE ADVANTAGE IN SPEED.
BUT...!!
WHMM
WHMM
WHIRL
!!
A LEFT TWIST?!
RGH!!

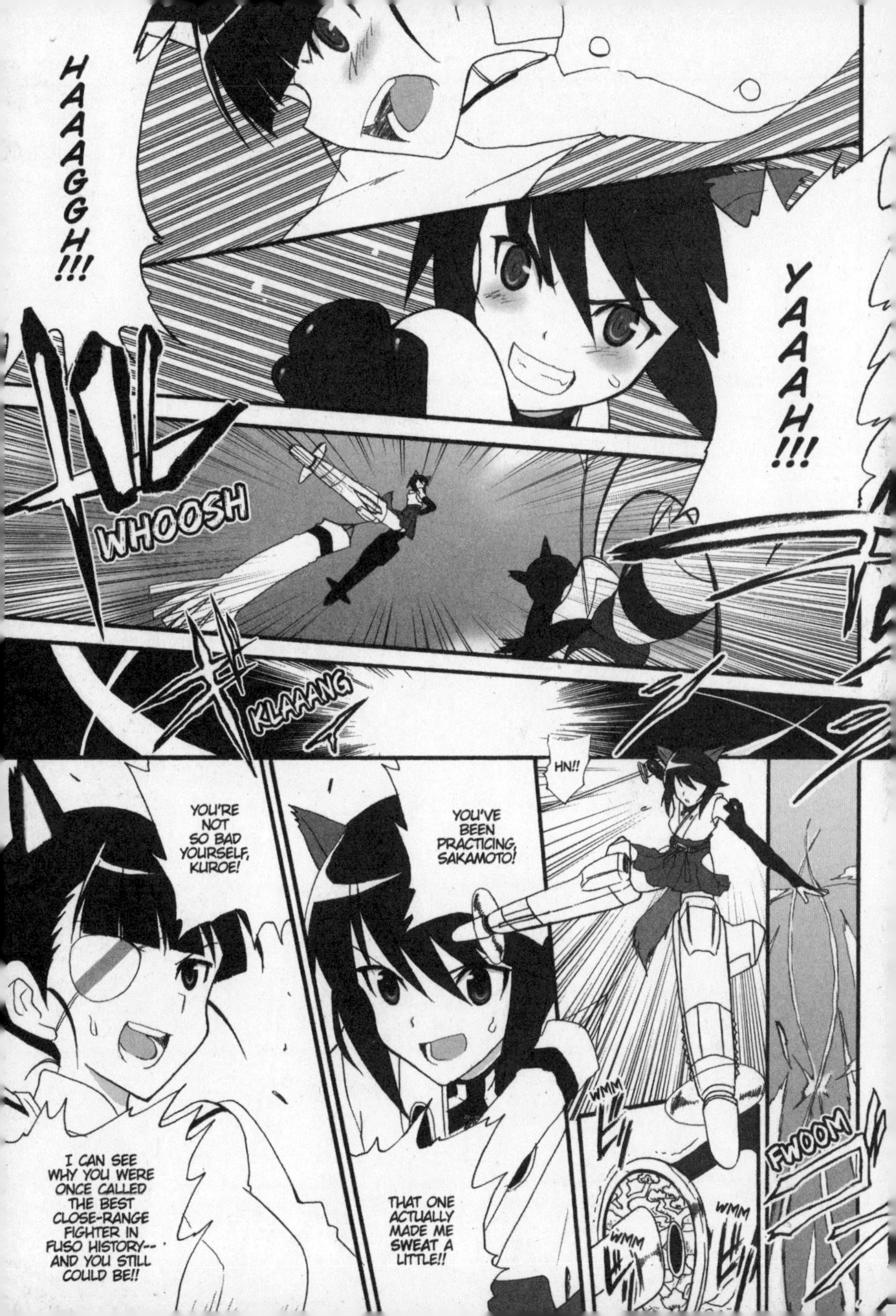
HAAAAGGH!!!
YAAAAH!!!
WHOOSH
KLAAANG
HN!!
WMM
FWOOM
WMM
WMM
YOU'VE BEEN PRACTICING, SAKAMOTO!
THAT ONE ACTUALLY MADE ME SWEAT A LITTLE!!
YOU'RE NOT SO BAD YOURSELF, KUROE!
I CAN SEE WHY YOU WERE ONCE CALLED THE BEST CLOSE-RANGE FIGHTER IN FUSO HISTORY-- AND YOU STILL COULD BE!!

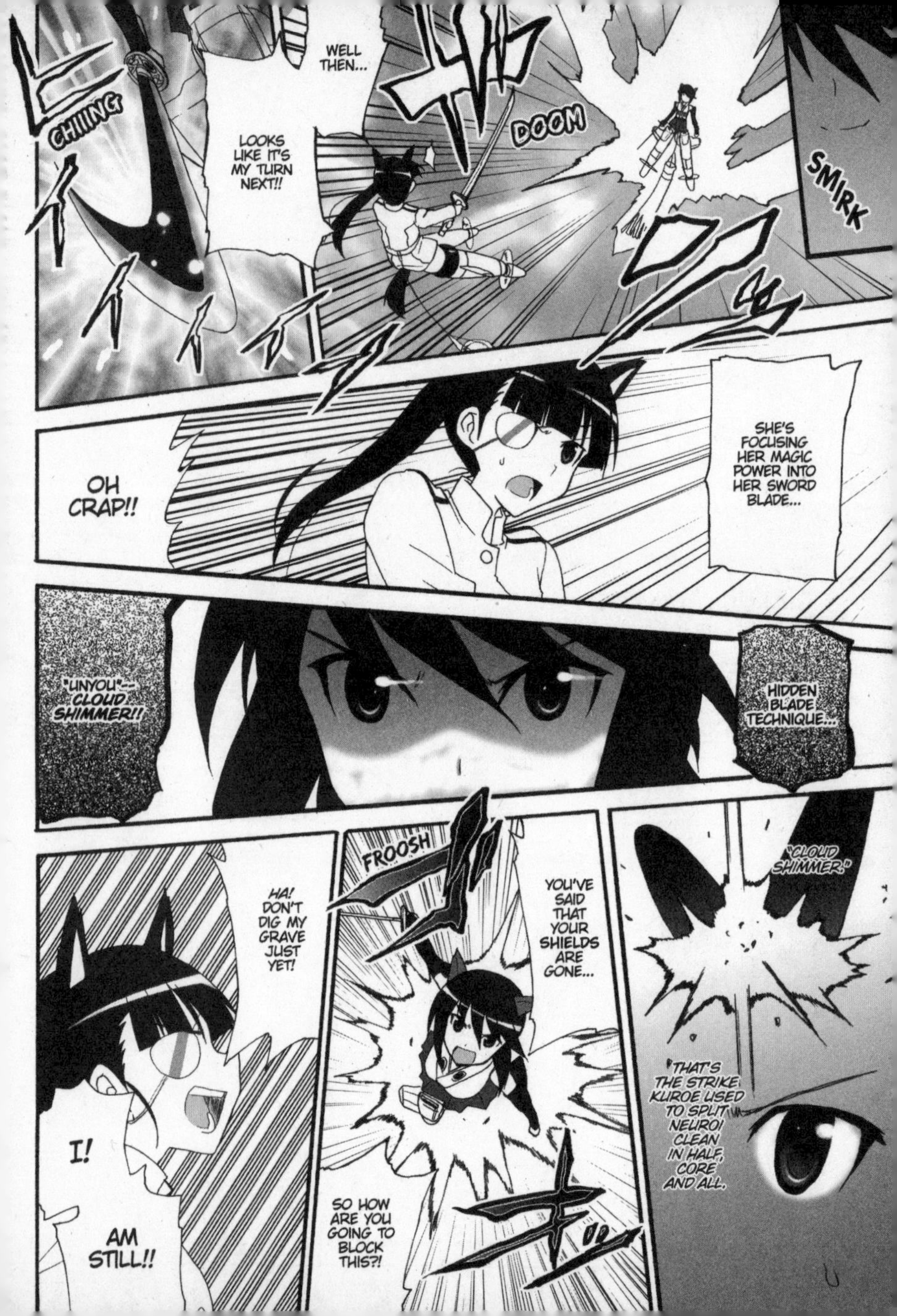
SMIRK
WELL THEN...
LOOKS LIKE IT'S MY TURN NEXT!!
DOOM
CHIIING
SHE'S FOCUSING HER MAGIC POWER INTO HER SWORD BLADE...
OH CRAP!!
HIDDEN BLADE TECHNIQUE...
"UNYOU"-- CLOUD SHIMMER!!
"CLOUD SHIMMER."
THAT'S THE STRIKE KUROE USED TO SPLIT NEUROI CLEAN IN HALF, CORE AND ALL.
YOU'VE SAID THAT YOUR SHIELDS ARE GONE...
FROOSH
SO HOW ARE YOU GOING TO BLOCK THIS?!
HA! DON'T DIG MY GRAVE JUST YET!
I!
AM STILL!!

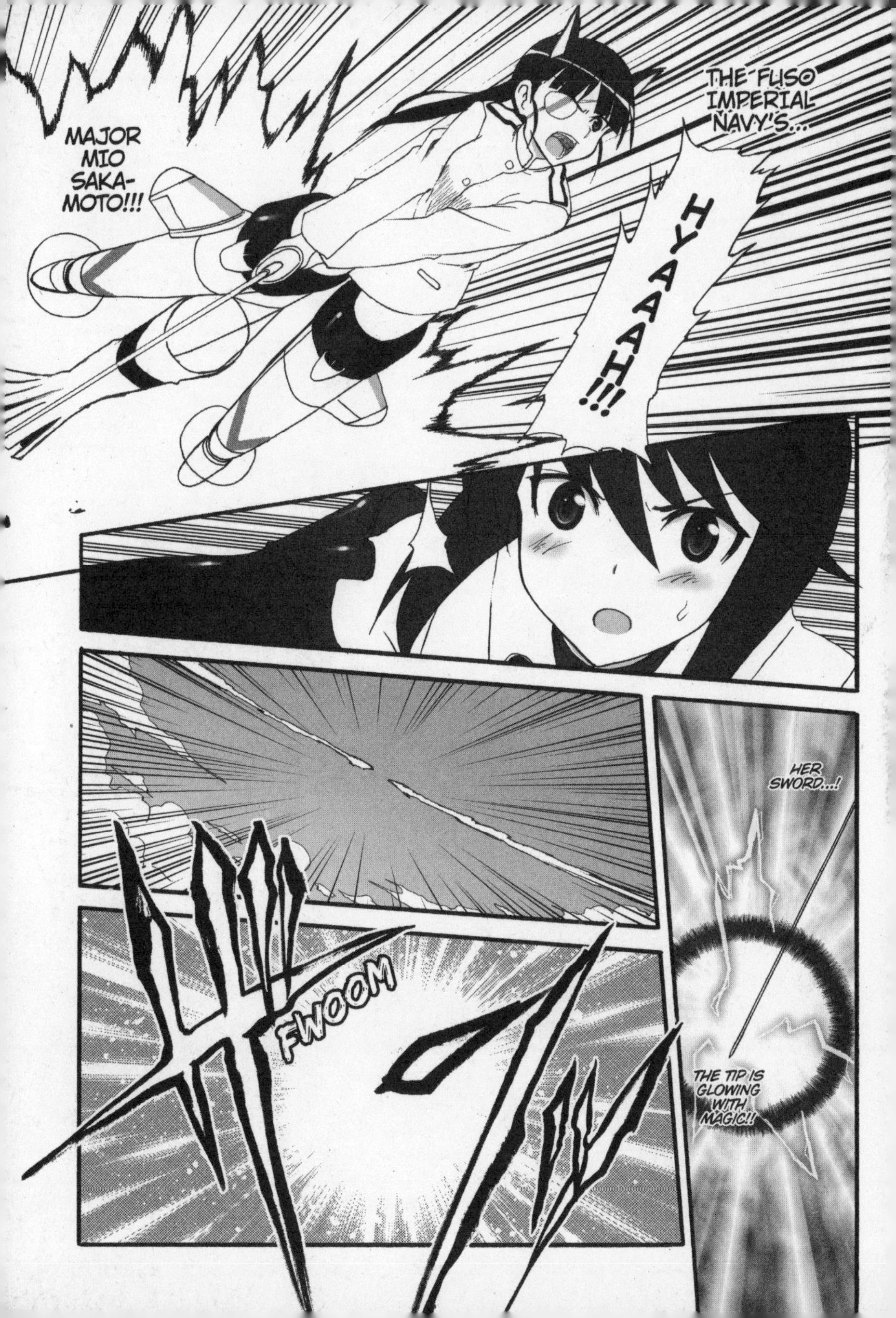

THE FUSO IMPERIAL NAVY'S...
MAJOR MIO SAKA-MOTO!!!
HYAAAAH!!!
HER SWORD...!
THE TIP IS GLOWING WITH MAGIC!!
FWOOM

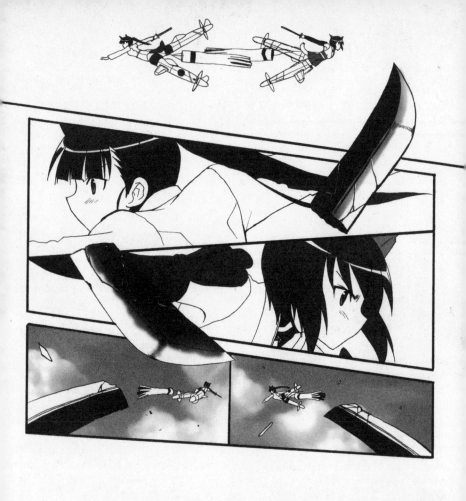

WOW.
I DIDN'T
KNOW YOU'D
LEARNED
CLOUD
SHIMMER.

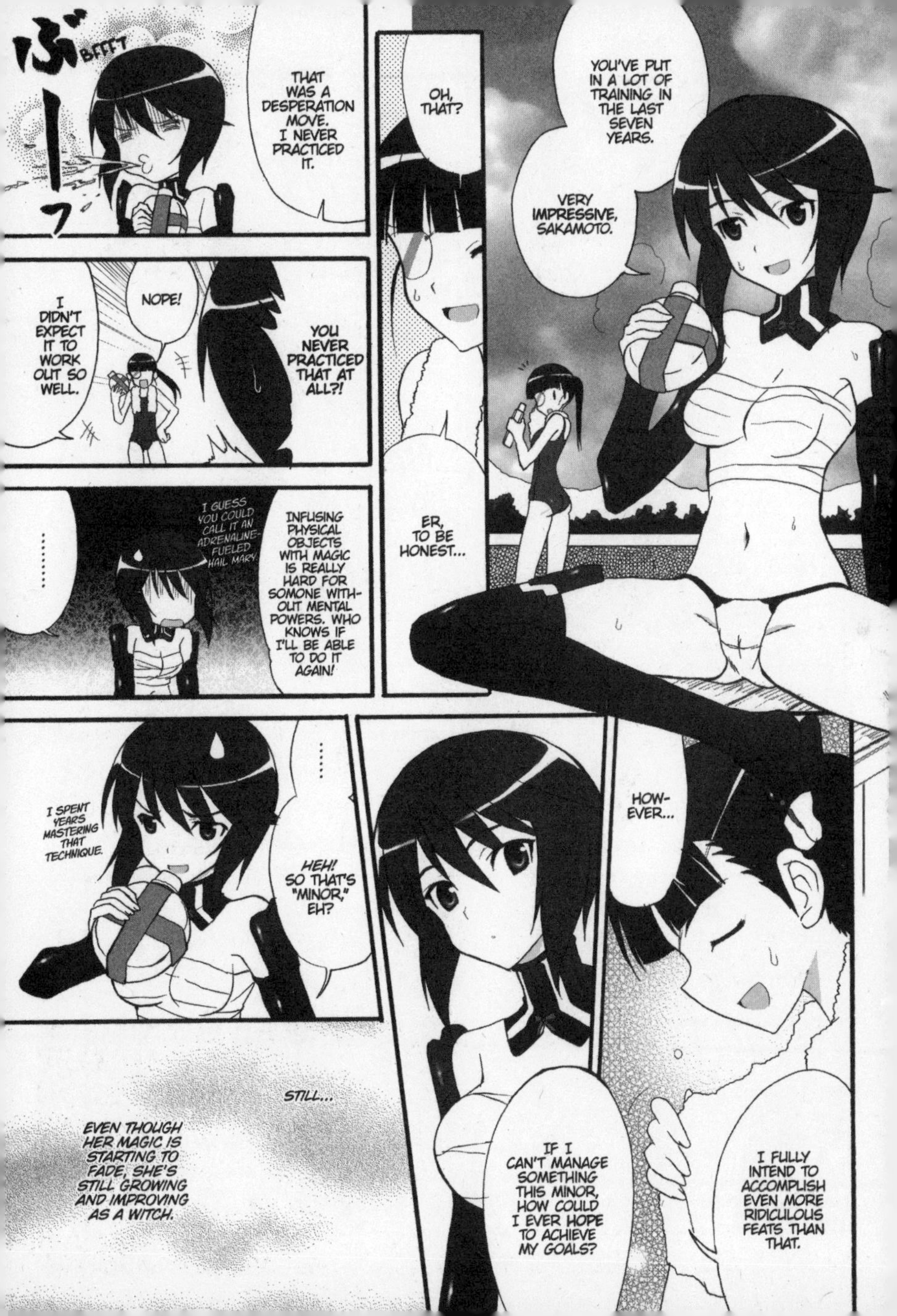
VERY IMPRESSIVE, SAKAMOTO.
YOU'VE PUT IN A LOT OF TRAINING IN THE LAST SEVEN YEARS.
OH, THAT?
THAT WAS A DESPERATION MOVE. I NEVER PRACTICED IT.
ぶーっ
BFFFT
YOU NEVER PRACTICED THAT AT ALL?!
NOPE!
I DIDN'T EXPECT IT TO WORK OUT SO WELL.
ER, TO BE HONEST...
INFUSING PHYSICAL OBJECTS WITH MAGIC IS REALLY HARD FOR SOMONE WITH-OUT MENTAL POWERS. WHO KNOWS IF I'LL BE ABLE TO DO IT AGAIN!
I GUESS YOU COULD CALL IT AN ADRENALINE-FUELED HAIL MARY.
....
HOW-EVER...
IF I CAN'T MANAGE SOMETHING THIS MINOR, HOW COULD I EVER HOPE TO ACHIEVE MY GOALS?
I FULLY INTEND TO ACCOMPLISH EVEN MORE RIDICULOUS FEATS THAN THAT.
......
HEH! SO THAT'S "MINOR," EH?
I SPENT YEARS MASTERING THAT TECHNIQUE.
STILL...
EVEN THOUGH HER MAGIC IS STARTING TO FADE, SHE'S STILL GROWING AND IMPROVING AS A WITCH.

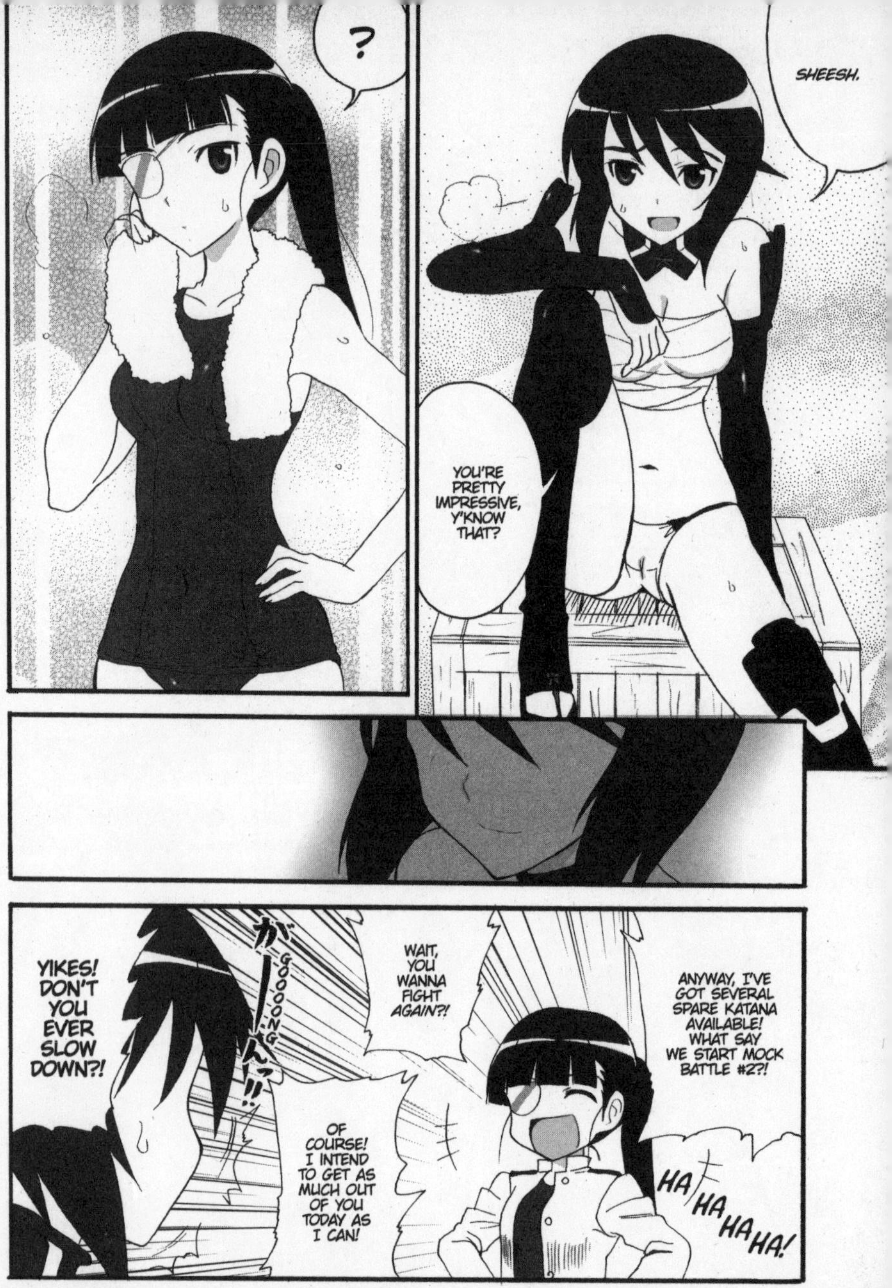
SHEESH.
YOU'RE PRETTY IMPRESSIVE, Y'KNOW THAT?
?
ANYWAY, I'VE GOT SEVERAL SPARE KATANA AVAILABLE! WHAT SAY WE START MOCK BATTLE #2?!
HA HA HA HA!
WAIT, YOU WANNA FIGHT AGAIN?!
OF COURSE! I INTEND TO GET AS MUCH OUT OF YOU TODAY AS I CAN!
GOOOOONG
YIKES! DON'T YOU EVER SLOW DOWN?!

WITCHES GRAFFITI

**Shimada Humikane &
Projekt Kagonish**
illustrated by
Kyougoku Shin

Junko Takei

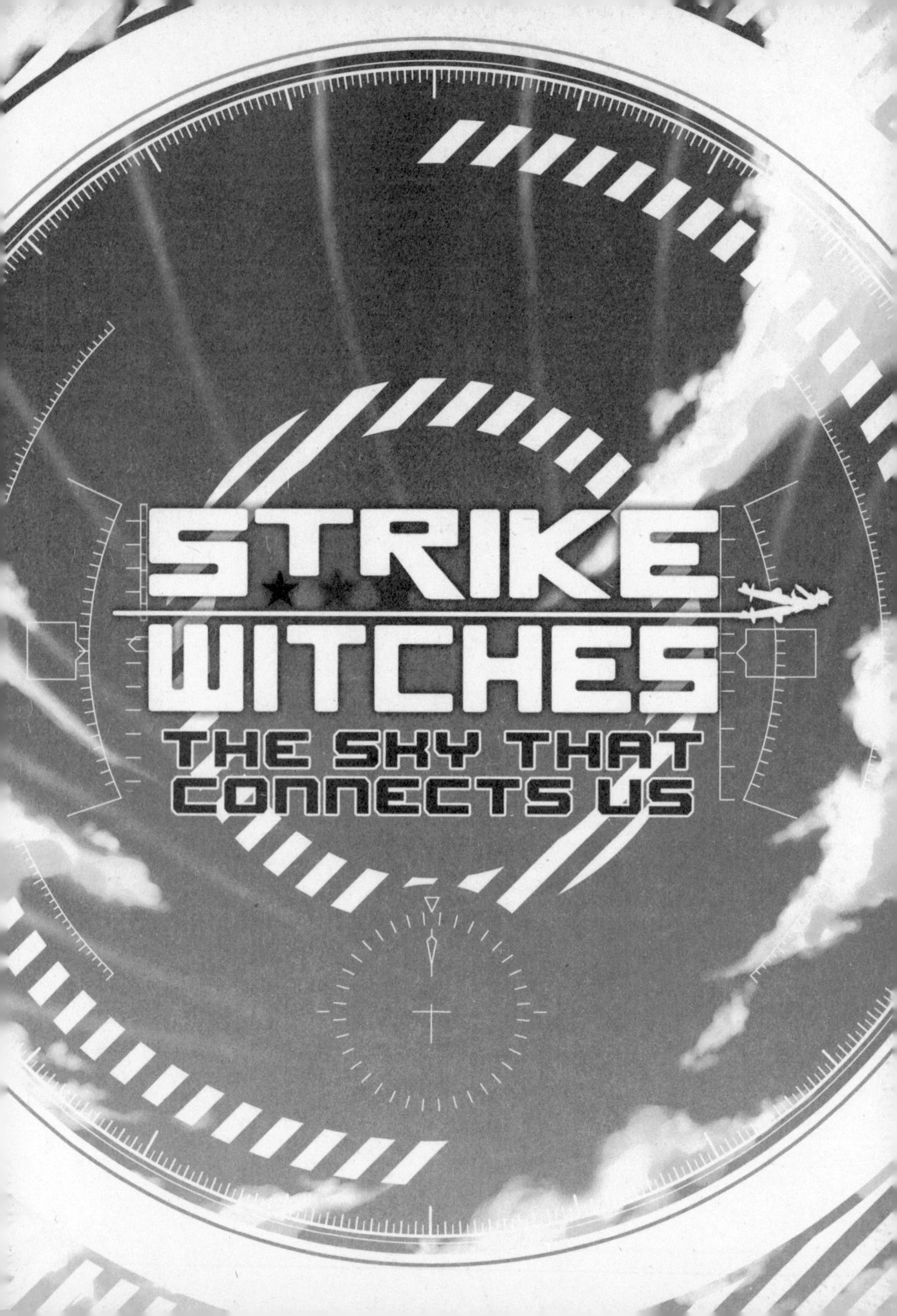
STRIKE WITCHES
THE SKY THAT CONNECTS US

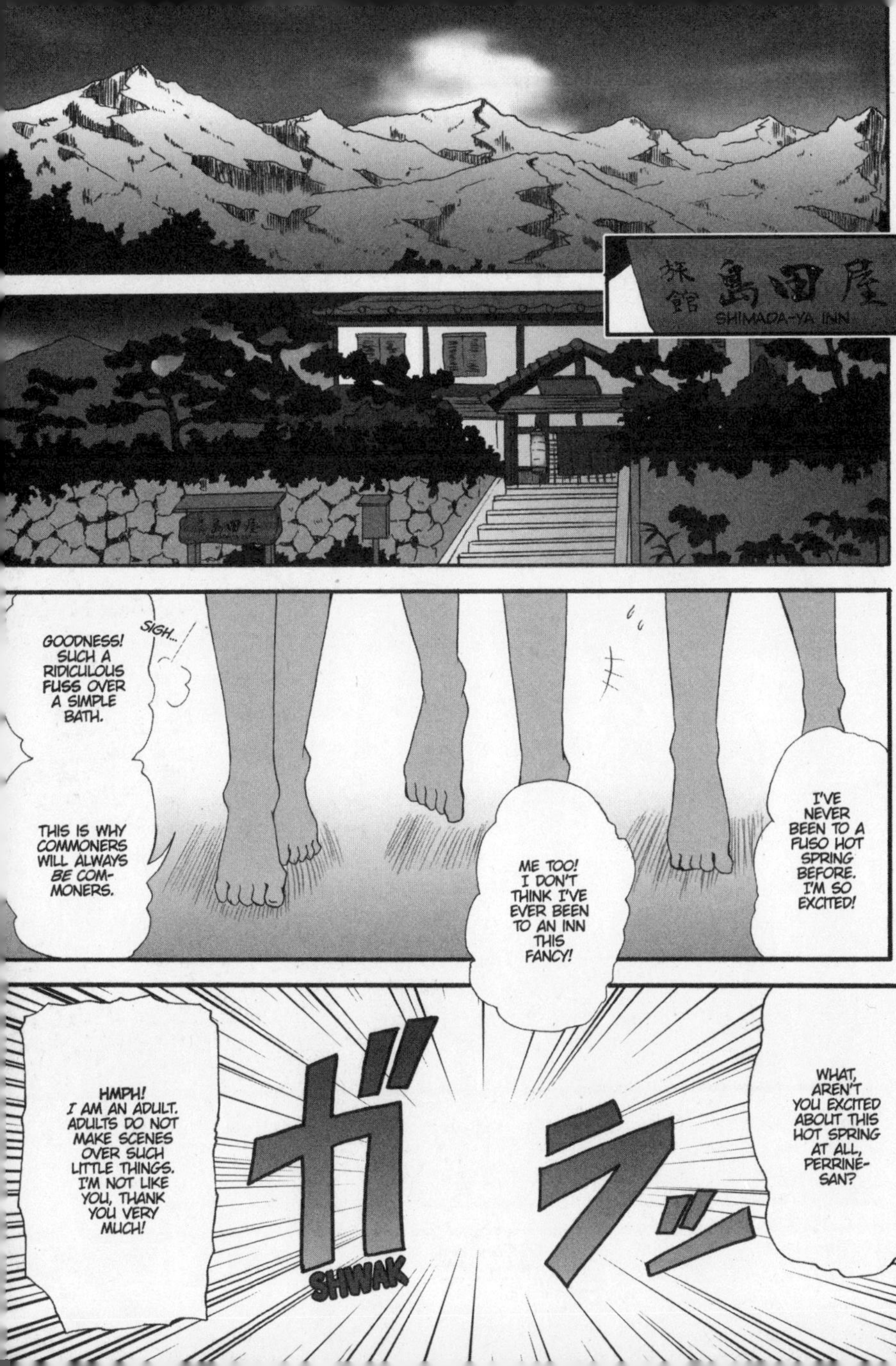
旅館 島田屋
SHIMADA-YA INN
I'VE NEVER BEEN TO A FUSO HOT SPRING BEFORE. I'M SO EXCITED!
ME TOO! I DON'T THINK I'VE EVER BEEN TO AN INN THIS FANCY!
SIGH...
GOODNESS! SUCH A RIDICULOUS FUSS OVER A SIMPLE BATH.
THIS IS WHY COMMONERS WILL ALWAYS *BE* COMMONERS.
WHAT, AREN'T YOU EXCITED ABOUT THIS HOT SPRING AT ALL, PERRINE-SAN?
ガラッ
SHWAK
HMPH! I AM AN ADULT. ADULTS DO NOT MAKE SCENES OVER SUCH LITTLE THINGS. I'M NOT LIKE YOU, THANK YOU VERY MUCH!

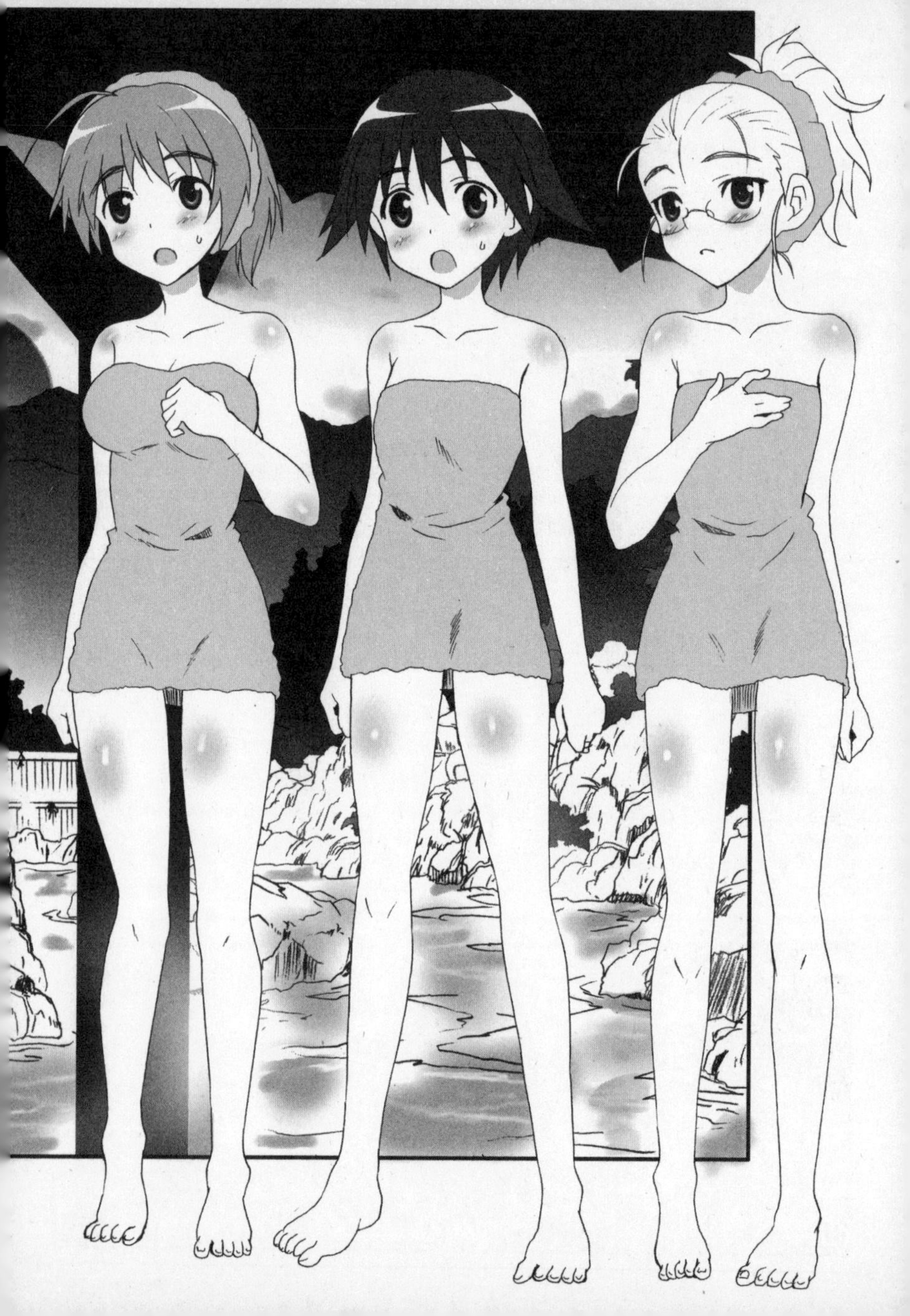

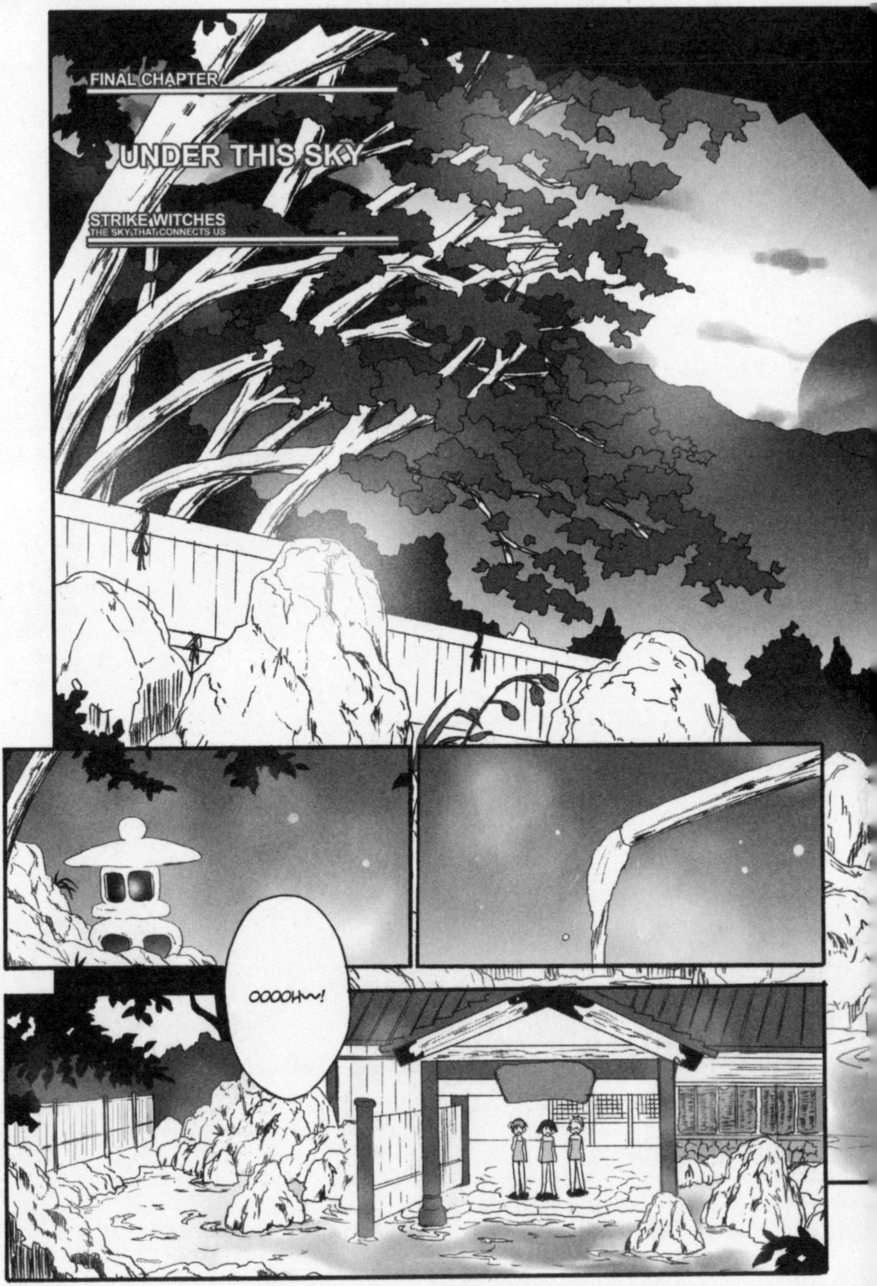
FINAL CHAPTER
UNDER THIS SKY
STRIKE WITCHES
THE SKY THAT CONNECTS US
OOOOH~!

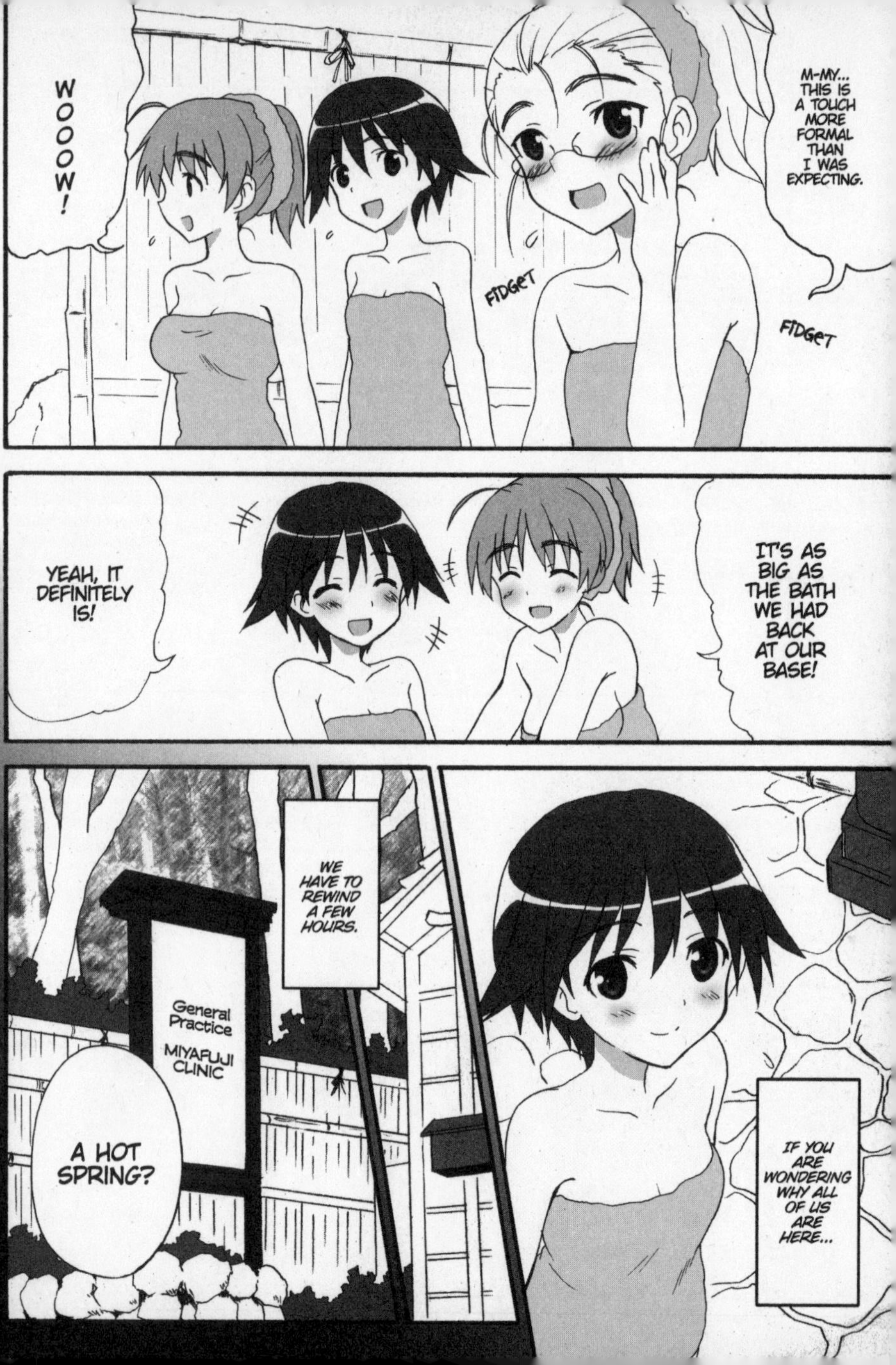
M-MY... THIS IS A TOUCH MORE FORMAL THAN I WAS EXPECTING.
WOOOOW!
FIDGET
FIDGET
IT'S AS BIG AS THE BATH WE HAD BACK AT OUR BASE!
YEAH, IT DEFINITELY IS!
IF YOU ARE WONDERING WHY ALL OF US ARE HERE...
WE HAVE TO REWIND A FEW HOURS.
General Practice
MIYAFUJI CLINIC
A HOT SPRING?

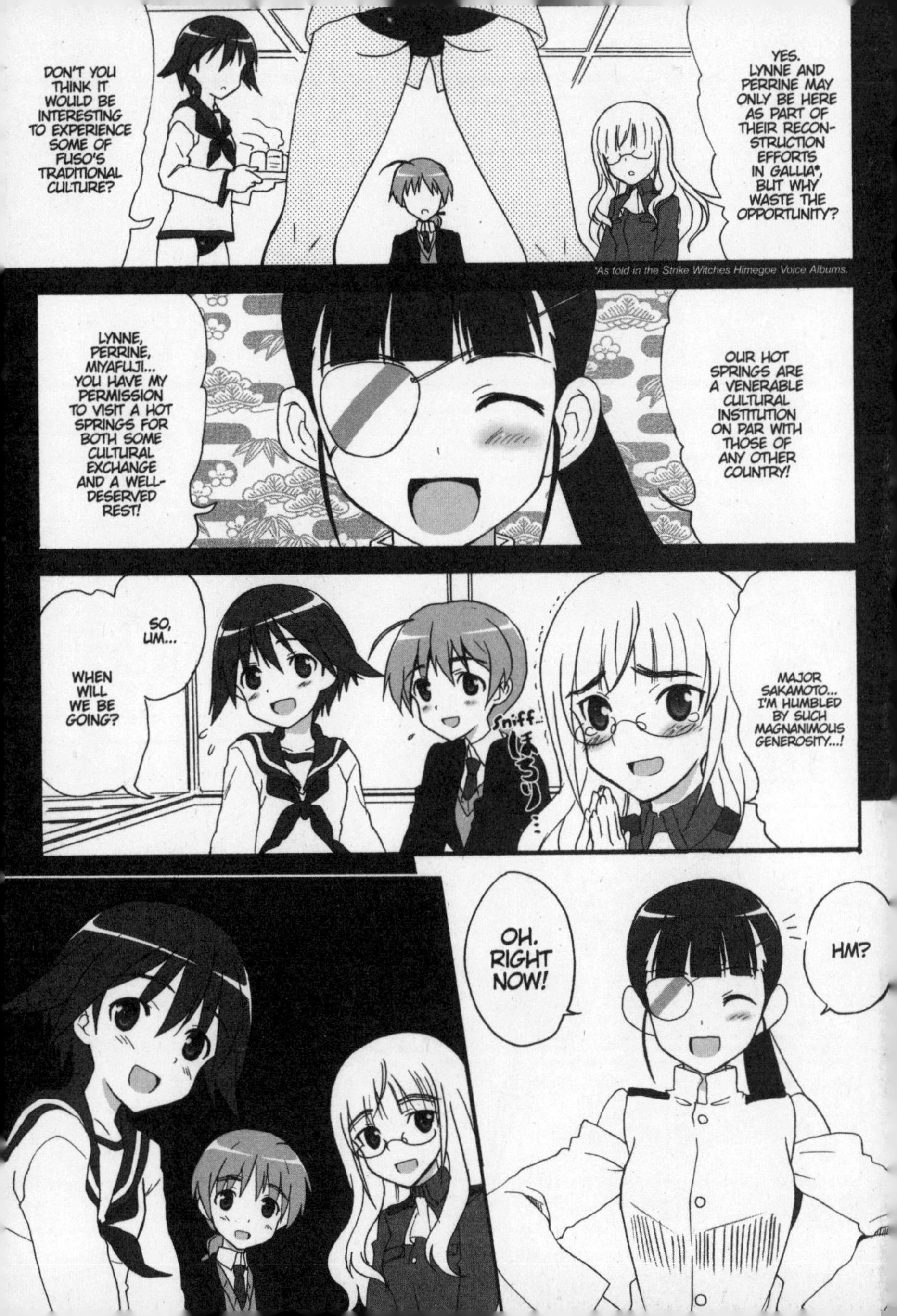
YES. LYNNE AND PERRINE MAY ONLY BE HERE AS PART OF THEIR RECON-STRUCTION EFFORTS IN GALLIA*, BUT WHY WASTE THE OPPORTUNITY?
DON'T YOU THINK IT WOULD BE INTERESTING TO EXPERIENCE SOME OF FUSO'S TRADITIONAL CULTURE?
OUR HOT SPRINGS ARE A VENERABLE CULTURAL INSTITUTION ON PAR WITH THOSE OF ANY OTHER COUNTRY!
LYNNE, PERRINE, MIYAFUJI... YOU HAVE MY PERMISSION TO VISIT A HOT SPRINGS FOR BOTH SOME CULTURAL EXCHANGE AND A WELL-DESERVED REST!
MAJOR SAKAMOTO... I'M HUMBLED BY SUCH MAGNANIMOUS GENEROSITY...!
Sniff... ほろり...
SO, UM...
WHEN WILL WE BE GOING?
HM?
OH. RIGHT NOW!
*As told in the Strike Witches Himegoe Voice Albums.

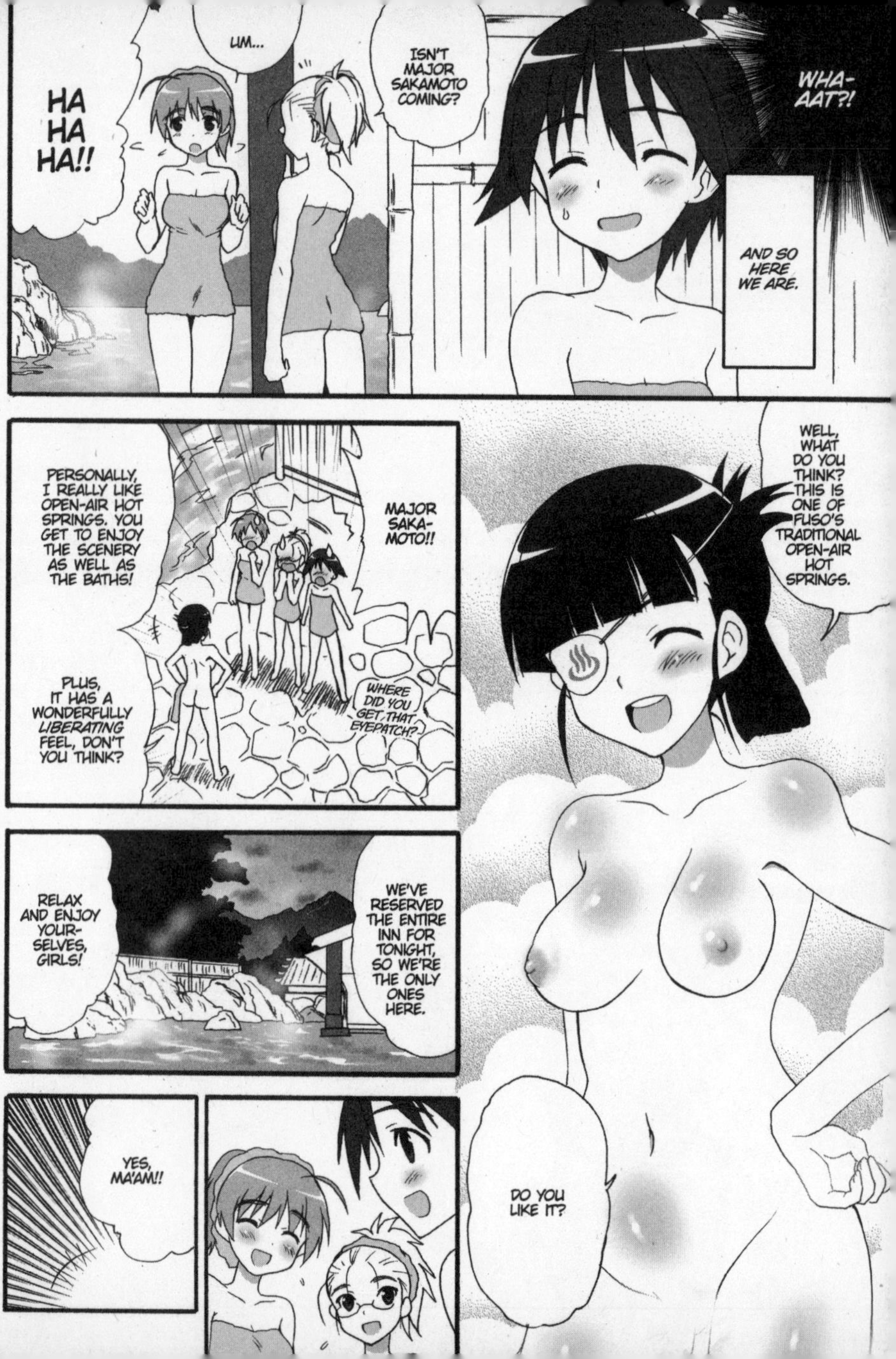
WHA-AAT?!
AND SO HERE WE ARE.
ISN'T MAJOR SAKAMOTO COMING?
UM...
HA HA HA!!
WELL, WHAT DO YOU THINK? THIS IS ONE OF FUSO'S TRADITIONAL OPEN-AIR HOT SPRINGS.
DO YOU LIKE IT?
MAJOR SAKAMOTO!!
PERSONALLY, I REALLY LIKE OPEN-AIR HOT SPRINGS. YOU GET TO ENJOY THE SCENERY AS WELL AS THE BATHS!
WHERE DID YOU GET THAT EYEPATCH?
PLUS, IT HAS A WONDERFULLY *LIBERATING* FEEL, DON'T YOU THINK?
WE'VE RESERVED THE ENTIRE INN FOR TONIGHT, SO WE'RE THE ONLY ONES HERE.
RELAX AND ENJOY YOURSELVES, GIRLS!
YES, MA'AM!!

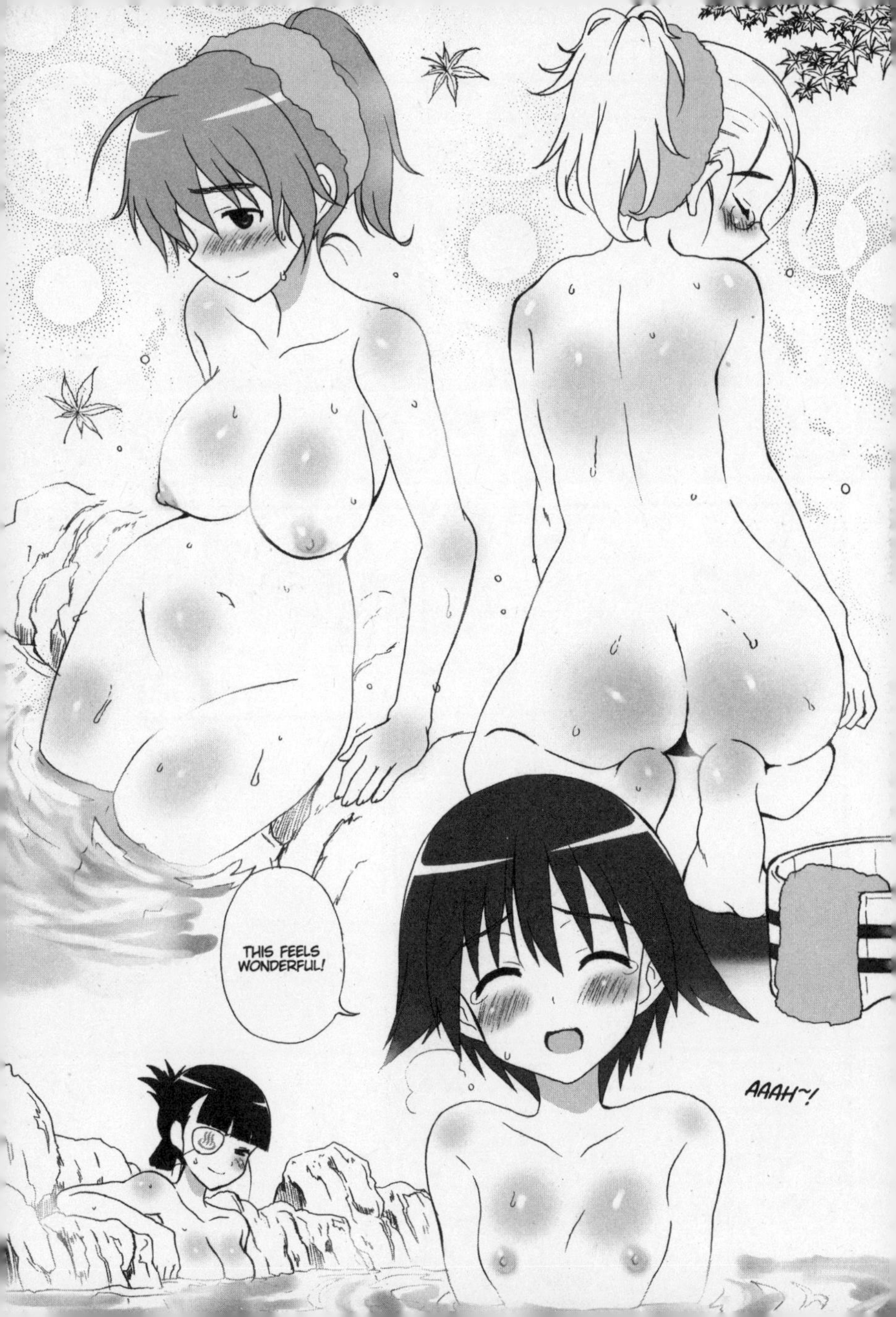
THIS FEELS WONDERFUL!
AAAH~!

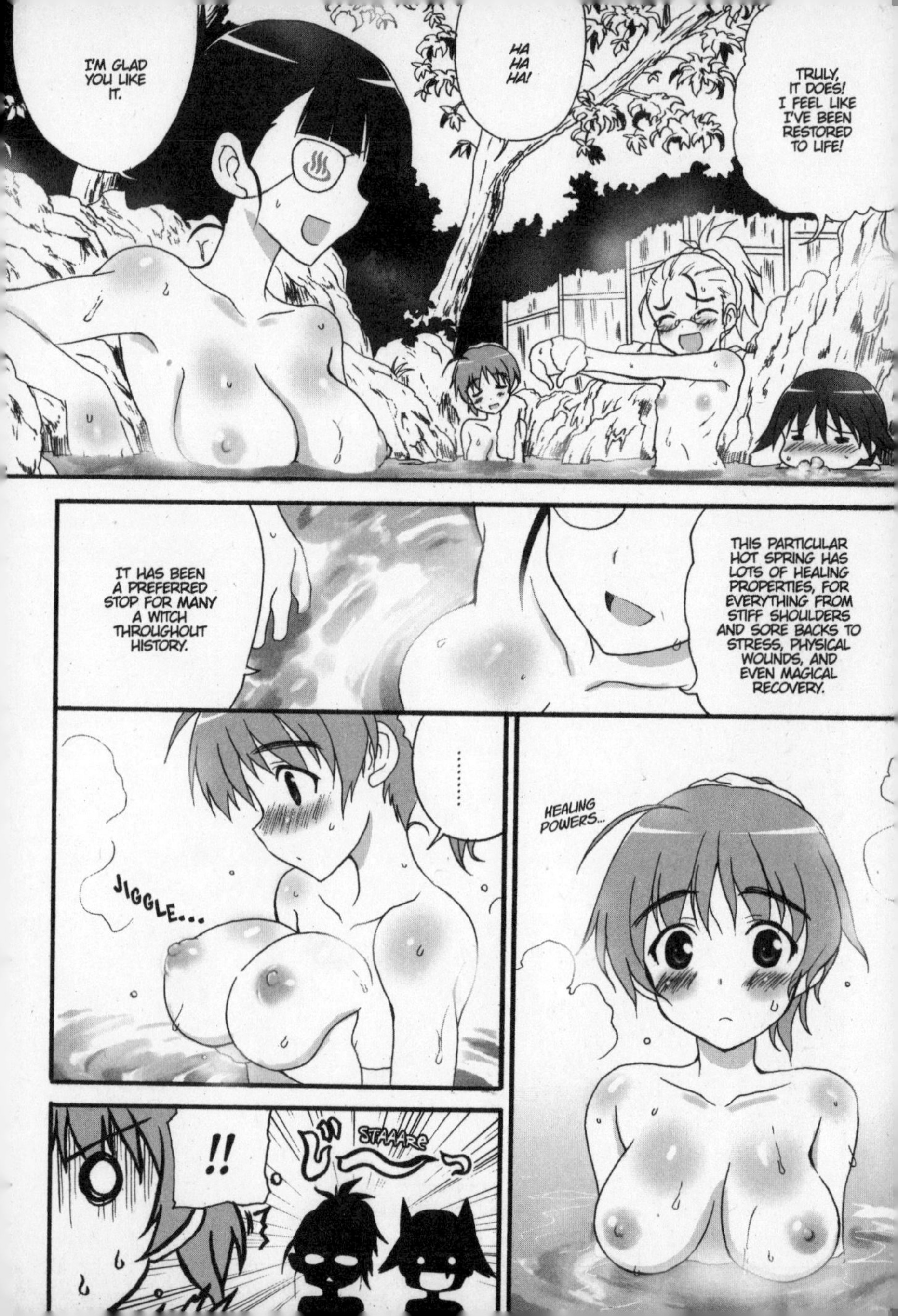
TRULY, IT DOES! I FEEL LIKE I'VE BEEN RESTORED TO LIFE!
HA HA HA!
I'M GLAD YOU LIKE IT.
THIS PARTICULAR HOT SPRING HAS LOTS OF HEALING PROPERTIES, FOR EVERYTHING FROM STIFF SHOULDERS AND SORE BACKS TO STRESS, PHYSICAL WOUNDS, AND EVEN MAGICAL RECOVERY.
IT HAS BEEN A PREFERRED STOP FOR MANY A WITCH THROUGHOUT HISTORY.
HEALING POWERS...
......
JIGGLE...
STAAARE
!!

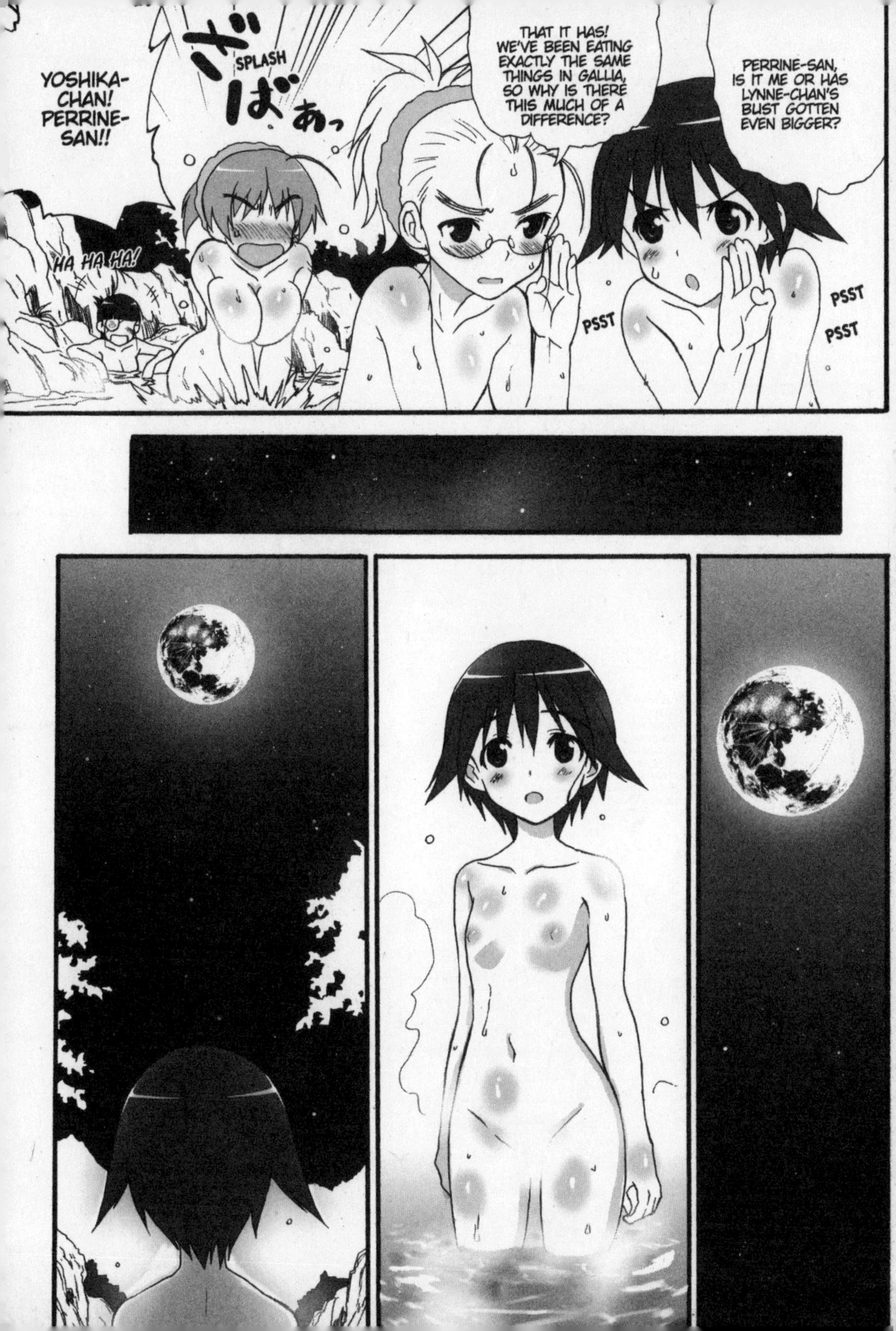
PERRINE-SAN, IS IT ME OR HAS LYNNE-CHAN'S BUST GOTTEN EVEN BIGGER?
PSST
PSST
THAT IT HAS! WE'VE BEEN EATING EXACTLY THE SAME THINGS IN GALLIA, SO WHY IS THERE THIS MUCH OF A DIFFERENCE?
PSST
ざばあっ
SPLASH
YOSHIKA-CHAN! PERRINE-SAN!!
HA HA HA!

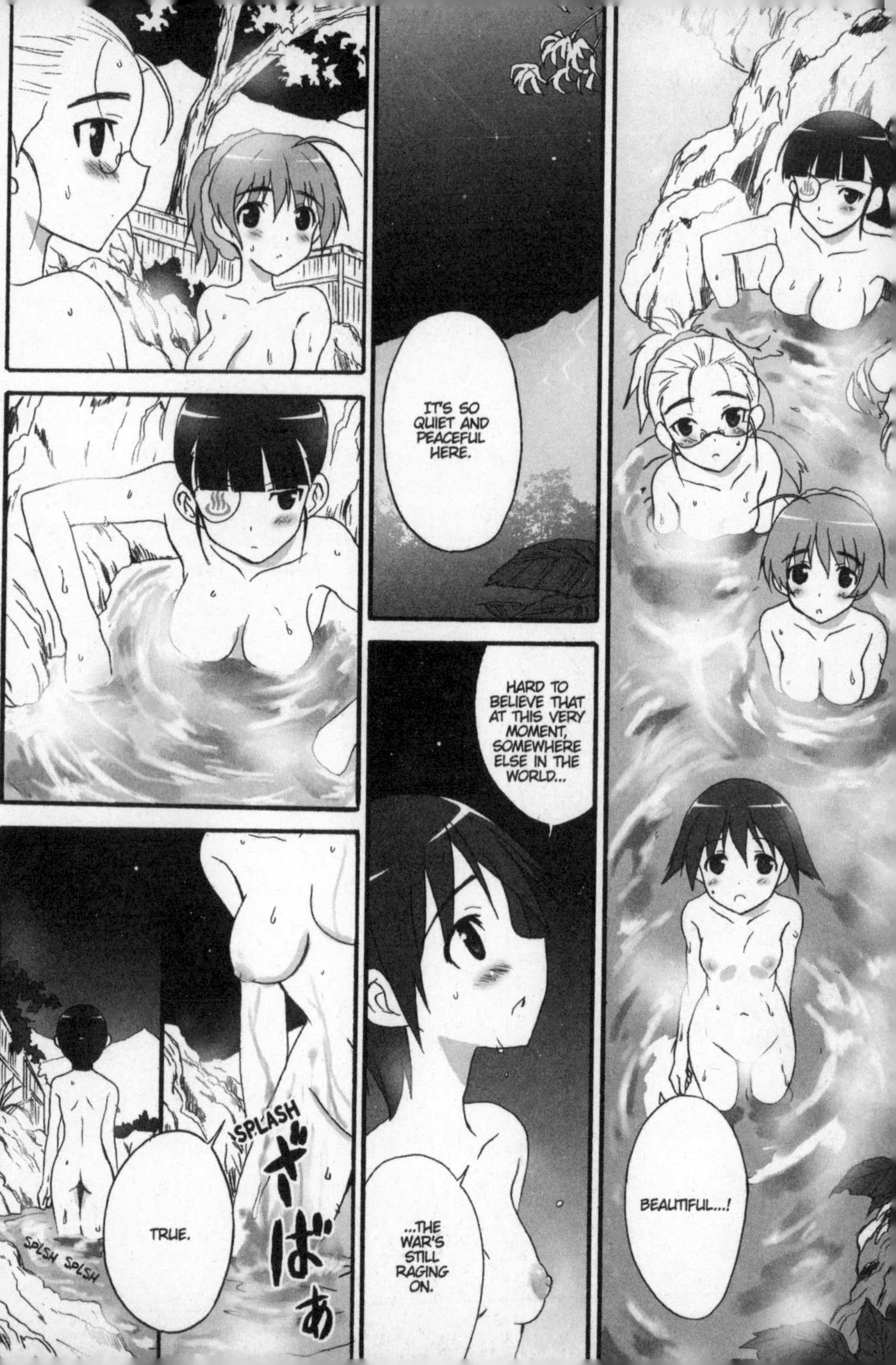
BEAUTIFUL...!
IT'S SO QUIET AND PEACEFUL HERE.
HARD TO BELIEVE THAT AT THIS VERY MOMENT, SOMEWHERE ELSE IN THE WORLD...
...THE WAR'S STILL RAGING ON.
SPLASH
ざばぁ
TRUE.
SPLSH SPLSH

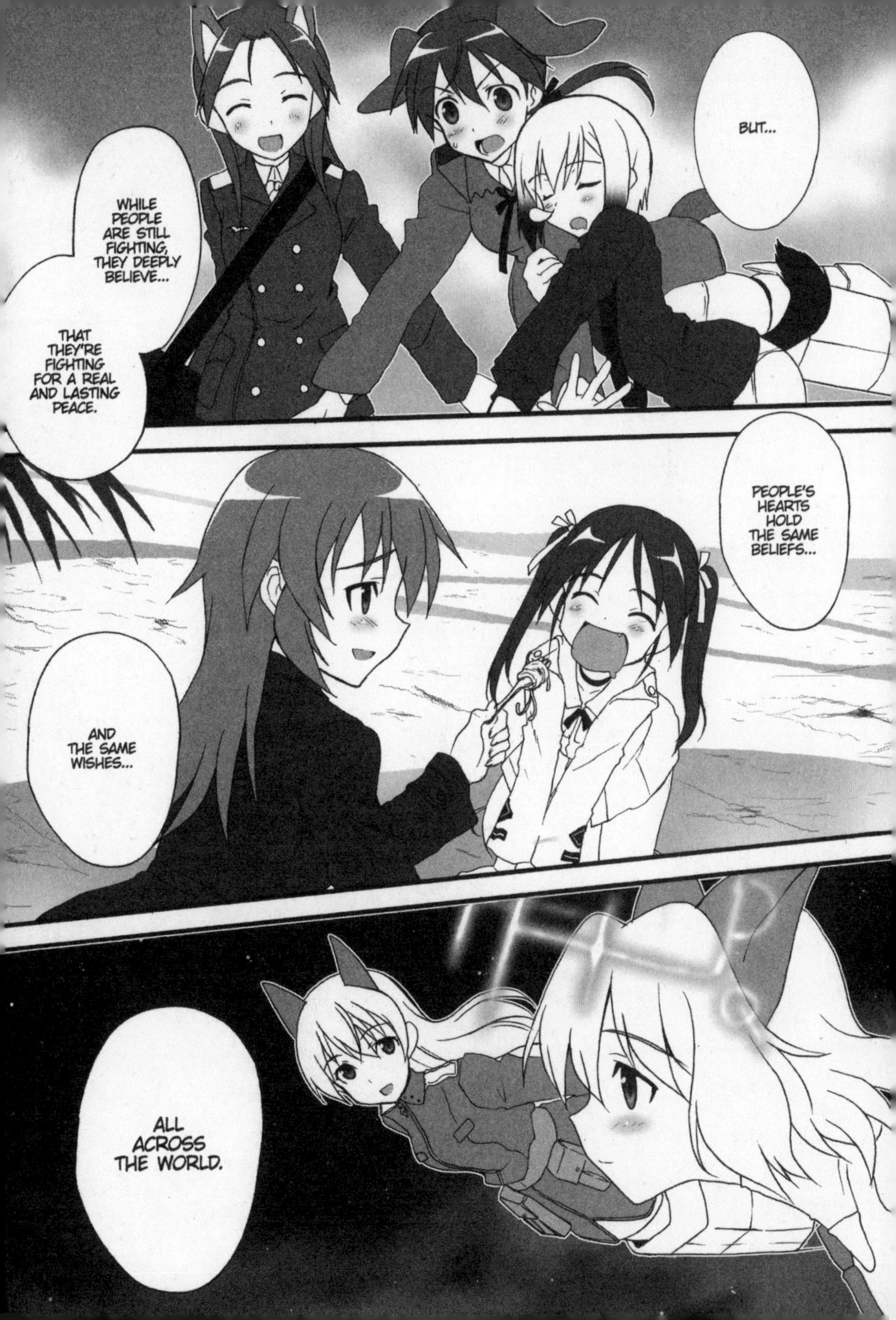
BUT...
WHILE PEOPLE ARE STILL FIGHTING, THEY DEEPLY BELIEVE...
THAT THEY'RE FIGHTING FOR A REAL AND LASTING PEACE.
PEOPLE'S HEARTS HOLD THE SAME BELIEFS...
AND THE SAME WISHES...
ALL ACROSS THE WORLD.

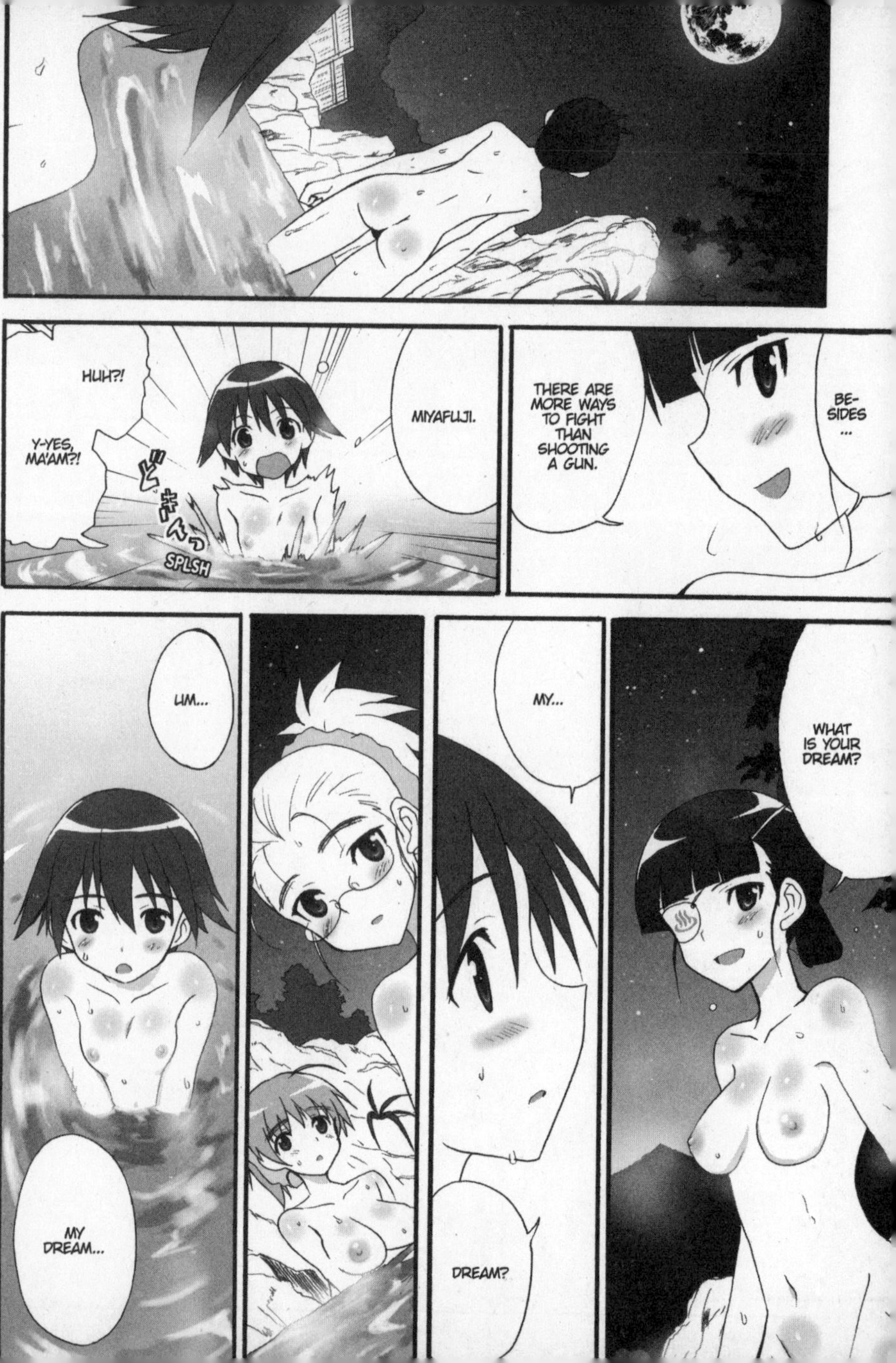
BE-SIDES...
THERE ARE MORE WAYS TO FIGHT THAN SHOOTING A GUN.
MIYAFUJI.
HUH?!
Y-YES, MA'AM?!
どきんっ
SPLSH
WHAT IS YOUR DREAM?
MY...
DREAM?
UM...
MY DREAM...

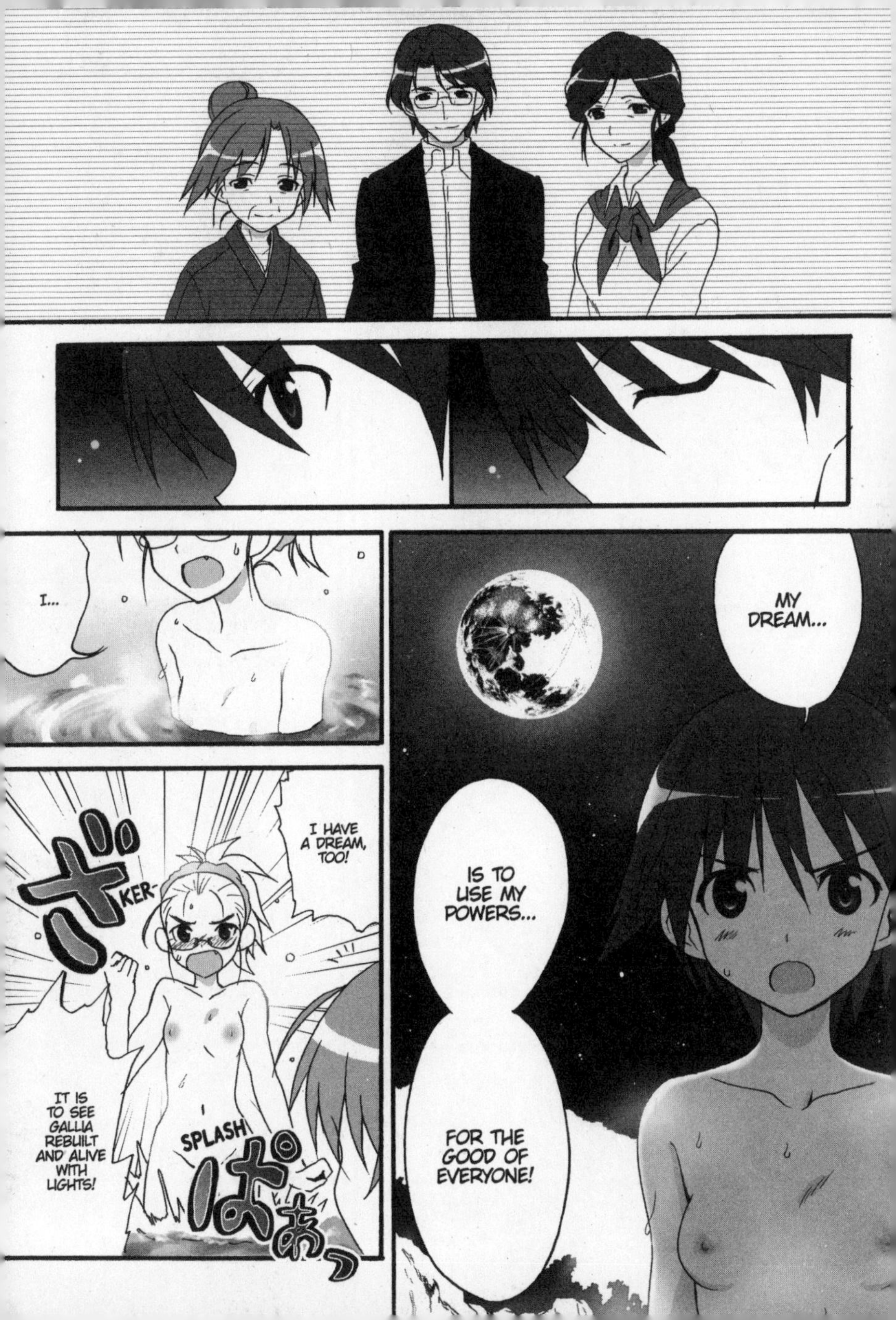
MY DREAM...
IS TO USE MY POWERS...
FOR THE GOOD OF EVERYONE!
I...
I HAVE A DREAM, TOO!
ざっ
KER-
IT IS TO SEE GALLIA REBUILT AND ALIVE WITH LIGHTS!
SPLASH
ぱあっ

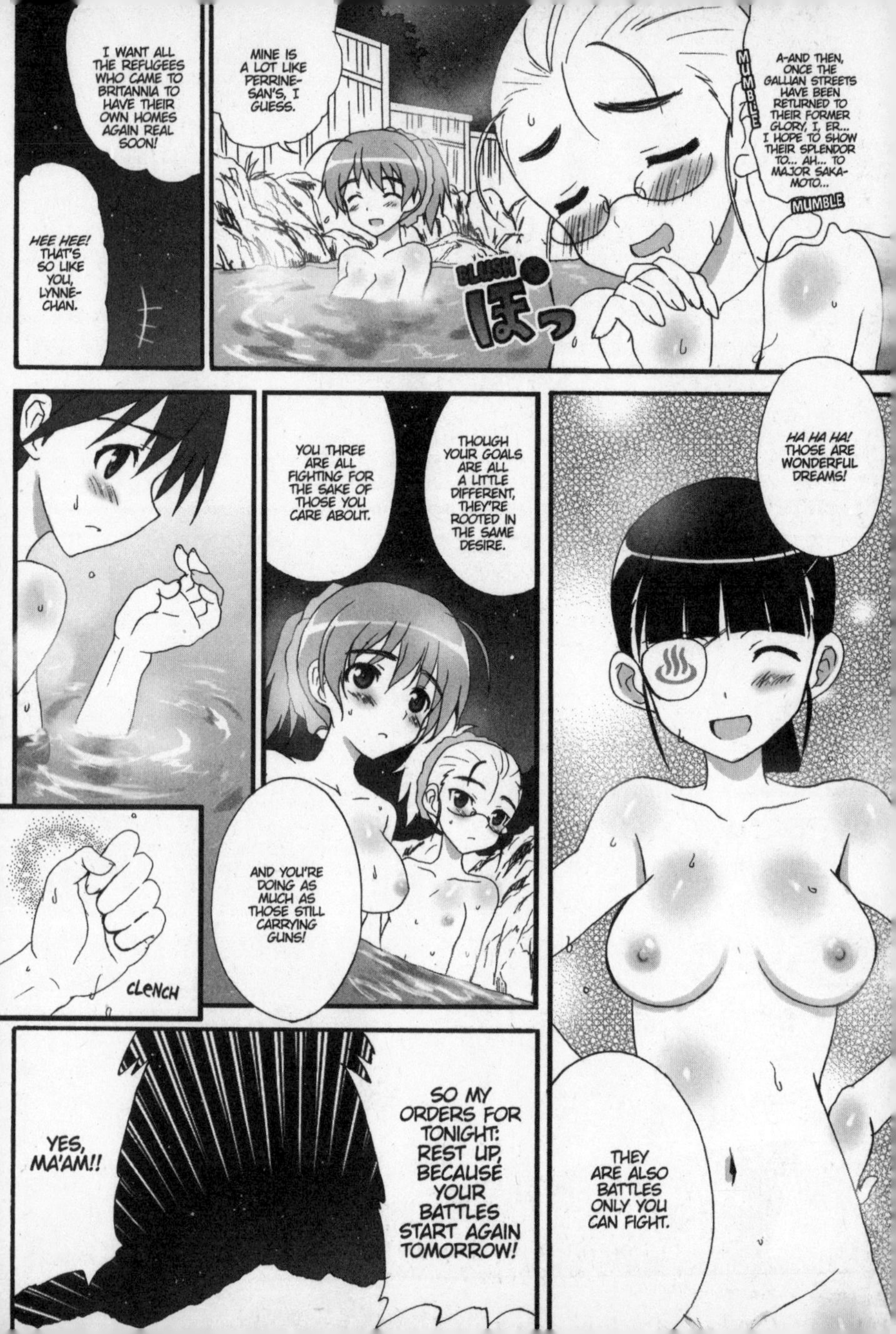
A-AND THEN, ONCE THE GALLIAN STREETS HAVE BEEN RETURNED TO THEIR FORMER GLORY, I, ER... I HOPE TO SHOW THEIR SPLENDOR TO... AH... TO MAJOR SAKAMOTO...
MUMBLE
MUMBLE
BLUSH
ぽっ
MINE IS A LOT LIKE PERRINE-SAN'S, I GUESS.
I WANT ALL THE REFUGEES WHO CAME TO BRITANNIA TO HAVE THEIR OWN HOMES AGAIN REAL SOON!
HEE HEE! THAT'S SO LIKE YOU, LYNNE-CHAN.
HA HA HA! THOSE ARE WONDERFUL DREAMS!
THEY ARE ALSO BATTLES ONLY YOU CAN FIGHT.
THOUGH YOUR GOALS ARE ALL A LITTLE DIFFERENT, THEY'RE ROOTED IN THE SAME DESIRE.
YOU THREE ARE ALL FIGHTING FOR THE SAKE OF THOSE YOU CARE ABOUT.
AND YOU'RE DOING AS MUCH AS THOSE STILL CARRYING GUNS!
CLENCH
SO MY ORDERS FOR TONIGHT: REST UP, BECAUSE YOUR BATTLES START AGAIN TOMORROW!
YES, MA'AM!!

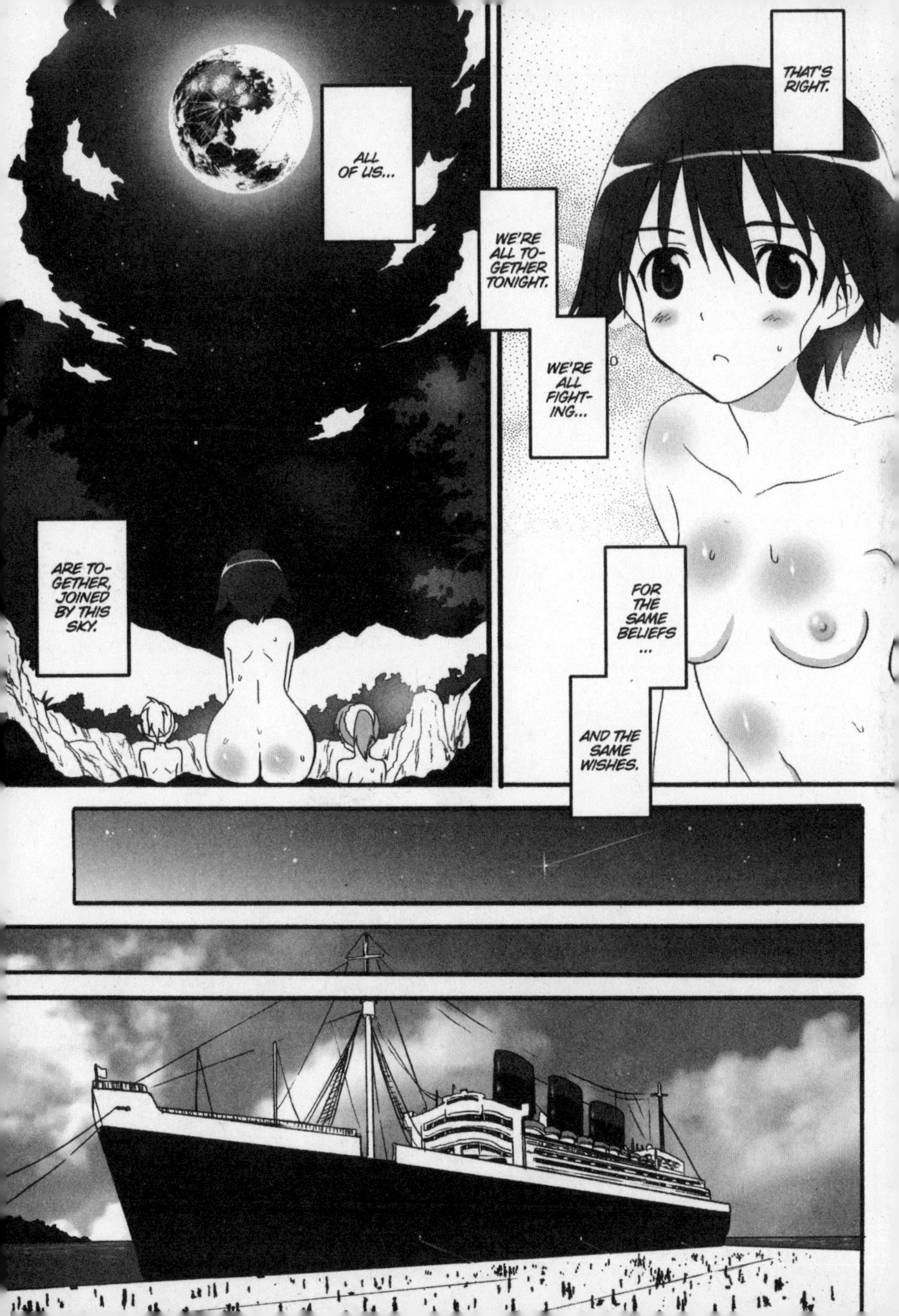
THAT'S RIGHT.
WE'RE ALL TO-GETHER TONIGHT.
WE'RE ALL FIGHT-ING...
FOR THE SAME BELIEFS...
AND THE SAME WISHES.
ALL OF US...
ARE TO-GETHER, JOINED BY THIS SKY.

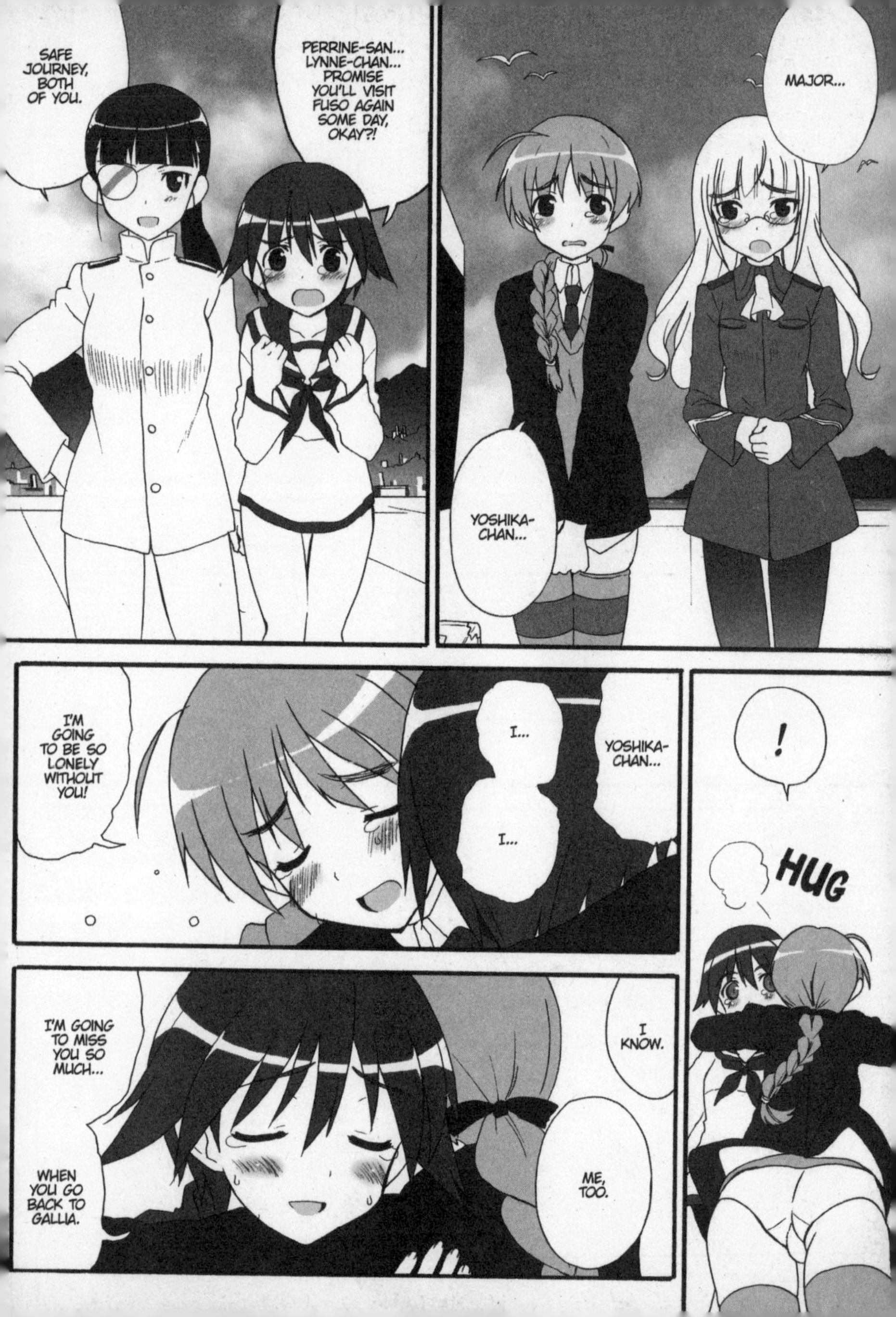
MAJOR...
YOSHIKA-CHAN...
PERRINE-SAN... LYNNE-CHAN... PROMISE YOU'LL VISIT FUSO AGAIN SOME DAY, OKAY?!
SAFE JOURNEY, BOTH OF YOU.
!
HUG
YOSHIKA-CHAN...
I...
I...
I'M GOING TO BE SO LONELY WITHOUT YOU!
I KNOW.
ME, TOO.
I'M GOING TO MISS YOU SO MUCH...
WHEN YOU GO BACK TO GALLIA.

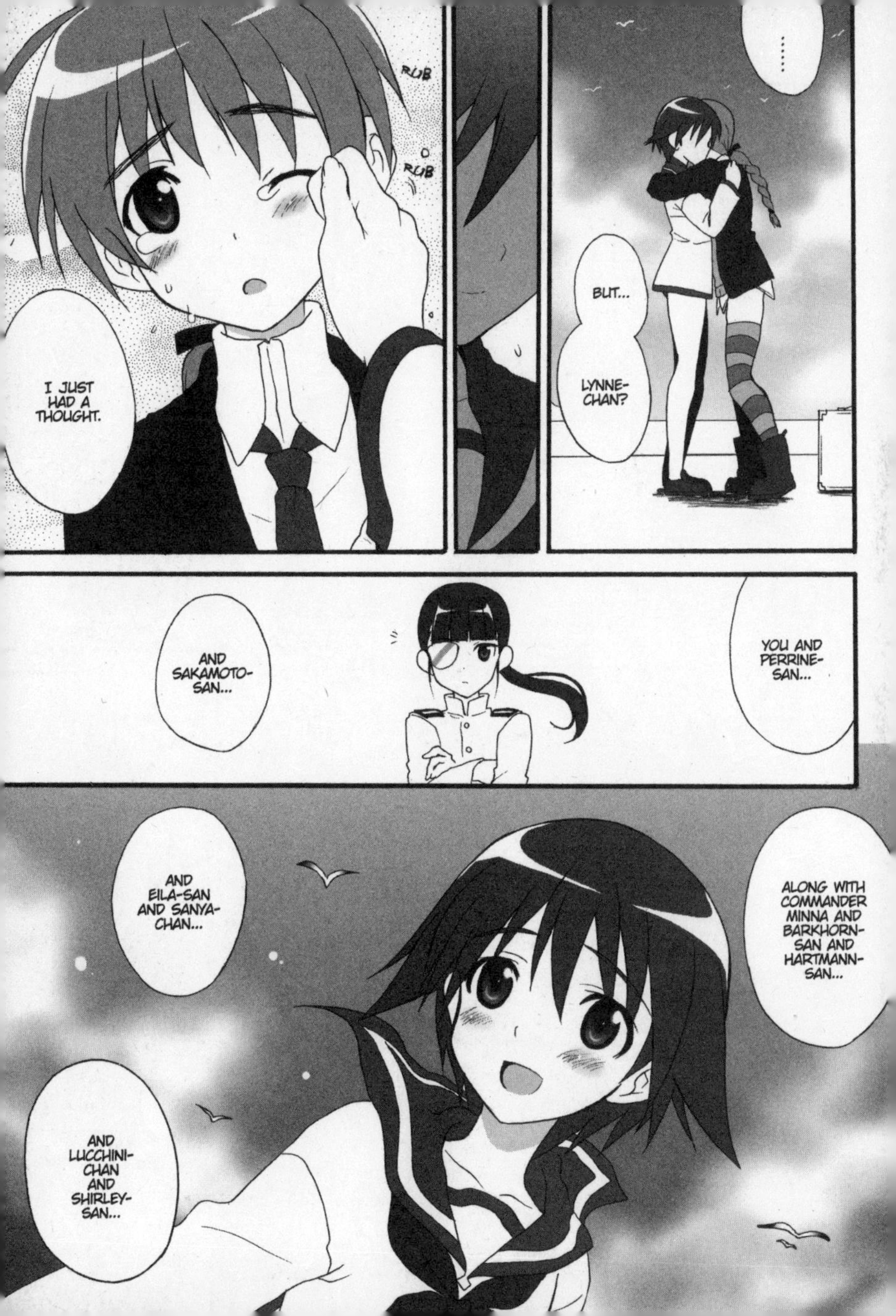
......
BUT...
LYNNE-CHAN?
RUB
RUB
I JUST HAD A THOUGHT.
YOU AND PERRINE-SAN...
AND SAKAMOTO-SAN...
ALONG WITH COMMANDER MINNA AND BARKHORN-SAN AND HARTMANN-SAN...
AND EILA-SAN AND SANYA-CHAN...
AND LUCCHINI-CHAN AND SHIRLEY-SAN...

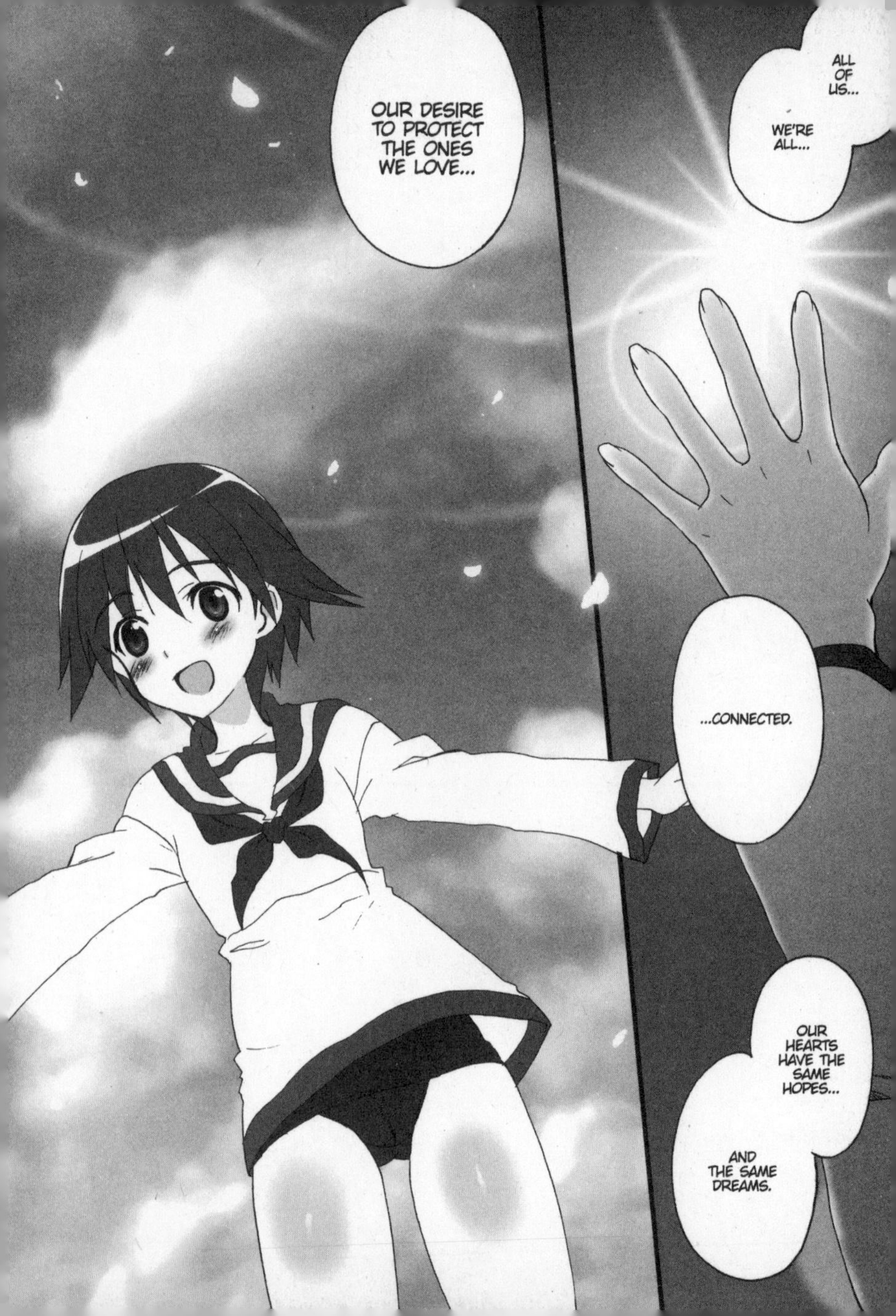
ALL OF US...
WE'RE ALL...
...CONNECTED.
OUR HEARTS HAVE THE SAME HOPES...
AND THE SAME DREAMS.
OUR DESIRE TO PROTECT THE ONES WE LOVE...

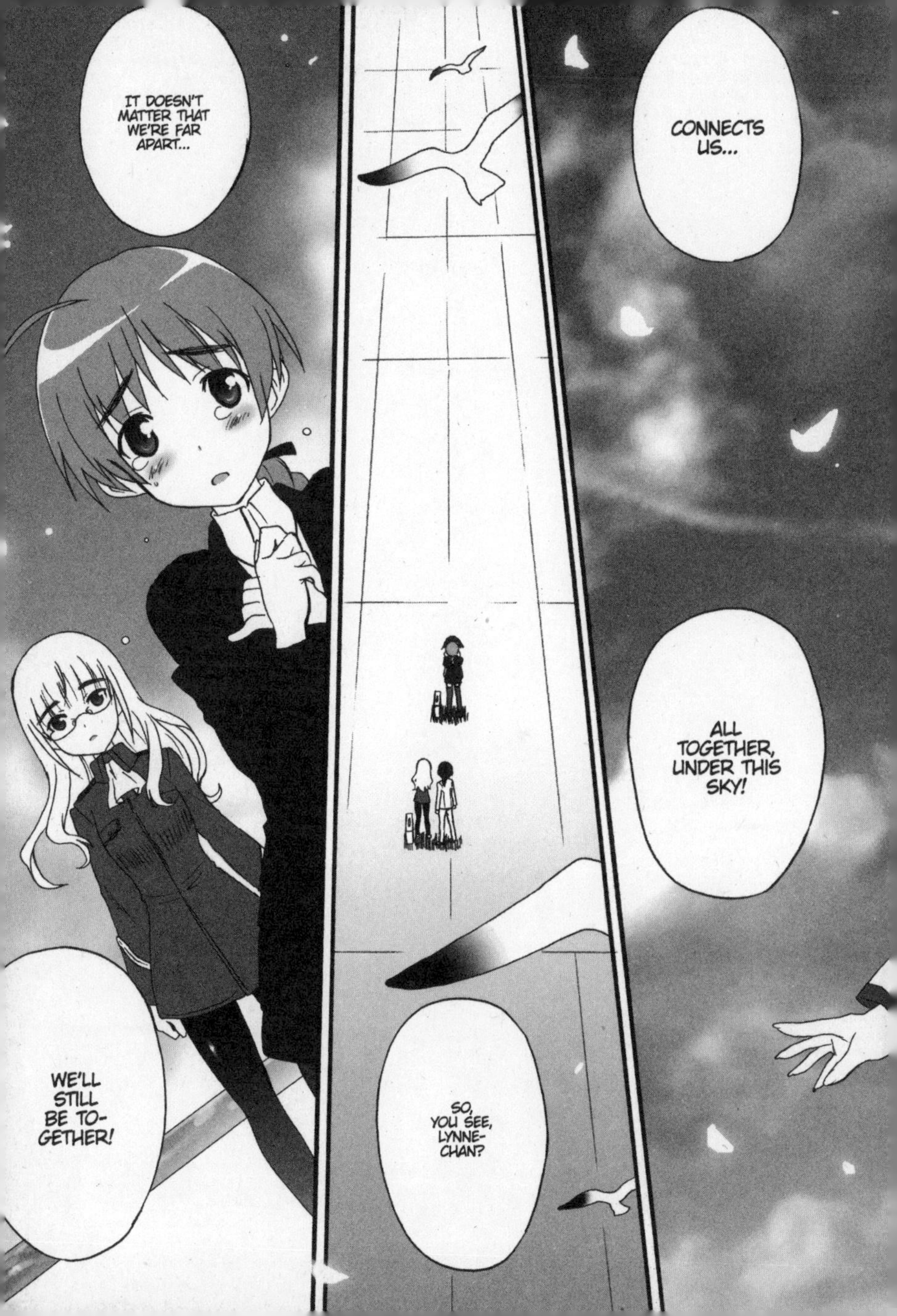
CONNECTS US...
ALL TOGETHER, UNDER THIS SKY!
SO, YOU SEE, LYNNE-CHAN?
IT DOESN'T MATTER THAT WE'RE FAR APART...
WE'LL STILL BE TO-GETHER!

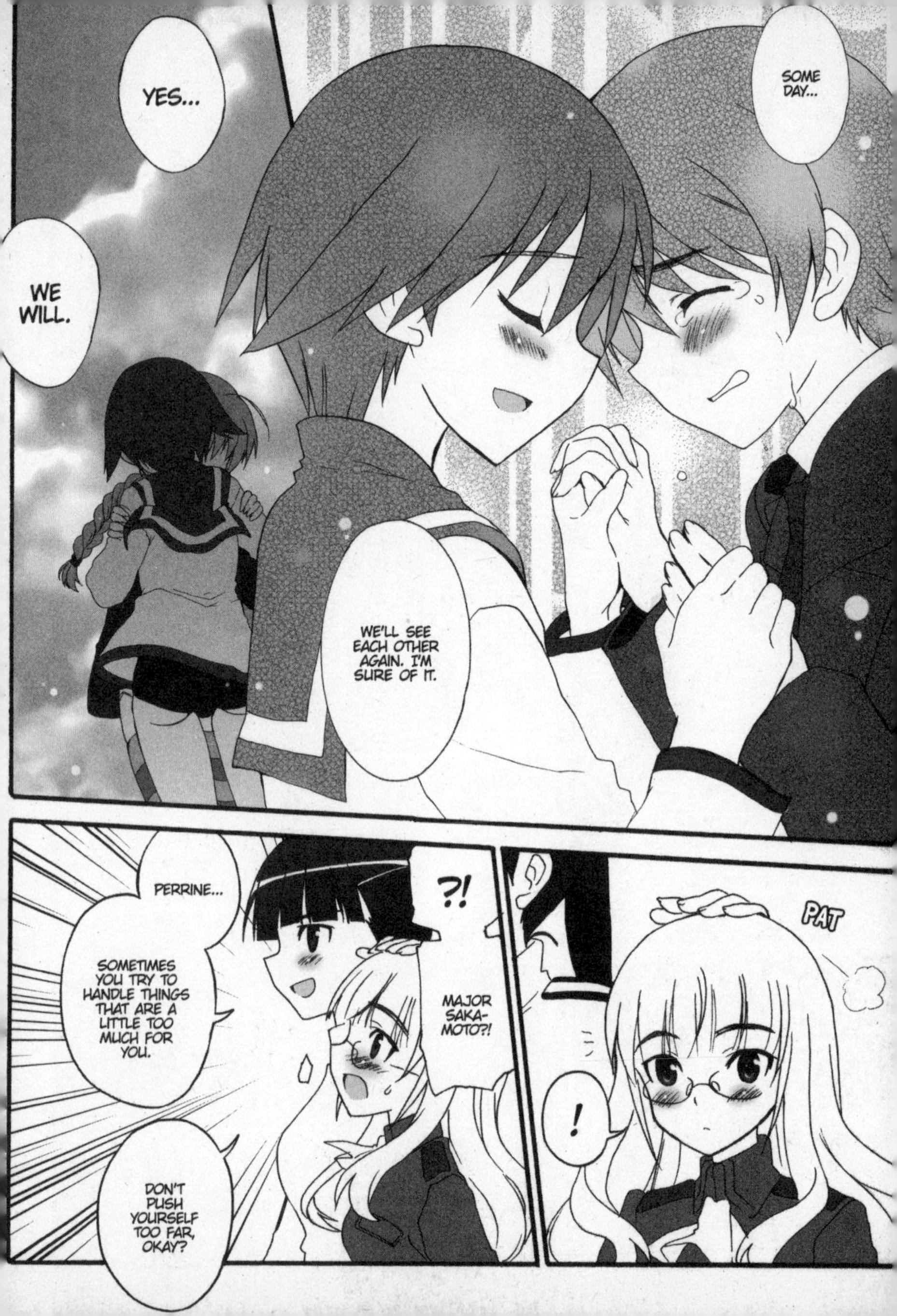
SOME DAY...
WE'LL SEE EACH OTHER AGAIN. I'M SURE OF IT.
YES...
WE WILL.
PAT
!
?!
MAJOR SAKAMOTO?!
PERRINE...
SOMETIMES YOU TRY TO HANDLE THINGS THAT ARE A LITTLE TOO MUCH FOR YOU.
DON'T PUSH YOURSELF TOO FAR, OKAY?

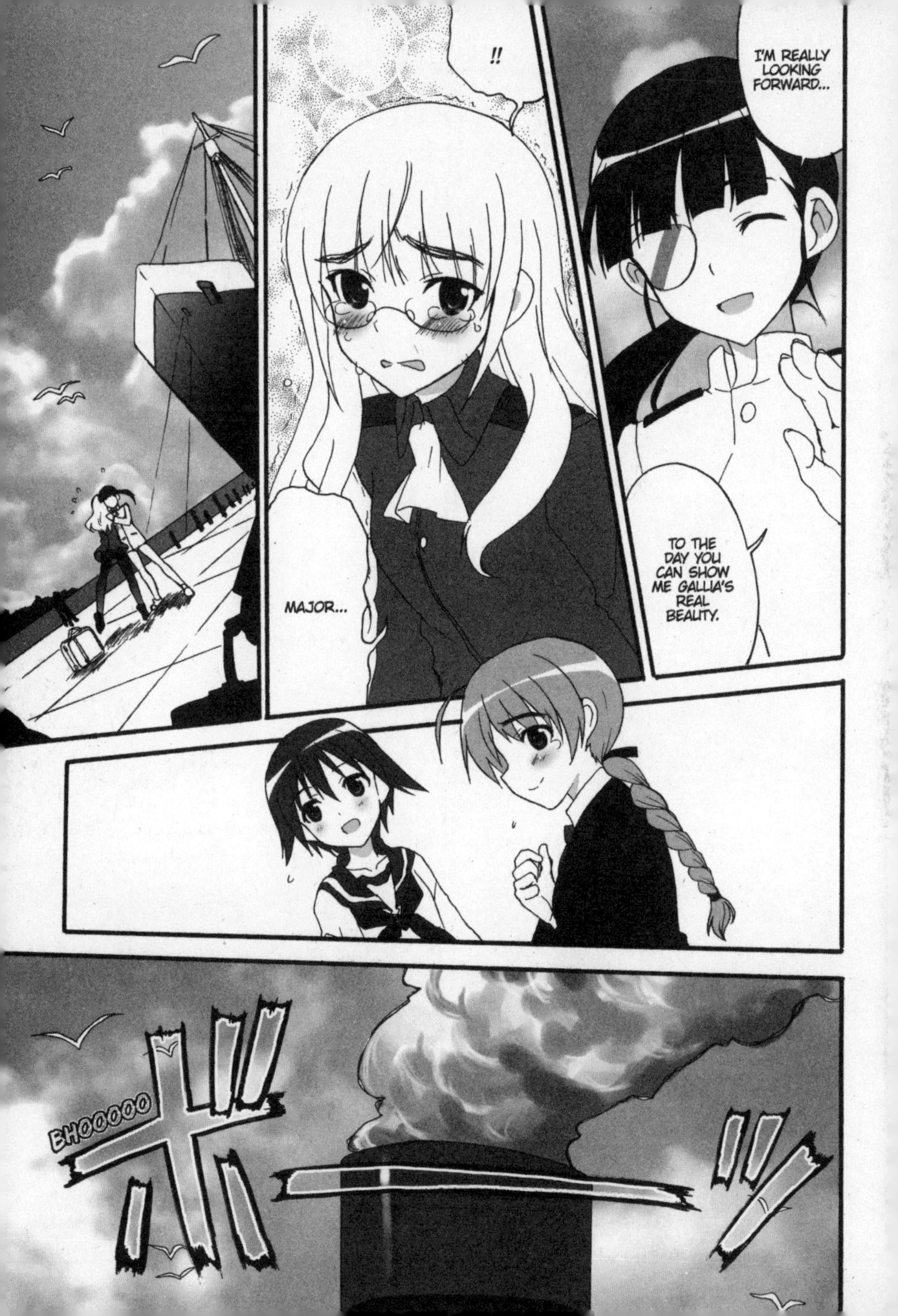
I'M REALLY LOOKING FORWARD...
TO THE DAY YOU CAN SHOW ME GALLIA'S REAL BEAUTY.
!!
MAJOR...
BHOOOOO

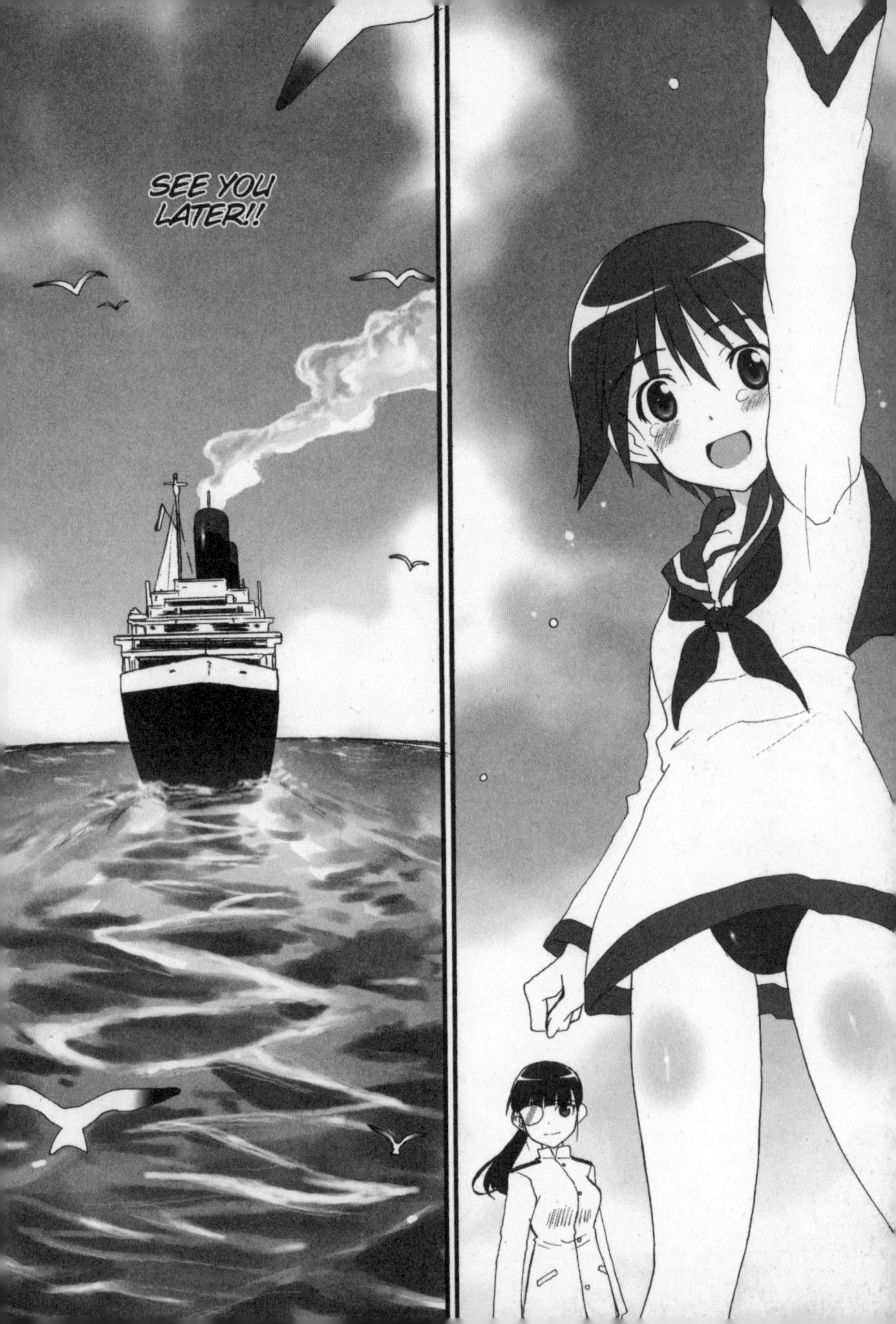
SEE YOU LATER!!

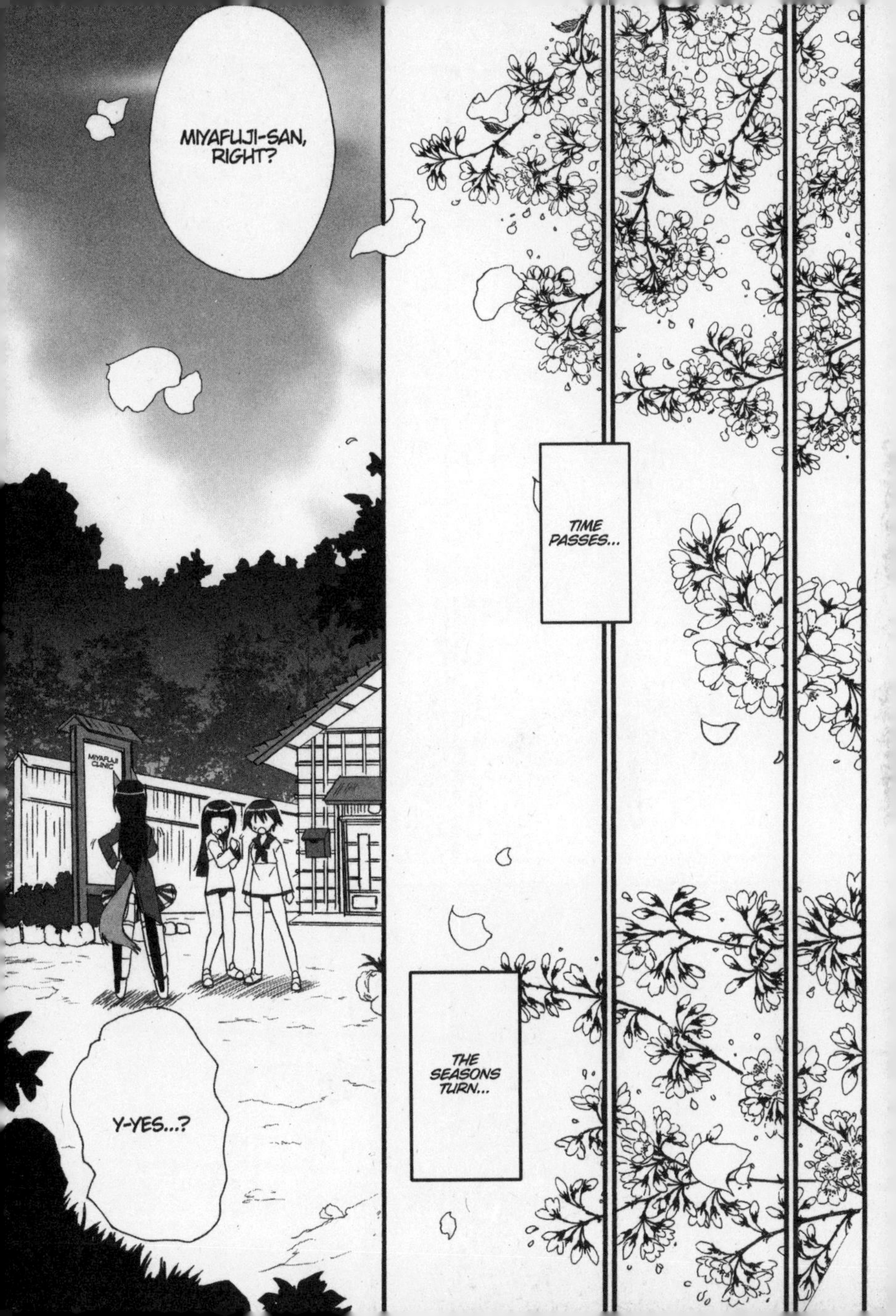
TIME PASSES...
THE SEASONS TURN...
MIYAFUJI-SAN, RIGHT?
MIYAFUJI CLINIC
Y-YES...?

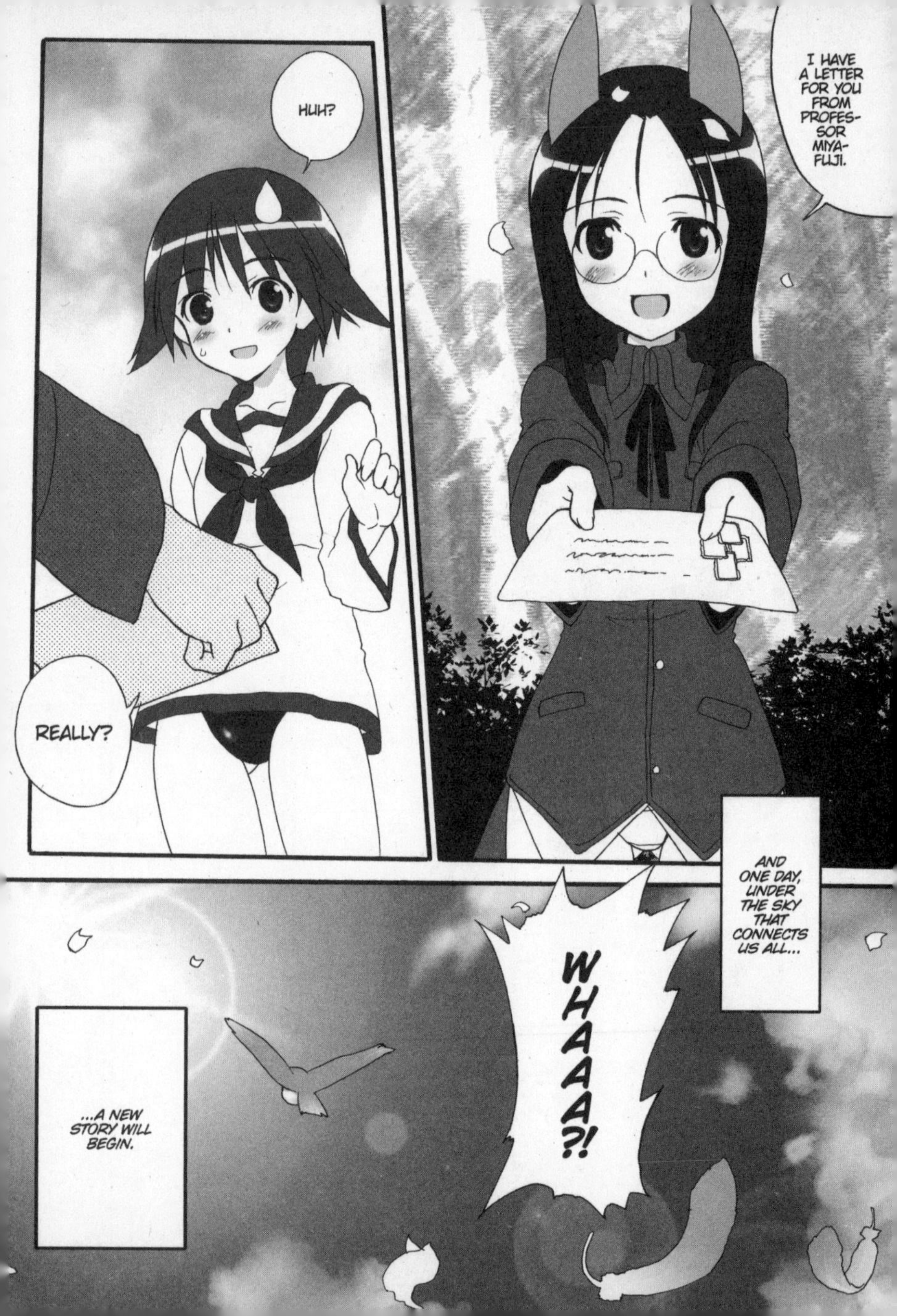

I HAVE A LETTER FOR YOU FROM PROFESSOR MIYAFUJI.
HUH?
REALLY?
AND ONE DAY, UNDER THE SKY THAT CONNECTS US ALL...
WHAAAA?!
...A NEW STORY WILL BEGIN.

501st JOINT FIGHTER WING

STRIKE WITCHES

501st JOINT FIGHTER WING
STRIKE WITCHES

Fin

The story continues in the
Strike Witches 2 anime!

STRIKE WITCHES
THE SKY WHICH IS CONNECTED TO YOU

Humikane Shimada &
Projekt Kagonish
comics by
Shin Kyogoku

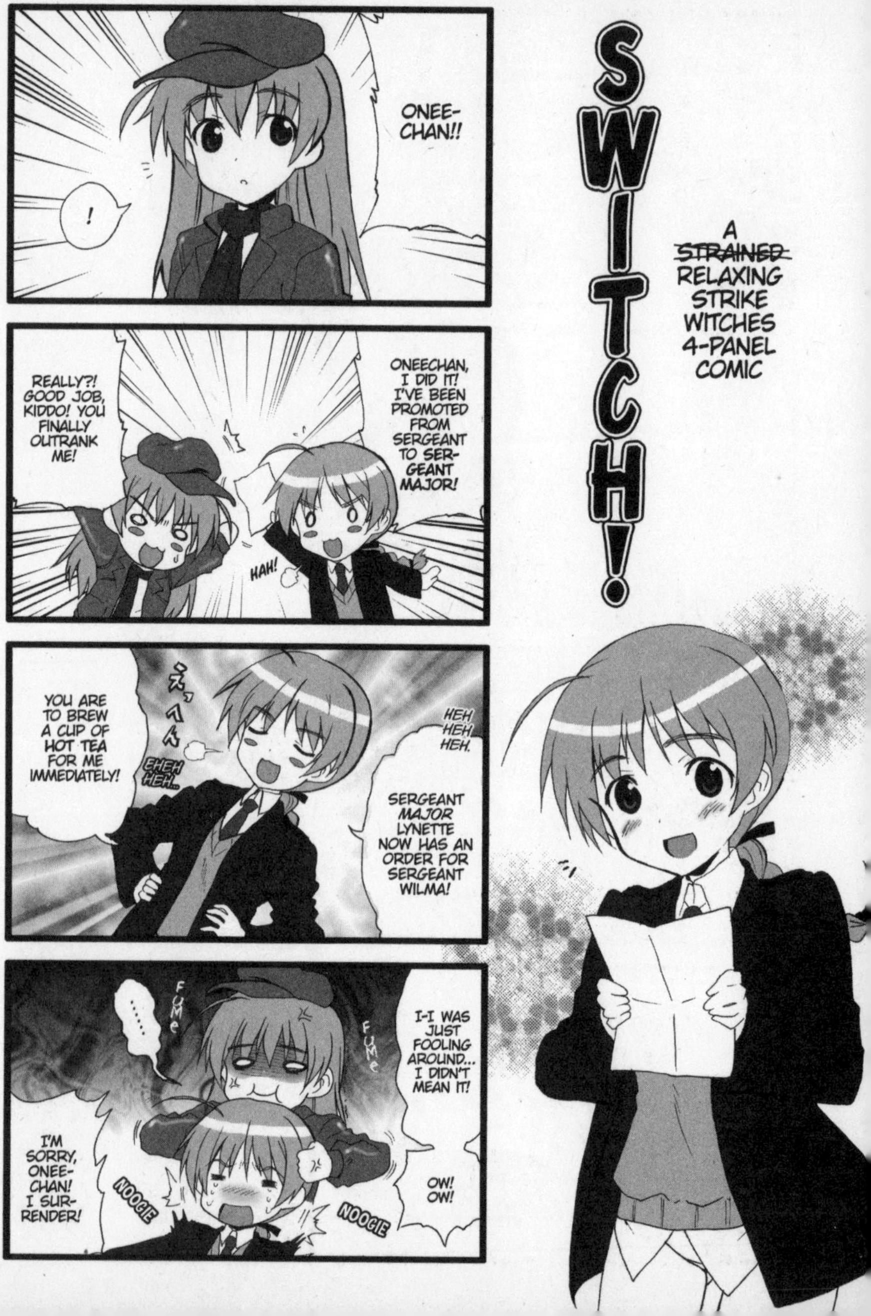
SWITCH!
A ~~STRAINED~~ RELAXING STRIKE WITCHES 4-PANEL COMIC
ONEE-CHAN!!
!
ONEECHAN, I DID IT! I'VE BEEN PROMOTED FROM SERGEANT TO SER-GEANT MAJOR!
REALLY?! GOOD JOB, KIDDO! YOU FINALLY OUTRANK ME!
HAH!
HEH HEH HEH.
SERGEANT MAJOR LYNETTE NOW HAS AN ORDER FOR SERGEANT WILMA!
えっへん
EHEH HEH...
YOU ARE TO BREW A CUP OF HOT TEA FOR ME IMMEDIATELY!
I-I WAS JUST FOOLING AROUND... I DIDN'T MEAN IT!
FUME
......
FUME
OW! OW!
NOOGIE
I'M SORRY, ONEE-CHAN! I SUR-RENDER!
NOOGIE

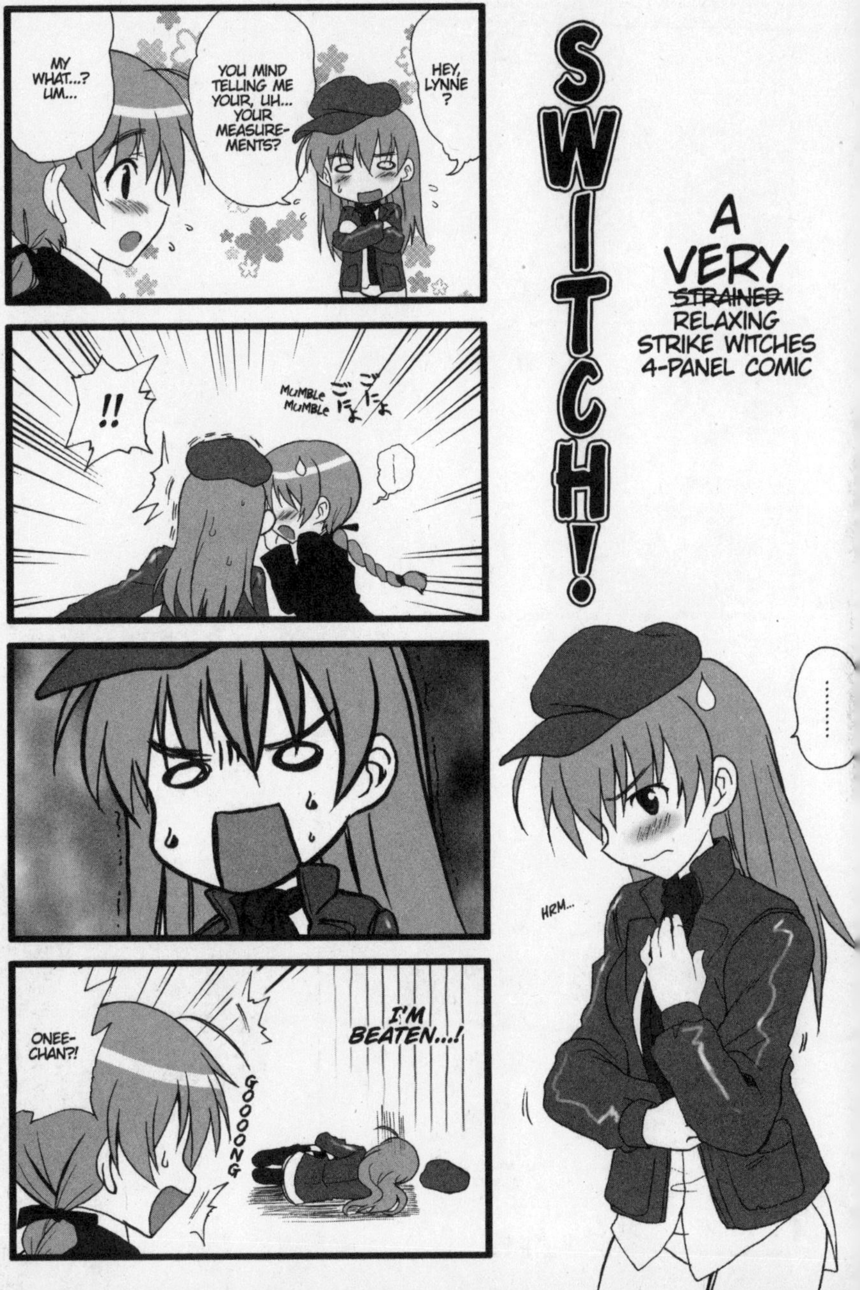
SWITCH!
A VERY STRAINED RELAXING STRIKE WITCHES 4-PANEL COMIC
......
HRM...
HEY, LYNNE?
YOU MIND TELLING ME YOUR, UH... YOUR MEASUREMENTS?
MY WHAT...? UM...
MUMBLE MUMBLE ごにょごにょ
!
!!
I'M BEATEN...!
GOOOOONG
ONEE-CHAN?!

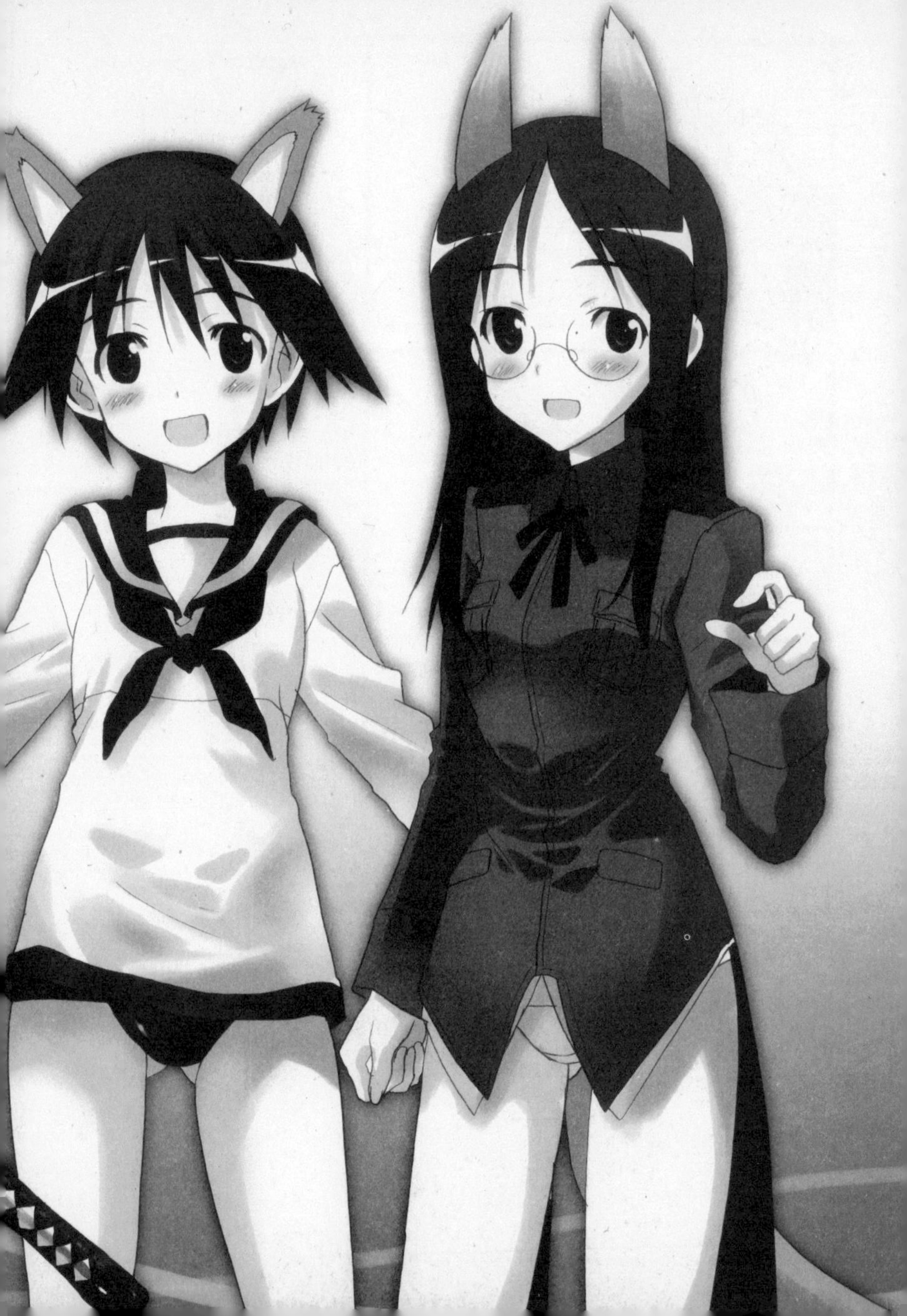

扶桑

FUSO

Thank you very much for reading Strike Witches: The Sky That
Connects Us. It was with the help
of a lot of people that I was able
to come this far. I really hope this
volume helps expand the world of
Strike Witches for you.

Thank you to Humikane Shimada-
sama, Takaaki Suzuki-sama, Ka-
zuhiro Takamura-sama, my younger brother and assistant, Amaga-
ta-sama, all of the editors at Mu-
sumeTYPE Magazine, and all of
the faithful readers out there.
Thank you, thank you, thank you
so much!!

-Shin Kyogoku

STRIKE WITCHES

THE SKY THAT CONNECTS US

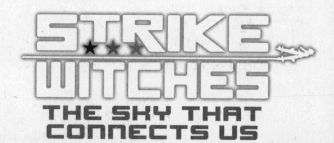

SEVEN SEAS ENTERTAINMENT PRESENTS

STRIKE WITCHES
THE SKY THAT CONNECTS US

art by **Shin Kyogoku** / story by **Humikane Shimada + Projekt Kagonish**

TRANSLATION
Adrienne Beck

ADAPTATION
Shanti Whitesides

LETTERING AND LAYOUT
Alexandra Gunawan

COVER DESIGN
Nicky Lim

PROOFREADER
Janet Houck
Conner Crooks

MANAGING EDITOR
Adam Arnold

PUBLISHER
Jason DeAngelis

STRIKE WITCHES: KIMI TO TSUNAGARU SORA
© Shin KYOGOKU 2010, © 2010 501st JOINT FIGHTER WING
Edited by KADOKAWA SHOTEN.
First published in Japan in 2010 by KADOKAWA CORPORATION, Tokyo.
English translation rights arranged with KADOKAWA CORPORATION, Tokyo
through TOHAN CORPORATION, Tokyo..

Seven Seas books may be purchased in bulk for educational, business, or
promotional use. For information on bulk purchases, please contact Macmillan
Corporate & Premium Sales Department at 1-800-221-7945 (ext 5442)
or write specialmarkets@macmillan.com.

Seven Seas and the Seven Seas logo are trademarks of
Seven Seas Entertainment, LLC. All rights reserved.

ISBN: 978-1-626920-38-5

Printed in Canada

First Printing: June 2014

10 9 8 7 6 5 4 3 2 1

FOLLOW US ONLINE: *www.gomanga.com*

READING DIRECTIONS

This book reads from *right to left*, Japanese style.
If this is your first time reading manga, you start
reading from the top right panel on each page and
take it from there. If you get lost, just follow the
numbered diagram here. It may seem backwards at
first, but you'll get the hang of it! Have fun!!

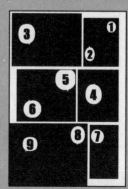